Debugging Java

Troubleshooting for Programmers

Will David Mitchell

D1307951

Osborne/**McGraw-Hill**

Berkeley / New York / St. Louis / San Francisco / Auckland / Bogotá
Hamburg / London / Madrid / Mexico City / Milan / Montreal / New Delhi
Panama City / Paris / São Paulo / Singapore / Sydney / Tokyo / Toronto

Osborne/**McGraw-Hill**
2600 Tenth Street
Berkeley, California 94710
U.S.A.

For information on translations or book distributors outside the U.S.A., or to arrange bulk purchase discounts for sales promotions, premiums, or fund-raisers, please contact Osborne/**McGraw-Hill** at the above address.

Debugging Java: Troubleshooting for Programmers

1234567890 VFM VFM 019876543210

ISBN 0-07-212562-4

Publisher	Brandon A. Nordin
Vice President and Associate Publisher	Scott Rogers
Editorial Director	Wendy Rinaldi
Project Editor	Mark Karmendy
Acquisitions Coordinator	Monika Faltiss
Technical Editor	Marian Corcoran
Copy Editor	Dennis Weaver
Proofreader	John Gildersleeve
Indexer	Jack Lewis
Computer Designers	Jani Beckwith, Lucie Ericksen, Liz Pauw
Illustrators	Michael Mueller, Bob Hansen
Series Design	Peter F. Hancik
Cover Design	Dodie Shoemaker

This book was composed with Corel VENTURA™ Publisher.

Soli Deo Gloria

About the Author

Will David Mitchell has worked with computers since 1973. While teaching computer science at the University of Nebraska, his research showed that people who learn debugging skills first, master computer languages markedly faster. As a result, he stressed debugging techniques the second week in his classes. Whereas no other classes in the university reached the 73 percent mark on standardized tests, Mr. Mitchell's invariably scored in the 80–82 percent range. The only difference was his early emphasis on debugging. In *Debugging Java: Troubleshooting for Programmers*, the author reveals the secrets that can make you a Java master in record time.

Mr. Mitchell began writing magazine articles in 1971 and has authored more than a thousand technical manuals, articles, and papers since. In recent years, he has written five high-tech thriller novels for publication. His popular Web site for authors is http://weblications.net. Besides being an author and computer scientist, he is an independent computer consultant, a jet pilot, a mathematician, an artist, and a musician. He and his family reside near Omaha, Nebraska.

Contents

Acknowledgments

Only God knows the names of all of the people who have contributed to this book. It would take yet another book just to list them. I feel uniquely and undeservedly blessed.

Carol, my wife, and Christie, my daughter, excel at the author's craft. They, and Andrew, my young son, shared time that was rightfully theirs with this book, proofing chapters, bringing surprise snacks, and offering enormous encouragement. Theirs is the greatest sacrifice of all, and adequate words do not exist to express my gratitude and love.

Bill Slater, my brother and fellow computer scientist in Chicago, who redefines the word 'outstanding,' has contributed to this book in a hundred powerful ways, as well as in a few that he knows about. I'm also privileged to have as a close friend and neighbor, Scott Novotny, another genius, who has the unique ability to make observations that penetrate perfectly to the kernel of a matter.

My revered parents, Will and Nelda Mitchell, taught me and my siblings enthusiasm, diligence, honor, music, art, and above all, how to love God and humanity. All of my siblings, Delle Jacobs, John Mitchell, Paul Mitchell, and Kathi Richardson, are fine writers.

Co-workers far too numerous to mention have given me examples and shown me the humor that helps erase the pain of finding bugs. Close personal friends such as Galen, Barb, Robert, Frank, Lonnie, Bill, Lou, Ted, Gary, Steve, Sue, Evelyn, Clarke, Joe, Sam, Roy, Sandy, Dennis, Russ, Don, and several people named Mike, John, and David—you'll see their contributions scattered through this book, and I thank every one of them.

The brilliant people who invented Java, and who have brought it to its current state as the second most popular computer language in the world, drew upon the expertise of those who developed C++, whose knowledge sprang from the art of the C language developers. All of these people deserve my thanks.

Hundreds who have taught me about computer science, these are all contributors, and I wish I could thank each one personally. I'm compelled to mention four of the very wisest: Marilyn Mantel-Guss, Hsing Liu, Stan Wileman, and Matthew Payne.

I mention the following people last, only to add emphasis to their contributions. Osborne/McGraw-Hill should surely be proud of their people. Acquisitions editor, now promoted to editorial director, Wendy Rinaldi, who recruited me to write *Debugging Java*, is the perfect advocate for such projects as this. Her overflowing of remarkable ideas and her enthusiasm have 'made' the series. Her able assistant, Monika Faltiss, coordinated the myriad details of scheduling. I was fortunate, indeed, to get the unsurpassed Mark

Karmendy as the project editor. When I reviewed the final cover for the book, I thought it was one of the 2 or 3 most attractive book covers I had ever seen. William Voss and Dodie Shoemaker designed it. Sincere thanks, also, to authors Chris Pappas and William Murray who conceived the Debugging series, and whose excellent book on Debugging C++ is the series' flagship.

Debugging Java would be far less than it is, except that each of these wonderful people and hundreds more helped create it.

Introduction

What aspect of computer science causes you, your supervisor, and your customers (internal or external) the most pain? Bugs? You're not alone.

The most powerful marketers on the planet got that way by discovering what causes people the most pain, and then by working hard to alleviate the hurt. For the same reason, the world's most respected programmers achieved hero status by producing painless, bug-free code. Many of the best techniques are counter-intuitive, but *Debugging Java* reveals them. It shows you how to:

- Prevent bugs from the start

- Write code that shuns bugs

- Locate and squash the few that get away

- Build a better bug trap

- Write the perfect error message

- Use automated power tools to strip bugs from programs

- Make your users love you

Bugs cause pain because they are inordinately expensive. Consider the double-digit billions spent on the so-called millennium bug, or the cost of replacing a space probe that mistakenly crashes into Mars. While it's mathematically impossible to test for all bugs, it's quite feasible to prevent them from hatching in your Java code. *Debugging Java* reveals a master programmer's powerful secrets for doing that. While this book concentrates on Java and related products, the author's principles apply to any project, even those outside the realm of computer science.

Debugging Java shows you the sources of Java bugs and clever ways to crush them. Here are three examples:

- **Deadline Pressure**   In "Never Miss Another Deadline," this book demonstrates Risk Factor Analysis (RFA) to the public for the first time. RFA lets you estimate project costs three times more accurately than the rest of the industry can manage. RFA estimates are convincing and defensible, letting you win firm, reasonable deadlines from your bosses and clients. By avoiding deadline pressure, you remove a whole class of bugs.

- **Scope Creep**   In "Write Your User Manual First," the author shows you how to turn a user manual into a set of program specifications your user can understand. This 'backwards' approach removes your user's fear of committing to a legal-looking document and makes it easy for you to obtain user sign-off. Then, you simply write and test your programs according to the user manual.

- **Threads**   Threads are inherent to Java. Their raw power enables a seldom-used class of parallel processing algorithms, and their attendant bugs. Such bugs are related to time, data, differing virtual machines, or even how fast you double-click the mouse! Most only occur at the rare moment when two or more threads are in mutually conflicting states, making such bugs very difficult to reproduce. The author reveals the special tactics needed to track, locate, and squash such bugs.

- **Automation**   Most companies test less than a third of the code they sell! The results are roundly cussed and discussed at the world's lunch counters. Java has spawned a score of extremely capable, automatic power tools to help you debug your programs. Using these tools, you can ensure all of your code is tested. You can know that it is tested more thoroughly than any code could have been tested a few short years ago. *Debugging Java* shows you how to use many of the best automated tools.

Truly, your motto can be, as the author's has been for two decades, "Software Guaranteed to Specs Forever."

Chapter 1   Asserts, and informally proves, that no amount of testing can find all bugs. Thus, you must write code that shuns bugs from the start.

Chapter 2   Delves into the psychological and physiological reasons bugs exist. In so doing, it helps you become more creative, or more organized, at your whim. It makes a strong case for writing the documentation before the code, and shows how to turn that documentation into a solid programming specification. Doing so relieves you of most deadline pressures, but the chapter forges on, to introduce Risk Factor Analysis for the first time in a book. This potent tool lets you estimate effort twice as accurately as is possible without it. Moreover, you can defend your estimates, making user signoff a snap.

This chapter shows how to sequence your programming tasks, so that nasty surprises occur early, when you can most easily handle them.

Chapter 3   Begins with how to build a better bug trap. It shows how to instrument your Java code, so that it will tell you when problems occur.

C++ introduced, and Java borrowed, an advanced mechanism for catching errors, that doesn't bury the original source code inside error traps. This chapter shows how and how not to use that mechanism.

It concludes by encouraging you to practice generating bugs, to be familiar with them. Bugs flee from knowledge faster than roaches flee the light.

Chapter 4   Details Risk Factor Analysis (RFA), showing you exactly how to employ it to the best advantage. Programmers must become experts in estimating how long it will take to do something they don't know how to do. What a hoot! Only something like RFA gives you a fighting chance.

Chapter 5   Explains editors and Integrated Development Environments (IDEs). Using a project to teach some of Java's more tricky points, this chapter shows how to turn Microsoft Word into a very capable Java editor, with dozens of automated tools built in. Then, the chapter explains the better Java editors available on the market.

It shows how to make many kinds of errors stand out as if highlighted in red. It shows how to extend your Windows clipboard in ways that prevent whole classes of bugs from hatching.

You can have a Java-oriented spell checker.

"Holey" 3 × 5 cards can organize your project in ways only a computer program can duplicate, but in far less time.

IDEs are scorned by some purists, who write magnificent Java code. However, an IDE can out-type any programmer 10,000:1 and make one-thousandth as many errors in the process. This chapter shows ways to use the most popular IDE editors. Some IDEs are freeware.

Chapter 6   Classifies Java bugs, showing innovative ways to detect and handle them. Some are common to other languages. For instance, during the design phase, any time you have an odd number of conditions to consider, such as men, women, and children, you've likely missed one.

Bugs cluster in specific places. Knowing how to find those places lets you expend 20 percent of your time finding 80 percent of the bugs, instead of the other way round. Those places are different for various classes of bugs: mathematical, logic, syntax, Boolean, data-driven, memory, thread, operator, shifts, string, and others. This chapter shows how to detect such bugs efficiently and to flush them into the open.

Java was specifically written to avoid many banes, such as the nuisances that pointers in C/C++ can become. Java's threads, however, introduce new classes of bugs that you must handle.

Chapter 7   Compares debugging to the fictional Sherlock Holmes' best practices. The chapter returns to philosophy and physiology to show you how to think inductively or deductively, as a matter requires. It shows when and how to use depth-first bug searches, and when to employ the breadth-first tactic.

Personal coding standards are powerful error preventers, and this chapter shares the author's personal set. The important thing is not to adopt these particular standards but to adopt an inviolate set of your own.

Chapter 8   Explains automated debuggers. These potent tools can write test sets for you, analyze your code before you compile, analyze running code, ensure all branches are tested, check for memory leaks, predict thread conflicts, profile for performance or memory hotspots, and do it all unattended, hundreds of times, while you sleep. Since an error might only occur every 100 runs, this advantage can be huge. You can analyze the method calls, the heap, the stack, the RAM, the IO, the ports, and more. You can set break points and watch points that let you see the contents of all threads and variables whenever anything interesting happens. You can change the code on the fly, recompile, and continue, or restart the program.

You can debug a Macintosh in Chicago, a Pentium in Rome, and a VAX in Brisbane, all from a Solaris in San Diego and all at the same time, as they interact with each other. You can detect and repair bugs automatically that you'd never be able to find manually.

Chapter 9   Introduces grand debugging strategies. It's interesting that this book exists in a near-vacuum. There is almost no published information on debugging Java, and not much on debugging in general. Debugging, like testing, benefits from doing things the smart way, and from using the best resources available.

This chapter digs into various kinds of reasoning, as they pertain to debugging. It shows how to employ binary searches to improve debugging, just as they improve file searching. It shows that bottom-up testing, while seldom used, is the most efficient means of producing accurate code.

The chapter cautions against regression errors, and shows how to avoid them. Then it shows how to write test stubs that simulate modules that have not yet been written, so you can test incrementally.

Chapter 10   Scrutinizes testing. Black-box tests are concerned only with input and output. Oppositely, white-box tests look at the code's innermost workings.

The chapter proposes and gives specifications for six automated analyzers for you, or commercial companies to build and sell. Some of these are already incorporated into commercial products, and several are entirely new.

Would you like to know how many bugs remain in your code? There are ways to find out, long before you have located all bugs. This chapter details two ways, leaving a third for Chapter 13.

The chapter concludes with a strong argument that you need a second computer. Compared to the extreme cost of bugs, and even compared to your salary, the price of another computer is insignificant. The same money, invested in savings, would have to garner an interest rate five to ten times the best available.

Similarly, the price of software is shown to be insignificant, compared to what its bugs cost you. This chapter shows why you, and your customers, should always choose robust software, regardless of its price. It's cheaper.

Chapter 11   Explains threads and how they interact. You can't get away from Java threads. They have the reputation of complicating programs, but actually, they simplify everything. Threads emulate how people think and live. Even though we're programmed to write sequential code, the threaded environment makes life easier, because we can look to our humanity for design examples.

However, threads can collide. They can deadlock. They can enter into data races, such as the classic case that might allow two people $1,000 each from a bank account that only has $1,000 in it in the first place, by acting simultaneously. Threads can die, leaving other threads that depend on them, stalled. Whole libraries, notably Swing, are not thread-safe.

Java's **synchronized** statement can prevent data races, and expose the same code to deadlocks. Furthermore, a **synchronized** block runs at about 25 percent speed. Spin locks, monitors, semaphores, polling, multiplexing, schedulers, and other coding methodologies are often more efficient than **synchronized** blocks. This chapter shows how to implement such advanced procedures.

Chapter 12

Helps you ensure that your users remain loyal. Pity the poor user who has to get a report to the CEO in an hour, but who's staring at a little box that reads "Invalid Page Fault." The user knows that the computer's going to crash. Then, the CEO will blame the user, not the real culprit who wrote the buggy code.

Why should we have to back up files anyway?

This chapter shows how to word error messages so the confused user will love you and not search for a rope to kill you. You can even enlist the user's sage advice for free. It all depends on how you present the error.

Answering the basic questions of who, what, why, when, where, and how, is necessary, but can overwhelm. Thus, you should present most of that information in a unique fashion that's most beneficial to you and to your user.

And for Heaven's sake, never let a misspelled word enter an error message!

You should log most error messages to your user's hard disk, in a circular queue that avoids consuming the drive. This chapter shows the easiest way to implement such a queue, and how your tech support team can use it to deliver astounding service, affordably.

Chapter 13

Returns to testing, in the light of new thread knowledge. It shows how most kinds of testing can be automated, to various degrees.

This chapter discusses another ten kinds of tests, such as stress testing, fault insertion, and backup testing.

It concludes with a way to include automated testing into the new paradigm that tells you how many bugs you have left. If you can estimate the number of bugs left, you can decide whether or not to drive the number to zero. The decision may be out of your hands, for economic reasons. On the other hand, lives may depend on your code being bug-free.

Appendix A

Lists a large number of commercial software titles that relate to Java.

Appendix B

Tells you where you can find great volumes of information in books, magazines, newsgroups, Web sites, and commercial training businesses.

Appendix C

Gives you my "21 Laws of Programming," a thought-provoking bit that pokes at a few sacred cows.

Appendix D

Is a glossary of Java-related terms used in this book, along with many not used herein.

Appendix E

Gives the source code for a number of powerful Microsoft Word macros. These macros help you turn Word into a very useful Java editor, with a few features no IDE has so far.

Just for Fun...

Turn the pages to Chapter 1 and see why it's impossible to write a set of tests that will find all bugs. Enjoy!

PART I

Begin with Bugproof Code

CHAPTER 1

You'll Never Catch 'em All!

Bugs, that is.

I'll begin with a rash-sounding claim. In even the smallest program (that has input, output, and processing), it's impossible to construct tests that will locate all bugs!

Now, if that's true, is perfection but a dream? Should we abandon hope and resign ourselves to producing poor-to-mediocre code? God forbid! We who have learned one of the hottest programming languages in history must now strive to create programs so clean that the chances of anyone finding a bug are nil. That's why this book exists. Testing is one of the programmer's best tools for writing master-level code, but as you shall see shortly, testing is insufficient. For example, just before Christmas, 1999, astronauts upgraded the Hubble telescope's computers from 386 to 486 technology, while Pentium-III computers were flying off the shelves. NASA couldn't use newer CPUs because they needed four years to test the chips' imbedded firmware. After four years of testing, NASA still didn't claim their tests were exhaustive. Rigorous testing is not enough. I'll try to prove that statement.

The Proof

You may recall Heron's formula from high school trigonometry. Give Heron's formula the three sides of a triangle and it reveals the area. This formula is just complex enough to challenge early computer students, but we'll use it for a different purpose.

Pretend your task is to use input and output to test a computer program that implements Heron's formula. You are to build test cases. What kinds of data would you input and what would you expect for output?

For example, you might input

- Integers 3, 4, and 5, and expect an integer area of 6.
- Integers other than 3, 4, and 5, expecting a floating-point answer.
- Various floating-point numbers as input.

Please put the book aside for ten minutes at this point and see how many kinds of input and output test sets you can devise. Use the worksheet on the facing page for your work. Further into this chapter, I'll present a rather long list, which is by no means comprehensive.

WORKSHEET

(In grade school, they taught us never to write in a book. Finally, in college, I realized that if I took notes in the margins, I could find and correlate those notes far more easily than if I had to rummage through boxes of papers. Do write in this book! After all, it's yours.)

Neither Debugging nor Testing Finds All Bugs

Teaching university computer classes, I would give the students a ten-minute, ungraded quiz, asking them to devise all the kinds of test data they could for the hypothetical Heron's formula problem. Then we'd tabulate the results. Most classes found 15–18 examples. Occasionally, succumbing to the ultimate bug, a student would write a computer program to solve Heron's formula! That always got a laugh.

After ten minutes, I'd propose a few clever ideas found by previous classes and challenge the students to find more. In the ensuing fun, they would invariably expand the list to 30 or more, and I'd add a couple of items to my personal list. I did this as much for research as for teaching.

One conclusion is that testing is a highly creative and intuitive process. It is quite difficult to think of an exhaustive set of tests. None of my students or colleagues ever did, nor have I. Without an exhaustive set of tests, how can testing find all bugs?

Even if a tester could write an exhaustive set of test classes, such a set is insufficient. For example, one of my best students discovered something amazing about the Pascal compiler. At random, he input 16, 20, and 12.50613300415 into his Heron's formula program, and his program printed 101.001. So far, so good.

The second part of his assignment was to round the results to two decimal places. He expected 101.00 and got an erroneous 101.01 instead. The Pascal compiler rounded incorrectly! However, 101.002 rounded correctly. So did 101.0001, 101.0011, and 101.005.

He proved it was the compiler at fault, and then wrote a new program to test the compiler for further errors. His new program compared the compiler's rounding function with the standard algorithm that rounds numbers. If the comparison revealed a discrepancy, his program printed it.

The first design was to step through all possible floating-point numbers allowed by the quad-precision VAX compiler. When it became apparent this program would consume the VAX for most of the semester, he restricted the program's range. In four evenings, checking billions of possibilities, 101.001 was the only erroneous example it found. We wrote a letter to Digital Equipment Corp. (DEC) and received a kind response. Later, we received a note that DEC had fixed the problem.

The point is that only sheer, random luck let one person isolate a bug that existed in nearly every VAX Pascal program that involved rounded numbers, worldwide! Since the set of floating-point numbers in a VAX can be practically infinite, it takes an infinite number of tests to discover all bugs.

This is not the only such case in history. Remember the problem with early Pentium CPU chips? They didn't calculate floating-point numbers correctly, some of the time. My early Hewlett-Packard (HP) calculator embarrassed its makers with what I recall was an erroneous 17th digit when it calculated pi. I didn't know about it until HP offered to send me a new calculator.

Granted, the above "proof" lacks a certain mathematical rigor, but it demonstrates that no practical amount of testing will certainly find any given bug.

Many semesters of classes compiled this list of test cases. You can probably invent several more kinds of input to try.

- Positive integers like 3, 4, and 5.
- Positive, floating-point numbers like 3.1, 4.1, and 5.1.
- One, two, or three negative integers.
- One, two, or three negative, floating-point numbers.
- All the permutations of positive and negative integers and floats.
- Symbols of numbers with infinite precision like pi and e.
- Rational numbers like 3/7, 4/7, and 5/7, expecting an area of 6/7 instead of about 0.857142.
- Logarithms.
- Letters instead of numbers. The program should still act rationally.
- Special characters, such as $, & and *. The program shouldn't swear back.
- Phrases and words, especially words like "three," "four," and "five," expecting "six."
- Mixed data, such as 3 feet, 4 feet, and 5 feet, expecting 6 square feet in this case.
- Four or more numbers instead of three.
- One or two numbers instead of three.
- No data whatsoever, expecting a message such as "Nothing to do."
- Impossible triangles, such as 3, 4, and 8. Skeptics might try drawing one!
- Points on a plane, such as (3,3), (4,4), and (5,3).
- Points on a sphere or other 3-D surfaces.

- Points in free 3-D space, such as (3,1,2), (4,1,1), and (5,2,2). Notice that in this case, there may be insufficient information, because the space needs to be defined.
- Points in *n*-dimensional space. I'm glad the seventh-grade prodigy who suggested that one is on our side! She didn't mean space of any finite number of dimensions. There's a difference, she pointed out.
- Points in fractional-dimension space, such as is inhabited by the Mandelbrot or Julia Set, and Cantor's Dust.
- Isosceles triangles with one side equal to zero. The area should be zero.
- Triangles with two sides equal to zero and one nonzero. Such triangles can't exist.
- 0, 0, 0, which is different from no data whatsoever.
- Null strings.
- Booleans and other types of data.
- Very large input numbers, smaller than the maximum, designed to give an area slightly smaller than the maximum.
- Very large input numbers, smaller than the maximum, designed to give an area larger than the maximum.
- One or more input number larger than the maximum allowed by the computer.
- Very small, nonzero numbers, approaching the limits of precision.
- Programming objects, such as list boxes, or their contents.
- Two huge sides and one extremely small side, which make a valid triangle.
- Two huge sides and one extremely small side, which make an invalid triangle.
- The outputs of functions and other processes.
- Input data from various external processes.
- Binary, octal, and hex numbers.
- Numbers in other systems, such as septuadecimal or duodecimal.
- Mixed systems of numbers, such as binary, octal, and decimal.
- Encrypted data.
- Zipped numbers, such as from PKZIP.

- Imaginary numbers, such as 3i, 4i, 5i.
- Numbers on the complex plane, such as (3 + 3i), (7 + 3i), (7 + 8i).
- Numbers from programs like WordPerfect which strip off the 8th bit.
- Cells from a spreadsheet.
- Memory addresses of numbers.
- Thousands of combinations of the above.

Obviously, many of these tests yield invalid triangles, but the program should handle invalid results as sanely as valid ones. For instance, Heron's formula cannot handle 3, 4, and 8, which comprise an impossible triangle. Give it those numbers and it tries to calculate the square root of (-59.0625). At that, it balks. The program should not abort, or even say that it cannot perform the calculation. It probably should not throw the usual Java exception. Instead, it should detect the problem and emit a proper, user-friendly message. Chapter 12 discusses how to emit the perfect error message.

Incidentally, I'm still waiting for a student to mention a test case that presents the points in one of the most common of all measurement systems: latitude and longitude. Yes, finding test cases is a highly creative process.

It Gets Worse

I haven't even mentioned the fact that input / output testing has another difficult task. It must also identify all the cases of invalid input data.

The difficulty worsens by orders of magnitude when a program gains a database. Now, the results of a current test can depend upon every other test that has been performed, because the remembered data can affect what paths the program will take. As a trivial example, a program will generally follow one path when there is no data—that is, it will collect information and build data tables. When there is data, it won't build tables, because they are already present. A valid reservation for an airplane flight might depend on many things, such as these data-driven items, and scores more:

- Do the airports exist?
- Is there a flight between those airports at that time?
- Is the credit card any good?
- Is the ticket agent authorized to sell this ticket?

- Is the flight filled?
- Are there first-class seats available, if first class is desired?
- Is the airplane operational?
- Is the fare correct?

If you're writing test conditions for a new Java compiler, your chore takes a wild, new turn. Exhaustive tests must detect all good syntax, and all bad syntax. They must check all possibly valid Java programs, and must ensure no syntactically invalid Java program compiles cleanly.

Code Must Shun Bugs from the Start

Even if it were possible to find all the bugs in a real-world program, such an extravagant testing process would be prohibitively expensive. Project managers must manage costs, and cannot allow testing to consume a project's entire budget. So, again, does this mean programmers should abandon hope and not test their code? Far from it! This chapter's exercise is an example of *black box* testing, and only shows that black box testing, alone, is insufficient. There are many other, powerful ways to prevent bugs, including other methods of testing.

White box testing is the opposite of black box testing in one important aspect. Black box testing hides the source code. It tests by inserting input and examining the output. In direct contrast, white box testing exposes the source code. The idea is for a small team of programmers, usually including the developer, to examine the code in detail. Best practice has the developer explain everything in the code to a team, which includes a recorder / secretary, one or two programmers from another project, perhaps a couple of trainees, one or two peers, and at least one highly experienced developer.

The team leader sets the stage by noting that all code has bugs, and that a successful white box test is one that finds bugs, not one which fails to find them. In other words, the idea is to find bugs, not to hope there are none. When I conduct such tests, I award small prizes for bugs found, with the developer getting double prizes.

White box testing finds bugs that black box testing would miss. However, white box testing is also insufficient. Recursion is particularly difficult to test in a white box environment, because the program's paths depend on input data and prior decisions the program makes. The limits of the human mind, as well as limits of patience, prevent white box testing from exercising all paths in a complex program.

Java identifies and disallows dead code at compile time, so it does some *path testing* for you. However, at compile time, it is impossible for the compiler to foresee all possible data conditions and program decisions. By examining all possible paths, you can find code that will not execute, but that the compiler would allow. However, such testing might well miss design errors.

Attempting to pare the infinite number of tests down to manageable size, developers have tried various versions of *decision coverage*. The idea is that all branches of each decision, and all procedure entry points, should be traversed at least once. However, aberrant code that has loops with multiple entry points would not be tested properly by decision coverage. Fortunately, a Java programmer might have to think a while to devise a loop with two input points. A more difficult bug for decision coverage to test is one involving misuse of DeMorgan's Laws. For instance, if a programmer uses 'and' where 'or' is proper, and hasn't done that at least once, decision coverage might fail spectacularly when the erroneous operator takes the program down the wrong paths.

Java makes testing easier by removing whole classes of bugs. However, Java introduces new classes of bugs in the autonomous threads it can generate. These bugs are driven almost by coincidence. Thread conflicts such as deadlocks, stalls, and deadly embraces might be possible in a program and not occur for years. Then again, they might occur ten minutes later but not again for a month. Exhaustively testing for such anomalies is as impossible as writing an exhaustive set of black box tests for Heron's formula.

As far as *unit testing* is concerned, I'll quote a wizened FAA check pilot before he awarded me my flight instructor's ticket. "I presume you can fly. If you cannot, this exam is over. I want to see if you can teach while you fly." All programmers must master unit testing, which is little more than a one-person white box test, even though unit testing is about the least efficient way to find bugs. The only method less effective is letting a chimp have the keyboard.

Users rightly demand bug-free code. World-class programmers, those who produce bug-free code, test their programs and submit their code to others for testing, because testing does find bugs. But, to attain and retain hero status, top programmers must do more than that. They must program to prevent bugs from the start, set better traps for those that hatch anyhow, and even enlist the user to find the few that might remain. Fortunately, Java programmers have powerful tools, techniques, and strategies for creating bugproof programs. The language, itself, helps you in the following ways:

- The Java language eliminates many bugs by forbidding pointer arithmetic. I've read two entire books that were devoted to trapping pointer bugs in C and C++.

- By disallowing the **goto** statement and requiring everything to be in classes, Java prevents most spaghetti bugs from hatching.

- By adopting the **try/catch/finally** ideas from ML and C++, Java's error trapping is as good as the state of the art allows.

- When the Java designers specified that primitive classes must always span the same numbers of bits, regardless of the computer platform in use, and that the language would be strongly typed, a host of numeric bugs fled, trailed by a deadly class of bugs caused by overwriting the wrong areas of RAM.

- Because Java checks array and string bounds for you, yet another class of bugs is squashed at runtime.

- Similarly, the way the language checks casts for legality kills another class of bugs at runtime.

- By automating most garbage collection, Java eliminates most, but not all, memory-allocation errors—the kind that can even crash an operating system and cause numerous memory leaks.

- By strictly specifying the byte-code verification process at the input of every Java Virtual Machine (JVM), by allowing digital signatures, and by specifying a clear "sandbox model" for Java to use when running unknown code, Java thwarts most security bugs and malicious attacks at the front door.

Sun, Inc., and third parties give away and sell scores of software titles to help you:

- Profile your code, identifying areas that consume inordinate amounts of time, RAM, CPU power, or disk space.

- Prove that all of your code is useful and has been tested.

- Analyze threads for potential conflicts.

- Prevent memory leaks that the garbage collector cannot discover.

- Regression-test your modified programs, to ensure you didn't introduce new bugs.

No language can prevent all bugs. No tool can find them all. However, a good programmer, using best practices and strategies, empowered by a language like Java, and using powerful tools, can write bug-free programs. This book is about testing, but also about using the tools, techniques, and strategies that go beyond testing. This book gives you the power to make your code as bug-free as possible. Read on to see how you can confidently "guarantee your software to specs forever."

CHAPTER 2

Prevent Java Bugs from Hatching

It's a subtle point that one of Java's finest aspects is its ability to multitask, or thread. It's subtle because threads emulate how people work.

People do several things at once. At this moment, I'm typing, hearing my wife and young son interact about dinner, thinking about thinking, hearing a fire siren, and gently rocking in a chair without falling out of it. My lungs and heart work almost autonomously. My eyes blink when dry, and if I want, I can reach over for a sip of soda. Without my realizing it, my brain is running thousands or millions of simultaneous threads, just as yours is.

Java appears to do that sort of multitasking, so it appears to be more 'alive' than any procedural language does. It helps developers create and organize programs as if they were everyday thought processes. All this thread activity frees Java programmers to develop software that acts more like a mind does. Thus, you can look to your humanity to find better ways to program. Why do you look for approaching cars before crossing a street? For the same kind of reason, safety, you might check whether or not a file is open before opening it.

Development Philosophy

Programming involves two psychological opposites: creativity and organization. Even the physiology of the brain separates the two processes. Devising a new method uses, primarily, the right hemisphere of the human brain, whereas the act of organizing and writing it down moves more to the left hemisphere.

Programming requires both activities to be effective, and most failed projects do so because of poor organization.

Similarly, devising software tests uses the brain's right hemisphere, whereas performing those tests uses the left hemisphere. Testing is a full-brain activity. In fact, creating a suite of software tests may be the most creative activity you will do. Testing requires a specific mind-set, one that seems uncommon among programmers. Some developers might say that a test is successful if it finds nothing wrong. That view is somewhat like taking your sputtering automobile to the mechanic and rejoicing when the mechanic's tests failed to find the trouble. Similarly, while nobody wants to hear the doctor say they're about to have a heart attack, not knowing is far worse. A successful computer test is one that locates as many bugs as possible, so they can be fixed.

A sound development philosophy considers these unusual elements, among many others:

- Creativity and organization are opposites.
- Finding bugs is a good thing.
- Risky elements take precedence.

Left Brain <==> Right Brain

To some degree, we create and organize at the same time. However, the creative and the organizational processes are opposites in the brain.

As mentioned, your brain is divided into two hemispheres—a left brain and a right brain, if you will allow. Connecting the two is a rich set of communicative nerves called the corpus callosum.

Studies on head trauma, epilepsy, and cancer patients have shown that a person can function quite well when missing one half of the brain! However, some abilities are diminished. Your left hemisphere, or left brain, contains most of your organizational ability, while your right hemisphere, or right brain, houses most of your creative ability. If you were to lose the left half of your brain, your creativity wouldn't be affected much, but your ability to organize those creative thoughts would drop significantly. You'd become what some might call scatterbrained. On the other hand, if you lost the right half of your brain, you'd still be able to organize with the best of them, but having a creative thought would be much harder. You'd become single-minded.

I happen to host a popular Web site (http://Weblications.Net) for authors that discusses this information in greater detail. Recently, I received a kind and complimentary email from a lady who had lost the left half of her brain in a cancer operation. Her letter said this explained why she was having such difficulty organizing her writing, although her creativity seemed to have increased significantly after her operation. She was quite relieved to know why, and sent a lovely poem for me to enjoy.

As you are developing code, you must use both hemispheres of your brain. You have to create new thoughts, and you must organize them into a cohesive pattern. In Java, as in other object-oriented languages, the pattern does not need to be linear, but it must be organized.

The left brain is jealously dominant. It hates losing control of your whole mind. While you are organizing, it is difficult to become creative. On the other hand, while you are being creative, it is quite easy to slip into your organizational mode. I believe this is due to early childhood training, but the corpus callosum seems to pass information more efficiently from the creative, right hemisphere to the organizational, left hemisphere than in the other direction. The result is that most people in our society are quite logical, and not very creative.

Or so they think.

Applying all of that to the art of writing bugproof code, consider this fact:

While you're developing, no matter how good your planning is, you'll think of new and better ways to do things. It's important that you do! However, doing so presents a dilemma.

If you stop what you're doing and work on the new idea, you lose your current stream of creativity and must restart it later. If you do that, the chances of design bugs creeping into your code grow enormously.

This is because your stream of creativity contains hundreds of links to things you need to do. You may have an entire algorithm in your mind, complete with:

- Several ways to implement it
- Several possible calls to library functions
- Declarations to make
- Types of loops to use
- How you need to count from one here and zero there
- And, of course, how this great system will "blow the socks off" your users

Half of these thoughts may not return a day or an hour later.

On the other hand, if you continue what you're doing and hope to recall that new idea later, you'll lose that new idea a significant portion of the time.

It is equally important to remember new ideas later when you need them, and to remember what you're doing at the moment, so you don't skip a critical step.

Say you're writing the comments of an intricate routine, when you think of another approach that might be even better. What do you do? Which thought do you want to risk losing?

Fortunately, you can keep both. Enter **QQQ** and write down just the germ of that idea, right there where you are. Make the comment complete, but neglect grammar, syntax, and even spelling, then hurry back to the original task. Just get a representation of that thought into a semipermanent medium so you can continue with the current creative process.

Why QQQ? There's no special reason, except that the string "QQQ" is unlikely to appear in a program. A friend of mine uses his initials instead of QQQ. Later, you can search for all instances of it, and your note will help you recall that lost thought.

A few minutes later, the thought might cross your mind that you need to check another mental thread. Again, enter **QQQ** and that idea. Then return to your first task.

If, instead, you chase the ideas as rapidly as they occur, you stand a chance of missing the intricacies of your original path. This is an opening for bugs to creep into your code. As you write, you are considering all the ways your code could succeed and fail, and you must catch all of the failure modes. Chase another idea and you're very likely to forget some failure modes.

On the other hand, if you ignore those side trails, you'll find yourself forgetting them long before you can return and investigate them. Many of those side trails are failure modes you need to investigate, or for which you must allow extra programming. It's imperative to return to each one. The QQQ comments will help you.

The very last thing before releasing your program is to search for all instances of QQQ. There should be none.

Commonly, while programming, I'll have an idea that applies to another project. I find that 3×5 index cards are perfect for capturing such thoughts. One thought fits nicely on a single card. The cards are easily sorted, easily inserted into books, and even fit above the keypad on your keyboard. At night, leave one stuck above the keypad, telling you where you quit and what is yet to be done. That removes yet another source of design bugs. My colleagues call me the 3×5 card king and I joke with them about it. Many of them have become converts, and the office supplies department has quadrupled their stock.

The whole idea is to enhance creativeness and organization, simultaneously.

Chapter 5 contains several useful 3×5 card tricks.

How to Become More Creative

Consider the word "think". That's a nice, logical, or left-brain word, isn't it? It's a word the left brain uses to assert its dominance. It's a word that the creative, right-brained person must distrust.

Temporarily replace it with the right-brain word "believe." Or "feel." Or "imagine." These are right-brain words.

Now, to start the creative juices flowing, you must move your mental processes out of the left brain, into the right. But how? The ancients would talk of creating when the muse struck. Some authors and artists have become alcoholics, because they found alcohol seemed to help them release their inhibitions and create. Some of their critics said what they wrote while under the influence of alcohol stank. Don't seek your muse in alcohol. You won't find her there for long, and shortly you'll lose her forever.

Instead, look to understanding your brain.

Since the left brain dominates, put the left brain to sleep, and the right brain takes over. Then create as long as you can. Ban any logical or organizational kinds of thoughts, or the left brain will awaken and you'll lose your creative streak.

So how do you lull your left brain to sleep? It's actually quite simple. The left brain gets bored easily, and when bored, it goes to sleep. Bore it to sleep.

Few things are as boring as a long automobile or plane trip. As soon as the novelty wears off, your left brain goes to sleep, and your right brain is ready to be creative. Take advantage of those times. If you're driving or piloting, get a pocket tape recorder and talk your ideas into it at random. Be prepared to drop the recorder when safety demands. If you're a passenger, take a notebook or a notebook computer.

One of the reasons we go to sleep at night is that the left-brain gets bored and drops off. Hundreds of successful writers keep notepads at their bedsides. In that wonderful right-brain half-sleep time called dozing, you can find thousands of creative ideas. Force yourself to consciousness enough to jot them down before they evaporate forever. Don't evaluate them and decide this one is worthy, or that one isn't. Doing so is a left-brain activity. Don't trust your left brain too much at such times. If you evaluate the ideas, you'll find you only rouse yourself to write down one in a hundred, missing 75 great (and 24 ungreat) ideas in the process.

It's noon, and you're sitting down to program. Now what? That deadline is in five days, and you have 3,000 lines to write by then. It's about time to panic, right?

Wrong! It's time to relax, as if you had all the confidence in the world.

As long as you're thinking of how you're going to have to panic, your left brain is in control. If you can relax, you can lull your left brain to sleep and, bingo, you'll find your right brain is ready to give you all 3,000 lines in record time.

Stop thinking, and believe for a while.

Plan to return to this little bug momentarily.

Go through a personalized, formal process of forcing your body to relax every time you sit down to program. Consider things like these:

- If you can, turn off the phone. Hang a sign on the door that you're creating and are not to be disturbed. Warn your coworkers or family that you keep a grizzly bear in there, and they must not open the door while you're creating.

- Sit down. Stretch all of your muscles, tense them, and relax them.

- Close your eyes. Pray. Meditate silently on things that are good, and lovely, and just, and kind, and of good report, thus allowing no distressing thoughts to enter your mind.

- Focus on breathing more slowly and deeply.

- Continue for ten to fifteen minutes, and then while you are still relaxed, begin to write—mostly comments or whatever comes to your mind. Start at the middle, or the beginning or end, or just somewhere in parallel with your subject.

- Let the creativity flow for as long as it will. Here are four tips to keep things flowing:

  - Don't evaluate anything. Just keep writing.

  - Don't correct anything—grammar, spelling. Just keep writing.

- Don't stop to think of the correct command or look up a reference. Just put down a word that's close, identify it with the letters QQQ, and keep writing, knowing that you can search for QQQ later and reorganize your thoughts.

- Whatever you do, *just keep writing*.

When you're done, believe you are not yet done. At that point, begin to read through what you've written—not to edit it, but to let it spark new ideas in your right brain. Ignore your left brain telling you that you should organize or correct your thoughts. You're still looking for ideas. As you get one, write it down, wherever you are. Beside it, insert QQQ.

You are trying to capture what your mind is thinking. Fortunately or not, you can think about seven times faster than you can speak. The fastest typist can speak about four times faster than he or she can type, and that's five times faster than you can push a pencil. So learn to type very fast. Even if you type at 80 words per minute, you're able to think 25–100 times that fast, but there's no sense in typing 20 words per minute and thinking 100–400 times that fast.

Every second you waste putting words on the screen is a second for a brilliant idea to vanish, never to return.

However, rereading helps you regain most of those evaporated ideas—until you let your left brain become dominant. Rereading seems to be the equivalent of rebooting your right brain, because most of the great ideas disappear in that process. Recalling them is like trying to recall details of a dream you had an hour previous. It may even be the same mental process.

Finally, your left brain just won't be able to stand it any longer, and will reassert itself by screaming, "I've absolutely got to get this mess organized."

Then, it's time. Creative time is over. Let your left brain do what it does so superbly. Let it organize your creativity into a cohesive piece of code, days before your deadline.

All of this is only magic, mirrors, and pixie dust unless you can believe that it works. Logically, it can never work unless you believe that it works, so logically, there's no evidence that it can work. So, logically, it truly can't work. Right?

Notice that word "logically"? Isn't it amazing how the left brain can deceive both itself and you?

Prove that the magic works. Take this simple writing test.

Get a clock with a second hand. Remember that little bug in the margin a couple pages back? Go back there and run through your right-brain process again.

When you're ready to write, note the time to the nearest second.

---

[1] The author types at 80 wpm and reads around 4,000 wpm, or 50 times as fast. Some people hit the 8,000 wpm reading rate, with as much comprehension as people who read at more leisurely speeds.

Your writing assignment is simple. Write for exactly six minutes, as fast as you can, on the subject of:

"Why I Program."

Count the number of words you wrote. Say it comes to 200.

Multiply by 10 and you have the number of words you write per hour. In this case, you'd be writing at a rate of 2,000 words an hour. That's astounding when you consider that an average novel consists of 80,000 words. In 40 hours, at that rate, you could draft the "Great American Novel." Think of how fast your documentation can fly out of your fingertips!

You'll find much more on that subject later in this chapter, because one of the better ways to prevent bugs is to write the documentation as early as possible.

Some other day, try it the other way. No relaxing. Write a paragraph, go back and massage it to get it right, then continue to the next paragraph, for six minutes. Your writing rate drops dramatically, probably to a few hundred words an hour. Moreover, you'll often find you acquire a case of writer's block.

Your grammar will be better in the second case, but anyone can correct grammar, and few people think they can write creatively. Ask them!

Writer's block never happens when you write with your right brain. It has a gazillion ideas in it that you can never find time to type into your keyboard, because people just don't live that long.

Is this exciting or what? No more writer's block, and your output jumps manyfold.

Not only that, you'll soon find that what you do write is far more creative and innovative than ever before, whether it's documentation or Java code. The reason is, you're writing from your heart, not your mind. Even if you're writing about mathematical logic, you need to write from your heart, from your passion, not from your mind. That I know, because all my university degrees are in math.

It's the best of all possible worlds.

Joy! The morning is fresh, the flowers are beautiful, and you just proved to yourself how very creative you truly are!

How to Be More Organized

Creation and organization are the twin difficulties programmers face. Good organizational skills help you write programs that shun bugs. Chapter 5 discusses a number of ways to improve your organizational skills, perhaps dramatically.

Programmers Build; Testers Break

While programming, you are trying to make things work for the first time. It's almost unnatural, trying to break the beautiful brainchild you have constructed so carefully.

Conversely, a tester's purpose is to break your program in any way possible. Testing seems mean-spirited in nature.

Some programming shops have tiger teams, which exist to test code. The supervisors realize that building and testing require opposite mind-sets. Tiger team members brainstorm diabolical new ways to break programs. Some go to the extreme of wearing black shirts and hats as a symbol of their esprit de corps. Despite hating the tiger teams, programmers do learn better coding techniques from them.

When you finish a function, consider the Heron's formula exercise. How many ways can you reasonably test it? Imagine your code sitting before the tiger team. How well would it fare? How would they try to break it? You're as creative and intelligent as the tiger team members, so put yourself in their shoes.

You'll save yourself some embarrassment, and you'll write a better function.

If you are the project manager, these paragraphs—especially the last sentence—should raise a red flag in your mind. I purposely wrote them in a negative light.

Never let embarrassment enter the picture if you want to keep the project moving steadily ahead. Otherwise, your creative people will become more and more reluctant to release their code to the testers. When they receive testing feedback, they will be defensive and unreceptive.

On the contrary, instruct everyone that when a test is successful—that is, when it finds bugs—this is a good event. The bugs are there. Recall the Heron's formula exercise? The idea is to find them, not to hope they remain hidden from that embarrassing tiger team, so the customer will find them.

Free your creative people to be more creative, instead of making them worry about what will happen when someone finds their bugs. Instill in your designers, analysts, and developers that the sin is not to have bugs, but to scorn practices that prevent them.

Documents First

Do you hate documentation? If so, you're in good company, because most developers do. Research convinced me that programmers who write the documents first have a huge efficiency advantage. They finish their code faster, it runs more efficiently, and it has far fewer bugs. There are many reasons why you should consider documenting first. Among them are the following:

- If you document your program before you write it, you've written it to a plan, because your documentation is your plan.

- Your documentation is also your test plan, so you don't need to write that.

- Writing documentation first is akin to performing the more risky tasks first. It's a relief to get them finished—and you have fewer headaches at the end of the day.

- When your program is ready to deliver, you don't have to write the documentation, and deadlines don't affect its quality.

- The way to get over hating documentation is to do it first.

Users often know what they want but not what they need. Unfortunately, it's seldom the programmer's job to tell them what they need. It is, however, the programmer's job to help users discover what they need, so that the needs can be communicated precisely into a set of specifications.

Without good programming specifications, it is difficult to give users what they need, or what they want. Then, after the program is finished, much of the work must be abandoned or redone because it doesn't satisfy the users' needs. What a waste of talent and time! What an expensive bug!

User Manual First

Your first major goal should be to solidify your programming specifications. In order to proceed, you need a road map to guide you, and a clearly defined end to tell you when you arrive. Specifications give you these things. However, the typical user has difficulty with a set of specifications written in legal or programming terms. Until there is understanding between users and developers, design bugs abound.

The innovative solution is to write the user manual first!

Ask your user to write large parts of the user manual. Present the idea as an ideal way for your user to show you exactly what kind of program to write. If your user cannot articulate what he or she wants, you can only guess. While guesses occasionally come out right, the odds are terribly skewed out of your favor. On the other hand, your user manual can become that road map, as well as your test plan. When your program does what the user manual says it does, your work is done.

Generally, you will have to write the user manual, but coordinate with your user very closely, and write it before you start programming.

Concentrate on input and output, leaving the processing for your technical documentation. Identify all the sources and contents of the input. Input is, of course, any information the program must know, whether coming from files, users, or the design. Programmers commonly forget to include two things: constants and filenames.

For output, design your screen and report presentations, and specify what information gets stored. The most common omission in this area is the set of error messages.

Identify any timing issues in the input and output. If inputting a certain file must precede generating a report, mention that fact. If files must be input in a certain order, or if they arrive on specific dates, include that data. Note when end-of-month reports and the like occur.

Watch for interface issues. Look for potential conflicts between asynchronous, threaded processes, especially when threads touch common data of any kind.

Before publication, manually try your formulas on real data. Test your algorithms to ensure they are not flawed. Consider alternative, similar formulas. For instance, you can find more than one way to calculate the standard deviation, as well as several mathematically equivalent formulas for each way.

If anything divides or averages, note that you must avoid division-by-zero errors there. For instance, if you average zero elements, you'll divide by the count, which is zero. If you take logarithms, watch for the fact that $\log(1) = 0$, and $\log(0)$ is a form of division by zero.

In reports, try to proceed hierarchically down the report, from heading, to detail, to summary. Reports that use other orders are inherently difficult and buggy. Reports with detail information in the summary or header are error prone. Besides, a hierarchical approach yields a more understandable report.

To help your user with colors and backgrounds, prepare a sampler. Create a dozen typical "looks" for your graphical user interface (GUI) and present them as separate screens in a special program. The user can choose one, and thus give you the preferred background, colors, fonts and icons, saving you from several common design bugs.

Obtain agreement, and create a gem.

Getting a Firm Signoff

When your manual is done, treat it as your set of specifications—and as your test plan. Approach your users with the idea that you'll deliver a program that does exactly these things, no more and no less, and ask if that will satisfy them. Remind them that if they come to you with enhancements later, those changes require a new manual, extra work, and extra time, all of which must be negotiated. So, the time to include enhancements is now!

Go through your new manual with your users. On each screen shot, show what will happen when they click a button. Follow every path in the manual. Scrutinize each screen and printout. Go through each formula. Few things can be more persuasive than such a walk-through, for showing that your program will do what the users want.

Nothing prevents scope creep—with its attendant deadline pressure, which causes its own class of deadly bugs—better than a firm set of specifications.

User Manual Becomes Programming Specifications

Your manual tells what the program will do, but not how. That's fine, because the "how" part of the equation is your responsibility. However, a user manual is not a complete set of programming specifications. You need to add some details. Fortunately, the user manual is already a framework for the specifications set. You should add such things as these:

- Time analysis—that is, what deadlines you are willing to accept. See "Risk Factor Analysis (RFA)" in Chapter 4. RFA lets you estimate timelines so accurately that you'll probably never miss another deadline.

- Cost analysis—that is, what resources (money, people, tools, hardware) you need for each part of the project.

- Algorithms you intend to consider.

- References to programming standards you've already established.

Then, take your cost analysis to your manager and your users, showing the resources needed for each piece of the system. Your manager or users may decide that certain pieces are too expensive and should be eliminated, or delayed for a new phase. However, when the users realize they'll get a program that does what they want, and if the price is right, they'll gladly authorize the work.

So much to do!

True, but the process becomes geometrically easier with practice. Sooner than you think, you'll write such things in an afternoon and be programming according to a map engraved in steel, with a lighthouse at the end that tells you when you're done. Few things make programming more fun.

Learn to Love Javadoc

Once, writing in COBOL, I was fortunate enough to pull a hat trick with my user manual. I was able to organize the manual the same way I planned to write the program. With a flash of inspiration, I copied the manual into a new file, and wrote a ten-line BASIC program that turned the whole thing into a set of line-by-line comments. Then, I began writing the COBOL code around the comments. I liked the results so well that I've tried that approach on nearly every project since.

The first benefit is organizational. Manuals are easy to organize, and it usually makes sense to organize a program the same way. Then, there's no need to reinvent the organization.

The second benefit is that when your method, class, or application is done, most of the comments are neatly in place. Generally, if there is a problem with the comments, it is that there are too many comments!

Have you ever been accused of that sin? Likely not.

Java is interpreted as well as compiled. BASIC and other interpreted languages suffer degraded performance when they have too many comments. The interpreter must read every line, comment or not, at runtime. Thus comments slow execution in most interpreted languages.

Java is an exception. Java has no performance penalty from comments, no matter what kind they are. The compiler strips them out while creating its bytecode. It is true that a plethora of comments slows the actual compilation process, but only a little bit, and never at runtime. Well-commented Java code runs at the same speed as the same code without comments.

More crucial is the fact that well-commented code is about five to ten times faster to enhance or maintain.

Two years ago, I inherited a huge, mission-critical, Visual Basic system that needed six months of enhancements—an aggressive schedule. A week later, I found there was a political struggle in the two layers above me. I discovered that when my manager walked in, requiring that I fully document the entire system in great detail before proceeding with the upgrades. Complying would completely subvert the deadline, so I began asking discreet questions.

It turned out that my enhancements and deadline had the rapt attention of stockholders, because a lucrative corporate merger was in the wind. This software was a key part of the company's value. If the enhancement schedule slipped, the company value would decrease correspondingly. If that happened, people higher up would be embarrassed, which some cynics speculated might be my manager's goal. If that happened, guess which scapegoat's neck would probably get the axe! However, it was clear that I'd also get the axe if I didn't meet my manager's documentation demands on time, and that would take two months. With my protests dissipating into the wind, I had to become creative.

Although this was a Visual Basic application, javadoc showed me the answer. The code was beautifully commented, so I wrote an application that documented the whole system. It relied on those good comments. It examined the source code for such keywords as **Sub**, **Function**, and **Dim**, as well as for comment delimiters. It collected the program's comments, the procedure names, and the variable declarations into a text file, adding a bit of formatting along the way. Then I tweaked the result with a word processor, making heavy use of macros.

Four days later, I could have placed the page-equivalent of five novels on my manager's desk. Instead, I dove into the enhancements and was fortunate to complete everything—documents and code—a few days ahead of schedule.

I merely implemented what javadoc does natively. When you use the /** style of comments, you enable javadoc.

The Java compiler treats javadoc comments just like ordinary comments, and, as mentioned, it strips them out at compile time. Thus, there is no performance penalty in using javadoc.

Javadoc prepares HTML formatted documentation that you can view with any browser. Several HTML files are produced, with hyperlinks between them. You can include HTML markup tags like <PRE> and <IT> to show code usage, but you should not add tags like <H3> <B> that alter the document's format. Chapter 5 will demonstrate automated ways to build a set of comments for each method header. Some of these comments, such as the class' or method's purpose, should be in javadoc.

Design Tip
*When you scan the list of special javadoc comments, that is, the ones that begin with the @ sign, notice that @version and @author can only be used with classes. @param, @return, and @exception can only be used with methods. Javadoc will disregard @author comments for methods, for instance. If you want to name the author of a method, leave off the @ sign and put the author's name in its own /** style comment.*

Error Watch
If javadoc cannot find your source code file, it produces a stub HTML file but does not warn you. When you take the trouble to get the command line right, go one more step and view javadoc's HTML output to be sure you created something usable.

Risky Elements Before Safe Ones

A typical project, at least one worthy of your talents, contains elements you can write directly, and others for which you will have to do some thinking. You may have to perform some research. There may be elements you are not certain are possible. Your program may need to go where no program has gone before, and for it to do that, you might have to invent a new paradigm.

Java came into being because of that last kind of situation.

It makes sense to solve risky elements first. Otherwise, you might expend weeks or months of effort before you discover that a particularly risky element kills the project.

Handle Surprises Early, Not Late

Solving a particularly risky element may be impossible. Alternatively, it may be feasible, but it may consume more than the entire project's budget. Knowing that at the start helps you and your manager keep things flowing smoothly. For instance, you might do any of the following:

- Cancel the project, expending the resources elsewhere
- Delay the project until a new tool or paradigm comes along
- Purchase and learn to use an existing software tool
- Find an expert who excels at doing this particular risky thing
- Eliminate the high-cost element but retain the valuable remainder
- Move the risky element to the next project phase

The ubiquitous 80:20 rule holds here. It states that 80 percent of the elements will require 20 percent of the effort, and 20 percent will require 80 percent of the effort. Those 20 percent are generally the risky ones. However, to be certain which they are, you should categorize your project into these subjective orders of risk:

A. "I've done this element many times before and know exactly how to do it."

B. "I've seen this done, or maybe I did it once, quite a while ago."

C. "I'm pretty sure my colleague knows how to do this, or else I'll need to perform a fair amount of research."

D. "It appears all the necessary information is available. I don't know how to do this, but I'm confident I can find a way."

E. "This may not even be possible, but I'll give it a jolly good go."

F. "Can't be done. And you want it delivered when?"

Then, work on the items in reverse order: F to A.

The primary reason for managing projects in this manner is bug defense. Bugs cluster into risky areas. This is because areas of low risk have already been subjected to considerable brainpower and experience. The potential bugs in those areas are well known and documented.

For example, the Java **for** loop has room for a classic bug. Most statements require a semicolon at the end, and the **for** loop allows one there, but in general, you don't want a semicolon there. Consider this Java program:

```
1: class ZeroToNine {
2:     public static void main(String[] arguments) {
3:         int i = 0;
4:         for (i=0; i<10; i++);
5:             {
6:                 System.out.println(i);
7:             }
8:     }
9: }
```

It only prints the number 10, not the promised list of numbers from 0 through 9, because the loop runs to completion before the **println** statement occurs. That's because the semicolon at the end of the **for** loop delimits the loop. When the loop is finished, i = 10 and the block executes. You knew that.

Remove the semicolon from line 4 and the **println** statement is inside the loop.

Incidentally, the **for** example is one argument for adopting coding standards. One preferred standard puts the left curly brace directly after the beginning of a loop, as a psychological reminder that no semicolon belongs there. Line 4, programmed this way, would look odd:

```
4:             for (i=0; i<10; i++); {
```

It is important to prevent bugs, and standards help. When you cannot prevent bugs, it is equally important to find them early, because it is cheaper to eradicate them early than late. When you cannot do that, you become prone to deadline pressure, which incubates the most deadly sorts of bugs found in code. They are caused because programmers don't have (or take) time to eradicate or prevent them.

Avoid Deadline Pressure

If you have two weeks' worth of work to finish by this Friday, and your job is on the line, you're going to produce buggy code. For one thing, you won't have the time to test it thoroughly. For another, while your right brain considers how to create the correct algorithms, your left brain dominates your thinking and won't let you create efficiently. Your left brain is considering survival: how to explain to the boss, how to reword the first paragraph in your résumé, what you'll say to your spouse who's going to make the mortgage payment, and a dozen other disaster-related thoughts. Your dominant left brain defeats itself by not letting your creative right brain program you out of trouble.

If your job isn't on the line, there's a good possibility that the amount of your next pay increase is.

Such is deadline pressure. Enlightened managers know this and avoid it for you. They place themselves squarely between your survival and those who might threaten it. They shoulder the responsibility and force others to accept the fact that the program will take the extra, unavoidable, two weeks. They know that if they don't do that, the program will probably take an extra six weeks and still be buggy when delivered.

Such managers manage projects and external forces much more than their people. If you have such a manager, the chances are good you're required to support him or her with something like Risk Factor Analysis (RFA).

If your manager focuses on managing you, then RFA may be your only hope for a defensive shield. You'll read about it in Chapter 4.

CHAPTER 3

Setting Java Bug Traps

Instruments. Flying a jetliner at altitude, a pilot without cockpit instruments has little idea whether the airspeed is 310 or 355 mph, or whether the altitude is 29,000 feet or 33,000 feet. Cockpit noise and the way the aircraft performs give small but insufficient clues.

Any qualified pilot can keep the aircraft topside-up when the horizon is in view. However, no pilot can keep the plane in a safe attitude for more than a few minutes in thick clouds without referring to cockpit instruments or using the autopilot. In fact, if the plane is one of the few that are stable enough, the best thing such a trapped pilot can do is release the stick and hope the craft will fly itself out of the weather. That's scary!

However, flying is safe. The reason is that an airplane has specialized instruments to show whether or not the wings, nose, and tail are level. Other instruments tell the pilot which direction is north, which way the destination is, and even that the #3 engine's oil pressure is just fine. You've seen a cockpit. There are hundreds of instruments in there, and the pilots are proficient in reading and interpreting every one, or they wouldn't be qualified to fly that aircraft. The ability to handle a crisis competently comprises at least 75 percent of piloting. The instruments tell the pilots what they need to know to fly safely.

Instruments are there, mostly, to give pilots negative information. If the exhaust gas temperature of #3 jet engine gets too high, the pilot needs to shut that engine down to prevent or extinguish a fire. When the radar altimeter beeps during the approach to a landing, it means the ground is very close. If the compass reads south and the plane should be going west, it's time to turn right. In each case, the pilot needs to evaluate the situation, often instantly, and take corrective action as needed.

Instrument Your Code

The situation is similar for programmers debugging code. We strive for the code to work, and need specialized code instruments for negative input. Without ways to see what's going wrong, we have no better chance of finding bugs than a pilot has of flying safely in the weather with no instruments. The greater the quantity and quality of code instruments available, the cleaner and safer the code can become.

Code Instruments

Code instruments come in several designs:

- Permanent Java bug traps, to help users. These are like a plane's ordinary cockpit instruments that tell the pilot when something is wrong.

- Temporary Java bug traps, for debugging only. These are like the special instrumentation installed for test flights.

- Code that prevents bugs. This is akin to an airplane's inherent stability.

Permanent Bug Traps

Pity the poor user. Frustrated by the traffic while driving to work and the pressure to get that report to the vice president by ten, or else, your resolute customer types a zero you didn't anticipate, and boom! The computer spits out a stack trace and terminates the program. The last hour's worth of input numbers dissipates as heat into some electrical resistor deep in the computer's insides. Well, perhaps the data is safe, but your user doesn't know that.

Your user hasn't a clue why, but it has happened before. The poor soul relaunches or reboots, this time vowing to save the data every 15 seconds! So, every 15 seconds, the program wastes another 15 seconds saving the data. Productivity has dropped at least 50 percent, all because nothing trapped for illegal input at a crucial point.

Permanent bug traps in your code give the user a chance. The last time the user typed a zero, and the time before that, the computer locked up. With better information and prompting, your user might have reported the bug. Those were opportunities missed. So, install permanent bug traps that give your user a fighting chance to get that report to the vice president by ten. See Chapter 12 for how to emit the perfect error message.

Two Categories of Bugs

At this point, there are two categories of bugs. There are bugs you can imagine and those you cannot. Each category has two subcategories.

If you can imagine a bug, you should try to prevent it. For instance, if a user should ever input a number less than zero, you can do the following:

1. Test the input.
2. Reject it if less than zero.
3. Tell the user the input must be zero or greater.
4. Send the code right back to that input box.

At that point, you might imagine another kind of bug. How can the user abort the input process, especially if continuing might corrupt the database? To fix that problem, you can build in a special code, such as null, or escape or click somewhere, to abort the routine.

Next, you might imagine yet another kind of bug. How does the user know how to abort the input? You might modify your error message and explain how.

Sometimes you can imagine a bug that you cannot prevent. Perhaps the user will have to make a judgment call, using information you don't have at design time. The user might even request that you install a warning at a certain point. For instance, if two medicines happen to be on the same prescription list at the same time, but they have potentially severe interactions, you might want a warning to appear. It could be that the physician prescribed those two medicines because despite the temporary side-effects, the patient would be cured. Or it could be that the physician erred. The pharmacist or other professional using your program might need a reminder at a critical point in the program.

Once, while building a hydraulic valve cross-reference program, my client requested that a flashing red box appear for certain combinations of valves. Such valve combinations were buildable, but probably were not what his customer wanted. When the program user clicked on the flashing box, it turned solid red to indicate that the potential error had been noted. I thought that was an excellent solution to a difficult design problem.

The design turned out to have an unusual bug. One of my client's customers was epileptic, and flashing red lights can trigger attacks! So now, a solid red box turns yellow when clicked off.

As in the flashing-red-box episode, there are bugs you cannot foresee, and they come in two categories: bugs you can trap and those you cannot.

Should you trap bugs you can't foresee? Well, if you don't, Java will do it for you, and it would be good to prevent that from happening. In most cases, when Java throws an unhandled exception, the error message is refreshingly meaningful to the seasoned Java programmer, compared to messages in older languages. Kudos to the Java design team for that boon! However, these messages confuse your users. Meant for developers, they are cryptic to users. Then, to make matters worse, the program terminates by showing a stack trace!

To keep your messages in the user-friendly category, you need to enhance what Java might tell them. To do that, you need to know how Java handles exceptions.

Java Exceptions, Detailed

Java exceptions, known as runtime errors in some other languages, are subclasses of a Java class named **Throwable**, which has two subclasses named **Exception** and **Error**. **Error**s are typically involved with disasters that your program cannot handle. **Exception**s are the classes that concern you on a day-to-day basis.

Java's object orientation has modernized error handling for you. In fact, whole categories of problems that used to plague programmers simply cannot happen in Java. For example, unreachable code is not allowed, and is itself an exception. This feature can cause its own kind of difficulties with improperly constructed error traps, as explained later in this chapter.

When Java detects an exception, it creates a Java object for that exception, and **throw**s it—that is, sends it to the runtime system inside of the method that did the **throw**ing. You can program that method either to handle the exception, or to pass it on, but somewhere, something in the program **catch**es the exception. If no program method **catch**es the exception, then the overall runtime system does. In effect, you might consider the entire program to be wrapped in code that eventually **catch**es the exception and handles it by default.

The exception object holds such information as the exception's type and the state of the program when the exception was thrown. This information makes it easy to track the exception back to its origin. Just as a roach, caught in the middle of the kitchen floor, is easy to eliminate, a localized computer bug is easy to fix.

Exception Keywords

You have five powerful keywords for managing exceptions: **try**, **catch**, **throw**, **throws**, and **finally**. They work together in the following way.

You establish a **try** block around the code you desire to watch for exceptions. If an exception occurs inside the **try** block, the **try** block sends the exception to a **catch** block to be handled. If you wish to create an exception of your own, you use the **throw** keyword. If you want a method to duck an exception, and let it be handled by some other method up the call chain, you say so with the **throws** keyword. Often, there is code that must execute before the method returns control to its parent, and you put that code in a **finally** block.

Without bothering with **throw** and **throws** keywords yet, the basic structure looks like this:

```
try {
  // Code being monitored for errors.
}
```

```
// No intervening code is allowed here.
 catch (OneException e) {
  // Handler for OneException.
 }
 catch (AnotherException e) {
  // Handler for AnotherException.
 }

// Other catches go here.

 finally {
  // Cleanup code that must execute before the try block ends.
 }
```

Six notes apply:

- You can think of OneException and AnotherException as placeholders where actual exception names will go. They are the names of exception types, like ArithmeticException, or exceptions you invent.

- **e** is just a variable name. In fact, most Java code uses this very name: *e* for error. You can use it to reference the exception, such as **e.getMessage()**.

- If you have a **try** clause, you must have at least one **catch** clause, or else you must have a **finally**.

- You cannot put any code between the **try** block and its first **catch**.

- The first **catch** that can, handles the exception; the others are bypassed, and code resumes after the final **catch** block for that particular **try**. Thus, you may place code between the final **catch** and its **finally** block, if there is one. Such code ultimately continues execution into the **finally** block, if not otherwise redirected.

- If you use more than one **catch** statement, exception subclasses must come before their superclasses. A superclass will catch exceptions of its subclasses. Thus, if a subclass follows a superclass, the subclass **catch** cannot possibly be reached. As mentioned earlier, the Java compiler does not allow unreachable code! Remember, "subs before supers."

Specialized Use for **finally**

Incidentally, because the **finally** block always executes before its **try** block ends, it has an important use that is not related to exceptions. You can install a method's housekeeping chores in your **finally** block, knowing they certainly will be executed. You can release locks, sockets, descriptors, or handles. You can commit or roll back data, etc. There is no overhead to surrounding statements in a **try** until an exception gets thrown.

A Poor Use for **try** and **catch**

I have seen **try** and **catch** used for loop control. It's possible to install a **try** block around the loop, and **catch** an exception to get out of the loop. You might **catch** the fact that something went past end of file, or even manually **throw** an exception to break out of the loop. It works, and is very efficient, but it's poor design and generally lazy thinking. However, I can think of at least one case (spin locks) where there is no other option without resorting to nasty-looking code. Even in that case, one should modify the code if some later version of Java opens other opportunities.

Exceptions Advance the State of the Art

One of the ways C++ improved the C language was in handling exceptions.
Java's exceptions are no, uh…

Sorry, but I just can't bring myself to finish that last sentence with the obvious word! Java's exceptions are a strong improvement over C's error-trapping mechanisms, for these main reasons. They:

- Segregate Java's core code from the error code.
- Percolate upward, to be handled by the method most interested in them.
- Cluster naturally into logical groups.

Segregating Core Code from Error Code

The beauty of Java's system is that the error handlers are separate from the core code. The core code is inside a **try** block, whereas the error handlers are inside **catch** blocks immediately below the **try** block. Error systems such as CoBOL, C, or Visual Basic might use, can nearly obscure the code with error tests. It makes little sense that the most commonly executed piece of code hides in a mire of error traps that hopefully never run. So, Java separates the two, making programs much easier to understand. Understandable programs are inherently less error-prone.

Consider this example. Say you have a function that reads a file into memory. In pseudocode, your function might read:

```
readFile {
  openFile;
```

```
    determineSize;
    allocateMemory'
    readFileIntoMemory;
    closeFile;
}
```

This code seems straightforward but has serious deficiencies. What should the program do if:

- The file won't open?
- The length of the file can't be determined?
- There is insufficient memory?
- The read fails?
- The close fails?

The traditional way of handling these potential errors creates a function with error codes, something like this. For reference, the original lines are in bold text. Look at that code bloat!

```
errorCodeType readFile {
  initialize errorCode = 0;
  openFile;
  if (fileIsOpen) {
    determineSize;
    if (gotFileLength) {
      allocateEnoughMemory;
      if (memoryAllocated) {
        readFileIntoMemory;
        if (readFailed) {
          errorCode = -1;
        }
      } else {
        errorCode = -2;
      }
    } else {
      errorCode = -3;
    }
    closeFile;
    if (fileDidn'tClose && errorCode = = 0) {
      errorCode = -4;
    }
  } else {
    errorCode = -5;
  }
```

```
  return errorCode;
}
```

The original's 7 lines have grown to 27, and you still have to handle the various errors. But the worst part is that the original code (in boldface type) is lost in the error traps. It's hard to tell if the code is even correct! One hard-to-spot misplaced semicolon or curly brace and things can go terribly wrong inside there. Think of returning to the code a year later to modify it. How easy would that be? Of course you could do it, but you'd have to expend some unnecessary mental energy. Look at the elegant solution Java gives you, in the form of exceptions. This example is also from the Java.Sun.Com Web site.

```
readFile {
  try {
    openFile;
    determineSize;
    allocateMemory;
    readFileIntoMemory;
    closeFile;
  } catch (fileDidNotOpen) {
    handle_Error;
  } catch (sizeNotDetermined_ {
    handle_Error;
  } catch (memoryAllocationFailed) {
    handle_Error;
  } catch (couldNotReadFile) {
    handle_Error;
  } catch (couldNotCloseFile) {
    handle_Error;
  }
```

This bit of code is only about 2.7 times the size of the original, whereas the traditional method is nearly 4 times the original's size. That's significant, but the greater beauty is that you can see what is happening. The core code is intact, and the error handlers are clustered neatly below it. Moreover, the **catch** blocks will clearly say what happens if each exception occurs.

Of course, you still must detect, report, and handle the errors, but look at how much cleaner and more logical the process has become!

The Java designers borrowed this clever idea from C++, which borrowed it from an obscure language named ML, or Meta Language.

Percolating Up the Call Stack

Exceptions travel up the call stack more efficiently than older error-handling methods could allow. If a method five deep in the call stack throws an exception that only the top method is interested in handling, traditional error handlers require each intervening method to consider and handle the error, even if handling it only means passing it up the chain.

On the other hand, Java lets disinterested methods "duck" the chore of handling the exception merely by listing them in the **throws** clause. Error handling, code bloat, and logic obfuscation are roughly halved.

Errors Fall into Natural Categories

Java exceptions are objects that belong to class hierarchies, which group naturally. For example:

```
Object
|---etc.
|---Error
|    |---etc.
|    |---AWTError
|    |    |---etc.
|    |    |---VirtualMachineError
|    |    |---OutOfMemoryError
|    |    |---StackOverflowError
|---Exception
     |---RuntimeException
     |---|---etc.
     |---|---ArithmeticException
     |---|---NullPointerException
     |---|---IndexOutOfBoundsException
     |---|---|---ArrayIndexOutOfBoundsException
     |---|---|---StringIndexOutOfBoundsException
     |---IOException
          |---etc.
          |---EOFException
          |---FileNotFoundException
```

Where Java doesn't already group them for you, you can create subclasses of **Throwable**, or of its subclasses, ad infinitim, for your own exceptions. You can also create subclasses of your subclasses, as deep as you desire. You can have exceptions with no subclasses. You can create groups, which have subclasses of logically related exceptions. Organization is as easy as drawing a hierarchy chart.

No more obscure error code numbers to memorize, or for you and your users to research. Your user manual doesn't have to contain a complicated error-codes list.

Java's hierarchy of exceptions even lets you create a general exception handler with a line like:

```
catch (Exception e) {
```

but I don't recommend it. That line will succeed in **catch**ing all exceptions that are subclasses of the class **Exception**. That set of exceptions includes all that are not of the class **Error** and are not subclasses of **Throwable** that you might create. It's a huge group, containing about any exception you could handle. The problem is that you'd have to handle them all in one spot, and it would be too easy to miss something. Worse, your error-handling processes would no longer be in proximity to the methods most interested in them. During code maintenance, the poor developer (you?) would have to page all over the place working on the exceptions. Java's natural hierarchical approach is better.

Order of Execution

If the thrown exception matches the first **catch**'s argument, then that **catch** block handles it. If not, the exception tries to match the second **catch**'s argument, etc., down the line.

If no **catch** was appropriate, the **finally** block, if there is one, executes, and the method acts as if there were no **try** block at all.

Next, the parent method regains program control and receives the exception. If it has a **try** block with a **catch** block that fits the exception, that **catch** will handle the exception. Otherwise, the **finally** block, if there is one, executes, and that method acts as if there were no **try** block either. The next parent method regains control, etc., up the call stack.

If the exception percolates to the top of the call stack without finding a fitting **catch,** then the top method stops executing and emits a message.

If, however, some **catch** along the way fits the exception, then the code in that **catch** block executes. It may or may not be possible for you to prevent a program abort at that point. Certainly, if possible, you should prevent the abort. If you cannot, then perhaps you need to revise the lines of code that threw the exception.

Eliminate RuntimeException Bugs

If your program is throwing actual runtime exceptions—that is, subclasses of the class **RuntimeException**—then you have serious work to do. You should weed these bugs out of your code immediately and fully. Table 3-1 lists these subclasses.

There Is No goto Statement

While the Java designers cleverly reserved the keyword **goto**, they did not use it in the language. They may have reserved it for future use, or possibly they wanted to prevent you from defining and using it as a method, probably both. You cannot install a **goto** inside a **catch** statement. It won't work. When the

Exception Name	Explanation
ArithmeticException	Some kind of arithmetic error, such as division by zero, or log(0).
ArrayIndexOutOfBoundsException	The array index is either less than or greater than its limit.
ArrayStorageException	An array element's type is incompatible with the data being assigned.
ClassCastException	The cast is invalid.
IllegalArgumentException	A wrong argument is being used to call a method.
IllegalStateException	The application's state or the computer's environment state is wrong.
IllegalThreadStateException	The current thread state is incompatible with the requested operation.
IndexOutOfBoundsException	An index is too high or low.
NegativeArraySizeException	An array has been created with a negative number of elements.
NullPointerException	A null reference has been misused.
NumberFormatException	Invalid string to number conversion.
SecurityException	Something attempted a security violation.
StringIndexOutOfBounds	The string index is either less than or greater than its limit.
UnsupportedOperationException	The operation is not supported by Java.

Table 3.1   Subclasses of Class RuntimeException

method that catches an exception finishes its **catch** block, the **finally** block (if there is one) executes, and then the method returns control to whatever called it. You can't use a **goto** to subvert that chain of events.

The classic **goto**, or jump command of other languages does not violate structured programming principles! Skeptics can read Dijkstra and Knuth. However, the use of a **goto** in other languages needs to have restrictions. One should not use it for these purposes:

- To enter a loop at several points
- To return to a place earlier in the code. However, menus implemented without jumps are nasty to code, because the programmer has difficulty knowing where the user will click or hotkey next.
- To construct loops. However, such loops are usually the fastest you can construct.

In many languages, **goto** is especially useful in error trapping, but the Java designers gave you a more elegant paradigm in the **try-catch-throw-throws-finally** set of commands. **goto** is simply not necessary in Java.

Compiler Enforces Exception Checks

Another beauty of how Java handles exceptions is that the compiler enforces exception checking when you use libraries. Each library method you use has already declared the exceptions it might throw. For instance, the various file IO methods are liable to throw various **IOException** class errors. When your code calls such methods, it must allow for each of these exceptions or you will get a compile-time message something like this:

```
SanDiego.java:25: Exception java.lang.IOException must be caught
or it must be declared in the throws clause of this method.
```

The message means exactly what it states. Either the method causing the error must have a **catch** block matching the exception (and a corresponding **try** block, of course), or it must list the exception in its **throws** clause.

As you know, most compilers alert you to problems with the number and type of arguments used in calling something—a method in this case. Compilers can do that because the arguments are formally declared in the subroutine's header. In Java, methods use the **throws** keyword to formally declare to the compiler (and the maintenance programmer) which possible exceptions they can **throw**. Thus, the compiler can check that your code, which calls these methods, will handle the exceptions. This feature makes Java more robust in error handling than its predecessors could ever be.

It gets better. You don't have to memorize which methods throw what exceptions, or even research a manual. The compiler checks for you. It alerts you and others who use your methods as to what exceptions to handle.

Checked and Unchecked Exceptions

Java defines several exception classes in **java.lang**. Since **java.lang** is automatically imported into all Java programs, most exceptions that are subclasses of **RuntimeException** are available by default. The compiler does not check to see if a method handles or **throws** most of these exceptions, so you don't need to include them in any method's **throws** list. These exceptions are usually called "unchecked exceptions."

Java has a number of "checked exceptions" defined in **java.lang**. You must include these in the **throws** list of your methods, or **catch** them when appropriate. Table 3-2 lists these checked exceptions.

Exception Name	Explanation
ClassNotFoundException	Java didn't find the class being referenced.
CloneNotSupportedException	Tried to clone an object that does not implement the **Cloneable** interface.
IllegalAccessException	Access to a class was denied.
InstantiationException	Illegally tried to create an object of an abstract class, or interface.
InterruptedException	Caused when one thread interrupts another.
NoSuchFieldException	Field does not exist. (Check for typos.)
NoSuchMethodException	Method does not exist. (Check for typos.)

Table 3.2   Checked Exceptions in java.lang

Coding to Handle Exceptions

So how do you code your program to handle exceptions? You have two things to do:

1. Surround your code with a **try** block. This is called protecting your code.

2. Deal with each exception in a **catch** block.

In the **catch** block, the variable "e" (Java programmers commonly use **e**) may be disregarded, but you can use it with lines like:

```
System.out.println("Error: " + e.getMessage());  //Prints error message.
System.out.println(e.toString());   //Prints exception name also.
```

Other useful exception handling methods are as follows:

Method	Action
PrintStackTrace()	Prints the stack trace upward from the point of the error.
GetLocalizedMessage()	Creates a description of the error or exception that a subclass can use in overriding the message, thus producing a message specific to this method.
FillInStackTrace()	Inserts the state of the stack for this thread into the exception object.
PrintStackTrace(PrintStream)	Prints a stack trace relative to the specified print stream.

Chatty Error Messages

The **getMessage()** method exists in all exceptions, and is somewhat more verbose. You can always use it to get, and present, the text of the error message. However, you should read that error message to ensure it's appropriate for your particular users. Write a simple stub to throw that particular error if you can't find the message's text in a reference. For example:

```
class TestDivisionByZero {
  public static void main(String args[]) {
    int a=0, b=1, c=0;
    try {
      a = b / c; // Deliberately throw division by zero exception
    }
    catch (ArithmeticException e) {
      System.out.println(e.getMessage());
    }
  }
}
```

Coding the **catch** Block

Your **catch** block should prevent a fatal abort, if possible. To let it do so, you might reset variables, close files, open files, or correct innumerable things that might have caused the error. For instance, if you have a program that divides a by b, assigning the result to c, and b becomes zero before the division occurs, you'll have a division-by-zero error. Your **catch** block might emit an error message, ensure some very large number gets assigned to c, and continue.

Error Watch   *Division by zero only throws an exception on integer and float types, not long or double. In those cases, /0 sets the result to POSITIVE_INFINITY or NEGATIVE_INFINITY as appropriate. If you divide by negative zero, you get NEGATIVE_INFINITY if the dividend is greater than zero, and POSITIVE_INFINITY if the dividend is less than zero. As expected, 0.0 / –0.0 is NEGATIVE_INFINITY as is –0.0 / 0.0. Both 0.0 / 0.0 and –0.0 / –0.0 are POSITIVE_INFINITY.*

Your program doesn't abort merely because an exception was thrown and caught. If the result of a/b is headed for the database and shouldn't go there when b = 0, then you can use the **catch** block to prevent that database write.

Our small son recently asked us what it was like living in "the olden days." In the olden days, just five years ago, your code would return a flag. Today, you would let Java handle things for you. For instance, if you calculate a/b and then write to the database, but have the whole thing inside a **try** block, and b = 0, this happens:

1. Your **try** block catches the **ArithmeticException**.

2. Control jumps to your **catch** block, which handles the exception. To do that, your code jumps around the process of writing to the database.

3. Your **catch** block handles the exception and merely omits writing to the database. Bug squashed!

4. When your **catch** block finishes, the **finally** block (if there is one) executes and then the method terminates, allowing the rest of the method to continue running.

5. If the method is finished after the **finally** block finishes, then the parent (the calling method) continues running.

Thus, your task is to create a **catch** block that resolves the exception as if it never happened.

For instance, there are eight ways to insert a floppy disk, only one of which is interesting. I've actually had to use needle-nosed pliers to remove such a misinserted disk, and no, it wasn't me who jammed it into the PC. Your program might throw an exception, by design, when your user attempts to read a floppy disk that is poorly inserted. Your **catch** block probably should tell the user that there is no disk in the a: drive, let the user correct the problem, and try again. There are several ways to let the user correct the problem, among them:

- Emit a friendly message like "There is no diskette in the a: drive.", and use **throws** to pass the exception back to the method that requested the filename. Let that method request the filename again, or abort if the user enters nothing.

- Merely request that the disk be inserted and that the user click Retry or click Cancel.

- Let the user browse the hard disk for the file, or cancel.

- Emit the error message and let **finally** finish the method.

The choice is yours. Whatever you choose, you should look at the heading "Emit the Perfect Error Message," in Chapter 12, for additional ideas.

Nesting the **try** Block

A **catch** block and its **try** block are atomic—that is, they cannot be divided. A **catch** block cannot **catch** an exception thrown in a different **try** block, except when you nest the **try** statements.

You can nest **try** statements within the same method. Also, when one method calls another and both have **try** blocks, you get implied nesting. In those cases, a subordinate method (or **try** clause) can **throw** an exception, fail to **catch** it, and have it caught by its parent. If the parent doesn't **catch** the exception, it still percolates on up the call stack. If the exception remains uncaught, the Java runtime system handles matters by emitting an error message and a stack trace.

throw

Java cannot possibly consider all of the exceptions you might want to program, so it lets you **throw** your own, with a line like this:

```
throw MyException;
```

MyException must be an object of type **Throwable**, or a subclass of **Throwable**. This type does not include simple types like **char** or **int**, or non-**Throwable** classes like **Object** or **String**. When throwing an exception, you have two options:

- Enter a parameter into your **catch** clause.
- Use the **new** keyword to create such an object.

Here's an example that demonstrates both:

```
class Dallas {
  static void subroutine() {
    try {
      throw new ArithmeticException("MyString");
    } catch(ArithmeticException e) {
      System.out.println("Caught inside Dallas.");
      throw e; // throw the exception outside subroutine
    } // Note that finally is optional because there are catch clauses.
  }
  public static void main(String args[]) {
    try {
      subroutine();
    } catch(ArithmeticException e) {
      System.out.println("Caught: " + e + " in main.);
    }
  }
}
```

The output of this program is as follows:

```
Caught inside Dallas.
Caught: java.lang.ArithmeticException: Mystring in main.
```

Notice that "MyString" came from the **throw new** line. When you construct a **new** instance of your exception, you can specify a "describing string" and display it when the object is used as an argument to **print()** or **println()**. That describing string is one way to tell the user something valuable. However, code you install in the offending method's **catch** block is more versatile.

The throws Keyword

To annul any remaining confusion between **throw** and **throws**:

- You **throw** an exception intentionally in your code.
- A method **throws** an exception out of itself, so it will be caught by its hierarchical parentage.
- A method that has no interest in **catch**ing an exception that it knows a method it calls might **throw**, signifies that lack of interest with the **throws** list.

This third idea is just tricky enough for an example. Say that the following three items are true:

- **myMethodA** calls **myMethodB**, which calls **myMethodC**, which calls **myMethodD**.
- **myMethodD** throws **myException**, and has no reason to handle it.
- **myMethodC** is not interested in handling it either, but **myException** is of vital interest to **myMethodB**.

In that case, **myMethodC** must cite **myException** in its **throws** list, with a line like this:

```
public Boolean myMethodC (int x, int y, int z) throws myException {
// etc.
}
```

The meaning is that **myMethodC** can toss **myException** right out of there, to let its parentage (myMethodB or above) handle it.

If there are several possible exceptions, list them, comma separated:

```
public Boolean myMethod (int x) throws Exception1, Exception2, Exception3 {
// etc.
}
```

To avoid listing numerous exceptions in a **throw**s clause, you can use a superclass of a group of exceptions to state that your method can, but will not necessarily, **throw** any subclass of that exception. For example, **IOException** has numerous subordinate exceptions. You could state the following, and any of those subordinates of **IOException** would be thrown out of myMethod:

```
public Boolean myMethod () throws IOException {
// etc.
}
```

There is a way to go wrong. Don't use the **throws** keyword in a method that cannot actually **throw** that exception, unless the method calls a subordinate method that can do the deed. The compiler will check up on you! The method that actually does **throw** the exception can be buried several subordinate levels deep, but it must be down there somewhere.

You don't have to use **throws** to specify every possible exception your method can **throw**. You need not (but certainly may) list exceptions of the class **Error**, or of the subclass **RuntimeException**, or any of their subclasses. Java programmers call these "unchecked exceptions," or "implicit exceptions":

- **Error**s are typically exceptions you can do nothing about anyhow, and probably didn't cause problems in your program.

- **RuntimeException**s, those listed in Table 3-1, will be handled by Java if you don't handle them.

Since you can do little, if anything, about **Error**-type exceptions, there's seldom a reason to list them in a **throws** statement—although you may.

Design Tip *If Java's runtime environment handles a **RuntimeException** for you, your poor user will see a somewhat cryptic message and a stack trace just before your program terminates. That's no way to treat a user!*

Here is an important philosophical design point. If **myMethodC** calls **myMethodD**, and **myMethodD** declares that it **throws** a particular exception, then **myMethodC** must either **catch** it or specify that it **throws** it on up the call chain (or both). Somehow, **myMethodC** must handle the exception.

Similarly, if **myMethodD** actually does **throw** an exception, it must declare that it **throws** it, or the compiler will object.

That's complicated. Another example is in order:

```
// This generates a compile-time error.
class Denver {
  static void throwDemo() {
    System.out.println("Trying to throw an exception");
    throw new WillThisCompileException("Thrown inside throwDemo");
  }
  public static void main(String args[]) {
    throwDemo();
  }
}
```

The code above looks normal, but on closer inspection, **throwDemo()** tries to **throw** the exception named **WillThisCompileException**. The trouble is, **throwDemo()** doesn't say it **throws** anything. One possible correction is for **throwDemo()** to say, in its declaration line:

```
static void throwDemo() throws WillThisCompileException {
```

The other possibility is for **throwDemo()** to have its own **try** and **catch** clauses for that exception, thus handling the exception locally.

If **throwDemo()** throws the exception out, as in the modified declaration line above, then main must **try** and also **catch** the exception. The corrected program might look like this:

```
// No compiler generated errors here!
class Denver {
  static void throwDemo() throws WillThisCompileException {
    System.out.println("Trying to throw an exception.");
    throw new WillThisCompileException("Thrown inside throwDemo");
  }
  public static void main(String args[]) {
    try {
      throwDemo();
    } catch (WillThisCompileException e) {
      System.out.println("Caught " + e);
    }
  }
}
```

The program now compiles, and produces this output:

```
Trying to throw an exception.
Caught java.lang.WillThisCompileException: Thrown inside ThrowDemo
```

Why is this an important Java design point? The Java compiler enforces these rules to prevent design bugs, and also to let it deal with exceptions more efficiently. A method that "ducks," or **throw**s, an exception further up the chain only needs to invest a few program cycles doing so, instead of investing a lot of time handling and rejecting the exception.

It's possible to subvert Java's wisdom at this point, but don't. A method can always catch an exception and do nothing about it. Instead, if a method has no business dealing with an exception thrown upward from a submethod, use the **throws** keyword and pass the exception further up the chain to where it should be handled.

Bugs Hiding Phantom Bugs

In the college computer lab, a sophomore was showing enormous frustration with a program. Fearing for the equipment, I walked over to help and saw that the compiler was indicating four bugs, so I suggested how to attack the first one in the list. The student declared a variable and recompiled. Suddenly, there were about 50 new bugs! I was shouting hallelujah, while my student was ready to drop the course. So, I continued the explanation. Most of those new bugs were actually phantoms, caused by other bugs. A parenthesis was missing, so the compiler thought most of the code had syntax errors. It didn't. We fixed that syntax bug and about 40 phantoms disappeared. Then it was time for class, and the student decided to attend—after all. Nobody claims that programming lacks frustration! However, that person got an A- and has become a top-notch programmer.

The incident personified to me the frustration of bugs hiding phantom and real bugs.

Bugs often hide other bugs in a linear fashion. Generally, the best strategy for clearing them out is to do it linearly. Fix the first one you see, not the first one you know how to fix, because you're fairly certain that the first one you see is not a phantom. You don't know that about many of the others. Then recompile and fix the first bug you see, iteratively.

You should modify that strategy when you can identify other bugs down the list that you know are not phantoms. For example, you might see an **ArithmeticException** caused by a divisor being zero. That case probably needs to be handled, even (especially!) if your top bug was what caused the divisor to become zero. You could fix the first bug with confidence and never see that /0 **ArithmeticException** again, until you found yourself at the end of a trouble call when some bad data drove that same divisor to zero.

Practice Generating Bugs

Until you're proficient at correcting syntax bugs, they can be as frustrating for you as for my sophomore student. One way to avert the frustration is to practice generating bugs! Build a simple "Hello world!" kind of program and get it to run exactly right. Then play with it. Mess with the parentheses, the braces, and the semicolons. Become intimate with the kinds of compile errors you get, and with their meanings. Expand on the "Hello world!" program and try generating other kinds of exceptions. See what happens if you try to run an applet as a program and vice versa. Generate a bug by **catch**ing a superclass exception before a subclass one. Comment out the import statements. Misname a class. Make capitalization errors on variables and methods.

Believe me, you will learn more from that exercise than from merely reading a chapter of this book!

Carry the idea of this exercise into your production programming. When you are unsure about something, test it. When you have a strange bug, see if you can generate it with only a small piece of code—like one of my students did when proving the Pascal compiler had a bug rounding 101.001 to two decimal places. When you want to call an ill-documented method, write a small program to test it every way you can, and write your own documentation about it.

Keep a notebook.

Autolog the Results

"O dream of dreams," sang the harried help-desk appointee. "If I could but see the screen you see. O but to see your exact error messages."

PC software products like Carbon Copy, Reach Out, and PC Anywhere are boons to consultants. From your quiet office, you can run your program on a client's machine and see exactly where the program stalls. A bug isolated is a bug nearly squashed. If only we all had the budgets to install such programs on all customer machines!

You can build a near equivalent. Write an error-message logger. Whenever your program throws an exception, log the available information to your customer's hard disk. Here's what you should consider logging:

- Something unique, so a technician can go straight to the line(s) of code causing the bug.

- The entire text of the message, in case you have (wisely) enhanced that error message. Please don't expect users to become familiar with Java exceptions. They utter their pronouncements in terms you and I understand, not in user-ese. That's not a pejorative statement, incidentally. Users know a ton more about their jobs than I do, and I don't speak actuarial lingo very well.

- The time and date, to appropriate precision. If your error message is associated with threaded processes, you might want to get down to the millisecond. Otherwise, the nearest minute might be plenty.

- The states of other threads, as best you can.

- The username, if appropriate and available. You might have to glean that from the operating system or network, even via an API call. You might capture it in the program at some appropriate point, such as a login screen, and save it in case there's an exception.

- Other environment information that might be available, such as status of the network and the PC.

- Possible notes to the technician saying what might cause this bug. However, if you can pull that rabbit out of the hat, you can probably install a bug trap that prevents the error from occurring in the first place.

- The status of appropriate open data files or queries, the record being manipulated, etc.

Next, consider how to make this information useful. Ask yourself: "Who would want it?"

Why, the person on the other end of the trouble call, that's who!

You may or may not want the user to break out of the program, load an editor, and locate that log file, which might even be locked by the still-running Java program. Instead, how about an invisible hotspot on your program's main screen or possibly on each screen? If the customer right-clicks there, up pop the last 100 error messages—latest at the top. If the program hasn't stalled, your help technician can offer runtime assistance based on actual events, not events filtered through imperfect human memories.

There are numerous ways to build a hotspot. For instance, you can insert a clickable object in the upper-left corner of the screen or under a logo. You might color that object the same as its surroundings and eliminate its border. Voila, a hidden place the user can click.

You don't want error messages to consume your customer's hard disk, so limit them to some finite number, such as 100. To do this, implement a circular queue. You could declare an array of 100 elements. Write the new message to the first array element, and use a loop to load the array's next 99 elements (or to end of file) with information from the log file. Then write the whole thing back to the log file, thus letting the filing system destroy any information beyond array element 100.

You probably don't want anyone to become curious and remove the log file, so name it something unique that doesn't attract attention and which Windows won't automatically open on a double-click. You might even go to the extreme of setting the log's hidden attribute so it won't normally appear in the Explorer or at the DOS prompt.

Appendix E gives the Java code for a minimal autologger such as this. You can customize it for all of your Java projects. Be glad you bought the book and got this valuable code, if for no other reason!

CHAPTER 4

Never Miss Another Deadline!
Risk-Factor Analysis

Deadline pressure causes bugs. That overstates the obvious, but evidently not to some who set your deadlines.

In fairness, when the high-level decisions are made to create software projects, the decision makers are seldom aware of the intricacies involved. So, they have to make best-guess estimates long before you have the time to do a full analysis.

Then, based on the estimates, marketing, advertising, production, and other departments build their plans. By the time you can tell the higher ups that your team's part of the project will take six months, not three, too many decisions have been set. Contracts have been let. Advertisements have proclaimed public promises. The CEO has spoken. You're stuck.

It should not be so, but it is, even in the best corporations.

So, you and your team rush around. You try the standard ideas. You can't change the deadline, so you try to change the scope, but that's not allowed. Advertisements have promised those features, after all. You must deliver. There's one thing left to change—the resources. You try hiring on new team members. You try the 80-hour week, including bonuses and pizza on the house every noon and midnight. You look for new software tools, all the while knowing three rules are immutable: (1) No matter how many hours a person works, they can't produce more than about 50 hours worth of quality code in a week. (2) If a crew of five can build a house in a month, 150 cannot build it in a day. (3) Any new tool entails a learning curve.

Somewhere I read a study that said output increases as the square root of the team size. It takes four people to double one person's output. If that's so, you must quadruple your team size to cut the schedule in half. My experience tells me that the study is correct. More people to supervise means more coordination, more meetings, more reports, more sick time, more email, more phone calls, more everything.

The deadline approaches, and two things become lost in the panic: testing and documentation. The end result is as predictable as gravity. While narrowly averting a few heart attacks and strokes, you and your team produce a mediocre product, 20 percent late. Soon thereafter, you lose your two best people to a less stressful environment.

Deadlines cause bugs. There is not a doubt. However, deadlines let people synchronize the huge array of tasks involved in getting a product out the door. The pressure helps keep people sharp and on task. When it comes time to enumerate the necessary evils, deadlines will be good candidates. No competitive environment will ever be devoid of them.

The trick is to manage deadlines reasonably. Books like *The Death March* should be part of every programmer's reading memory because of the stark portrayals of reality they present. Every time I hear of a death march project, I shudder, because there is a better way. There is a way to estimate completion dates accurately when only about 10 percent into a project. Before Risk-Factor Analysis (RFA), I had to be 40 percent of the way into a project before having a good idea of how long it would take. By then, all the top-level decisions were made. Now, I'm consulted early, and a number of department heads use RFA in their own estimates. It works for any kind of project, or part of a project.

Use Risk-Factor Analysis (RFA)

Earlier, I recommended writing the user manual first and then treating it as your specifications document and your test plan. Once you have agreement on the user manual, try to treat it like the holy writ. The canon is closed. When your users want to creep the scope a little, merely insist that it involves a new project—or at least a new phase. That means a new time and dollar estimate. In integrity, you must be sure to state that fact up front before you and your user agree to the project. Let your user know that if changes occur, you'll insist on a new time and dollar estimate, and learn to say "no."

Politically, realize when you cannot say "no."

How do you derive that estimate? And once derived, how do you stick to it? How do you convince everyone that it's accurate and inviolate? That's a tough chore for most programmers. Old hands consider themselves very good if they can consistently estimate within 25 percent of the final time and cost when 25 percent of the way into the project. There is a better way, which I call Risk-Factor Analysis.

How RFA Began

Early in my computer career, I was vice president of a small consultancy. We struggled mightily with a dilemma. By the time we had defined a project to everyone's satisfaction, we had expended half of the total time needed to develop it. However, few customers were willing to give us money for an undefined project. Several times we exerted effort designing fine systems, only to find the customer asking other vendors to bid on the project, based on our free specs! We lost most of those projects to the competition because our bid had to recoup development costs and theirs didn't.

After I moved on, the unsolved dilemma continued to bother me, until I arrived at the idea behind RFA. RFA now lets me consistently estimate the time required to complete a project within 8 percent. Before I began using and teaching it, I felt good when I came within 25 percent of the estimate, either side. Here's how it works.

How RFA Works

Divide the project into tasks. Use whatever granularity is comfortable and appropriate. For example, you might decide a smallish project will use ten screens, four reports, and fifteen special functions for unique calculations. Of the screens, six might be ordinary in scope, two might be quite special in some manner, and two might be trivial. Let's say you have no idea how to write two of the functions, but you're fairly certain you can find a way. Two of the functions are in some library you've seen somewhere. You're certain you know how to do the rest because they are things you've done repeatedly in the past three months. Sound rather typical? Begin RFA this way:

1. List all of the tasks.

2. Decide how much time each task would require if you knew exactly how to complete it. That's a big "if," but estimate as if you knew exactly how to do it. You're not estimating research time here, just the raw time needed to complete the task.

3. Decide how risky each task is, based on the following rather subjective criteria, and assign a letter to each task:

   A. I've done this task many times and know exactly how to do it. I won't even consult a book on the syntax. No research is required.
   B. I've done this before, but I don't recall exactly how things go together. I'll probably have to look something up or consult the JDK Help system.
   C. I've seen this done, or I've read about it somewhere. Probably, Jane or Joe knows how to do it.
   D. It looks like all the information is available to solve this problem; that is, a solution exists. However, I don't know how to find out how to do it yet.
   E. Beats me how to do it, but I'll give it a jolly good go.
   F. I think this is impossible, but I can't prove it yet.

4. Now, assign those letters A–F values according to powers of 2:

   $$A = 2^0 \text{ or } 1$$
   $$B = 2^1 \text{ or } 2$$
   $$C = 2^2 \text{ or } 4$$
   $$D = 2^3 \text{ or } 8$$
   $$E = 2^4 \text{ or } 16$$
   $$F = 2^5 \text{ or } 32$$

5. Multiply your time estimates by the assigned numerical values 1 to 32. You'll arrive at the average times for your tasks.

6. Sum the times and you have your project estimate.

I have never had a client or supervisor question my task estimates. I often get a few raised eyebrows on specific tasks, and sometimes we jointly decide that a particular bell or whistle isn't worth the expense. That's good, because that was probably a risky item and not strategic to the project. Removing it reduces the entire project's risk, which invariably improves the overall estimate's quality.

Occasionally, a client will offer an idea or the services of someone who happens to be expert in a high-risk area. In that case, a D item might become a C or even a B item, reducing costs.

Strongly resist the idea of "gaming" your estimates. It becomes tempting to think that since Jane or Joe have done something, you can do it out of hand, so you can award a B or an A letter to the task. Sometimes you can make up time that way. Just as often, you'll find that neither Jane nor Joe is available, or worse, that they only did something that looked similar on the screen. Your C item might just become a D item!

Besides, do the math. If you have four C items and one becomes a B and another becomes a D, you're way behind! Your gut feeling is about as close as you'll ever come until you get more information.

Do not be afraid to redo your estimate when you obtain better information, especially when the information changes your project's scope. If you must add grains, that is, screens, reports, formulas, and database tables in the previous example, you need to perform the same analysis on them. However, if you discover an easy way to do a particularly risky item, be aware that an easy item might sandbag you and turn out to be tougher than you guessed.

On the other hand, you should never try to build in extra slack time, not in today's competitive environment, because being first to market is of paramount importance. Your speed to market is one of the primary things managers will remember when it comes time for a salary review. Rapid, high-quality work is what makes you more valuable than your peers.

Why RFA Works

RFA breaks your project into two aspects: known and unknown. For the A tasks, there is no unknown aspect. For all the rest, there is a considerably expensive unknown aspect, and that's the additional time most programmers underestimate. The additional time is taken up by research, whether it means reading part of a book, consulting technical services, calling on Jane or Joe, calling your professor at the university, or merely experimenting with a few dozen undocumented possibilities until the right one works—consistently. All of those kinds of research consume time.

As computer scientists, we aren't expected to know everything. If someone anointed you with all computer knowledge this instant and you set to learning everything as it was generated, you'd be hopelessly outclassed. There are millions of highly inventive programmers in the world generating software thousands of times faster than you or anyone else could possibly learn to use it.

Thus, we must become experts in estimating how long it will take to do something we don't know how to do. What a hoot!

The best we can do is apply something like RFA, which lets us rely upon averages.

Why Is RFA Important to Debugging Java?

It helps you prevent deadline pressure. It doesn't help prevent deadlines, just deadline pressure. Deadline pressure causes some of the worst kinds of bugs. When it's more painful and career destructive to miss deadlines than to let the possibility of a few bugs slip through, programmers tend to let the maintenance group catch the rest of the bugs. Unfortunately, the maintenance programmer doesn't know the mind of the code's original author, and must spend extra time trying to decide what the code should have done in the first place. That's not an efficient process.

Many of our favorite and least favorite large software houses release programs they know are buggy, and I point a finger at their shame. The reasoning is that they must beat their competitors to market. It's perceived that the lesser evil is buggy code, and the greater one is delay. They believe their customers are so eager to receive new features, they'll forgive the bugs.

So, the houses manage their bugs. They categorize known errors, fix most of the critical ones, and forego the non-critical ones to the next release—which they plan to sell to you, of course. Some bugs they never intend to fix. Some, they seem to intend to fix only after their customers beta test their new software, and then, only if the magazines cry loudly enough about it.

Many software houses have discovered that the idea of fixing bugs just before the software is released is a siren concept. When deadlines are of paramount importance, when it becomes more important to keep the project on track, then developers merely catalogue bugs. If a bug would delay delivery of a module, the bug goes into a list. The module is delivered on schedule, knowing it has bugs. The bugs are to be fixed after delivery, but the project stays on schedule, and people are happy.

After all, if module J must be completed before module K can pass its 50 percent mark, then the entire module K team cannot be idled because module J is late, can it?

The trouble is that module J isn't done until it's done, and that means the critical bugs are fixed. Otherwise, the module K team is liable to be spinning wheels, backtracking because of design changes, and actually repairing bugs in module J, when they should be writing their own code. Worse, the module K people are unqualified to fix the bugs, because they don't know the code and aren't privy to its original specifications.

It works better to fix bugs as quickly as possible.

First, however, check that such bugs are strategic to the program. If they are enhancements, and especially if the project sponsors did not request them as features, consider holding them for the next enhancement.

I had a manufacturing client who wanted a vacation-calendar program. They keep several large three-ring binders of vacation-calendars, one sheet per employee, per year. These are worksheets. As an employee requests vacation time, a clerk annotates that person's sheet in pencil and calculates by hand the vacation time left. It's a simple process that has worked for years.

My client wanted me to automate the process of printing those calendars, taking into account employee tenure, adjustments due to sick leave, company holidays, and a strict formula of how vacation was accrued. The output was to be a printout which they would install in the three-ring binders.

A number of interesting enhancements suggested themselves. Instead of using paper worksheets, the computer program could track vacation accrued, requested and taken. That would require a couple more input screens and another table of data. However, those enhancements were not strategic to the project. Even though the client was interested in getting them next time, the enhancements would have delayed the project a critical few days, and would have cost the client a few days more for training, and not just in human resources. All of the factory employees would have to be told of the new processes.

The core requirements were strategic, and they had to be perfectly rendered before I released the software. The program had to produce flawless printed pages, each with a company logo. It had to input the list of employees and their amounts of sick leave from two flat files. It had to provide a screen to manage company holidays. It had to have a menu screen to manage the various functions. Those items were strategic to the project.

I fixed strategic bugs as I came to them, and listed ideas for enhancement for our regular phone conversations. Even though my client had little hope for success at the start, the project was completed on time and considerably under budget. Had I added the features, the project would have been late.

Fixing bugs as they are discovered might seem to run counter to my earlier advice to insert QQQ in the code and press on; however, it's not. The QQQ idea serves to keep creativity flowing, not to delay bug fixes. It gives you a quick way to catalog a potential problem area without stopping to investigate it at that moment.

The idea of using a QQQ notation is that you can finish the current set of ideas, then immediately return to your QQQ areas and work them while they are fresh in your mind. Occasionally, you'll need to forego working on one, because you don't have the knowledge yet, but most of the time, you can resolve your annotated areas before closing that module for the day. Even when you cannot, they are easy to locate the next day.

As long as you don't let the number of QQQ annotations in your code build continuously, you're fixing bugs at the proper time.

The idea of "fixing bugs later" is an inducer of buggy, late projects—when it doesn't kill them. Every time scientists study the subject, they conclude that the longer it takes to discover a bug, the more it costs to fix it. If you can prevent bugs, discovery time is zero.

One of the best ways to prevent bugs is to use a great Java editor, or to roll your own. Chapter 5 demonstrates both.

CHAPTER 5

Write to Shun Bugs

If you can kill every termite that approaches your house before it begins chewing wood, obviously you'll never have to repair termite damage. Termite exterminators spray bands of insecticide around your home to kill, or at least discourage, the pests from entering your property. They drive long-lasting termite stakes into the ground as a defense perimeter. The whole idea is to keep the critters out, because once they establish a nest inside your wooden structure, they hide, weakening the wood until something reveals them. Then, significant parts of the home must be replaced—at major expense.

As you know, it's similar with computer bugs. The later you discover them, the more expensive it is to fix them. A good set of development tools helps you prevent bugs before they hatch. Moreover, such tools help you write code that shuns bugs. Some tools even write most of the code for you, a fact that can be a mixed blessing.

Common Word Processors

Word processors are so powerful that they actually make good specialized editors, if you take the time to learn them and to train them.

Today's powerful word processors can even become programming languages. I'm not merely saying you can use a word processor to write code for a Java compiler. The word processor actually has a full-fledged language built into it. In the case of Microsoft Word, the language is VBA, which is similar to Visual Basic. Star Office's StarWriter has StarBasic as a programming language. It makes sense to use a word processor as a language if your software needs the particular kind of word power already built into word processors.

As an example, a recent application I wrote uses Word 97's VBA as a programming language and as the project's driver. Word calls Microsoft Access 97 for its database activities. It mail merges selected data into a series of ordinary Word documents. It calls Excel for a bit of spreadsheet action, and a third-party barcode program for barcode images. I might have used Java, Visual Basic, or C / C++, but then I'd have had to write a miniature word processor. Word as a language provided the shortest route to a completed project in that case.

Since you can do nearly anything in a word processor that you can do in Java, why not program the word processor you already own to help you create bug-free Java code from the start? The only adverse answer to that idea is that many commercial tools are inexpensive. On the other hand, you can customize your word processor to do anything you desire, including several things commercial tools don't do.

Your word processor can do wonders for your Java code, making it hard for you to insert bugs. For example, you can make it finish your typing, or not, at your option. When you type the four characters:

for(

your word processor can change what you typed to the following three lines, and wait for you complete the blanks:

```
for ( ; ; ) {

}
```

On the other hand, if you type the five characters:

for (

you get exactly what you type.

Your word processor can also:

- Spell check your code. You can create a special dictionary that holds all Java keywords, as well as names of library classes, methods, interfaces, etc. Each time you type something that's not in your dictionary, your word processor can underline it in red. You can perform a spell check, and at your option, add each red word to your dictionary, gradually building a personal Java dictionary.

- Search globally or locally, for any string of characters, and if you desire, change them to any other string of characters. This makes it easy to rename a variable, especially if you have misspelled it about half of the time. There are clever search-and-replace tricks you should know. See Table 5-1, which automates many of theses tricks.

- Keep several windows loaded in the computer and switch back and forth between them. You can actually drag and drop code from one program file to another, by having simultaneous copies of your word processor active on the screen. You can use the copy buffer to clone pieces of code from one file to another. A large, high-resolution monitor facilitates this process.

- Establish a bookmark in your code, leave that page, and return to exactly the same spot.

- Sort selected lines of code, based on any character positions. Major and minor sorts are possible.

- Turn all keywords one color, comments another, etc.

- Hide special comments so they won't be printed or seen on the screen.
- Remove all text of a particular color or with a particular attribute such as "hidden" and save the results to a new file. That file can be for production, for internal testing, or the source for a demonstration CD, for example.
- Reveal (or hide) all tabs, linefeeds, spaces, etc., helping you with indenting.
- Automatically indent items.
- Record sets of keystrokes and play them back later.

Word, other full-fledged word processors, and powerful editors like Multi-Edit contain full programming languages, so you can use them as the basis of your personalized Java Integrated Development Environment (IDE). Many of these things are beyond any commercial IDE. However, most IDEs do some things you'd find it nontrivial teaching your word processor to do. Color coding comes to mind.

Using Microsoft Word

Word Perfect and Ami Pro users please forgive me, but the scope of *Debugging Java* doesn't allow me to write these pages for more than one word processor. If you're a fan of Star Office, as I am, please accept my apology for not using it in the next example.

Word currently has the greatest user base, so I'll use it for the demonstration. The idea is not to hype any particular product, but to show how you can build a great Java editor from a word processor. You can do the same thing with StarWriter, WordPerfect and Ami Pro.

Error Watch *You can use the 24 × 7 sidebar information to remove macro viruses, since they usually propagate via Normal.Dot. However, you'll need to remove such viruses from any infected documents as well.*

24×7 Restoring All Word Defaults

In the very unlikely event that you ever get Word totally wrapped around the axles, there is a simple and safe way to restore everything to its original defaults. Merely search for the file named Normal.Dot and rename it. The next time you run Word, it sees that the Normal.Dot file is missing, and rebuilds it from scratch. Since rebuilding it removes all of the Normal.Dot macros, keep an updated copy of Normal.Dot in another folder. You can overwrite a corrupted Normal.Dot with your saved copy and restore Word to its former glory.

The first hurdle to overcome is a simple one. Word wants to save your program with an extension of its own choosing. Sorry, but ".java" is not on its list. If your program is named Median and you try to save it as Median.java, Word insists on trying to save it as Median.java.doc, which usually generates an error.

A cute trick gets you around that difficulty. Merely click File | Save As... and put double-quotes around your entire Java filename, like this:

```
"Median.java"
```

That trick works with many other software products when you want to give files nonstandard names or embed spaces they won't otherwise allow.

Some of the things useful in a custom Java editor would make Word less useful for writing other kinds of documents like books and business letters. To prevent difficulties later, create a special template for Java, another for books, a third for business letters, and another for generic word processing, etc.—as many as you want. We'll begin with how to create and save a special Java template. The process is for Word 2000, but the steps for Word 6 and Word 97 are similar.

Creating a Template

Follow these steps:

1. On the main menu, click File | New. Don't use the New File icon on the toolbar, because it bypasses the tabs you need in the next step.

2. You'll see a number of tabs. Select the General tab.

3. Click the Template radio button and select the Blank Document, then click Okay. You've created a new, blank template, which will become your new Java editor. It's a separate entity within Word.

4. Save the template in the default directory. Give it the name of JavaEditor (or choose your own name) and let Word add the extension of .DOT to the filename.

5. Close everything and then reopen JavaEditor.Dot.

You're ready to build your editor. You'll customize the menu, the font, and the toolbars. Then you'll add programming macros and attach them to the toolbar. Finally, you'll build hotkey combinations for the more common commands.

Customizing the Word Menu

Be sure you're working on your Java template, the one you saved as JavaEditor.Dot. Word should say so in its title bar.

You'll want to customize your menu, because Word has many useful commands that are not readily available on the standard menus. First, I'll show how to build or modify a menu, and then I'll present a list of items you might want to install there.

Menus contain categories and commands. Categories are the names like File, Edit, View, Insert, Format, Tools, Table, Window, and Help along a menu bar. Menu commands are the subitems in menu categories. In the File category, you'll find commands like Open, Close, Save, etc.

First, enable menu editing. Click Tools | Customize | Commands.

To add a new category of commands to the menu, drag any command to the menu and place it where you want. At that moment, it's only a command, so in the Customize window, click Modify Selection. In the drop-down, click Begin a Group. That turns the Command into a category. Now, clicking it will no longer execute the original command. Instead, clicking will make the category present a box that currently has no commands in it.

You can rename your new category to something like &Web. The ampersand before the W tells Word to underscore the W, so that ALT-W will open that category. With the ampersand, the category's name becomes Web. Ampersands are optional, and you can install them on commands too.

To remove a category from the menu, merely drag it off the menu, anywhere into the opened Customize window.

Design Tip *Surprisingly, you can remove Word's default categories and commands, as well as those you have added. In other words, you can create a brand new template and totally redesign the menu bar.*

To add a command to any menu category, first drag it to a menu category. Immediately, that category will open, exposing all the commands there, so drag your command down to the desired spot and release the button. As easy as that, you have a new command in your menu's category. Add all commands that seem reasonable, because you can remove them so easily.

Here are some additional commands I find useful in Java programming:

Under the File category	New Web Page
	Close All
	Save All
	Save Version
	Properties
Under the Edit category	Find Next
	Previous Edit
	Next Edit
Under the View category	Magnifier
	Fit to Window
Under the Insert category	Field
	Symbol
	From File
Under the Format category	Hidden
Under the Tools category	Spelling
	Tools AutoCorrect Exceptions
	Compare Documents...
	Record Macro / Stop Recorder
	Security
	Visual Basic Editor
	Microsoft Script Editor
Under the Table category	Sort Ascending
	Sort Descending
	Find in Field
Under a new Web category	Address
	Open

	Open Favorites
	Search the Web
	Web Toolbar
Under a new AutoShapes category	Line
	Arrow
	Rectangle
	Oval
	Autoshapes
	Lines
	Basic Shapes
	Block Arrows
	Flowchart
	More Autoshapes
Under a new Java Fonts category	Courier New
	OCR A Extended
	Symbol
	Times New Roman

You can remove any commands you feel should not be part of your Java editor. Have no fear of removing them, for you can replace them by dragging them back to the menu.

Error Watch   *Be sure you don't remove the commands that let you drag them back to the menu! If you make that mistake, rename Normal.Dot and begin again from scratch. See the Design Tip earlier in this chapter.*

Editing the Word Toolbars

You'll want commonly used commands available at the click of a Word toolbar icon. Some, such as File Open, are already there. Others, such as Close and Close All are easy to drag there. Here's the two-step process:

1. Click Tools | Customize | Commands.

2. Drag any command you desire to any toolbar you desire.

You can make new toolbars via the Toolbars tab and drag any command to them. Click Tools | Customize | Toolbars | New. Name your toolbar, choose JavaEditor.Dot for its residence, and check it to make it visible. Then drag commands to it.

You can remove any command from any toolbar merely by dragging it down into the Customize window. Some of the more useful tools you might want to add are as follows:

- FileCloseOrCloseAll (Yep, that's a real command name!)
- Symbol
- Hidden
- Tools AutoCorrect Exceptions
- Record Macro / Stop Macro

Using Macros to Increase Word's Functionality

A number of excellent tools found in other word processors and editors are missing from Word, or require too many keystrokes. For these handy items, you can build macros, which you can execute from the toolbar or from hotkeys.

When I wrote DOS-based programs, I fell in love with Multi-Edit's bookmarking system. Hit F7 and you install a bookmark onto a stack. Later, via SHIFT-F7, you can return to any bookmark. For some reason, Microsoft has never installed an easy-to-use bookmarking system in Word, so I build one, which admittedly is still not as good as Multi-Edit's.

A few times an hour, I need to check a reference elsewhere in a document or piece of code. I click an icon or press a key, and navigate elsewhere. If I suspect I might return to that new spot, I install another bookmark when I get there. Then, I can flick between two spots in the same document at the click of a mouse. Here's how to insert such a system in your new Java editor. The process is nearly identical for Word 6 and 97.

The BookMark Toolbar Icon

The idea is to establish two bookmark icons and two goto icons. Here's how to build a bookmark icon for your toolbar:

1. Click Tools | Macro.
2. Click Record New Macro.
3. Name this new macro BookMarkA and click OK. Of course, you can name a macro anything you desire. (Do not assign your macro to the toolbar or keyboard yet. You'll do that momentarily.)

Error Watch   *You probably don't want to give a macro the same name as a Word command. Just as Java can override a method by reusing the method's name but specifying different parameters or return type, your new macro supersedes the Word command until you delete the macro from Word.*

4. The recorder is now on. Every keystroke and mouse click is being captured. A new, small toolbar containing two tools has appeared. If you rest your mouse cursor over the rectangle tool, (without clicking) you'll see that clicking the rectangle would stop the macro you're recording. The tool button on the right pauses the recording of that macro. Don't click either button yet.

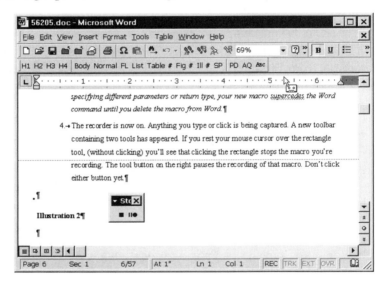

5. On the main menu, click Insert | Bookmark. Name the bookmark A and click Add.

6. Click the Stop Recording tool in the new macros toolbar to stop the recording. Your macro is finished, so it's time to install it.

Error Watch   *If you click the X in the recorder toolbar, you'll close the toolbar, but the recorder will still be running, and you'll have recorded the wrong stuff. In that case, you should stop the recording and begin anew.*

7. Click Tools | Customize | Commands.

8. Scroll down, if necessary, to select Macros in the Categories window.

9. You'll see Normal.NewMacros.BookMarkA or just BookMarkA in the window. Drag it to your Word toolbar. That will install a new icon where you release the mouse button. A good place is just left of the zoom window, which probably displays 100%. Your new toolbar button is huge and you'll want to change it to an icon, so before you leave this window, click Modify Selection. In Word 2000, if you don't do this now, you will not have another chance later.

Error Watch *In Word 2000, if you don't click Modify Selection at this point, you'll have to remove the macro from the toolbar, and then move it back to the toolbar. Otherwise, you won't be able to modify the selection.*

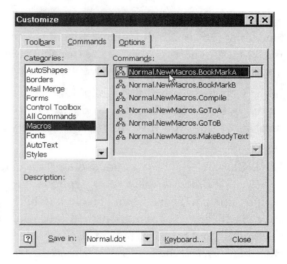

10. Select Default Style. That gives you a single icon without that long name in it. Don't exit the window yet.

11. Now choose an image for your icon. To do that, click Modify Selection | Change Button Image, and select an image. I like to use the pushpin image for this macro.

12. Optionally, edit the macro's image. I like to draw the letter A (or B) in it. To do this, click Modify Selection, click Edit Button Image, and modify the image. Click OK when you're happy with your artwork.

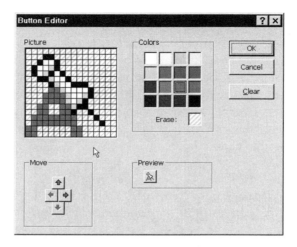

13. One thing remains. Build a hotkey for this icon. Since it's named BookMarkA, the ALT-A key is a reasonable choice. It has no default assignment. Still in the Customize window, click Keyboard.

14. In the Categories window, highlight Macros. In the Macros window, highlight BookMarkA. Click inside the Press Shortcut Key window. Now press ALT-A, and you'll see that ALT-A was previously unassigned. Click Assign.

15. Click Close, click Close again, and try your macro. Unless you have bookmarks turned visible (Tools, Options, View tab, check Bookmarks), nothing much happens when you click it, but what you can't see is that you have established a bookmark named A at your cursor, or wrapped around any highlighted text. Next, page elsewhere and then click Edit | GoTo | Bookmark, select the bookmark named A, and click GoTo again. You'll immediately return to that bookmarked position.

The GoTo Toolbar Icon

That's cool, but you need another macro to take you back to that bookmarked position with a single click, not five. The installation process is nearly identical:

1. Follow steps 1–3 above. At this point, you're recording every keystroke and mouse click again.

2. Record these actions into your macro: Click Edit | GoTo | Bookmark, highlight A, and click GoTo | Close. Those are the actions you want the macro to remember.

3. Follow steps 5–14 above. This time, name your macro GoToA. When you install it on the toolbar, put it just to the left of the BookMarkA icon and give it a different icon. I chose the icon that looks like footprints and edited a red A into it. For the keyboard hotkey, use ALT-CTRL-A, instead of ALT-A.

To test your macro, install a bookmark, navigate several pages away, click there to move the cursor, and use the GoTo icon or ALT-CTRL-A key combination to return.

Additional BookMark and GoTo Icons

Obviously, you can install as many Bookmark and GoTo icons as you desire. I've found two pair to be necessary, and usually adequate. Merely repeat the two previous processes, substituting B for A.

If you're a bit more adventuresome, you might write some Visual Basic for Applications (VBA) code to implement a stack of bookmarks.

Editing and Adding Hotkeys

Word already uses a number of hotkeys for various functions. You know about CTRL-X, CTRL-V and CTRL-C, of course, for the clipboard. CTRL-F and CTRL-H launch the Edit Find and Edit Replace processes, respectively. You can get a list of Word's hotkeys, including any changes you have made but excluding hotkeys you have assigned to macros. Do this:

1. Click Tools | Macro | Macros.

2. Inside the Macros in box, select Word commands. You'll have to use the drop-down arrow to find the selection.

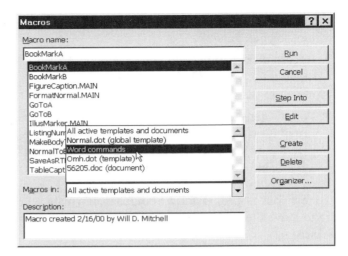

3. Inside the Macro name box, select ListCommands.

4. Click Run.

5. In the List Commands dialog box, click "Current menu and keyboard settings."

6. Click File | Print.

You can also assign hotkeys to macros. You don't need to print a list of keys in order to choose unused ones, because Word will tell you at key assignment time. Notably, the ALT function keys are reserved for your use.

Search and Replace Tricks

During searching and replacing, Word adopts a few odd-looking conventions for ordinary whitespace. Spaces are spaces, but the ENTER key is denoted as ^p, for instance. You actually type the carat ^ and then the letter **p**. The entire list of conventions is available by clicking Edit | Find | Special. When you select a special character, Word enters it into the Find or Replace box. Alternately, you can type it yourself. Here are a few useful characters to memorize:

Special Character	Representation
New paragraph (ENTER)	^p
Tab	^t
Any character (wildcard)	^?
Any number (wildcard)	^#

Special Character	Representation
Any letter (wildcard)	^$
Any whitespace (wildcard)	^w

Error Watch *When you replace text, beware of using Replace All. It will, indeed, replace every instance of the Find text with the Replace text, and that might not be what you want. It's safer to replace things one at a time.*

If you do replace some things by mistake, your Undo command will save the day. Its hotkey is CTRL-Z, a combination that has saved my bacon scores of times.

Word's case sensitivity during Find and Replace operations bears a bit of explaining.

Some things are obvious. If you specify case sensitivity and seek "Java", Word will not find "java". One thing is not so obvious. If you have several places where myVariable needs to be replaced with MyVariable, you must specify case sensitivity and take care to put "myVariable" in the find block. If you put MyVariable in both the Find and the Replace blocks, the replace will fail. That wasn't the case with earlier versions of Word.

If you do not specify case sensitivity, Word tries to match the formatting of the found text. For example, if you replace "QQQ" with "trix", you get "TRIX."

Sorting Lines of Code

Say you have some program lines like this to sort:

```
String a = "Wilson, Diana A. Omaha, NE";
String b = "Jones, John P. Tacoma, WA";
String c = "Taylor, Jones R. Dallas, TX";
String d = "Wilson, Neil B. Omaha, NE ";
```

Prior versions of Word required you to convert the information to a table, sort it, then convert it back to text.

In Word 2000, you can highlight the text and click Table | Sort, choose your options, and click OK. You can sort by the whole paragraph, left to right. Or, you can choose words for your sort. Below, I specified a space as the word delimiter, and then sorted ascending on words 7 (city), 4 (last name), and 5 (first name) in that order:

```
String c = "Taylor, Jones R. Dallas, TX";
String a = "Wilson, Diana A. Omaha, NE";
String d = "Wilson, Neil B. Omaha, NE ";
String b = "Jones, John P. Tacoma, WA";
```

Changing Colors and Formatting

Macros can make Word as powerful as you desire. Very little functionality can escape them, for they are programmed in a full-featured language. You can record a macro to get hints of how to use the underlying language (VBA) and then edit the macro for greater functionality. The appendices include several useful macros, among them the following.

KeywordsGreen   Finding all keywords and changing their color to, say, green, is a simple task. Disregarding keywords in strings and comments is not rocket science, but neither is it trivial. Either task requires a bit of VBA coding. The appendices provide a macro that will search a Word document and turn all Java keywords green, unless they are in strings or comments. It presumes that all Java keywords are surrounded by whitespace or curly braces.

QQQtoHidden   If you adopt the QQQ idea (or something similar), a macro can seek all comments containing QQQ and treat them in a special way. For instance, it can remove them or make them hidden text. A macro in the appendices seeks comments that contain QQQ and asks whether you want to remove them all, or turn them all into red, hidden text. Then, it complies.

RemoveHidden   Another macro in the appendices removes all hidden text and requests a SaveAs… filename. Although you can tell Word to suppress hidden text from printouts and from the screen, you can't tell it to suppress hidden text from a file you're saving. This macro removes such text and saves the results under a new name you specify, without modifying the original file.

Recording Keystrokes

One thing Word has never mastered is the idea of a macro running another macro, perhaps because of the possibility of a recursive runaway. So, it may not be possible in Word to build a macro that opens a new macro, which records keystrokes.

   When you want to record keystrokes, click Tools | Macro | Record New Macro. Then, if this is a throwaway macro, accept the default macro name and start typing. Anything typed is recorded for you. The small toolbar shown in the margin appears while you are recording. It has a Stop button and a Pause button. The latter changes into a Resume button if you pause the recording.

   If you want to highlight something with the mouse while recording a macro, you'll find you cannot. However, there is a trick you can use. First, you may

want to pause the recording process, because arrow key actions are recorded. Use the arrow keys to move your cursor to the area you want to highlight. Resume the recording if necessary, press and hold the SHIFT key, and use your arrow keys to move the cursor. That highlights the text. Now, you can use the highlighted text in your recording, perhaps by copying and pasting it.

When you're done, stop the recording. You can give the recording a new name, install the macro on a toolbar, or give it a hotkey, as shown previously. Alternately, you can click Tools | Macro | Macros, select your macro, and click Run.

Use the Best Java Editor You Can

A great editor helps you shun bugs. Some editors and most word processors are configurable, and some, such as Multi-Edit come pre-configured for Java, or other languages you select. Most Integrated Development Environments (IDEs) include excellent Java editors. You can program your word processor to do things no IDE currently does. However, the makers of your IDE are reading this book too, and you may find some of these features in your next upgrade package.

Any text editor that can save files with four-character filenames will work. That includes nearly all editors. Here are some general-purpose editors I have used with Java:

- I have enjoyed Multi-Edit (ME), a product of American Cybernetics, since the days of dBase-II and Clipper. Some of its advanced features from a decade ago still are not incorporated into programs like Word. The current GUI version has a Java template, which you can extend at will. It also includes templates for about 30 other languages. The templates let you configure all kinds of things, such as your preferred indent style.

- NotePad is from Windows 3. Aside from its 64K file-size limit, and its inability to edit multiple files, it does yeoman service in Windows.

- WordPad is also bundled with Windows.

- Write is actually a pretty good word processor. It's bundled with Windows.

- vi is one of two standard editors for various flavors of UNIX. It works on DOS computers. While it has a steeper learning curve than most, it is extremely capable. vi masters can edit faster in it than in anything else, partly because there's never a need to waste time moving one's hand to a mouse.

- EMACS is the other standard UNIX editor. Its source code is free for downloading, and the editor is extensible. You can customize it to your taste.

- Edit (at the MS-DOS prompt) works fine, except for cut, copy, and paste commands between it and Windows programs. For some reason, it's difficult to copy part of a Web page into the Windows buffer and then paste it into Edit. Other kinds of copying seem to work perfectly. Of course, you cannot program Edit to do all the special tricks more modern editors can perform, but it's free, and available when you're programming at the DOS prompt.

- Some of my older editors, such as Technical Edit and Professional Editor, refuse to save four-character extensions. Possibly newer versions work okay, but before you acquire an editor, be certain it doesn't restrict you to the 8.3 filenaming convention. Otherwise, you'll have to rename each .java file after you save it!

Editing Tricks

The following over-complicated SQL code was designed to find duplicate data in a table. It has a bug. It's an actual piece of SQL I inherited one day. It's written in MS Query, but scan it just long enough and you'll see that finding the bug might take a while. As a hint, I'll give you all the information I had: The SQL runs, selects the correct fields, and orders the rows properly. It just doesn't select the right set of rows. Oh, the **IsNull()** function returns **true** or **false**, depending on whether or not the referenced field contains a null value.

```
SELECT DISTINCTROW tblAllDbfInfo.PLANT_CODE, tblAllDbfInfo.ING_CODE,
tblAllDbfInfo.SUPPLIER, tblAllDbfInfo.TRK_CAR, tblAllDbfInfo.DATE_REC,
tblAllDbfInfo.NUTR_1, tblAllDbfInfo.NUTR_2, tblAllDbfInfo.NUTR_3,
tblAllDbfInfo.NUTR_4, tblAllDbfInfo.NUTR_5, tblAllDbfInfo.NUTR_6,
tblAllDbfInfo.NUTR_7, tblAllDbfInfo.DATE_LOG, tblAllDbfInfo.NUTR_8 FROM
tblAllDbfInfo WHERE (((tblAllDbfInfo.PLANT_CODE) In (SELECT [PLANT_CODE] FROM
[tblAllDbfInfo] As Tmp GROUP BY [PLANT_CODE],[ING_CODE],[SUPPLIER],[TRK_CAR],
[DATE_REC],[NUTR_1],[NUTR_2],[NUTR_3],[NUTR_4],[NUTR_5],[NUTR_6],[NUTR_7],
[NUTR_8] HAVING (Count(*)>1) And [PLANT_CODE] = [tblAllDbfInfo].[PLANT_CODE]
And [ING_CODE] = [tblAllDbfInfo].[ING_CODE] And [SUPPLIER] =
[tblAllDbfInfo].[SUPPLIER] And ([TRK_CAR] = [tblAllDbfInfo].[TRK_CAR] Or
(IsNull([TRK_CAR]) And IsNull([tblAllDbfInfo].[TRK_CAR]))) And ([DATE_REC] =
[tblAllDbfInfo].[DATE_REC] Or (IsNull([DATE_REC]) and
IsNull([tblAllDbfInfo].[DATE_REC]))) And ([NUTR_1] = [tblAllDbfInfo].[NUTR_1]
Or (IsNull([NUTR_1]) and IsNull([tblAllDbfInfo].[NUTR_1]))) And ([NUTR_2] =
[tblAllDbfInfo].[NUTR_2] Or (IsNull([NUTR_2]) And
IsNull([tblAllDbfInfo].[NUTR_2]))) And ([NUTR_3] = [tblAllDbfInfo].[NUTR_3] Or
(IsNull([NUTR_3]) And IsNull([tblAllDbfInfo].[NUTR_3]))) And ([NUTR_4] =
```

```
[tblAllDbfInfo].[NUTR_4] Or (IsNull([NUTR_4]) And
IsNull([tblAllDbfInfo].[NUTR_4]))) And ([NUTR_4] = [tblAllDbfInfo].[NUTR_5] Or
(IsNull([NUTR_5]) and IsNull([tblAllDbfInfo].[NUTR_5]))) And ([NUTR_6] =
[tblAllDbfInfo].[NUTR_6] Or (IsNull([NUTR_6]) And
IsNull([tblAllDbfInfo].[NUTR_6]))) And ([NUTR_7] = [tblAllDbfInfo].[NUTR_7] Or
(IsNull([NUTR_7]) and IsNull([tblAllDbfInfo].[NUTR_7]))) And ([NUTR_8] =
[tblAllDbfInfo].[NUTR_8] Or (IsNull([NUTR_8]) And
IsNull([tblAllDbfInfo].[NUTR_8]))))))) ORDER BY tblAllDbfInfo.PLANT_CODE,
tblAllDbfInfo.ING_CODE, tblAllDbfInfo.SUPPLIER, tblAllDbfInfo.TRK_CAR,
tblAllDbfInfo.DATE_REC, tblAllDbfInfo.NUTR_1, tblAllDbfInfo.NUTR_2,
tblAllDbfInfo.NUTR_3, tblAllDbfInfo.NUTR_4, tblAllDbfInfo.NUTR_5;
```

Spot the error? Small chance, without some serious eyestrain.

The following version almost makes the error pop out at you, even if you're not current in the language. The code is the same, except for a few judiciously placed line-feeds.

```
SELECT DISTINCTROW tblAllDbfInfo.PLANT_CODE, tblAllDbfInfo.ING_CODE,
tblAllDbfInfo.SUPPLIER, tblAllDbfInfo.TRK_CAR, tblAllDbfInfo.DATE_REC,
tblAllDbfInfo.NUTR_1, tblAllDbfInfo.NUTR_2, tblAllDbfInfo.NUTR_3,
tblAllDbfInfo.NUTR_4, tblAllDbfInfo.NUTR_5, tblAllDbfInfo.NUTR_6,
tblAllDbfInfo.NUTR_7, tblAllDbfInfo.DATE_LOG, tblAllDbfInfo.NUTR_8
FROM tblAllDbfInfo

WHERE (((tblAllDbfInfo.PLANT_CODE) In (

SELECT [PLANT_CODE] FROM [tblAllDbfInfo] As Tmp
GROUP BY [PLANT_CODE],[ING_CODE],[SUPPLIER],[TRK_CAR],[DATE_REC],
[NUTR_1],[NUTR_2],[NUTR_3],[NUTR_4],[NUTR_5],[NUTR_6],[NUTR_7],[NUTR_8]

HAVING (Count(*)>1) And

[PLANT_CODE] = [tblAllDbfInfo].[PLANT_CODE] And
[ING_CODE] = [tblAllDbfInfo].[ING_CODE] And
[SUPPLIER] = [tblAllDbfInfo].[SUPPLIER] And

([TRK_CAR] = [tblAllDbfInfo].[TRK_CAR] Or
(IsNull([TRK_CAR]) And IsNull([tblAllDbfInfo].[TRK_CAR]))) And

([DATE_REC] = [tblAllDbfInfo].[DATE_REC] Or
(IsNull([DATE_REC]) And IsNull([tblAllDbfInfo].[DATE_REC]))) And

([NUTR_1] = [tblAllDbfInfo].[NUTR_1] Or
(IsNull([NUTR_1]) And IsNull([tblAllDbfInfo].[NUTR_1]))) And

([NUTR_2] = [tblAllDbfInfo].[NUTR_2] Or
(IsNull([NUTR_2]) And IsNull([tblAllDbfInfo].[NUTR_2]))) And
```

```
([NUTR_3] = [tblAllDbfInfo].[NUTR_3] Or
(IsNull([NUTR_3]) And IsNull([tblAllDbfInfo].[NUTR_3]))) And

([NUTR_4] = [tblAllDbfInfo].[NUTR_4] Or
(IsNull([NUTR_4]) And IsNull([tblAllDbfInfo].[NUTR_4]))) And

([NUTR_4] = [tblAllDbfInfo].[NUTR_5] Or
(IsNull([NUTR_5]) And IsNull([tblAllDbfInfo].[NUTR_5]))) And

([NUTR_6] = [tblAllDbfInfo].[NUTR_6] Or
(IsNull([NUTR_6]) And IsNull([tblAllDbfInfo].[NUTR_6]))) And

([NUTR_7] = [tblAllDbfInfo].[NUTR_7] Or
(IsNull([NUTR_7]) And IsNull([tblAllDbfInfo].[NUTR_7]))) And

([NUTR_8] = [tblAllDbfInfo].[NUTR_8] Or
(IsNull([NUTR_8]) And IsNull([tblAllDbfInfo].[NUTR_8])))
)))

ORDER BY tblAllDbfInfo.PLANT_CODE, tblAllDbfInfo.ING_CODE,
tblAllDbfInfo.SUPPLIER, tblAllDbfInfo.TRK_CAR, tblAllDbfInfo.DATE_REC,
tblAllDbfInfo.NUTR_1,
tblAllDbfInfo.NUTR_2,
tblAllDbfInfo.NUTR_3,
tblAllDbfInfo.NUTR_4,
tblAllDbfInfo.NUTR_5;
```

If you haven't seen the bug yet, there's a spot where NUTR_4 should be NUTR_5. If you look vertically eight characters in from the left margin, you'll see the numbers: 1, 2, 3, 4, *4*, 6, 7, 8, an obvious giveaway.

It takes some drudgery, but any time I come across a long SQL statement, I spend a few minutes and edit it into a more readable format, just to have a chance of understanding it. Several times, I've found bugs in code that was supposedly running fine.

A very recent case entailed a bit of dynamic SQL that had been in use for nine years. While inspecting it for an entirely different reason, I saw how a typo prepended a zero to months 1–10, instead of only to 1–9. Thus, October's month number became 010. The SQL discarded the trailing zero, coming up with 01, or January. For nine years, a few hundred salespeople had been getting about 8–12 percent higher commissions in October (month 10) than they deserved, because the program duplicated their high-volume January commissions into a lower-volume month, October.

For some reason, no salesperson ever complained!

Changing the format to include line-feeds helped reveal the error.

Make Typos Identify Themselves

The Java compiler will help you find many kinds of errors, because Java requires you to declare variables and methods. If you misspell or miscapitalize a name, the compiler will complain and become recalcitrant. That is, it will refuse to compile your code.

Naming standards help. Most Java programmers begin variable names with lowercase characters, capitalizing interior words, thus: *thisIsANewVariableName*. A variable name like the following should be suspicious:

thisIsaNewVariableName.

The previous vertical alignment trick made a typo stick out. Obviously, the numerical sequence 1, 2, 3, 4, *4*, 6, 7, 8 has an error, and the vertical alignment helps one spot that error. Vertical alignment helps in other ways. If you had to initialize five similarly named variables to zero, vertical alignment might help you spot one whose variable was missing a capital letter. It's actually easier to write code in vertical alignment than other ways. If you need to initialize a dozen array elements to the letters A through L, write a line like this, and replicate it eleven more times:

```
myVariable[0] = "A";
```

Then change all the indices from 0 to their proper value and the A's to their proper letters like so:

```
myVariable[0] = "A";
myVariable[1] = "B";
...
myVariable[11] = "L";
```

It's surprising how rapidly and accurately you can use two hands to change a long list of array indices by typing the key sequence **A**, **left arrow**, **down arrow**, **B**, **left arrow**, **down arrow**, **C**, **left arrow**, **down arrow**... etc.

Of course, one should use a loop in this trivial example, but sometimes you can't use a loop—or should avoid one for clarity. For example, you might need to add a special comment to each of the lines. You can't do that with a loop.

Sometimes line length identifies a problem. If ten lines are aligned vertically and the fourth is one character longer than the others, it stands out. It might have a typo. Similarly, the line lengths might be vastly different, but the first 22 characters might be identical. In that case, vertical alignment lets you quickly scan the first 22 characters of each line, seeking errors, but first, you must construct that vertical alignment.

Extend Your Copy/Paste Buffer

People who do a lot of editing soon discover the Windows cut/copy/paste buffer. Unfortunately, fewer people use its mouseless hotkeys CTRL-X, CTRL-C, and CTRL-V, respectively, which work with every Windows-based application I've used for a decade.

You can use the mouse to highlight just about anything on a Windows screen, and then press CTRL-X or CTRL-C to put that "thing" into a special parcel of RAM, called the clipboard, which Windows has reserved.

For example, writing this, I highlighted this text, above: CTRL-X, CTRL-C and then pressed CTRL-C, so my buffer now contains "CTRL-X, CTRL-C," complete with the drop-case formatting. In the last sentence, I used CTRL-V twice to avoid typing that specially formatted text. The original text remains in the previous paragraph because I used CTRL-C, to make a copy.

If you use CTRL-X, or cut, to install something in the buffer, that object disappears from your document as it enters the buffer.

You can position your mouse cursor anywhere else and press CTRL-V to paste the contents of the buffer there. CTRL-V is a copy from the buffer, not a move, so you can use CTRL-V multiple times to make dozens of copies anywhere you want. So, how many times do you suppose I've pressed CTRL-V and modified the result while writing the last four paragraphs?

Using those keystrokes is about seven times faster than using the mouse. That is, you can type CTRL-V at least seven times in the period it takes you to grab the mouse and click Edit, click Paste.

In Word and most (but not all) other applications that can use the buffer:

- CTRL-X is the same as clicking File | Cut.
- CTRL-C is the same as clicking File | Copy.
- CTRL-V is the same as clicking File | Paste.

Incidentally, notice the adjoining positions of the characters X, C, and V on your keyboard. That positioning makes it easy to recall which is which. X means cut and C means copy, and V for paste is right next to the other two.

Most people find the clipboard useful when they want to reuse code from another file. You should consider reusing code from within your current file as well. When declaring and initializing your variables, take care with their initial order, because you might be able to reuse part of that typing later. You might have to strip off the = 0 part of a declaration, but you might save retyping the variable name—with the attendant typo problems that can entail.

Copious use of the clipboard makes it easier to use long, descriptive names for variables and methods, another practice that enhances code legibility.

Consider building a standard comment stub to paste into the beginning of each method or class. Although your shop may use a different format, such a stub might read:

```
// Purpose:
// Input:
// Output:
// Date:
// Author:    John Q. Public
// Mod Hist:
```

By using such a stub, you won't forget to add a Mod Hist: placeholder, for example. You'll save a lot of typing, and the attendant typographical errors. Open another window and use the buffer to copy your comment stub into each new method.

Alternately, use a clipboard extender to keep items like your comment stub always at hand. Described next are several clipboard extenders that are more versatile than Microsoft's.

Clipboard Extenders

In Windows 95, CTRL-X or CTRL-C seems to overwrite any prior information in the buffer, but that's not strictly so. The buffer can contain one piece of text and one picture, for example, without either overwriting the other. However, the buffer is severely limited by the fact that there's only one spot for text and one for a single image. Authors who take screen shots would also find it useful to be able to capture 20 screens at a time, but they cannot.

Windows 98 introduced the Clipboard Viewer with added features, such as the ability to save the clipboard's contents to a file. You can find the viewer by clicking the Start button, then selecting Programs | Accessories | System Tools | Clipboard Viewer.

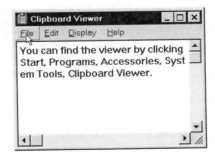

If you plan to use the clipboard viewer a lot, install an icon on your desktop, the Office toolbar, or your Windows Quick Launch toolbar.

Inexpensive and free shareware utilities do the job much better. They let you cut or copy an essentially unlimited number of items, of any type, into the buffer, then save them to disk. Most use CTRL-X, CTRL-C, and CTRL-V. Here are the three best I've found, and they're free:

Internet Source: http://www.	Very Short Description
cyber-matrix.com/clipmag.htm	ClipMagic. Freeware. The most capable of the lot. Edit your clips, save multiple files. Does it all.
easysoftwareuk.com	Classic version 1. Freeware. Save up to 3,000 clips, view them about 100 at a time, and paste any clip with just two mouse clicks. Save multiple files. CTRL-F1–CTRL-F9 make often used clips immediately available. The $25 version is even better.
thornsoft.com	ClipMate. No-nag shareware. Unlimited number of files. Capture with CTRL-X or CTRL-C, paste with CTRL-V. The pay version is as capable as they come.

Teach AutoCorrect to Cut Errors and Save Typing

How would you like to type the four characters **for(** and have your editor automatically change what you typed to the following text, complete with the blank line?

```
for ( ; ; ) {

}
```

Modern word processors contain AutoCorrect features, which can do that for you. These features masquerade as automated spell checkers, but they were really invented for Java programmers. Well . . . perhaps not, but we can put them to excellent use. Here's how to build that special, autocorrecting **for** loop. The example is for Microsoft Word 2000. It uses an officially supported feature that seems to be so poorly known that I've explained it to five separate Microsoft Word technicians, which is doubly odd because I got it from one.

1. Open any ordinary, new document in Word.
2. Type the text you want to appear automatically. In this case, you are using a loop, so enter two spaces on the line between the curly braces. That way, you will get automatic indenting.

3. Use your mouse to highlight all of the text you typed. Surprisingly, you don't need to install the highlighted text into the copy-and-paste buffer. Word uses whatever you've highlighted, not what's in the buffer.

4. Now, click Tools and click AutoCorrect in the menu. If you're using Word 2000, you may have to click the bottom of the drop-down box to see the lesser-used menu options.

5. You'll see a semblance of the highlighted text appearing in the With box. You won't see things like the tab or paragraph marker (ENTER key), nor multiple lines, but they are present.

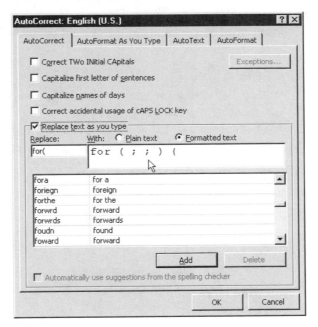

6. Type **for(** in the Replace box, without the quotes. Note that there's no space between the "r" and the "(". That's important.

7. Click Add (or click Replace if you are correcting an existing entry) and exit the screen.

8. Test it by typing your replace characters. Type **for(** and immediately Word will autocorrect it to your desired text.

In step 6 above, you did not enter a space between the "r" and the "(" characters. Here's why. If you want to construct your own **for** loop without help from Word, type the same thing, except insert a space after the "r". Word will keep exactly what you typed. It won't autocorrect because the space makes it a different string.

Some people abhor such conveniences, preferring to type all those characters and to correct the occasional typographical error. If you're of that ilk, more power to your fingertips, but if you'd like your Java editor to do a bit of work for you, give this idea a try.

Here is a good starter set of AutoCorrect entries. For added clarity, Table 5-1 displays dots for spaces and ^t for tabs. Notice the //class entry, which automatically adds a number of comments to your code's header. I use similar entries that create JavaDoc stubs. You can standardize the comments list any way you choose. Word can even insert the current date if you desire.

Replace	With
	. (dot) means space in this table, so don't type them into your AutoCorrect entries
`/*`	`/*..`
	`*...`
	`*/`
`for(`	`for.(.;.;.).{`
	`..`
	`}`
`do{`	`do.{`
	`..`
	`}.while (.);`
`while(`	`While (.).{`
	`..`
	`}`
`if(`	`if.(.).{`
	`..`
	`}`
`Else(`	`Else.{`
	`..`
	`}`
`Else.if(`	`Else.if.(.)`
	`..`
	`}`
	`else.{`
	`..`
	`}`

Table 5.1 AutoCorrect Entries

Replace	With

`/**`	`/**`
	`.*`
	`**/`

`try{`	`try.{`
	`..`
	`}`
	`catch.{`
	`..`
	`}`
	`finally.{`
	`..`
	`}`

QQQ	/*.QQQ.*/

`//class`	`//.class.constants`
	`//.class.variable`
	`//.instance.variables`
	`//.class.methods`
	`//.constructor.methods`
	`//.instance.methods`
	`//.main.method`
	`//.Function:^t`
	`//.VersDate:^t`
	`//.Author..:^t`
	`//.Mod.Hist:^t`
	`package`
	`class.{`
	`..public.static.void.main.(String[].args).{`
	`....`
	`..}`
	`}`

Table 5.1   AutoCorrect Entries *(continued)*

Train Your Spell Checker

Build a special Java dictionary for your word processor. To do that, use actual Java programs from any source that is similar to the style you will use. The JDK has a good set of demo programs. While editing Java code, turn on your Java dictionary, and it will underline in red any word or command it doesn't understand.

As you build new classes and name them, and as you name variables and constants, you can tell your Java dictionary to remember those names for next time.

The beauty of using a Java dictionary is that when you misspell a variable name, the word processor flags the error. The result is fewer typographical errors in your code at the start, when it's easier and cheaper to correct them.

Here's how to train your spell checker:

1. Click Tools | Options and select the Spelling and Grammar tab.

2. Click Dictionaries | New, type **Java**, and click Save. Your new dictionary will be named Java.Dic.

3. Check the Java.Dic entry and uncheck the Custom.Dic entry. You'll see a warning window that says this may affect other applications that use Word's dictionary. That's okay, unless you want to use something like Outlook at the same time you're editing in Java. Even then, the main Office dictionary remains active, so your spell checking still works. You've only disabled your other custom dictionaries.

4. Get a list of Java keywords and type them into Java.Dic. To open Java.Dic for data entry, click Tools | Options and select the Spelling tab. Then click Dictionaries, highlight Java.Dic, and click Edit. If Word asks permission to convert from a Text document, answer yes.

5. Open several listings of Java code in Word and use the spell checker. Each time Word comes to something it doesn't understand, such as java.awt, it will underscore the word in red. When you press F7 to perform a spell check, you will have the opportunity of adding each such word to your dictionary.

6. One problem remains. Word insists on using its main dictionary in conjunction with your Java.Dic dictionary. Microsoft has confirmed to me that as in prior versions, you can't disable the main dictionary in Word 2000. However, you don't have to use an English language main dictionary! If you change to a language that's very unlike English, such as Japanese or Swahili, only in very rare instances will the main dictionary confuse a mistyped word for a correct one. Changing dictionaries may require you to insert your original setup CD, because your installation probably didn't install all the languages Word supports. It's not a perfect solution, but it works.

Write in the First-Last-Middle Sequence

Most Java constructs have three parts: beginning, end, and middle. That's the best sequence for writing most of your code, because it saves you time at the end.

You don't have to page back to recall just where the closing curly brace belongs on a line, and you don't need to figure out how many closing curly braces to install at the end. Best of all, you don't need to worry about a line of code that might go between the last two, or the second and third from the last. Misplacing such a line will probably break your code in subtle ways.

Of course, if you miss a brace, the compiler will catch your error, but then the problem is that you're expending energy to fix a bug you didn't need to create in the first place. Moreover, bugs tend to cluster. Your chances of fixing that bug erroneously are about ten times greater than your chance of introducing a bug by writing in first-last-middle sequence.

In this almost trivial example, when you begin a **for** clause, you might type this much:

```
for (long i=0; i<maxIterations; i++) {

}
```

then arrow upward one line and complete the middle.

The first-last-middle idea becomes vastly more important when you write the larger constructs, such as intricate methods that contain numerous nested loops or **for**, **if**, and **switch** statements.

The QQQ Bookmark

In the "Left Brain <==> Right Brain" section of Chapter 2, I introduced the notion of creativity being an opposite of organization. I stated that when you are creating something, it's important not to break the stream of creativity until it is finished.

One way to keep the creative juices flowing is to develop "standard methods" that handle creative hurdles for you. One of these is the QQQ bookmark idea.

When programming creatively, most people think in a top-down mode. They have the overall structure in their minds and work out the details as they write. The trouble comes when they have to divert their attention (switch to left-brain mode) to research a detail. They tend to lose track of the big picture.

A good, standard method for jumping that research hurdle is to type **QQQ** and keep on creating. Later, you can return to all of your QQQ entries and replace them with researched code.

If you want your Java to compile, you can put QQQ in a comment. I even went to the trouble of creating a hotkey, ALT-Q, in my Java template of Word, which writes this:

```
/* QQQ */
```

Not only that, if you're using the Java template in Table 5-1, typing the letters **QQQ** autocorrects to /* QQQ */.

Next to your QQQ comment, you should insert a note or question indicating whatever is on your mind at the time, no matter how ridiculous, because the note will help you recall what you were trying to think about at the time. For example:

```
/* QQQ Is this algorithm really what the user wants?? Ask Pat
about it. */
```

Design Tip *If you're concerned about someone seeing your QQQ comments after the code is released, consider not making them comments after all! That way, the code won't compile until you've removed every one.*

You might want to work with several levels of QQQ, by appending numbers or letters to the QQQ string. QQQ might mean things to fix in the overall schema. QQQ1–QQQ9 might represent things to fix at the method level. QQQx1–QQQx9 might be reserved for things another level deeper, etc.

Nearly all editors, word processors, and IDEs have "find" capabilities, which can locate all instances of QQQ for you, even if the three Qs have numbers or letters appended to them. One of the final steps before releasing code is to remove every instance of QQQ.

Error Watch *You can use CTRL-H to find every instance of QQQ and replace them with nothing, but this would be a poor time to use Replace All. You should inspect each QQQ and resolve them manually.*

Holey 3 × 5 Card Trix

Creativity and organization seem to hate each other inside the brain. Unfortunately, organization will win every confrontation between them. Our society trains us that way. This, in part, is why 97 percent of the people believe it is so difficult to be creative.

Creativity occurs mostly in the right half of the brain, and organization occurs mostly in the logical, or left half, of the brain. The problem with creative writing is often this: The writer gets a dozen great thoughts down on paper, and then feels the need to organize them. That feeling is the logical, left half, of the brain trying to take over. The unsuspecting writer starts organizing, and gentle creativity loses yet another battle.

The trouble is, many people have great difficulty lulling their logical left half of the brain back to sleep so they can become creative again. While you're being creative, why not remain that way a while? Don't stop and organize; let that happen later. I'll show you a trick next, but for now, just create, using 3 × 5 cards. Use the spiral-bound ones. I'll explain why in a moment.

The idea is to write a separate thought, or perhaps two, on each card, and sort the cards later.

What this does is separate a predominantly right-brain (creative) activity from a predominantly left-brain (logical) activity. In doing that, it prevents the dominant, logical (left) half of the brain from suppressing the recessive, creative (right) half of the brain.

Pick up a card and write down one idea on it. Quickly. Don't think. It might be as simple as "Pat needs to verify the DSS algorithm", or even simpler: "DSS Algo, see Pat". Pick up the next card, and write another idea. It's fine for one idea to spark another. Just pick up another card and write the next idea on it. It's important to write as fast as you legibly can.

When you're done, go back through the cards. Don't read them with a thought of how you'll organize them. Just read them for sparks of other ideas. When you get another idea, and you will, pick up a new card and write.

Here's why you use spiral bound 3 × 5 index cards. Make them "holey." Remove the spiral wire, because you have a unique need for the holes. Just unbend one end of the wire with pliers, and screw it out of the card deck. You can discard the wire, but keep the cards and use them for your ideas. Mead #63130, or Pen-Tab 78178 cards work perfectly. Each brand has 20 holes. You can also get 4 × 6 cards and other sizes, spiral bound.

Here is how you can organize your cards in dozens of ways. One card will be an index for all the rest. On that card, next to the holes, write your organizational categories. If you have 10 or fewer categories, you might want to use every other hole. Your index card might look like the left-hand card shown in Figure 5-1. If you're right-handed, put the holes on the right.

Find an ordinary, hand-held, single-hole paper punch.

Read each card and see what categories fit it. Perhaps the first card contains something about the screens. Use your index card to see which hole that is. Use your paper punch to remove the paper between that hole and the edge of the card (don't punch your index card). Now, next to SCREENS, you have a sort of V-shaped channel where a hole there used to be.

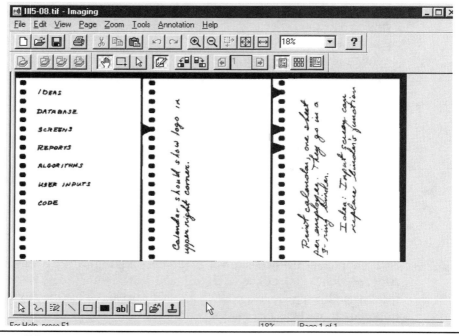

Figure 5.1   Organizing your index cards

Punch out other categories, as appropriate. If you need to, add more categories to your index card—as many as you need. Does this still sound mysterious? Hang in there a minute.

Do the same for all your cards. Some cards may receive multiple punches. Perhaps you have a card that mentions the screens and a book that contains useful algorithms. Make a punch for SCREENS and one for ALGORITHMS. If the card relates to the ideas, make a punch for IDEAS, too.

Okay, here's the trick. Stack your cards back into a deck with the Index card on top. It's time to find all the "Screens" cards. Stick a nail through the Screens holes and shake the deck. With a little encouragement, all the Screens cards will fall out. Simple as that!

You can have compound selections. If you want all the Screens cards that are also Algorithms cards, just stick your nail through the Algorithms hole of the Screens cards you just shook out, and shake that deck. If you want all the Screens cards that are not Algorithms cards, do the same thing, but this time use the cards that don't shake out.

The power of this trick is subtle. You might have thousands of cards before you're done with a project! You can sort the whole deck in a minute, instead of a full day! If you don't care for that selection, you can put the deck back together and re-sort an entirely different way, in only a minute.

The subtlety is this. Since you only spend a fraction of a minute selecting and sorting cards, your right brain can stay in control, and you stay creative. Double tricky, eh?

Of course, you can add new punches later. Just annotate the index card. The 20 holes in the Mead 63130 or Pentel 78178 cards allow up to 20 categories, but you can even have more.

Say you need 30 categories, and for some reason, they are named 1, 2, ... 30.

Use two ranges: 1–15 and 16–30. If a card is in the first range, punch out the first hole, but not the second. If a card is in the second range, punch the second hole instead. Now make another punch in each card to indicate where in the range that card falls.

For 1 or for 16, punch the third hole. For 2 or 17, punch the fourth hole, etc., to the end of your ranges.

You might create one index card for the 1–15 range, and a second index and for the rest.

So, if you want the 19 category, check your index card. It should say to put a nail in the second hole, and from that shaking, put the nail in the sixth hole. Voila!

There's a limitation to consider. You can't have a single card that has holes in both the 1–15 range, and in the 16–30 range to boot. You should be able to arrange your categories so that's no problem. If you just can't, then use one of your spare holes for a new, combination category.

Are 36 categories not quite enough? You can double it to 72 easily. Your first two holes are your superindex. For another 18 categories, punch holes 1 and 2. For another 18, punch neither hole. Go to a three-hole superindex and you can get 136 categories.

It's actually possible to generate 524,288 separate categories with your 20 holes, but then each card can only be punched for one category. That should be enough for most projects. If it's not enough, remember a card has two sides! And 4 × 6 cards have more holes!

I've also been known to create a database and a Java program to organize a project. However, I used to have a 3 × 5 card taped to my desk that read "Never write a program to replace a 3 × 5 card deck."

Use a Known Subset of Java

I doubt that you or I will ever understand everything about Java. After all, Java 2 comes with more than 5,000 classes! Even if you and I were suddenly blessed with all Java knowledge, a few days later a million smart people would have generated far more knowledge than we could learn in that span of time. The only sane defense is to find what works, stick with it, and expand that sea of knowledge into areas needed for current projects. You can do 90 percent of your Java work using only about 200 classes, so it makes sense to become intimate with the core classes and refer to documentation for the rest, when necessary.

It also makes sense to seek favorite paradigms in Java. Here is a trivial example. A **for** loop can do about any loopy thing you want, although it probably uses a few more cycles than a **do** or a **while**. You might consider always using a **for** loop, unless a **do** or a **while** is absolutely necessary. On the other hand, if you're happier with **do** and **while**, you might consider relegating **for** to the nether regions of your programming habits.

No matter what kind of loop you prefer, form special habits for loops that must execute at least once, and loops that need not execute.

You can probably type the phrase "public static void main" in your sleep. As you know, there are several equally valid ways to finish the phrase, for you can put the square brackets on either side of the array name and include whitespace there. Choose one method and stick to it.

Java is a rich language that grows dramatically in power with every release. If you use libraries, and you should, the possibilities tend to boggle the mind. For instance, there are numerous ways to create a text box. The java.awt contains a good one. Most third-party Integrated Development Environments include extended text boxes, which give you more properties to customize but which involve larger footprints. You can even write your own custom text box. Find one that works for you and stick with it. Doing so will save you some research every time you need to install a text box.

Realize that when you start iterating at zero, you almost always want to count to one less than the total number of iterations, so you want to use the $<$ sign, not the $<=$ sign. That means the first line of your **for** loop can become nearly standard: for (int i = 0; i < max; i++) {. Along those lines, avoid starting your iteration count with 1, although there are times when you should start at 1, such as to bypass a header record.

Comment First, Code Later

A second-semester Pascal student once asked me what I considered the most important thing to learn as a programmer. I baffled most of the class with the declaration "Comment first, code later." I didn't know that my boss had taught most of them exactly the opposite the previous semester!

For their first assignment, I suggested that the students do this: They were to type in the programming assignment exactly as I gave it to them. Then, they were to rearrange the requirements as appropriate and turn them into comments. Next, they were to apply whatever overhead coding it took to make the whole thing compile. Of course, the program would do nothing at runtime. Finally, they were to write code to support the comments.

Some did, and others did not. A few days later, those who had followed my suggestions were assisting the others with their assignments, a practice I encouraged and rewarded.

On the next assignment, most of the students commented first and coded later. The few that did not, lagged behind. The tactic works.

The reasons it works are manifold. For one thing, typing the requirements into source code as comments ensures that they are read, if not understood, fully. In class, I made it a practice to leave two or three important details ambiguous in the set of requirements, because after academia, that's real-life programming. Typing the requirements as comments tended to pinpoint those ambiguities for students. However, the main advantage was the fact that the students quickly had a solid set of specifications for their assignments. Armed with that, coding the program was easier.

If you comment first, you gain several advantages:

- You have a firm program plan before you begin coding.
- You don't have to return to the code to write all those comments at crunch time.
- Your program has excellent comments.
- There is less frustration, especially if you hate to write documentation.

Memorize the Differences Between Languages

Java is like C and C++ in many ways. It resembles Visual Basic and ASP in other ways. In the extreme, Java resembles Cobol and even APL, because all languages have several things in common. They share certain keywords, they loop, they have recursion, they have conditionals, variables, processes, etc. Well, Cobol doesn't support recursion natively, but I've implemented Cobol recursion. You merely write and use stacks, but I admit that's stretching a point.

If you're a C/C++ programmer, it's easy for you to be blind to some places where C and C++ differ from Java.

Java and C/C++

It's not by accident that Java resembles C and C++. The designers could have used any set of keywords, but they wanted Java to be easy to learn. There is a vast body of C/C++ programmers who might like to learn it. Thus, if you know C and/or C++, Java looks familiar.

Of course, Java is neither of those languages. There are many important differences. People who know C/C++, and who learn these differences, learn to program in Java quickly. Here are some of the primary differences that tend to cause or eliminate Java bugs:

Pointers

C and C++ pointers are powerful, but with that power comes the greatest amount of bug trouble. Approximately eighty percent of one of the most useful books I have read on C is devoted to managing errant pointers.

Java has no pointers, per se. However, Java classes and arrays are reference types. References to classes and arrays are similar to C pointers. In C, you can convert a pointer to a primitive type. You can also increment or decrement it, moving to the next array element, for example. In Java, you increment or decrement an array index, not the pointer to the array element. Nor can you examine a reference by converting it to a primitive type. Java has no equivalent of C's address-of operator (&) or dereference operator (*), or for that matter the sizeof operator.

C lets you pass the reference to a function into other functions. Java does not permit this, but it's a handy idea. Java lets you do the same thing by passing in an object that implements an interface.

Along those lines, Java does not include the **typedef** keyword of C. Without pointers, Java's type-naming processes are more elegant than C's, and those processes were the most common kinds of places where C programmers used **typedef**.

Garbage Collection

A fair amount of C and C++ overhead involves memory management. Poor memory management is responsible for memory leaks and another entire class of bugs. Java manages garbage collection automatically, preventing memory bugs from hatching. Thus Java has no equivalent to alloc, malloc, etc.

This is not to say memory leaks are impossible in Java.

The goto Statement

Technically, Java has a **goto**! Actually, the Java designers have reserved that keyword, but have elected (so far) not to implement it. This might be so you cannot use it, eh?

The tenets of structured programming do not forbid **goto**, as is popularly believed. On the contrary, even the earliest papers by Knuth and others allow its use, but they restrict the misuses of **goto**. Notably, every procedure should have exactly one entry point. With certain exceptions, every procedure also should have exactly one exit point.

However, **goto** is very useful for breaking out of a procedure when an unforeseen error occurs. It also helps a programmer exit a loop early, speeding processing. The **goto** keyword simplifies implemention of menu systems. There are other ways of doing these things, but the **goto** keyword implements the tightest loops possible because of its close relationship to an assembly language jump command.

Java does not implement **goto**, but it lets the programmer break out of procedures and discontinue loops early with keywords like **break**, **continue**, and the entire **try** series of commands. The compiler implements loops efficiently and GUI menus are a snap to program. Thus, **goto** is seldom, if ever, useful in Java.

Preprocessor

Java does not have a preprocessor, so there is no equivalent to C's #define, #ifdef, or #include kind of directives. This is almost never a deficiency. Two of the main reasons for conditional compiling in C and C++ are (1) debugging and (2) making allowances for varying machine platforms, because an int on one machine is longer than an int on another. Java's platform independence means that conditional compiling is almost never needed.

C's constant definitions have a Java counterpart in static final.

Java does not have C's macro definitions, which are unnecessary because of the advanced Java compiler.

Object Orientation

C is not an object-oriented language. C++ is, and Java is. Of course, it's possible to use C to program using objects. Similarly, it's possible to use C++ to program procedurally. It's even possible to program procedurally in Java. Just put everything in one humongous class and method. Technically, you would have an object, but in practice, you would have subverted the whole idea of object-oriented programming. Don't do that, lest your colleagues invent new four-letter words to describe your coding style.

Objects are native to Java, but not to C.

Compiling and Linking

Java is an interpreted language, and for a very good reason. As such, it can run on the Java Virtual Machine, which compiles Java bytecode into machine-specific instructions. This brilliancy lets identical Java programs run on any platform, without a single change in the Java source code!

A typical compiler has three major parts, sometimes called the front-end, the middle, and the back-end. The front-end understands the specific language syntax, the middle contains the compiler's logic and state machines, and the back-end produces object code, which a linker can understand. The linker then translates object code into machine code for a specific platform.

The following is a gross oversimplification, but what Java has done is combine the back-end and linker into a platform-specific Java Virtual Machine (JVM). Every platform—be it an IBM mainframe, a Sun Solaris, or a PC—has a different JVM, and that is how Java makes allowances for varying platforms.

The Java front-end and middle produce Java bytecode. It's the job of each Java Virtual Machine to understand this highly standardized bytecode, and then to finish the compiling and linking processes to generate machine code for the hardware.

All of this is why the Java "compiler" still begins with a line interpreter, and why anyone trying to build a true Java compiler has a difficult task ahead. The output must be in bytecode that the JVM understands, not object or machine code, so that the Java language can retain one of its most prized features. Sun states that feature well with their copyrighted motto: "Write Once, Run Anywhere."

C and C++, on the other hand, are compiled languages. While it usually takes longer to compile and link their source code, the result runs faster. The compiled results are not platform independent. The executable runs only on the kind of machine for which the compiler and linker were written.

Compilers can optimize the machine code better than interpreters—thus the difference in runtime speed. However, Java designers have invented Just In Time (JIT) compilers that largely or completely erase the C/C++ speed advantage. JDK 1.2.2 (Java 2) ships with such a JIT compiler.

main()

Every Java program must have at least one class definition. For applications, as opposed to applets, one class must define a method called **main()**, with the following prototype (with some allowed variances in syntax):

```
public static void main(String args[])
```

C and C++ must include **main()** as the program starting point, but **main()** need not return void.

Java must return void from its **main()** method. A Java application cannot return a value that is to be passed back to another application, at least not with the return statement.

Error Watch *You can call **System.exit()** if you want to return a value from a Java program, but beware of platform dependencies in this case. Also, note that **System.exit()** stops everything, even other threads that might be executing.*

Environment Variables

Unlike C and C++, Java cannot read environment variables directly from the operating system. To allow this would be to destroy some of Java's vaunted platform independence, because different systems manage their environments differently. Java can read the system properties list, however, via **System.getProperty()**. There are several standard system properties that Java defines for you. You can add to this list by invoking the interpreter properly.

Variable Declarations

In C, you must declare variables before they are used, generally at the beginning of a block or function. In Java, you can declare them anywhere.

Some people insist it's better to put all declarations in one place, while others believe it's better to sprinkle declarations throughout the code, near the points that they are first used.

- Java is a strongly typed language that requires every variable to be declared. This makes misspelling a variable name difficult, so many programmers prefer placing all variables at the top of a method.

- Other people observe that a variable is less likely to cause a bug if it is readily visible near the code that uses it, where you can easily refer to its type.

- One counter to the latter argument is you can prepend a few characters to each variable name. These characters state the kind of variable. For example, sName or strName would be a String. iEmployeeID or intEmployeeID would be an int.

- Other programmers disdain the idea of prepending the data type to variables. So, the jury remains out.

Header Files

In C, functions must be declared before they are used, typically in header files with a .h extension. Java, with its look-ahead compiler, has no such requirement. A Java method must be defined, but it can be used first and defined later.

Class, struct, and union

Java has no struct, nor union. It accomplishes the same purposes in a more elegant manner with classes.

Variable-Length Argument Lists

In C and C++, library functions like **printf()** and **scanf()** can have a variable number of arguments. They do this by building specialized parsers for the arguments, right within the functions. Java doesn't allow this particular practice. However, you can use overloaded methods to accomplish the same job.

Overloaded Methods

Java has added the ability to have many methods with identical names. You merely declare different parameter lists for the methods. C does not allow this advanced practice.

Global Scope

Java does not use global variables or methods. Every variable and method is declared within a class, which is within another class or a package, but variables cannot have scope outside the boundaries of their classes. This means you must structure your programs, which is not a bad thing!

Filenames

Java source code always has the extension of .java. There is no header (.h) file, as allowed in C/C++. Compiled Java programs must have the same filename as the class or interface they define, and they bear the extension of .class.

Data Types

In C and C++, variables of type short, int, and long have varying sizes, depending on the machine. Preprocessor directives let the programmer ensure the code operates properly on various machines. In Java, short, int, and long always have the same size, eliminating a whole class of bugs at the start.

Major Differences Between Java and Visual Basic (VB)

Java and VB are vastly different in syntax. VB shares many gui objects with Java, however. Several Java Integrated Development Environments have adopted and enhanced the best of the excellent VB development environment.

Since many VB developers are migrating to Java, and debugging tactics differ between the languages, I'll cover the major differences between the two. I'll focus on the differences that are more liable to spawn bugs.

Case Sensitivity

Java is a case-sensitive language. VB is not. Two Java variables MyName and myName are entirely different entities, whereas in VB they would be the same. Actually, in VB if you declare a variable, all instances of it take on the capitalization of the declaration. In Java, you must declare every variable as if you had declared Option Explicit in VB. If you misuse a variable's capitalization, Java will tell you the variable is not declared.

Variable Types

This table compares variable types between the two languages. Note the case sensitivity in the Java terms:

Java	Visual Basic	Representation
boolean	Boolean (capitalized)	true or false only
byte	Byte	8 bits, signed

Java	Visual Basic	Representation
short	Integer	16 bits, signed
int	Long	32 bits, signed
long	None	64 bits, signed
float	Single	32 bits, signed
double	Double	64 bits, signed
char	No equivalent	16 bit unicode character
String	String	16 bit unicode characters, even in 32-bit VB and Windows
No equivalent	Variant	Can hold most objects

Declarations

In Java, this line defines three double precision variables:

```
double a, b, c;
```

In VB, this similar line defines c as Double, but a and b as Variant types:

```
Dim a, b, c as Double
```

IsNull() vs. NaN

The VB **IsNull(x)** function returns **true** if *x* is null, and **false** if not. *x* can be a number or a string. The Java equivalent is NaN, or "Not a Number", for numerical types only. NaN is not a function.

Numerical Constants

Consider the Java statement:

```
x = 5;
```

In this case, the number 5 is of type int, so *x* must be of type int, or else *x* must be compatible in the implicit cast made by the equal sign. You can implicitly cast an int to a long, so if *x* is a long, everything is fine. However, if *x* is a byte, for example, you would have to perform an explicit cast like so:

```
x = (byte) 5;
```

If you have x = 5.0; the number 5.0 is automatically a double in Java.

In Java, you can designate floats, longs, octals, and hexadecimals this way:

```
float interestRate = 6.85f;   //float
long value = 12345678L;       //long
```

```
long octalNum = 03552;      //Octal
int hexColor = 0x10FFC0;    //Hexadecimal
```

Note the trailing f and L; and the leading zero and 0x.

Design Tip *Please don't use a lower case letter "L" to indicate a long number, because it looks too much like a numeral one. For example, is 12345678l an eight-digit or nine-digit number?*

Error Watch *Don't fall into this innocent-looking Java trap:*

```
float x = 5.0;
```

The problem is that 5.0 is a `double` *and the equal sign tries to assign it to a* `float`*. Instead, you would have to use*

```
float x = 5;
```

or employ a cast like

```
float x = (float) 5.0;
```

Comparisons and Assignments

VB overloads the equal sign for both comparisons and assignments. C, C++, and Java use the equal sign for assignments, but a double equal sign for comparisons. Moreover, C, C++, and Java assign from right to left, whereas VB assigns from left to right.

a = b = c is allowed in VB, and is the equivalent of a = (b = c). In this statement, *a* is assigned **true** or **false**, depending on whether or not *b* equals *c*.

a = b = c; in Java assigns the value of *c* to *b*, and then the new value of *b* to *a*, so that all three variables end up with the same value. That's totally different from how VB acts.

Arithmetic Operators

The more common operators are common to VB and Java, but the lesser-used ones are not. Moreover, the order of precedence is different. This table explains:

Java	VB	Operation
+	+	Signed summation
-	-	Unary negation and subtraction, depending on context
*	*	Multiplication
/	/	Division. In Java, 3/5 = 0, because 3 and 5 are ints. In VB, 3/5 = 1.5 However, in Java, 3.0 / 5.0 = 1.5
%	Mod	Modulus, or remainder after division
&	And	Bitwise And
|	Or	Bitwise Or
^	Xor	Bitwise Exclusive Or
~	Not	Negation, or one's complement. Don't confuse this with Java's != for not equal
>> and >>>	No equivalent	Two forms of right shift
<<	No equivalent	Left shift
++	No equivalent	Increment by one
--	No equivalent	Decrement by one

Conditionals

Java conditions must be surrounded by parentheses and the **if** keyword has an implied then. VB requires then, and parentheses are optional around conditions.

Both Java and VB have multiple conditional constructs, but they operate differently. In VB, when a valid Case condition is found, the code there executes and the program exits the Select – End Select block. In Java, things are different. When a valid case condition is found, the code there executes, and the program continues on through the rest of the case statements within that **switch** construct until the program counter drops out of the bottom of the code block or it encounters a break; statement. Thus, most Java case statements in Java include break; lines.

Both have defaults. VB uses Case Else, whereas Java uses default:.

Comparisons

Java can use either & or && for the And comparison, and there is a subtle difference. With a single & sign, both conditions on either side of the comparison are evaluated every time. With &&, the right condition is not evaluated unless necessary. With And logic, if either condition is **false**, the whole thing is **false**, so the right-hand condition need not be evaluated.

Similarly, Java can use either | or || for the Or comparison. If the left condition is **true**, then the entire expression is **true** and it's not necessary to evaluate the right condition. | evaluates both conditions, and so || is smarter.

In Java, != means not equal. However, ~ is the logical not. You would read this statement:

```
a = ((x != y) && (~z));
```

as something like this: "if the condition (x is not equal to y) is **false**, then assign **false** to a and do not evaluate (~z). Otherwise, if the statement (not z) is **false**, then assign **false** to a. However, if both conditions are **true**, assign **true** to a."

VB uses <> for not equal, and the word Not for Boolean negation.

Error Traps

Java has an elegant way of making code blocks atomic, that is, indivisible. VB has no analog. Java uses the five keywords—**try**, **catch**, **throw**, **throws**, and **finally**—for error trapping.

Loops

Java and VB loops have complete analogs between the two languages, although the syntax is different, and VB can form **goto** loops.

There is one major difference between Java and VB loops. In Java, it is common and excellent practice to declare variables within the loop. This strictly limits the scope of the variables to within the loop's code block, and prevents them from clobbering (or being clobbered by) other similarly named variables. The following might begin a Java **for** loop:

```
for (int i = 0; i < max; i += 2) {
```

The VB equivalent would be something like this, with a critical difference. The loop counter remains active, consuming a bit of RAM and remaining able to interact with other parts of code.

```
Dim i as integer
For i = 0 to 9 Step 2
```

In the Java loop above, you would have to redeclare *i* next time you used it. In the VB loop, you would not have to declare *i* again; thus, you could miss an initialization and wonder why you had a bug.

Integrated Development Environments (IDEs)

Earlier, this chapter showed how to turn Word into an excellent Java editor. If you prefer, a number of other products are available. This is an introduction to several of the more popular IDEs. You'll discover more about them further into the book.

Java programmers are blessed with a mature set of IDEs, an order of magnitude more numerous and more powerful than were available for other major languages when they were so young. Even in its infancy, Java already has better tools available than most other languages ever will. Some are expensive, and some great tools are even free!

As mentioned at the start of this chapter, when you use an IDE, whether it be one you develop or one you purchase, your chances of introducing bugs into your code drop tremendously. IDEs write syntax-free code for you, and the most difficult thing you need to do is come up with a killer design.

Among the most popular and capable, and in alphabetical order, are the following.

JBuilder

By Borland, a division of Imprise Corp., JBuilder is a complete Java development system. A free version is available from http://www.borland.com. It doesn't contain all of the features of their for-sale product, but it's quite capable.

The "Getting Started" book that comes with JBuilder contains the clearest 80-page description of Java I have read!

JBuilder is far more than a great editor and IDE as described below. Chapter 8 details its powerful debugging tools.

Top Features

JBuilder is scalable and component-based, which means you can use it for all levels of projects, including:

- Web- and browser-based applets
- Stand-alone computer applications
- Applications with networked database connectivity
- Client/server
- Enterprise solutions
- Distributed multitier computing solutions

JBuilder supports 100-percent pure Java, or not, at your option. It supports JavaBeans, Enterprise JavaBeans, Servlets, the Java Development Kit (JDK) from version 1.1 forward, Java Foundation Classes (JFC) / Swing, Remote Model Invocation (RMI), Common Object Request Broker Architecture (CORBA), Java Data Base Connectivity (JDBC), and Open Data Base Connectivity (ODBC) via some bridge software. It supports all of the major corporate database servers.

It includes several third-party sets of controls, so you have a number of ways to create text boxes, for instance. Some of the text boxes are more capable than others and, of course, have larger footprints.

JBuilder also gives you a flexible open architecture, so you can add new JDKs, third-party tools, add-ins, and JavaBeans.

The Multi-Edit editor interfaces natively with JBuilder.

Debugging with JBuilder

Java's threaded (parallel) processing paradigm introduces a number of new classes of bugs, some of which are quite difficult to isolate. JBuilder has a powerful debugger that lets you:

- Debug multiple applications at the same time
- Debug code running on remote machines, even if they are different kinds of platforms
- Debug code running in various versions of the JDK from 1.1.x forward.

Please see Chapter 8 for a more thorough discussion of JBuilder's debugging power. Threads are covered in Chapter 11.

Wizards to Generate Code

JBuilder writes much of your code for you. Unlike every code generator I've seen in older languages, JBuilder writes clean, nonbloated code.

JBuilder extends the best ideas of Visual Basic and Visual C++ for its graphical user interface. It incorporates two-dozen wizards to build bug-free code or code stubs for you. They are as follows:

- JavaBean Wizard, which builds a JavaBean for you to customize, and offers BeansExpress to help you do it.
- Project Wizard, which begins a Java project for you.
- Application Wizard, which starts a new Java application shell, including a frame into which you can drag and drop controls.

- Applet Wizard, which creates an applet stub and the HTML code that contains the applet.

- BeanInsight Wizard, which checks a class to see if it is a valid JavaBean or not.

- Data Migration Wizard, which imports and exports data between desktop database tables and SQL database servers. This wizard only comes with the Professional and Enterprise editions.

- Deployment Wizard, which archives a selected project into a .jar or .zip file.

- Desktop Pane Wizard, which creates a new desktop pane.

- Enterprise JavaBean Wizard, which creates an Enterprise JavaBean component. This wizard only ships with the Professional and Enterprise editions.

- Generate CORBA Server Wizard, which builds a CORBA server to make a CORBA object available to the Object Request Broker (ORB.)

- HTML Wizard, which writes an HTML file.

- Implement Interface Wizard, which creates code that makes a class accessible via a particular Java interface.

- Internal Frame Wizard, which creates a new internal frame.

- Javadoc Wizard, which builds a Javadoc HTML file from appropriate Java source code.

- New Frame Wizard, which creates a new frame for your application or applet.

- New Dialog Wizard, which begins a dialog box.

- New Panel Wizard, which creates a panel for dropping in controls.

- New DataModule Wizard, which creates a data module. This wizard only ships with the Professional and Enterprise versions.

- New Class Wizard, which begins a new class for you.

- Override Methods Wizard, which creates a stub to override a method that is in a superclass.

- Package Migration Wizard, which updates applications using JBCL and Swing components to their new package names.

- Resource Strings Wizard, which puts resources into separate classes to aid localization.

- Servlet Wizard, which creates a server-side application. This wizard only comes with the Professional and Enterprise versions.

- Use DataModule Wizard, which lets your application use a selected data module. This wizard only comes with the Professional and Enterprise versions.

The JBuilder Editor

This editor does most anything you want. It highlights your syntax as you type code and includes a number of popular key mappings you can choose.

You'll find the usual essential functions, such as undo, redo, find, and replace. You can make, rebuild, compile, and run your program with a JBuilder toolbar button, instead of jumping to the DOS prompt. In fact, you never need to leave JBuilder, until your project is complete.

One of the best features is how the editor helps you write Java. As you type, the editor will complete lines for you, unless you turn that feature off. It can pop up suggestion boxes that give you parameter lists. It will evaluate expressions that lie under your mouse cursor. It will try to highlight illegal class references and statements, which import packages that it cannot find. You can even see a list of all available packages.

You can customize this editor and store those settings in an .ini file.

JDK Commander

This is a zero-cost alternative to a commercial Java IDE. It provides an easy-to-use graphical user interface to Sun's JDK for Microsoft Windows, relieving the developer of the pain of using DOS windows and command-line interfaces. Obtain this excellent freeware at http://www.geocities.com/jdkcommander/.

Mojo

Mojo is inexpensive, and it's a powerful Java IDE. It contains a fine GUI so you can drag and drop objects into place on your screens.

VisualCafé

By WebGain!/Symantec, the highly intuitive VisualCafé is one of the original, most powerful, and best-selling IDEs. It's big, requiring a minimum of 96 megs of RAM (128MB recommended) and half a gig of HD space. In print, it has been called the near-perfect IDE, with good reason.

These paragraphs talk about how the VisualCafé IDE helps you write bug-free code. VisualCafé also includes a great debugger, which is discussed in detail in Chapter 8.

My copy of VisualCafé arrived with an outstanding wall chart that shows the 15 core Java Class Libraries. I studied it and immediately mounted it near my computers.

Taking a note from Sun's famous motto, VisualCafé has adopted the philosophy of "Write Once, Debug Anywhere" from a single computer. If you're based in Atlanta and during a company trip to Orlando you get a trouble call, your chances are excellent of fixing the problem via your logged-in laptop while still in Orlando, even if the problem is on a Chicago computer.

VisualCafé writes in pure Java, for complete platform independence.

Top Features

When you're developing large enterprise-wide systems, VisualCafé helps you perform at your best with features like these:

- An open, extensible architecture.
- Supports CORBA, Enterprise JavaBeans (EJB), Java 2, JavaBeans, JFC/Swing, and Remote Model Invocation (RMI.)
- Version control is easily managed via bridges to most third-party versioning tools, such as Merant's PVCS, Microsoft's SourceSafe, Rational Rose's ClearCase, and StarBase Versions.
- Performs local, distributed, and remote debugging from the same machine, so you can exploit some of Java's most valuable features with solid code.
- Full support for client/server environments.
- At design and testing time, VisualCafé interfaces with third-party modeling and testing tools using VisualCafé's Open API.
- Debug into external multiple-platform environments. This task can be particularly difficult and time-consuming without a product like VisualCafé.
- Accomodates many existing tools and enterprise applications, because VisualCafé understands Solaris, Tru64 Unix, HP-UX, Linux, Windows NT, AIX, etc.

- Write Internet interfaces to your corporate data and applications.
- Supports various versions of the Java Development Kit (JDK).
- Handles multiple Object Request Brokers (ORBs).
- A number of wizards hide the underlying RMI and CORBA object networking.
- Other wizards provide connections to all the major databases and simplify the task of writing database applications. With such wizards, you can write in an hour what might otherwise take a week to design, develop, and debug. Moreover, the wizards will produce proven, robust code every time.
- Interfaces to the Enterprise JavaBeans of the powerful BEA WebLogic Applications Server.
- Supports all of the standard drivers in JDBC.
- Probably has the fastest Java compilers available. It ships with Just In Time (JIT) 4 and native x86 compilers.

Debugging with VisualCafé

VisualCafé sports what they term "Single View Debugging." This means that from one machine, you can debug many simultaneous processes that are distributed across many machines, of varying kinds, using many different operating systems.

Most earlier languages could not accomplish that feat at all, and even Java developers find it difficult without a product like VisualCafé. Such power can save a tremendous amount of time, frustration, and, of course, money. Chapter 8 has more.

VisualCafé's Editor

This editor highlights your keywords as well as checks your syntax as you type. It has all of the bells and whistles you'll want, including suggestions for syntax and parameter lists in its Java Code Helper.

The debugger and compiler are fully integrated with the editor, so you never need to leave your editing environment to debug or test code. You'll love this feature, because if you have the Professional or Enterprise edition, you can even edit running code! VisualCafé recompiles, rebuilds, and saves your files automatically. If you don't have one of those editions, restarting the debugger, after breaking out to edit, is only a two-click process.

Wizards to Generate Code

Wizards build robust code in a flash. You'll find VisualCafé wizards that let you simplify such things as:

- Creating JavaBeans
- Visually editing JavaBeans
- Building interactions between JavaBeans and components
- Automatically managing distributed communications
- Debugging
- Building, debugging, and deploying servlets

Classes of Bugs

Chapter 6 classifies bugs. It shows how to prevent most from hatching, and gives reasons why some will hatch anyhow. For those that will hatch, it shows how to isolate them so you can squash them as early and inexpensively as possible.

PART II

Removing Java Bugs

Classes of Bugs

Dennis lunged back in his chair and threw his hands into the air in exasperation. "Why is it that we have to fall through the holes in the floor in order to find them!" he exclaimed. He wasn't amused, even if the rest of us were.

He had just discovered a design bug that had hidden from our team for three months.

Design Bugs

You can hardly have a worse bug lying hidden than a design bug, because having one means you've worked for nothing. The earlier your bugs creep in, the more work you have to redo. Moreover, most debugging tactics are useless against design bugs.

The key to preventing design bugs is adopting the inquiring mind of an ace detective. Few details escaped the fictional Sherlock Holmes. Doyle gave him amazing ability to probe, as well as to integrate facts into a conclusion. It was his attention to detail that laid the foundation for such astounding prowess. It was his well-honed ability to sort and select facts that cemented it. Secretive to all but Dr. Watson, Holmes seemed uncanny to his associates. To us, his readers, Holmes was marvelous at using his left brain or his right brain when the situation demanded. This chapter is about becoming a lot like Holmes.

During a typical brainstorm meeting, people are at their creative best. Very bright people toss good and bad ideas into the fray, feeding on each other's ideas. Brainstorming is an arch example of right-brain activity.

Sooner or later, however, those grand schemas must be set into the concrete of source code, and that requires organization. More than anything else, organization —a left-brain activity—is what prevents projects from failing. Organization is a slower-paced, often solitary activity. While organizing, you have more time to seek Dennis' proverbial "holes in the floor."

Design bugs result from failure to use both halves of the brain.

Conditions Come in Powers of Two

Here is a designing trick that has served me well for decades. It's the fact that the number of possible combinations is the product of the various category counts. I'll explain with an example.

Say part of your design statement reads: *"account for men, women, and children who either are ill with or have been exposed to tuberculosis (TB), and have or have not been immunized."*

Since you have three kinds of people (men, women, children) and two pair of Boolean conditions affecting them, your code should account for 3 × 2 × 2 or 12 possibilities. If your **switch** statement has ten **case** entries, the chances are excellent that you've missed two.

That's an accurate, but insufficient, observation. You have probably spotted an error in the design statement above. At least one entire condition is missing. The design statement didn't account for people who have not been exposed and don't have TB. Perhaps that's not a problem, but at design time you must inquire.

More properly, we have three kinds of people, multiplied by two states of immunization, multiplied by the following three possibilities:

- Not exposed and don't have TB
- Exposed and don't have TB
- Exposed and have TB

There should be 3 × 2 × 3 = 18 elements in your **switch** clause.

The fact that there are three possibilities should raise another question, however, because three is an odd number. Powers of two are never odd. Is there a fourth condition? In fact, there is: people who have not been exposed, but yet who have TB.

That last possibility seems physically impossible, so the design can probably disregard it. If you were to ask people on the design team, you'd probably find they all had considered and rejected the possibility.

However, at design time it's crucial to consider that possibility formally. For one reason, the word "exposed" might not mean the same to you as to the physician. Exposed might mean "contact with a known TB patient," or it might mean "exposure to the TB bacillus." These are two entirely different things! If exposed means the former, you have four conditions. If it means the latter, your code can safely disregard that condition, unless you need to perform a chicken-and-egg routine and account for the very first person ever to contract the disease. For example, where did that first TB bacillus come from? Did it come from some pretuberculosis illness? If the latter is true, then someone did actually have TB without being exposed to a bona fide TB bacillus. Perhaps the program can disregard that person, or perhaps not.

At design time, always seek that extra condition, especially if you have an odd number of them.

In the previous example, we considered men, women, and children: three conditions, another odd number. The designers must also ask the question: "Would it be better to consider men, women, boys, and girls?"

If so, the actual number of combinations to consider is 4 × 2 × 4 or 32, a far cry from the original 12.

Usually when you count conditions privately during a brainstorming session, you'll agree that some possibilities are trivial and some are ridiculous. However, that sort of inquiry leads you to the hidden design bugs so easily overlooked during right-brain activities.

Sometimes, an odd number is correct. If your switch statement needs to account for the days in the week, then the odd number 7 is the correct number.

It's important for someone to assume the role of an odd duck that quacks at seemingly inappropriate times, and for the others to withhold their ridicule. It's important for design-team leaders to reward such inquiring behavior. When I host a design meeting, I hold out the daily "odd duck" award as the highest honor a team member can win. The winner is the person who quacks at the most ridiculous possibility, but whose quack nevertheless uncovers a valid design bug.

The "Why Didn't That Work?" Mindset

When you have a rough design on paper, consider each element in turn, and imagine that some user just complained the element failed. That's all the user can tell you. It just didn't work right. Your imaginary task is either to prove that the element did not fail or to find out how it did.

About the time IBM's president proclaimed that there was no reason anyone should ever own a personal computer, I was designing an ultra high-gain amplifier on paper, while on vacation. I had no tools and no components to assemble for experiments, so I looked at the completed design and asked myself, "Why didn't that circuit work?" Almost immediately, I spotted a transistor drawn backwards. I redrew the circuit, and asked myself the same question. This time, I saw where a capacitor was needed to block voltage and pass a signal. I went through at least 12 more iterations before finally deciding my design would work. I was shocked when it did work, exactly as designed. It was my first such design that did.

The "Why didn't that work?" mindset will help you find innumerable design bugs. Adopting it almost feels like picking up a different tool, perhaps a chisel instead of a screwdriver. The mindset of a designer is to find something that will work, but it's a mindset that overlooks the details.

Most bugs are in the details. The question "Why didn't that element work?" forces your mind back to the details. If you can convince yourself that the design is correct, then progress to your next element.

What is an element? If you have a flowchart, an element is anything with a box drawn around it, as well as every connecting line. Have you accounted for all connections? Do you have redundant ones? Do any connections go to the wrong spot, or do they go the wrong direction?

In most designs, even the white space on the flowchart is an element, for it represents things the flowchart cannot indicate. For instance, if you're considering a functional diagram, what about the data flow? It's in the white space on a functional diagram. If you're viewing a data-flow diagram, what about the functions? If you're considering either, what about the people involved? How can their inevitable failures keep your design from working?

At design time, be your own worst critic lest your users assume the role for you.

Syntax Bugs

I would rather have a syntax bug than any other kind, because the compiler can identify it.

Occasionally, the compiler will identify good code as buggy because a syntax error elsewhere tricked the compiler. Because bugs hide bugs, you should generally fix the one at the top of the screen first.

There's an important exception. Each time your code doesn't compile, take a minute to scan down the list of errors. Occasionally, you'll see, and be able to fix, a bug that the compiler won't uncover unless another bug points it out! For example, if you forget to reinitialize a variable, the compiler may not tell you. If failure to reinitialize that variable sets it to zero and you find a division-by-zero error further down the list of bugs, you might not otherwise see that /0 error until runtime. Fix it now, so your user won't find it later. Then repair your errant variable.

Code Generators

An early scientific article on computers bore the title "Teaching Computers to Program Themselves." The article described a new generation of computer languages (assemblers) that generated machine code. Today, at a different level, the idea of a self-programming computer is still an intriguing concept.

One of the driving forces behind the invention of C was to avoid writing all that assembler code! Any chance I get, I write scripts, macros, and programs that write snippets of source code for me, because it's usually faster and more accurate to write that way.

Question: When do 1 and 1 make 25?

Answer: When one is a template and the other is a code generator.

Two weeks into a new job, I needed to turn out 25 CoBOL reports in record time. They were similar, so I wrote and tested one report during the week before a business trip.

While at 33,000 feet, seated halfway back in an airliner, I wrapped each line of that CoBOL source code, including the comments, inside a QBASIC **Print #1,** statement that would generate that particular line. In 20 minutes, I had a QBASIC program that would clone the source code for my already written CoBOL report. A DOS differences program proved the original and the clone were identical.

Big deal. So I could generate as many perfect copies of the source code as I wanted. So what? It would be faster to use DOS and make copies, as if I needed them. Besides, I already had that report written.

The next part was a bit sweeter, however, because the idea was to use that report as a template to generate 24 more. I looked for the places the CoBOL program would change from report to report, and broke them out of the **Print #1,** statements. For lack of a better name, I called them source variables. Next, I turned them into valid variables and concatenated their contents back into the static parts of the code. These were not mere CoBOL variables found in PIC statements. They were a step back from that. They were things like the names of those CoBOL variables, the targets of loops, the names of variables that would hold filenames, etc.

Then I designed input screens for all of the source variables. Within an hour, I had generated 14 of the CoBOL reports. While the plane was over Missouri, I finished a simple layout format that extended the generator to 21 reports. The final four reports were odd enough that I needed to generate them partially, and finish them by hand. When I landed in Arkansas, I presented my boss' boss with the source code for all but four reports, and by the end of the day, he had all 25.

A homegrown report generator typed an inch-thick package of source code for me, making no typographical and no syntactical errors. Of all those reports, the only ones with bugs were the four I had to finish by hand.

I arrived back home with a custom report generator that I expanded over the next five years and used to write about 100 reports. It had nowhere near the flexibility of the standard CoBOL report generator, but I found it much faster to use because it was fine-tuned for my particular environment.

One of the important lessons I learned was that you can use any language to write source code to compile in any other language.

You can even use Pascal or Lisp—or Java, for that matter—to write a Java compiler.

I used QBASIC because that was all I had running on my 286 laptop. Today, I might use Java to write that CoBOL source, or even use CoBOL itself!

Java is a lot like C. Just as C automates Assembler, and code generators exist for C, Java automates the writing of bytecode, and code generators automate much Java code. Code generators save typing, but more importantly, they increase production rates and devastate entire classes of bugs.

Autoconverting Visual Basic and Access to Java

Are you a Visual Basic programmer? You can get a forward-thinking tool that converts VB and Access code to the Java equivalent. DiamondEdge's Applet Designer does the magic. It generates Java code in the style you prefer. Appendix A tells how to obtain the software.

The name Applet Designer belies the product's full potential. It builds more than applets. The code it produces will run either as an applet, or as a full application, on clients or servers, and, of course, on Web servers. You can implement sophisticated databases and publish them on the Web. And, you can tweak the Java source code Applet Designer produces.

Applet Designer installs a VB toolbar, displaying these four buttons:

Make Java Applet   Converts VB code to Java and launches javac to compile the result. The new Java source code is available for inspection or modification. A report window shows conversion status, number of files successfully compiled, and any syntax errors found.

Run Java Applet   Uses the Java Virtual Machine (JVM) to run the compiled Java application. Of course, you can run the application via any of the other standard methods.

Data Access Wizard   Automatically generates a VB data access procedure for an applet or application, which is subsequently converted into Java source code when you click the Make Applet toolbar button. For that database, you can enter:

- A new procedure name for the automatically generated VB procedure that will retrieve data from the specified Java data source (next bullet)
- Java data source, from a drop-down list of valid JDBC data sources
- Username, if required, to log on to the database

- Password, if required
- SQL table in the data-source database, the one you want to use as a source for the generated applet or application

Options Dialog   This button contains:

- The Environment tab, letting you:
  - Specify directories for tools, along with their options
  - Manage the Web server environment
  - Change the Java "Look and Feel" emulation for Windows, Sun, etc.
  - Specify an IDE like Visual Café or JBuilder, to be used for later development
  - List the output directory
  - Name the Java runtime .Exe
  - Specify a different Java compiler, such as J++
- The Database tab, where you specify:
  - Any previously defined JDBC data-source specification, such as the JDBC-ODBC Bridge
  - DAO vs. ADO
  - JDBC drivers
- The General tab, which lets you specify:
  - Four types of conversions
  - Coding style—that is, where curly braces go
  - Indenting amount
  - Save Before Run, or not
  - Java integer type (number of bits)
  - GUI control set, such as Swing or AWT
- Online help, which gives comprehensive help along with a list of all supported VB features

Java cannot and should not support 100 percent of VB's possible code; thus, Applet Designer does not either. For one thing, Java has no **goto**, but VB does. For another, the VB command **On Error Resume Next** results in extremely ugly equivalent Java code. In essence, Java would have to surround every line with a separate **try** block, along with a **catch** or **finally** that would direct the program to the next line of code. So, Applet Designer does not support the VB **Resume** command in any of its forms. Nor would I want it to do that.

To my mind, all of the important VB processes are supported, except for financial functions and a few useful file functions. You'll find most controls, including a set from Sheridan, most database objects, and the form objects that you might want to modify in code.

Data-bound controls, including ADO, are supported in both the VB and the Access version.

Java employs security restrictions that VB does not enjoy, so if you are deploying an applet on a Web server, you must abide by the Java security violations. When converting a VB file application to Java, you can either change to a stand-alone application or use a database instead of files.

Among several fascinating files that come with Applet Designer:

- objects.vb2java contains the rules Applet Designer uses to convert VB's properties and methods into equivalent Java objects.

- custom.vb2java shows how to extend Applet Designer into unsupported arenas. You can place your own customizations here.

- constants.vb2java contains conversion rules for constants.

- swing.vb2java lists rules for converting most Java 2 Swing controls.

You can use information in these files to extend Applet Designer to third-party controls and APIs without modifying the Applet Designer compiler.

If you're fully conversant with Visual Basic or Microsoft Access, you will find Applet Designer to be an outstanding tool for learning the finer points of Java tactics. You can view the Java source code in any text editor and compare that with your original VB code. That's the same way I learned the arcane syntax of Word Basic, and Applet Designer has improved my Java techniques.

The Future of Code Generators

As RAM and hard-disk prices plummet, as CPU speeds increase, and as salaries soar upward, we can afford less efficient programs—especially when it takes less time to build them. More significantly, we can afford to use programs that are generic enough to run on multiple platforms.

Just as Java is a generic language, able to run on nearly any platform, code generators are generic in nature. A code generator can write all kinds of code for you. It may not write the most efficient code for the machine, but the most meager code generator can outtype you and me 10,000:1, while making 1/1,000 as many errors.

Code generators have some general traits; let's discuss some of them now.

Syntax Is Guaranteed Correct

Code generators, unless they have bugs or faulty input, generate code that will compile every time. Of course, this doesn't mean the code will be bug free. It merely means there will be no syntax bugs, and in the case of the Java compiler that several other classes of bugs are missing. Java code generators won't produce unreachable code, for instance, because the Java compiler won't compile a program that has truly dead code. There is a caveat here. The Java compiler can never detect some kinds of unreachable code. For instance, you can write code that only runs during the year 1984, knowing full well it will never execute. The compiler isn't quite that smart.

Correct Logic Is Not Guaranteed

At runtime, you might find errors in design or errors implementing algorithms. The process of getting the design and algorithms correct is your job.

Traditionally, programmers find code generators difficult to control, especially when asked to perform off-the-wall tasks. This is usually a good thing, however, because code generators tend to force programs into mainstream paradigms. They have a host of built-in options, but it is a daunting task for their builders to include more than about 80 percent of what developers want from a language. The more capable code generators get around this problem by giving you a large number of parameters with which to customize the output. Then, to finish the job, they let you tweak the output source code, supplying copious comments about what the generator actually did.

The logic is still left to your artistry.

Some Formats May Not Be Supported

If you want to produce a nonstandard kind of form or report—for example, with several kinds of summaries—you may have trouble using a code generator. A typical code generator will delight in giving you a nice heading, well-formatted details, subtotals based on your major-minor sort order, and a grand total, suppressing any or all of the above at your whim. Ask it for subtotals in the midst of your detail section, or try to make it resort and resummarize, and you may find grave difficulties. Of course, you could produce such code with native Java, but the report generator is liable to expect you to request a more normal report.

It could be, in this case, that you should listen to your code generator's complaints! I recall spending a morning on a rush job trying to get a code generator to jump through a particular hoop, while it steadfastly refused. Finally, inspiration hit and I reversed two subtotal areas to match the initial major-minor sort order, and the summaries calculated correctly. The only problem was to admit to the quality manager that I couldn't produce the exact report he needed to mail out to 20 plants that day. It would take me another day to modify the source code.

The quality manager's reaction taught me a valuable lesson. He actually wanted it the way the report generator wanted to produce it! When the report generator balked, I should have stopped, analyzed, and asked the user the obvious question.

Generators Are Prone to Code Bloat

Code generators are notorious for giving you bloated code. Code generators are generalists, so you can generally improve their code.

A refreshing exception is JBuilder 3, by Borland/Imprise. You can download their similar Jbuilder Foundations at their Web site. It's free (JBuilder 3.*x* Professional and Enterprise are not), and it doesn't time out after a month or so. Visit http://www.borland.com. Appendix A gives details of how to obtain it.

Lint-like Checkers

I never did learn how the C language checker, Lint, got its name. Perhaps it was because Lint is so "picky." Probably a hundred readers will send me email now!

Lint examines C programs for typical errors. Its rules can force your code to be nearly perfect before it ever compiles, although even Lint can be fooled. Lint has steered legions of C programmers toward better code practices.

JLint carries on the Lint tradition for Java. It and its companion, AntiC, check Java source code for bugs, potential bugs, inconsistencies, and synchronization problems. See Appendix A for how to obtain this shareware.

Another program, JProbe, by the KL group, is discussed in depth elsewhere in this book. It overlaps some of JLint's functions. JProbe does a wonderful job with threads. It also handles coverage, profiling, and memory debugging, topics that are beyond JLint. Appendix A tells how to get JProbe.

JLint and its companion program, AntiC, are written in C++ and will have to be compiled before use. Just about any C++ compiler will work, and the source code looks remarkably platform independent. You can examine the source code and can add new features if you desire. The author even asks that you do, and that you email your ideas to him.

JLint and AntiC check for many kinds of errors and potential errors. Most of those are listed next. Even if you don't use the programs, you should beware of the following potential bugs in your code. Note that most of them are merely suspicious, not provable bugs.

- There is a string that, perhaps, should be an octal number. Here, 123 looks suspiciously octal:

```
String a = "\0123";
```

- There is a string that, perhaps, should be a hexadecimal number. Here, 1234 looks suspiciously hexadecimal:

```
String a = "\1234";
```

- There is a string of unicode characters that perhaps should be a hexadecimal number. Here, ABCDE is possibly hex:

```
String a = "\uABCDE";
```

- There is an unusual escape sequence. Here, \x might be a typo for \n or some valid escape sequence:

```
String a = "\x";
```

- There's a possibility that the numeral 1 (one) has been substituted for lowercase letter l, or vice versa. In the next example, is the number an **int** with a value of 321 or a **long** with a value of 32?

```
a = 321;
```

 *When you append the letter L to a number to designate it as **long**, you should always use the uppercase L for clarity.*

- There is a potential operator precedence error. Here, the coder might have gotten the operator order of precedence wrong. You should always overparenthesize for clarity, and to show your reviewers that you got the precedence right. For instance, the following are legal, but they are suspicious, and would be flagged:

```
a = j * k + l % m / n;
a = a & b == c;
a = a || b = c;
```

- There is a potential logical operator precedence error. Similar to the last bullet, the coder might have made an error. Always overparenthesize for clarity.

```
if (a || b && c) {  // etc.
```

- There is a possible precedence error in bit manipulations. Should the & in the next example be &&? Or should == be =?

```
a == b & c
```

- There may be a shift operator precedence error:

```
a = a >> b - c;
a = a >> b & c;
```

- The programmer may have substituted = for ==. Note that if a and b are both type **boolean**, the following could perform a legal assignment, so Java would not flag it as an error, if the code should perform a comparison instead:

```
boolean a, b;
a = b = true;
if (a = b) {  // Potential for a bug here.
```

- There may be a misplaced semicolon. In this example, // code always executes, whether or not (a == b) is true, and the compiler can't flag an error because there might not be one:

```
if (a == b); {
  // code
}
```

- It appears that there are missing braces around the loop body. In this legal code snippet, there are no braces and, suspiciously, what appears to be a loop body is indented. JLint looks at indenting to help it decide when to flag suspicious code.

```
while (a == b)
  x++;
  y++;
// more code
```

- There may be missing braces around the conditional statement's body. In the next example, there are no braces, and the indentation suspiciously suggests there should be some:

```
if (a == b)
  x++;
else
   x--;
   y--;
// more code
```

- The **else** probably belongs to the wrong **if**. Here, indentation suggests that **else** belongs to the outer if (a == b) clause, but belying the indentation, it actually belongs to the inner if (c == d) clause:

```
if (a == b)
  if (c == d)
    x++;
else
  x--;
```

- The body of a **switch** statement is not a block of code. This probably means there is an error. Concentrate your attention on the second **switch** below. See the semicolon?

```
switch (a) {
  case 1:
    // code
  case 2:
    switch (x);
  {
      case 'y':
        // code
      case 'z':
        // code
  }
}
```

- A **case** statement is in a block that doesn't belong to a **switch** operator. This may be legal, but it is highly suspicious!

```
switch (a) {
  do {
    default:
      x++;
    case 1:
      y++;
```

```
  } while (x <= 10);
}
```

- A comment containing the word 'break' or 'fall' comes before a case statement, possibly indicating a missing **break** statement:

```
switch (a) {
  case 1:
    callAjax;
    //fall through
  case 2:
    callBell;
}
```

- A **switch** statement has too few **break** statements for its **case** labels. This is usually an unintentional omission.

```
switch (a) {
  case 1:
    x++;
    break;
  case 2:
    y++;
  case 3:
    z++;
}
```

Have you ever done the following? My wife and I try to avoid playing a game when it's time to leave. We call the game "waiting on you waiting on me." Each of us tells the other we'll be ready in a few minutes, and each of us then waits for the other to become ready. It's a deadlock until one of us gets up and heads for the car, asking the other to "come on."

It happens to computers. If a data server has one thread for each of several clients and one client is committing a transaction while another client adds a new class to the database, then a deadlock can occur. It can happen if this sequence of events occurs, in order:

1. Thread A opens and locks table A, and then
2. Thread B needs table A, but
3. Thread B has locked table B, that
4. Thread A needs before it can release table A.

At that point, a deadlock exists. Of course, the same could happen with three or *n* tables in a circle, each depending on another and none able to break the deadlock. Here is some code that can deadlock:

```
class DataServer{
  public TransactionManager transMgr;
  public ClassManager classMgr;
  // etc.
}
class TransactionManager {
  protected DataServer server;
  public synchronized void commitTransaction(ObjectDesc[] trans_objects) {
    // etc.
    for (int i=0; i<trans_objects.length; i++) {
      ClassDesc desc = server.classMgr.getClassInfo(trans_objects[i]);
      // etc.
    }
    // etc.
  }
  // etc.
}
class ClassManager {
  protected DataServer server;
  public synchronized ClassDesc getClassInfo(ObjectDesc object) {
    // etc.
  }
  public synchronized void addClass(ClassDesc desc) {
    ObjectDesc trans_objects;
    // etc.
    // Insert a new class in the database
    server.transMgr.commit_transaction(trans_objects);
  }
};
```

1. Client A invokes TransactionManager.commitTransaction, which locks this object.

2. Client B invokes ClassManager.addClass(), locking the ClassManager object.

3. Method TransactionManager.commitTransaction() tries to invoke ClassManager.getClassInfo() but must wait because this object is locked by another thread.

4. Method ClassManager.addClass() tries to invoke TransactionManager.commitTransaction() but must wait because this object is also locked by another thread.

Now, both client A and client B are on hold, waiting for each other. This hold condition also means that no other thread can address the locked objects. If these deadlocked threads have other objects depending on them, those objects are stalled. This condition has the potential to stall the entire computer.

Another form of deadlock occurs when one thread depends on another but the other thread dies first. The first thread cannot continue.

JLint also detects potential races. The classic example of a race condition is a bank account program. A race occurs when several threads seek the same resource and one fails to use it completely before another gains access. Here's some code that might enter a race condition:

```
class bankAccount {
  protected float balance;
  public boolean get(float checkAmount) {
    if (checkAmount >= balance) {
      balance -= checkAmount;
      return true;
    }
    return false;
  }
}
```

If thread A drains the account, and thread B tries to drain it between the time thread A checks the balance and recalculates the balance, thread B will succeed where it shouldn't. There's a solution, of course. You make the condition and the calculation atomic, that is, indivisible, with a **synchronized** command.

There are times you cannot use **synchronized**, because to do so would make your code prone to deadlocks. So, depending on the situation, you might need to employ some of the more sophisticated methods you will find in Chapter 11.

Programs such as JLint or JProbe cannot possibly guarantee that a set of code will deadlock or race. The mathematical algorithms for doing that have not been developed yet, and may never be because of the huge potential complexity involved. These algorithms probably belong to a mathematical realm known as NP, a class of problems whose answers can never be calculated, even if the answers are known to exist. However, software such as JLint and JProbe can point out suspicious code with good accuracy. They try to do so without confusing the issue by fingering good code more than necessary. That's a delicate balancing act.

The following things in your code should raise red flags:

- At the time a **wait()** method is invoked, more than one monitored object is locked by a thread. The **wait()** method might release only one object and leave the other locked.

- A method that is **synchronized** is overridden by a non**synchronized** method of a derived class. This can break up code that should be atomic.

- A non**synchronized** method can be called by more than one thread. This opens the possibility for a race.
- A thread locks at least two objects and is terminated by a method that calls **wait()**. The **wait()** may release only one of the two objects.
- A method is called from a non**synchronized** method.
- A non**synchronized** method implements a **Runnable** interface.
- A field that is not **volatile** can be accessed from different threads.

Some people tout inheritance as the Holy Grail. Visual Basic 6 did not have true inheritance, to the seeming glee of Microsoft detractors. Visual Basic 7 does, but probably would not have it except for their scolding. Despite the fact that inheritance improves the possibilities for reusing code, and thus speeding up production, inheritance brings its own basket of bugs to the programming table.

If you use line numbers, perhaps because you compiled with the debugger on, JLint does a good job of telling you where the bugs lurk. If you don't, the software still points to the first line of the offending method, or in the case of fields, the first line in the source file. As mentioned before, whether or not you use JLint, you should examine your code for the following kinds of potential inheritance errors:

- An **overrides** statement may be missing. For a method of base class A, there is a method of the same name in a derived class B. However, there is no method with the same name in class B that has the same number and types of parameters (signature) as that method in class A. JLint wonders if you have erroneously expected that the method in B overrides the method in A. It wonders if you might think that calling the method in B would execute the method in B, not A.
- A component in a derived class shadows one in the base class. For example, a field in a derived class has the same name as a field in its base class. The potential problem is that the programmer might expect the wrong variable to be used. You should usually use different field names.
- A local variable of a method shadows a class component with the same name. This is common practice, but can cause confusion. Accordingly, JLint does not throw a message when the class field is explicitly accessed with a **this** reference. The following example clarifies:

```
class Detroit {
  public int x;
```

```
public void bean(int x) {
  this.x = x;    // JLint ignores this line
}
public int corn(int x) {
  return x;      // JLint flags a possible bug due to 'x'.
  }
}
```

- Method **finalize()** doesn't call **super.finalize()**. It is good practice for **finalize()** to call **super.finalize()**, because it makes class implementations more independent.

- A method can be invoked with **null** as a parameter, and this parameter is used without checking for **null**. For example, this linked list code might fail:

```
class Node {
  protected Node next;
  protected Node previous;
  public void link(Node after) { // The value of 'after' can be null.
    next = after.next;
    prev = after;                // Oops, there's no check for null.
    after.next = next.previous = this;
    }
  }
//etc.
  }
```

- The value of a referenced variable may be null.

Error Watch *JLint can misreport this error on occasion.*

- A null reference is used. Here's an example where null is used as the left operand of the **. (dot)** operator:

```
public void printMessage(String msg) {
  (msg != null ? new Message(msg) : null).Print();
}
```

- One of the operands of a binary operation is zero. The assignment: $x = 0 + y$; would trigger this message. Only rarely would zero be a reasonable operand of any binary operation, because such an expression can nearly always be simplified, if it is valid.

- The result of an operation is always zero. Overflow, shifting all bits off, or clearing all bits via a masking **&** operation might trigger this message. So might multiplication by zero, or any expression of the form $(a - a)$.

- A shift count is suspicious. For instance, an **int** that is right-shifted by 32 or more, or a **long** that is right-shifted by 64 or more, should throw up the red flag. JLint also flags negative shifts, such as x >>= -3; the software looks at the possible range of shifts. An **int** should only shift within the range of 0–31, and a **long** should only shift within a range of 0–63. In practice, the amount of a shift is usually calculated, so JLint tries to confirm that the calculation results in a shift within the proper range. So should you!

- A converted value is outside the allowable range of the target variable. This might happen due to explicit conversions, or implicit ones such as are caused by an assignment. For instance, this will trigger a message:

```
int i = 123456;
short s = i;
```

- Truncation may result in loss of data. This message occurs when converting from a larger type to a smaller one, and can cost significant bits. JLint's rules help it determine which such operations are probably errors and which are not.

- Suspicious cast. You might have two integers multiplied together, ultimately resulting in a **long**. A problem can occur when an interim result of the multiplication will be an **int**, causing a temporary overflow before the result gets converted to a **long**.

- A comparison always produces the same result. Say you assign x the value of 10 and with no intervening changes to x, you test to see if x is greater than 100. JLint will flag it. Picky, eh?

- Compared operands can be equal only when both of them are zero. Here's an example where the left operand is always 0 or 1, whereas the right is always 0 or an even number, but never 1:

```
((a & 1) == (b * 2))
```

- A result is always equal to the first operand. At the end of the following example, c always equals a, so the % calculation is meaningless:

```
a = 3;
b = a + 1;
c = a % b;
```

- The code uses == to compare string objects. While this is legal, it is probably an error because usually the programmer means to compare the contents of those objects. The following code will always evaluate **false** because the strings reside in different objects and == compares the objects, not their contents:

```
String str1 = "ABC";
String str2 = "ABC";
if (str1 == str2) then {
  System.out.println("true");
}
else {
  System.out.println("false);
}
```

- Inequality can be replaced with equality. Doing so commonly clarifies the code. When it's possible to make such a replacement, the program may be erroneous at that point.

- A **switch** constant cannot be reached. This can happen when a **case** constant is beyond the range of the **switch** expression. For example, if you **switch** on a **char** named c, and one of the case constants is 256, that **case** will never be reached. Similarly, if you **switch** on even numbers by masking out the 1's bit, it's meaningless to use an odd number as a **case** constant.

JLint cannot find all errors, but it can find an inordinate number of them that many people miss. You will find JLint to be overly picky in that it will flag numerous pieces of code that are actually correct. However, if you change that technically correct code so JLint won't flag it, your program will read better and be more robust.

As always, how to handle each situation is in your hands.

Logic Bugs

"Turn right at the next corner," my passenger instructed. I turned left. Three blocks later, my passenger said, "I meant left," as we laughed about it. Actually, I wasn't reading their mind. Twice in a row, I had turned the requested direction, only to have to double back.

The computer will, of course, do what you tell it, with the occasional exception caused by buggy operating systems or cosmic rays. When what it does is not what you intended, you often have a logic bug. These come in several subspecies.

Actual Errors in Logic

Facts are stubborn things! They don't change merely because we perceive them wrong.

Two puzzles illustrate:

- A brick weighs 6 pounds plus half its weight. How much does it weigh? The obvious answer of 9 pounds is incorrect. Actually, the brick weighs 12 pounds.

- If a hen and a half can lay an egg and a half in a day and a half, how long does it take a hen to lay an egg? Again, the obvious answer is a day, but the correct answer is a day and a half.

Each of these puzzles is designed to obscure good logic, and each succeeds with most people who have never heard them. They deceive us into relying on inapplicable thought patterns.

Many of our daily problems involve things similar to taking an actual value and adding half of that value to get a result. At a restaurant, after a $10 meal, we mentally calculate that 10 percent of $10 is a buck, add 50 percent of a buck, and leave $1.50 for a tip. In the brick example, the actual weight of 12 pounds is obscured by the fact that it's the sought number, not a number that's given.

Another computational pattern we commonly use is proportion. If it takes 8 hours to drive to Chicago, and Omaha is twice as distant, then it takes 16 hours to drive to Omaha via Chicago. In the chickens-and-eggs puzzle, the pattern is that 1.5 chickens (on the average, of course) reduced by 33 percent to 1.0 chickens, and 1.5 eggs (again on the average) reduced by 33 percent to 1.0 eggs, should mean that 1.5 days will reduce to 1.0 days, and it's simply not so. Time doesn't apply to the formula.

Here's another. Say the earth was a smooth ball its present size, and you stretched a string tightly around the equator. Now, say you inserted 1 yard of string to the length and enlisted a zillion people to hold the string up from the equator equally. Would you believe that each person would hold the string about 1 foot off the globe? The actual value is 3/pi feet. The sphere's circumference cancels itself out in the equations, so the size of the sphere doesn't matter. We're not used to mixing planet-sized and yardstick-sized measurements.

The point is that our well-honed thought patterns serve us extremely well most of the time, and occasionally fail us because of the fact that they are patterns.

One of my "21 Laws of Programming" states that we make rules and laws so we don't have to think. We learn patterns so we don't have to examine every situation exhaustively every time. That would be impossible. So when a pattern fails us, we modify it slightly. Doing so is the very essence of learning, and it is our greatest power over computers.

Make no mistake: Rules and laws are good things! It's good not to have to think about everything. We place these patterns in our minds alongside sound logic, so we don't have to think through most deep logic problems every time.

And so, at times, we can deceive our very selves into wrong answers, wrong algorithms, and wrong conclusions. In Java, these deceptions can appear as logic bugs, of which there are several subspecies, such as the following.

Memory Leaks

Java has an efficient garbage-collection schema. When a resource is fully released, the garbage collector notices and sooner or later reclaims that resource.

What if you forget about a thread that keeps referring to that resource? The reference will prevent the garbage collector from doing its work, and you will have leaked some memory.

If the thread keeps making new instances of that object and relies on some other thread to release them, but the other thread fails to do so in a timely manner, you can have an ever-increasing memory leak—potentially leading to a crash.

You can instrument your code, but it can take a product like the JProbe Memory Debugger to isolate and fix such leaks.

Thread Conflicts

Chapter 11 discusses thread problems in much greater detail than the book will here. We multiprocess most of our daily thinking, but most of us have been trained to think sequentially (often called "logically") while we program. Programming with threads breaks that mold. Threads emulate, more than sequential programming, how the brain works. Moreover, the primary reason for writing a thread is so we can set it to its duties and forget it.

The garbage collector is an excellent example. We instantiate a new object, use it, and release it, not really caring when the garbage collector will reclaim it. In Java, we usually forget about garbage collection.

Unfortunately, forgetting about the garbage is not a totally reliable pattern because the garbage collector can be fooled. Some ace programmers go to the trouble of writing routines to release their objects manually, thus helping the garbage collector know when to reclaim their space. Even that procedure is flawed, though, because the Java specification falls short of guaranteeing when garbage collection will occur.

Do-Forevers

Some well-constructed programs rely on infinite loops. Can you think of two?

How about heart pacemakers? Hope so!

How about your operating system? A UNIX clone I once wrote in C employed this wrapper code:

```
while (true) {
  // The rest of the system
}
```

Since **true** is never **false**, the loop runs until someone unplugs something.

You can prove whether or not a running loop will terminate. You merely prove that the condition that keeps the loop running will change to **false** at some point, that the loop will subsequently test the condition, and that when it finds the condition **false**, the loop exits. Merely? That can be hard to do.

Here is a loop whose counter uses (1.0 / 3.0) as an increment value. The counter never does reach the exact target value of 5.0, and the loop merrily keeps running. However, when you change the target value to 10.0, the loop does terminate on a Windows PC! The example shows the danger of using floating-point numbers as loop counters and termination targets.

```
public class WhileForever {
  public static void main (String args[]) {
    double d = 0.0;
    while (d != 5.0) {
      d = d  + (1.0 / 3.0);
      System.out.println(d);
    }
  }
}
```

It also shows the difficulty of proving such an anomalous loop will terminate. In decades of programming, I have seen only one obscure case that required a floating-point loop counter.

It's not quite enough that the loop's entry condition turns to **false**. When that happens, the loop must test the condition and, when the test fails, send the program outside the loop. The following loop's iteration counter does reach 10, but is reset before the loop control mechanism can test it:

```
for (a = 0; a < 10; a++) {
  if (a >= 10) {
    a = 0;
  }
}
```

In the next loop, the condition (a < 2) becomes **false**, but there is no way to break out of the outer loop, because the **if** statement grabs tight control in the middle of the second iteration. In this example, the inner loop is obviously contrived, but you could replace it with any process that lacks a terminus. You might replace it with a thread that waits on a port for input that never arrives.

```
a = 0;
while (a < 2) {
  if ++a > 1 {
    while (true) {
    }
  }
}
```

Differences Between Actual and Perceived Operator Precedence

You should memorize the logical operator precedence, but not rely upon it. Instead, take pity on the person of lesser experience who will have to maintain your code. Overparenthesize your expressions. Better still, break complicated expressions into several lines. For example, take a moment to evaluate this obviously contrived program and decide what it will print. There are no syntax errors.

```
public class Logic {
  public static void main (String args[]) {
    int i = 0;
    boolean b1, b2, b3, b4;
    b1 = b2 = b3 = b4 = true;
    i = b1 | b2 & b3 ^ b4 ? i++: --i;
    System.out.println(i);
  }
}
```

The logical operator precedence (in Java) is: Not, And, Xor, Or. The preceding code relies upon that fact, excessively. Of course, most competent Java programmers can decode it, and the maintenance programmer seeking bugs in this unnecessarily complex piece of code probably knows the logical operator precedence.

What the maintenance programmer doesn't know is whether or not the original author knew that operator precedence! So, the maintenance programmer has two tasks: (1) decode the sixth line personally, and (2) discover whether or not the line is written correctly.

The sixth line would be better if parenthesized. This substitution performs exactly the same function:

```
i = ( b1 | (( b2 & b3 ) ^ b4 )) ? i++; --i;
```

However, why not do it the easy-to-maintain way? Then, the maintenance programmer can check the logic against the user's specifications more easily. Moreover, you can test interim results, proving that you don't have an obscure bug.

```
public class Logic2 {
  public static void main (String args[]) {
    int i = 0;
    boolean b1, b2, b3, b4;
    b1 = b2 = b3 = b4 = true;   // Set four booleans to true
    boolean tmp;                // Added
    tmp = b2 & b3;              // & takes top precedence.
    tmp = tmp ^ b4;             // alternately:  tmp ^= b4;
    tmp = tmp | b1;             // alternately:  tmp |= b1;
    if (tmp)                    // or the trinary:  i = tmp ? i++ : --i;
      System.out.println(i++);
    else
      System.out.println(--i);
  }
}
```

The examples print the **String** "0". It's a **String** because of **println()** and the output is "0" because the variable i is set to zero and printed before being incremented.

You do realize, of course, that the following code snip from the last program will print "0" instead of "1", because i++ is incremented after being printed:

```
if (tmp)
  System.out.println(i++);
else
  System.out.println(i--);
```

If performance were a problem and this routine happened to be at the heart of a nested loop, you should time the code with both versions, or use a profiler such as JProbe. Usually, the cleaner-looking code runs faster, but sometimes not. If you must use the original sixth line above, you should include a comment saying what it does. Several comment options suggest themselves:

- A statement in English

- An overparenthesized version of the original sixth line as a comment

- Comments like this:

```
// The next line is equivalent to this:
// tmp = b2 & b3;
// tmp ^= b4;
// tmp |= b1;
// i = tmp ? i++ : --i;
```

Solve All Mysteries

In the next program, the **if** statement is correct. It's worthwhile to test what errors occur with a malformed **if** statement so that when those errors crop up, you can recognize and fix them more quickly.

```
class IfTest {     // This code is correct.
  public static void main(String[] args) {
  int i = 0;
    if (true)
      i++;
    else
      i--;
    System.out.println(i);
  }
}
// Prints "1"
```

If you forget the required parentheses around the **if** statement's condition, the error message is clear, as shown here:

```
if true            // Parentheses missing.


IfTest.java:4 '(' expected.
    If true
        ^
```

If you misuse = for a comparison and have a type clash as well:

```
if (i = true)     // (1) need to use "==", (2) i is not a boolean.

IfTest.java:4: Incompatible type for if. Can't convert int to boolean.
    if (i = true)
        ^
IfTest.java.4: Incompatible type for =. Can't convert boolean to int.
    if (i = true)
          ^
```

If you mistakenly surround all of the **if** action with curly braces:

```
if (true) {
  i++;
else
  i--;
}  // Should be before the 'else', not here.

IfTest.java:6: 'else' without 'if'.
   else
   ^
```

That's because the block of code between the curly braces truly does not contain an **if** statement. The **if** statement evaluates and sends the program pointer into the block of code as a new statement. That new statement has no **if**, but it has an **else**—thus the error.

When you find a bug, it may be tempting to experiment a little, fix it, and proceed. However, you should investigate such bugs until you understand why they occurred. If time presses you too hard, pull out a 3 × 5 card and write yourself a note. Bugs that you don't investigate will revive themselves later to bite you in other programs. You don't want that to happen.

In the last example, one might remove the curly braces, realizing they were unnecessary, and the code would run perfectly. However the message "'else' without 'if'" is just bizarre enough to beg the question, "Why does Java think **if** is absent when it's not?" Each time you realize how Java is interpreting your source code, you become a better programmer. Granted, this example is purposely trivial, but the principle abounds in the more complex ideas.

Make it your professional practice to solve your mysteries, as well as to fix your code.

Mathematical Bugs

Humans do many things better than computers.

My family laughed when a TV actress played seven notes of an ancient Irish tune on a wind instrument and an ancient Irish tomb rumbled open for her.

Even today, that feat demands a set of extremely high-Q acoustical filters, along with a microprocessor and enough hydraulic power to slide a 10-ton rock aside. The ancients must have been formidable, indeed!

Or, did the show's writer stretch the imagination a little too taut?

On the other hand, computers perform computational math far faster and more accurately than humans do. When computers compute, humans tend to accept the results without question. Often, we can prove that a computer will produce a correct result without having to calculate the result by other means.

At times, however, our proofs are flawed, and errors can slip in. Here's an example.

Math Near the Limits

You've probably studied inductive proofs. Roughly, they state that for a continuous function named f, if $f(a)$ is true, and $f(a + 1)$ is true, then for all n, $f(a + n)$ is true. For example, consider the function commonly called doubling. Since there is an integer $x = 2 \times (a)$ and there is another integer $x' = 2 \times (a + 1)$, *then there is* an integer $x'' = 2 \times (a + n)$ for any integer n. In plain English, that merely means that since the set of integers is a continuous set, you can always double an integer.

Inductive proofs break down at the edges of loops because loops are not continuous functions. Loops are discontinuous at their beginnings and their ends—that is, at their limits. This is one reason you'll find bugs there.

Limits Attract Bugs Like Picnics Attract Ants

If a loop has errors, 90 percent or more will be within one iteration of the loop's beginning or end. Building a typical loop involves answering questions like these:

- Should your loop start at 0 or 1?

- If it starts at 0, can anything inside the loop divide by the counter on the first iteration? Does anything take the log of the counter on the first iteration? Log(0) is as undefined as division by 0.

- If it starts at 1, does anything divide by the term (counter - 1)? Does anything divide by the log of the counter? Log(1) is zero.

- Should it end at the maximum, or one short?

- If it iterates through an array, does it hit every element, or miss one at an end, or try to hit an element that doesn't exist?

- If, heaven forbid, the loop counter must hit the end exactly, is there any possible way it could miss, thus generating an infinite loop? This program, for example, iterates a very long time:

```java
public class WhileForever {
  public static void main (String args[]) {
    double d = 0.0;
    while (d != 5.0) {
```

```
    d = d  + (1.0 / 3.0);
    System.out.println(d);
  }
 }
}
```

The loop counter reaches 4.999999999999999, but never exactly 5.0. Interestingly, it does reach exactly 10.0, a fact that is actually an inconsistency in how computers use floating-point arithmetic. That fact introduces a very subtle bug. It is difficult to predict exactly how Java (or any language) will handle floating-point numbers, especially during division. What if you had a perfectly performing loop counting to 10, but someone needed it to count to 20. Would it still work? Only a test would tell. It's best never to use **float** or **double** numbers as loop counters, even if they appear to work.

Design Tip *For similar reasons, your loop condition should never be equality. Always use >= or <= for your loop condition, unless that's impossible.*

- Does the loop counter actually increment? It doesn't in the next example, because (1/2) evaluates to zero! It uses integer division.

```
public class WhileForever {
  public static void main (String args[]) {
    double d = 0.0;
    while (d <= 10.0) {
      d = d  + (1 / 2);
      System.out.println(d);
    }
  }
}
```

- If the loop marches through a string, does it hit each letter or word, or does it miss something at either end? Does it look for something that doesn't exist on either end?

- Is the string length correctly calculated, especially if it is in terms of words instead of characters? Do you need to consider the string terminator character or the word delimiters?

- If the words are space delimited, what about other punctuation? What happens if there is no space at the beginning or the end? In this case, the number of spaces is probably one less than the number of words.

Know the limits of calculations, and never approach them. If your calculation contains multiplication, be wary of exceeding a numeric variable's maximum size. If it contains division, check for division by zero and for exceeding a number's minimum precision.

Booleans

Java handles Booleans a bit differently than C and C++ do.

Legal and Illegal Boolean Comparisons

If you compare a Boolean with a number, you get a compilation error. Unlike C and C++, a Java Boolean doesn't have a numeric value. It only contains the value **true** or **false**.

You can compare any two different kinds of numbers. For example, (3 == 3.0f) evaluates **true**.

> **Question:** Should you beware of comparing an **int** or **long** with the result of a **float** or **double** calculation? For instance, is 1 == (3 * (1.0 / 3.0))) **true**?

Because of the parentheses, the first thing that happens is that (1.0 / 3.0) evaluates to about .333333 and then, multiplying by 3, you get about .999999, which is not quite equal to 1. Right? Be careful!

Surprisingly, that's not so! Examine the output of the following program:

```
public class Equal {
// Numeric comparison test.
  public static void main (String args[]) {
// This line prints: 1.0
    System.out.println((3.0f / 9.0f) + (3.0f / 9.0f) + (3.0f / 9.0f));
// This one does too:
    System.out.println(3 * (3.0 / 9.0));
// And this clause prints: Equal.
    if (1 == (3 * (1.0 / 3.0))) {
      System.out.println("Equal");
    }
    else {
      System.out.println("Not Equal");
    }
  }
}
```

I've performed a number of tests on numbers up to ten digits long, dividing various **float** and **double** primes by other primes, and multiplying back by the **int** or **long** versions of the divisors. I've found no aberrant behavior. Do I trust a comparison like the one above? Not unless I can test the algorithm exhaustively. Even then, I'd have to know I could rely on future versions of Java to act the same way.

Comparing Strings

Different string objects can contain identical values. If you try to use the == operator to compare them, the comparison will evaluate to **false**, because the objects are different regardless of their values. If you want to compare the objects' values, you must use **equals()**.

```
str1 = "ABC";
str2 = "ABC";
System.out.println(str1 == str2);
```

The above prints false, because str1 is not str2 regardless of contents. However,

```
str1 = "ABC";
str2 = "ABC";
System.out.println(str1.equals(str2));
```

prints true, because the values of str1 and str2 are identical.

The next three lines also evaluate to **true**, because in this case str1 and str2 are the same object:

```
str1 = "ABC";
str2 = str1;
System.out.println(str1 == str2);
```

Programming sainthood is in the details.

Comparing Objects

The most important comparison between objects is to see if one is an instance of another. For this, always use the **instanceof()** operator, and never use this operator with primitive types. Doing so will generate a compile error.

Assignments

The Java program immediately below will not compile:

```
class CompileFails {
  public static void main(String args[]) {
    byte b = 0;
    b = b + 2;     // There is a type clash here.
    System.out.println(b);
  }
}
```

But the similar one shown next compiles without error, for a subtle reason. The various assignment operators of the form *op* = automatically cast their result to the left operand's type. This happens with **+=, -=, *=, /=, %=, &=, |=, ^=, <<=, >>=,** and **>>>=** but not with **=**, which acts differently.

```
class CompileSucceeds {
  public static void main(String args[]) {
    byte b = 0;
    b += 2;     // This line has no error!
    System.out.println(b);
  }
}
```

The first program fails to compile because the assignment b = b + 2; tries to add an integer (2) to a byte (b). That's not allowed without casting. You may assign an integer to a byte because that action promotes the byte to an integer, but you cannot merely add an integer to a byte. You must first perform a cast, because the = operator does not perform an implicit cast.

However, b += 2; works just fine. The reason is found in the following sequence of events:

1. (b += 2) promotes b to type **int**.

2. It casts the result of (b + 2) to type **byte**.

3. It assigns the result to b.

The following program employs a cast and compiles cleanly:

```
class CompileNowSucceeds {
  public static void main(String args[]) {
    byte b = 0;
    b = b + (byte) 2;
    System.out.println(b);
  }
}
```

Unusual Operators: Shifts

With its roots in C, Java allows binary shifts, in which all bits of a variable's contents shift left or right. We don't exactly balance our checkbooks with shifts, but shifts are speedy ways to multiply and divide, especially by powers of the numerical base.

Everyone knows that if you want to multiply a decimal integer by 10, you append a zero to the right end. If there is a decimal point, you move the decimal point one place to the right. The effect is shifting the entire number one place to the left.

This principle holds for octal, hexadecimal, binary, and all other bases of numbers. You can multiply an octal number by 8 by appending a zero to the right end, or a binary number by 2 by adding a zero at the same place. Thus, the value 142 octal times 8 (decimal) is 1420 octal, and 1011 binary binary times 2 (decimal) is 10110 binary.

Similarly, to divide a binary number by 2, shift the binary representation's bits one place to the right.

Okay, I know. Just as there is no single-digit 10 in the decimal system, there is no 8 in the octal system, nor 2 in the binary system. Isn't it interesting, though, that decimal 8 is represented as 10 octal, and decimal 2 is represented as 10 binary? In any number system, to multiply by 10, you can merely attach a 0 to the right of the number, or equivalently, move the decimal point one place left.

Multiplying by 2 is far slower than shifting everything left one bit, unless the multiplication is carried out by shifting. Even adding a binary number to itself is far slower than shifting everything left a bit. Bitwise shifts are so fast because the CPU's machine language supports shifts, natively.

Many mathematical operations, such as multiplication and division, lend themselves well to shifts. For example, if you want to multiply a number by 17, it's quicker to shift left by 4 bits and add that number back in. Left-shifting 4 bits multiplies by 16, and addition is yet another fast operation at the CPU level.

This process of multiplying by 17 works because $17n = (16 + 1)n$, which expands further to $16n + n$.

All of this material, which anyone who has studied assembler languages knows blindfolded, introduces the problem of overflow.

As you know, a **short** contains 16 bits in Java, no matter what machine is in use. This lets a **short** range from $-2^{15)}$ or $-32,768$, through ($2^{15} - 1$ or $32,767$. So, what happens if you increment **short** 32,767, which is binary 0111 1111 1111 1111?

```
public class Overflow_1 {
  public static void main (String args[]) {
```

```
   short s = 32767;
   s = s + 1;
   System.out.println(s);    // prints -32767
  }
}
```

Java produces the binary result of 1000 0000 0000 0000, which it evaluates to –32,767 which is not quite what one would expect. Moreover, there's no exception thrown! Java perceives that you did exactly what you wanted to do.

Do the same thing to an **int** number, and the desired result prints.

```
int i = 32767;
i = i + 1;
system.out.println(i);
```

You get 32,768, a positive number.

The reason is not that the calculations go wrong, but that the representation of 1000 0000 0000 0000 in 16-bit binary evaluates –32,768 as a **short**, but 32,768 as an **int**. This shows the importance of using large enough primitive types.

In fact, except when you are concerned with your RAM footprint, you should not use **byte**, **short** or **float** at all. Be safe and always use **int**, **long**, and **double** numeric types.

Error Watch *Overflow does not merely reverse the sign without changing the value. That's just what it did in this unique situation. For example, if you try substituting x = x + 2; in the first example, you will get –32,766 instead of 32,769. Substitute x = x + 3; and you get –32,765, instead of 32,770. However, if you find an unexpected sign reversal, chances are excellent that you have an overflow condition.*

The point is that you can get results that look good but are wrong. It would be easy for a tester to miss the negative sign in the last example.

Multiplying by 2 is the same as left-shifting one bit. Consider this code:

```
public class Overflow2 {
  public static void main (String args[]) {
    short x = 32767;
    x <<= 1;     // Note: x *= 2; gives exactly the same result
    System.out.println(x);
  }
}
```

The result is –2.

This calculation takes the binary number 0111 1111 1111 1111. Because the left bit is 0 and the type is **short**, that number is positive. The calculation shifts all bits left one place, installing a zero on the right. This produces 1111 1111 1111 1110, which is a negative number in 16-bit binary, 2's complement. You know the result is negative by the fact that the leftmost bit is a 1, not a 0. Of course, in decimal numbers, 32,767 * 2 = 65,534, which is a positive number. Again, the problem is not the calculation, but the representation of 1111 1111 1111 1110. As an **int** or **long**, Java shows the desired value of 65,534.

It is interesting that when x is a **short**, $x <<= 1$; gives the same result as $x *= 2$; but $x = (x \times 2)$; produces a different result. This is because $(x \times 2)$ produces an integer, even if you try to cast 2 to a **short** first. The solution is to use this form: $x = (short) (x \times 2)$; which again results in 2. This is not the desired answer, but at least it is a consistent one.

The next example strives for the correct answer instead of consistency:

```java
public class Overflow {
  public static void main (String args[]) {
    short x, y, z;
    x = y = z = 32767;
// These three assignments are equivalent, but produce erroneous arithmetic
// results, due to overflow because the variables are shorts.
    x <<= 1;
    y *= 2;
    z = (short) (z * 2);
    System.out.println( x + " " + y +  " " + z );
// However, these int variables don't overflow, and compute correctly.
    int a, b, c;
    a = b = c = 32767;
    a <<= 1;
    b *= 2;
    c = c * 2;
    System.out.println( a + " " + b + " " + c );
  }
}
```

This program's output is

```
-2 -2 -2
65534 65534 65534
```

What happens if you multiply two large **short**s together? As you expect by now, the results may differ from what you want. If there is overflow, Java keeps the rightmost 16 bits and discards the extra. Here's an example:

10,000 decimal is 0010 0111 0001 0000 in binary notation. If you square 10,000 in decimal, you get 100,000,000. If you square the same binary representation, you get the right 16 bits of the result, or 1110 0001 0000 0000, from the full binary result of 0000 0101 1111 0101 1110 0001 0000 0000. You get –7,936.

If you do the same to two relatively large **int**s, such as by squaring 50,000, you will get a similarly erroneous result because the actual result of 2,500,000,000 exceeds the maximum integer's value of $2^{31} - 1$.

When you divide by, say, 16, the easy way is to shift the bits right four places. This process discards any bits shifted off the right end. The effect is to throw away the "decimal" part of the number—that is, the part to the right of the decimal point. That's how integer division works. If you need to preserve the ordinal part, you need to use **float** or **double** type numbers, or move the discarded bits into another number and evaluate them.

If you use shifting to divide a negative number like –65,280, which is 1111 1111 0000 0000 binary, by some power of 2, you may or may not want to preserve the sign bit. Say you want to divide by 32, which means right shifting five places:

a = - 65280 >> 5;

which evaluates this way:

1111 1111 0000 0000 >> 5 is 0000 0111 1111 1000 or +2040.

However, if you want to preserve the sign, it goes this way:

a = -65280 >>> 5;

1111 1111 0000 0000 >>> 5 is 1111 1111 1111 1000 or -2040 as a type **short**.

The Windows calculator evaluates 1111 1111 1111 1000 as 65,528 decimal. That's not a bug. It's merely because the calculator uses 32-bit calculations.

The moral of this story is, again, that you should use **int** and **long** numbers, not **short** or **byte**, unless you know there's no possible way to exceed the limits. Unless something modifies x later, a statement like this is safe:

for (byte x = 0; x<10; x++) {

There are similar arguments for using double precision instead of float.

Of course, if you're writing an embedded system for a new-generation cell phone and must concern yourself with the size of your RAM footprint, you'll want to consider using **short** and **float** even in calculations. Doing so introduces a whole new class of hungry bugs to your program.

In such cases, it is prudent to include tests in your code anywhere you suspect a number might range beyond its expected bounds—for example:

```
if (x < sqrt(32767)) {
  y = x * x;
}
```

or faster in this case, since sqrt(32767) is a little more than 181, you could write the following preceded by a comment explaining what the deuce 181 is:

```
if (x <= 181) {
  y = x * x;
}
```

Misconceptions

Before the DC-3 aircraft existed, there was a DC-2. The cockpit controls were similar; indeed, the entire aircraft was similar in most respects. It was easy for a DC-2 pilot to upgrade to the more powerful DC-3.

One difference was that the positions of the flap and landing gear levers were reversed, although the two controls looked the same. On today's aircraft, every gear lever has a knob like a wheel on it, and every flap lever physically looks like an aircraft flap. Nowadays, the FAA mandates that these shapes be there. On most planes, the controls are located far from each other. Usually, the flap lever is between the pilots and the gear handle is on the front instrument panel.

That wasn't so back in the days of the DC-2 and DC-3. Several DC-3 aircraft suffered misfortune because of those flap and gear levers. The pilots would land with flaps and gear down, then while taxiing in, they would raise the flaps. That was the normal procedure.

Occasionally (and you saw this one coming, didn't you), a DC-2 pilot who had recently upgraded to the DC-3 would instinctively reach for the flap handle and raise it, while taxiing in. Instants later, two expensive propellers were bending themselves noisily as they gouged the taxiway. One comedy of errors culminated a flight in which the plane lost an engine as the plane was about to land. The copilot feathered the wrong engine, killing it, and turning the plane into a glider. The pilot barely made it to the runway, at which time the copilot raised the flaps, or, oops, the landing gear. More than words were exchanged that day!

One of the problems United States astronauts might have had when visiting the Soyuz space station was with an emergency egress system. In the egress module, hidden around the pilot's knees were two identical ordinary toggle switches. One had to be turned on for egress to be successful. If the other were turned on, however, everyone would die. There were no labels on the switches, because it was extremely difficult to see them anyhow.

As you can imagine, United States astronauts spent ample time practicing which switch to flip!

In the movie *Apollo 13*, someone plastered a big sign NO over a critical control that must not be touched, lest in a tense moment an errant hand move it prematurely.

If you are from a non-C background, there are a few things to relearn about Java. One is how the assignment operator works. This code fragment illustrates:

```
int a = 0;
int b = 0;
int c = 5;
a = b = c;
System.out.println(a);
```

The output is 5, because in Java, assignments proceed from right to left. First, b is assigned c's value of 5, then a is assigned b's value of 5. Similar CoBOL code would give you an error. Similar BASIC or Visual Basic code would evaluate whether or not b equals c and assign the truth of the evaluation to a.

Unless Java is your first computer language, you probably have some programming baggage to unlearn.

Unusual Bugs

Once, I debugged a SQL statement designed to find duplicate data in two tables that contained records with 12 fields each. The SQL found 2,318 duplicate records, a number about what the user expected. However, I wanted to test it more rigorously. I duplicated one record exactly five times and the SQL statement failed to find those duplicates!

The errant SQL statement included a clause of the form:

```
WHERE
    [Table1].[Field1] = [Table2].[Field1] AND
    [Table1].[Field2] = [Table2].[Field2] AND (etc.)
```

The SQL was trying to test whether or not Field1 contained identical data in Table1 and Table2, and also whether or not Field2 had identical data in Table1 and Table2, etc.

The WHERE clause was yielding no data, even though in my test data, all of the fields had identical contents.

I used a binary search. I removed half of the fields from the SQL, then half of the remainder, finally localizing one offending field. That field had null data in both records.

Well, zero equals zero, but null doesn't equal null. That was Visual Basic and SQL. The solution was to use the **IsNull()** function. If A is null and B is null, the comparison expression (A = B) evaluates false. However, the expression (IsNull(A) = IsNull(B)) is true. In other words, the results of the **IsNull()** function compared as expected. The new expression took this longer but correct form:

```
WHERE
  ([Table1].[Field1] = [Table2].[Field1]) Or
(IsNull([Table1].[Field1]) And Isnull([Table2].[Field1])) AND
  ([Table1].[Field2] = [Table2].[Field2]) Or
(IsNull([Table1].[Field2]) And Isnull([Table2].[Field2])) AND (etc.)
```

Note	*Unlike in Java, the = operator is overloaded in VB. It's used for assignment and for comparisons.*

In Java, **NaN** means Not a Number. If you compare two variables that have **NaN** as their values, the comparison is **false**. You can test this with the following:

```
int A = NaN;
int B = NaN;
System.out.println(A == B);
```

If you assign 10 to either *A* or *B*, but not to both, *(A == B)* still evaluates **false** for two reasons. First, any expression containing **NaN** evaluates **false**. Second, 10 is not equal to **NaN**.

If, however, you assign zero to both *A* and *B*, you get a true comparison.

The expression *(10 != NaN)* evaluates **false**, and so does *(10 == NaN)*. For that matter, *((10 != NaN) == (10 == NaN))* also evaluates **false**, even though both major components evaluate **false** and, ordinarily, *(false == false)* would evaluate **true**. In Java, any expression involving **NaN** evaluates **false**, period.

As in most languages, zero is equal to zero, but Java's **NaN** is not equal to **NaN**.

Data-Driven Bugs

The **Available()** method of the **InputStream** class returns the number of bytes available to be read without blocking. You can use the **Available()** method to peek into an input stream to see how much data is there.

Some input streams always report 0 bytes available, even when there is data available. So, you must not rely wholly on this method to perform input, unless you don't care about platform independence and you know the method works with the systems you've targeted.

Java also supports **markable** streams. You can place a mark in a stream and return to it directly, not having to redo the search process. Such **markable** streams have memory buffers, but if a buffer's capacity is exceeded, the mark is invalidated.

The **flush()** method writes all buffered data to the output stream. Don't forget to **flush()** or the data may be lost or misrouted.

Similarly, it's important to **close()** streams, but more important to **close()** output streams than input. If you remember to **close()**, data in the stream is stored before the stream is deallocated. Otherwise, the data is lost.

Side-Effect Bugs

Some operators generate side effects. Like the interaction between certain medications and grapefruit juice, these can cause problems unless you are wary of them.

The **++** operator increments a variable. So the expression $y = ++x$; assigns one more than the original value of x into y, but it increments y in the process. The alternative line $y = x + 1$; does not increment x and has no side effects. If you write $y = ++x$; and expect x to have its original value next time the code comes through that line, you'll have a side-effect bug.

Ditto for the **--** operator.

The method invocation operator () is another example, provided that the method has side effects—and most do.

The **new** operator creates a new object, which consumes RAM and has other effects on the program. It tells the garbage collector that there is something open to collect at some point, for example. If the garbage collector becomes confused, and this is possible, the **new** operator is an impetus for memory leaks.

Optimizer-Caused Bugs

Long before I knew much about computers, I read a statement that intrigued me. Basically, it compared machine language, assembler code, and high-level language code. With each level of language abstraction, more and more generalizations must be made. Each generalization leads to code that is less efficient. In other words, the tightest, fastest programs possible must be written at the machine language level.

The trouble with this otherwise noble idea is that going to lower levels of language abstraction makes it more and more difficult to write, maintain, and enhance the program.

At the Java level, code optimizers can replace several lines of code with something else that acts exactly the same way, except that it runs faster, or has a smaller footprint, and sometimes both.

At the machine level, optimizers can do greater marvels. They can actually take advantage of a particular machine's peculiarities to improve performance or size. Code optimized for a Solaris workstation would be different from the same code optimized for Windows NT, and different yet from code optimized for a Mac—that is, at the machine level.

The trouble is, optimizing for particular computers destroys Java's vaunted machine independence.

This is not to say optimizers are useless. Far from it! Most commercial optimizers let you decide whether or not to preserve machine independence. Optimizers will generally improve your code until you learn to write the best possible algorithms.

That's another good reason to optimize. You will find ways to improve your craft. For example, if you find that your optimizer routinely changes the kind of loop you write, you'll begin considering the other kind.

Java supports multiprocessor computers, but it doesn't optimize well for them. If you had a loop that assigned 10,000 values from one array to another, one element at a time, and you had two CPUs in the box, that loop would have potential for optimization. One CPU might work upward from the 0 element, while the other CPU worked downward from the 9,999th element until the two met in the middle, getting the job done in about half the time.

Surely future versions of Java will support such automatic loop optimization on multiprocessor machines. When they do, another class of collision bugs awaits the unwary. For instance, the CPUs must decide which handles the middle array element(s). The solution is different, depending on whether the array has an even or odd number of elements. When three CPUs carve up a loop, there are six possibilities for such collisions and so forth, in geometric progression.

Optimizers are pretty good, but flawed. Many times, the most elegant, fastest, smallest Java code is undesirable because it's so difficult to maintain.

You want it lean, but you don't want it mean.

Always remember that program maintenance is a large part of the overall project cost. It does you no good to save 50K of disk space when nobody cares. Saving 2/10 of a second while a screen pops up does not impress your customer. If doing those things results in code that costs three times more to maintain than a clear program would, that will impress your boss!

Perhaps the correct word is: depress.

To savvy supervisors, maintenance difficulty, even when caused by lean, optimized, speedy code, is a huge bug.

Pseudo Bugs

Question: When is your buggy program not buggy?

Question #2: Does the computer have a virus?

Suffice to say that your Java program's pathological behavior might be due to something else, such as a virus. Ridding your computer of viruses is beyond the scope of *Debugging Java*. However, when you've ruled out the obvious, consider updating and running your antivirus software. Several hundred new viruses are created every month, although most are variants of a smaller number of classes. Most are macro viruses. Of the hundreds of new viruses, fewer make it "to the wild." Some do, and occasionally one spans the globe before the antivirus software vendors react to it.

The infamous Melissa virus was one such virulent bug. Before anyone had antivirus software that could recognize Melissa, it attacked the author's network and bounced right off. In fact, it's difficult to imagine how any macro virus could penetrate our net because of a unique countermeasure we happened to have adopted. I'll explain how it works, because you might be using Word as your Java editor, and macro viruses commonly focus on Word. The countermeasure is simple, and you can adopt it too.

Many of the new viruses are macro programs that infect such software as Microsoft Word, Excel, and PowerPoint (especially Word). Fortunately, there is a simple solution to preventing macro viruses from infecting your computer.

The unique solution relies on the fact that Microsoft produces free viewers for these three programs. The viewers are named, appropriately Word Viewer, Excel Viewer, and PowerPoint Viewer. Microsoft encourages their widespread use, not as antiviral software but so you can create a Word, Excel, or PowerPoint document and send it to someone who doesn't own the same software.

These viewer programs don't let you save documents, and more importantly, they do not understand macros! This means they are as immune to a macro virus as your pencil is.

Most computers become infected due to double-clicking or other automated ways of opening documents. If you double-click an infected file whose extension is .DOC or .DOT, Windows presumes you want to launch Word so you can read the document. Do that, and you're infected unless your antivirus software stops the virus. Melissa proved that a virus can outpace its countermeasures for a time, so you're never safe.

For your convenience, Microsoft has given permission to post these viewers on this book's Web site. Download them from http://DebuggingJava.Com or seek them on Microsoft's own Web site.

When you install each viewer, it will ask if you want Windows to use it as the default for opening files with various extensions. Answer Yes.

Error Watch *Be careful not to install these viewers in the same directories as their counterparts. That is, don't install Word Viewer in the same directory as Word. Doing so can overwrite crucial files. The viewers default to being installed in their own unique directories, so if you allow the defaults, you will be safe.*

Test by double-clicking a file bearing each kind of extension, for instance, .DOC. In this case, Word Viewer, not Word, should open and present the file. If you double-click an .XLS file, Excel Viewer should open the file instead of Excel.

You will not get a warning if there are macro viruses present, unless other antivirus software gives you one. However, you can be sure the document you are viewing in Word Viewer has no viruses in its present state. Opening the document in a viewer filters out all macros.

If you want to pass the document, or a modification, to someone else, you need to copy it into the copy-and-paste buffer, then open Word and paste it into Word.

Error Watch *There is a way to go wrong here. In its File menu, Word Viewer lists a way to reopen the same document in Word. Don't do that, because Word launches and then opens the original document, macros and all. If you want to edit the document, open it in Viewer and use the copy-and-paste buffer to pull it into Word.*

For reference, here's the process to use:

1. Double-click on the file.
2. Word Viewer (or Excel Viewer or PowerPoint Viewer) launches.
3. Your file appears.
4. Press CTRL-A, which selects the entire document. Alternately, you can click Edit I Select All.
5. Press CTRL-C, which copies the selected items into your copy-and-paste buffer. Alternately, you can click Edit I Copy.
6. Launch Word (or Excel or PowerPoint) separately, start a new document, and click somewhere inside it.
7. Press CTRL-V, which copies the contents of your copy-and-paste buffer to the new document. Alternately, you can click Edit I Paste.
8. Unless your copy of Word (or Excel or PowerPoint) was already contaminated, your document is still free of viruses. You can send it to a colleague, modify it, print it, or store it knowing that it is clean.

Of course, if you're using a different word processor, your chances of getting a macro virus are slim indeed. The vast majority of macro viruses only infect Word documents.

After reading a somewhat lengthy chapter that classifies Java bugs, you'll find the next offering more philosophical. Chapter 7 shows how to train your mind to think in bug-free ways.

CHAPTER 7

Mental Disciplines

Perhaps you recall a crack from Chapter 6 that "rules and laws only exist so people don't have to think." It's not a pejorative statement at all, and it certainly doesn't mean that rules and laws are for dummies. It's actually a piece of wisdom because, paradoxically, we find mental freedom in rules and laws.

How to Think Consistently

Rules and laws exist so we can save time by not reinventing the wheel with every thought we think. The people with the most rules and laws in their heads are usually the most creative, for they have more time to invent. Every time we decide to adopt a rule into our personal codes, we free ourselves to think more.

One might argue that rules and laws stultify creativity, but that only happens when people believe rules are made to be followed blindly. When you reach an impasse, when you find a rule hinders you from doing what you need to do, it's time to try to modify that rule and make it better. That's one definition of learning. Grace Hopper said, many times, words to the effect that when you can't ask permission, it's better to do something and apologize.

Rules and laws save us time and make us more creative, but the main reason we have them is to prevent errors. It's illegal to drive past my home faster than 25 miles per hour, for good reason. Small children play near the street there. A speeding driver might make a deadly error. A slower driver in the same situation might only make a lot of noise, as tires squealed on pavement.

Good rules and laws, when followed, force us into safe molds. Because a bill has to pass numerous tests, hurdles, and revisions before reaching enough of a consensus to become a law, bad laws are relatively rare. Programming ideas, after being blessed and modified by experience, trial, failure, and success, can become good rules to follow. They keep us safe as programmers.

Use Inviolate Personal Conventions

Once you've thought something through to completion, there's no need to do it again. You can accept the conclusion as fact. Remember, facts are stubborn things. They don't change.

For example, in Chapter 6, I mentioned an ace programmer who decided to write explicit routines that would tell the garbage collector when he had released objects. He thought it through, realized that the garbage collector operates as an autonomous thread, and realized that sometimes it has difficulty in reclaiming objects. He decided to help it every time he could.

Now, he doesn't bother to think about whether or not to help the garbage collector; he just does it. Every time.

The key is to do something every time.

I have a favorite adage about flying. "The superb pilot is so good because he never lets himself get into a situation where his superb skills are needed." Programming is the same. The superb programmer stays away from situations that would utterly test their skill. This means adopting standard practices, like the following.

Java Programming Standards

Caveat: You, your peers, and your bosses won't like all of these standards, and that's fine, because you don't have to adopt them. All that matters is that you develop a set that you do like, and that you hold strictly to them. Even when you've developed a set you personally like, your peers and your bosses won't like them all, and that doesn't matter either.

What matters is consistency. Personal consistency is paramount in programming. Consistency between peers is important, although not paramount, because peers will probably maintain your code, and you theirs. Consistency in a company is significant, but not crucial. Your personal set of standards needs to be more encompassing than the set to which your peers can agree. Your company needs standards too, but these need to accommodate far more people, programming a wider variety of systems, so company-wide standards need to have wider latitude.

With that huge caveat in mind, I present my personal set of Java programming standards. They comprise a target. Discard what you disdain, take what you like, and build on them to find your own set of preferences as well as a set for your group and another for your company.

Comments

All three kinds of Java comments are required in nontrivial code.

- A header, consisting of javadoc (/**) comments, begins every interface, class, and method.

- Nearly every declaration needs an inline (//) comment giving the declared item's purpose. Loop counters declared within their loops are obvious exceptions.

- Inline comments should be aligned vertically, where practical.

- Comments generally precede their subjects. Precede such a comment with a blank line and do not put a blank line after it.

- A javadoc HTML document or printout should read clearly enough that few people would ever need to read the code.

- A company standard copyright notice is generally required.

- Headers for classes and methods should be standardized throughout the enterprise. Include the applicable items listed next:

```
/** Detailed description should include the purpose, pre-conditions,
* post-conditions, dependencies, side effects, implementation requirements,
* callers, callees, overrides allowed or not, where super is located, and
* any required program states before or after the call.
*
* @param describes each parameter's purpose, any masks or requirements, and
* whether parameters are input, output, or both.
* @return describes the return's type, purpose, range, and error codes.
* @exception describes all non-system exceptions that the method throws,
* whether or not the exception is recoverable, and how to go about recovering
* if applicable.
* @author tells how to contact you.
* Date: the code originated.
* Usage: Optionally show a formal usage statement. A good alternative
* is to write a main(), because this assists in debugging as well as
* showing usage.
* Example: Optionally show a sample call
* Mod History: lists the names of all people who modify the code, when,
* and what modifications they made. Also, inline comments refer back to
* this section by initials and date.
* @See String, URL, or classname#methodname containing other documentation.
* Javadoc will generate HTML links to the referenced items.
*/
```

- Group your methods together to take advantage of comment blocks. For instance, you might group all of your I/O methods in the same area of the program, unless doing so would decrease clarity.

- Each individual line of block comments (/*) or javadoc (/**), except the first line of course, should begin with an asterisk (*).

- Comments are required to explain clever code, when clever code cannot be simplified.

- Comments should never be used to take the place of a good, descriptive variable name or method name, nor to explain the obvious.

- Rule of thumb: Write your comments as if they will be published in a magazine!

- The gross weight of the comments should be about 20 percent of the gross weight of the code.

Names

In a way, names are the most important of comments. They describe, succinctly. In Java, names are case-sensitive, so how you capitalize names can tell other programmers what kinds of names you are using.

- Package names are in all lowercase letters. They are single words, not combinations of words. There are enough words in the English language to describe all of the packages I'll ever write.
- Class names are in mixed case. The first letter is always capitalized. They are often combinations of words, such as MyClass.
- Interfaces should begin with the capital letter "I", such as IMyInterface.
- Member function names are in mixed case. The first letter is never capitalized, but each subsequent new word is capitalized. Whole words are in mixed case. They are often combinations of words, such as myMemberFunction.
- Static method names follow the member function naming convention.
- Special names for debug-only code begin with the word "debug". For example: debugmyMemberFunction.
- Names may almost never have $ signs nor underscores in them, even though Java allows them to be used. Because constants use all capital letters, constants employ underscores as word separators, such as MY_CONSTANT.
- Avoid using a variable name that is already used in a **super** class. This is nearly always an error.
- Each parameter should begin with a lowercase "a" or "an", and the rest of the words are mixed case. The name should reveal the type. For example: aButterflyIcon or anEagleIcon.
- Constants (**final**) use all uppercase letters with underscores between words, such as in MY_CONSTANT.
- Globals begin with a lowercase "g" or "global" and are mixed case. For example: gMyGlobal, or globalMyGlobal.
- Avoid using names like Temp1, Temp2, Temp3, which describe almost nothing.

Implementers, Factories, or Constructors

Here are some more naming conventions:

- The word "Factory", with its first letter capitalized, is appended to each implementer name—for example: PreambleFactory.
- Implementer methods begin with the word "Make", with the first letter capitalized—for example: MakeToDoList.
- Getters, except those that return Booleans, begin with the word "get", in all lowercase—for example: getPrivatePhone.
- Getters that return Booleans begin with the word "is" or "can", for example: isValidListener or canGenerateText.
- Setters begin with the word "set", in all lowercase—for example: setPortOn.

Code

How you should structure your code is a controversial subject, at least. There are the conventions I've adopted. They serve me well, but I find I must violate some of them occasionally.

- Overparenthesize any expression that contains a mixture of operators.
- Break up lines of code that have more than three kinds of operators.
- Declare variables with as small a scope as you can, realizing that you should seldom declare variables in the middle of loops. When possible, use declarations like this:

  ```
  for (int i = 0; i < max; i ++) {
  ```

- Declare most variables near the point where they are used so their types can be readily seen. If you feel you must collect all variable declarations at the top, duplicate the declarations as comments later.
- Put constants on the left sides of their expressions. For one thing, this improves the performance of some compilers, and for another, it improves the compiler's chances of finding assignment bugs.
- Don't let lines wrap around. The maximum line length is 78 to 80 characters, in most cases.
- Use two-space indenting.

- If you use tabs, be sure your IDE converts every tab to spaces. Otherwise, you may find that printers vary in how they indent your code.

- Always indent bodies of loops and conditionals. This helps programs like JLint find misplaced braces, parentheses, and semicolons.

- Be consistent with braces. Adopt a style and keep it. When working on someone else's code, use their style. The two accepted styles are listed later in this topic.

- When a closing brace is more than a page from its opening brace, place an appropriate comment after the closing brace. For example, if the brace closes a conditional or a loop, place the appropriate condition after the closing brace, as a comment.

- Always use braces, even for single-line blocks of code.

- A condition and its keyword go on the same line—for instance:

```
if (condition)
```

- Error traps should almost never be used for loop control. However, in cases of extreme performance need, remember that they are very fast.

- **Do-While** loop formats:

```
do
{
   statement;
}
while (condition);
```

or

```
do {
   statement;
} while (condition);
```

- If formats:

```
if (condition)
{
   statement;
}
else
{
   statement;
}  //condition
```

or

```
if (condition) (
  statement;
} else {
  statement;
}  //condition
```

- While loop formats:

```
while (condition)
{
  statement;
}  //condition
```

or

```
while (condition) {
  statement;
}  //condition
```

- Switch formats:

```
switch (condition)
{
  case 1:
    statement;
    break;
  case 2:
    statement;      // No 'break' is needed in the last 'case' clause.
  default:          // Required by this standard!
    statement;
    break;
}  //condition
```

or

```
switch (condition) {
  case 1:
    statement;
    break;
  case 2:
    statement;      // No 'break' is needed in last 'case' clause.
  default:          // Required by this standard!
    statement;
    break;
}  /condition
```

- Error traps:

```
try
{
  statement;
}
catch (ExceptionClass e)    // Optional if and only if there is a finally.
  statement;
}
finally    // Optional if and only if there is a catch.
{
  statement;
}
```

or

```
try {
  statement;
}
catch (ExceptionClass e)    // Optional if and only if there is a finally.
  statement;
}
finally {    // Optional if and only if there is a catch.
  statement;
}
```

- Use **Assert**s freely. These help you verify assumptions and aid in debugging. Remember that you can remove all **Assert**s from compiled code by flipping the debug flag in the **Assert** class. Here's an example of **Assert** usage:

```
String copyString (String strSource) {
  String isNull = "Source string is null.";
  String notEqual = "Source and target string lengths not equal after
copy.";
  Assert.PreCondition (NULL == strSource, isNull);
// Code to copy the string.
  Assert.PostCondition (strSource.length() != stTarget.length(), notEqual);
}
```

- Install **SelfTest** classes in packages. Every package needs a test plan, so implement it in a **SelfTest** class.

- It's a good idea not to use **import**, for an odd reason. Not using **import** forces you to use fully dot-qualified class references, a practice that avoids ambiguity. The downside is that you'll have to make more code changes if (heaven forbid) you change package names. The counter to that argument is that such changes are easy and quick via global replaces.

Don't Mix Depth-First Searches and Breadth-First Searches

When searching a tree of data, there are two primary methods one can use: depth-first and breadth-first.

With a depth-first search, you examine the top node, then a node on its next lower level, then a node on that one's next lower level, and so on until you reach the bottom. At that point, you pop up a level and look for unsearched nodes subordinate to that level. If you find one, you examine it, then search its subordinate nodes, if any. Otherwise, you pop up another level, etc. Sooner or later, you make it back to the top node, having searched the tree. See Figure 7-1.

With a breadth-first search, you examine the top node, and only go to a subordinate node when all nodes at the current level have been searched. See Figure 7-2.

When you are coding or debugging, you have a choice of depth-first or breadth-first searching. Your choice depends on your current needs.

Let's say you are seeking the spot where a variable erroneously goes to zero and you are stepping through code. You should probably choose a breadth-first search here, skipping over the function calls, until you find the function that sets the variable to zero. Then, you can examine that function in the same manner. This process will find your errant variable assignment faster than a depth-first search will, because you can eliminate most of the code quickly.

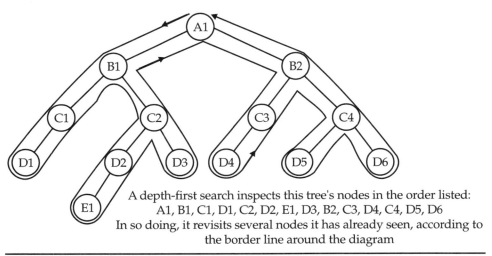

A depth-first search inspects this tree's nodes in the order listed:
A1, B1, C1, D1, C2, D2, E1, D3, B2, C3, D4, C4, D5, D6
In so doing, it revisits several nodes it has already seen, according to the border line around the diagram

Figure 7.1   Depth-first search

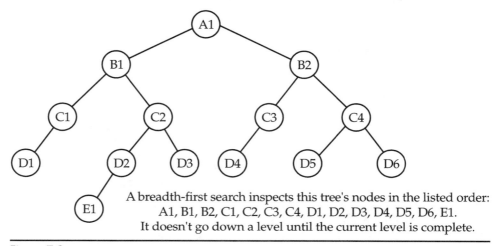

A breadth-first search inspects this tree's nodes in the listed order:
A1, B1, B2, C1, C2, C3, C4, D1, D2, D3, D4, D5, D6, E1.
It doesn't go down a level until the current level is complete.

Figure 7.2   Breadth-first search

If, however, you are conducting a code review, you might want to give a high-level overview, and then choose a depth-first search. One reason for this choice is that you can write down the contents of variables as you step into function calls, and easily return to those variable contents when you back out of the calls. That process makes it easier to keep track of the program's state.

What you should not do is mix the two kinds of searches. Doing so almost guarantees that you'll miss something, perhaps something critical. Both methods guarantee that you can visit every node, but if you mix the two, all such guarantees fail.

Instead, consciously adopt one search method or the other and follow it until your task is finished.

When to Debug

Debugging is like detective work. It's a process of gathering data and deducing information. Try to do it when you're sharp and fresh. For most people, that's not right after lunch, nor late in the afternoon. If you're working 80-hour weeks, you probably shouldn't take up debugging.

Keep moving while you're debugging. Get up from your chair, let the blood move around better, lean on the back of your chair and take a deep breath. Stretch and then start thinking again.

Vitamins are brain food. So are caffeine and sugar, it seems, from the looks of many programmers' desks, waste cans, and waistlines!

Debug all the time. Debug while you are coding, designing, testing of course, and even when addressing an audience. You don't need to tell your audience that you just thought of a way to break your gem, but be thinking about it. You will have adopted a different mindset while showcasing a program, and that mindset lets you think about things in different ways.

Writing a book, I find similar effects. While typing, I can see and correct most kinds of errors. However, when I use the screen to review what I've written, I expose other kinds of errors, primarily those in the area of clarity. Later, the printed page has the power to show me errors in grammar, spelling, and organization that I might miss otherwise. Different physical activities seem to predispose the mind to finding different kinds of errors.

While you are programming, seek ways to adopt different mindsets so you can think about debugging. Look at a printout. Look at the screen. Step through the code. Show it to a peer. Build a flowchart. Those diverse processes put your mind through different processes and let it operate from different perspectives. Your mind tends to uncover different kinds of bugs while operating in different realms.

Your Environment

Where your 'head' is while you debug is important. Distractions cost you dearly at such times. Here are some ideas you can use to improve your environment. Some are a bit over-the-top, but I've used them all on occasion.

- Never be debugging when you must be thinking about a meeting.
- Turn off your phone's ringer, or unplug the cord, letting voice mail take your calls. When I do that, I put a courtesy message on voice mail inviting callers to ring my cell phone or my colleague in the next office in an emergency.
- Review your voice mail first thing in the morning, right after lunch, and an hour before quitting time, but otherwise only on request.
- Turn off email notification on your computer screen. Review your email at the same times you return your phone calls.
- If you receive megabytes of email, ask or hire someone to filter it for you.

- Move to a more private area while you debug. If that area has a networked computer, and you can close the door, it's perfect.

- Get or make a small flagpole with a flag that can be raised, or lowered to half-mast. Post a sign reading: "Interruptible only when flag is at top-mast." People will respect your wishes.

- Take a printout and a red pen to the bathroom, your car, or the cafeteria, and hide. Put a 3 × 5 card on your keyboard saying that you're off somewhere debugging.

- Give up and socialize a while. Often, relaxing with your peers at the soda machine unshackles the mind, and by the time you return to the tube, you know exactly what to do next. However, be political about it. I have an apolitical friend who had a shirt made. It had these words written on the back, so they were visible when she arose from her chair, "I'm not socializing; I'm researching." Her boss was not amused, at least not publicly.

CHAPTER 8

The Awesome Power of Debuggers

When I began teaching computer science classes, I couldn't forget my recent frustrations as a student, trying to make programs work. It was only after I learned how to use debuggers that I began to understand the various languages. Before debuggers enlightened me, I could program in many languages, but I had only mastered one. Determined not to visit such frustration on my students, I spent the semester's second week detailing the debugger, and then delved into the language. Throughout the semester, I emphasized using the debugger to clarify knotty issues.

Then, an interesting phenomenon transpired. We had standardized, departmental, midterm, and final exams, prepared each semester in secrecy by two or three senior professors. For years, class scores had averaged between 67 percent and 72 percent on those exams, without exception. My first class averaged an astounding 81 percent, raising my eyebrows and those of a few others around the department. I was invited to explain to a dean's representative how this impossibility could be.

We discussed the syllabus, teaching techniques, and the large amount of time I spent in the computer lab with my students. All but accused of "teaching the test," I had to point out that I had no more access to the exam than my students, and that my class was the first to take it. To me, the difference was that I taught the debugger, a practice frowned upon by the department, but my inquisitor didn't think that would make a difference.

On the next exam, my class scored a tad above 82 percent. The next semester, the scores were a point or two higher. One other instructor tried teaching the debugger. His class scored 78 percent on the next midterm. Nobody else would try the idea, but suddenly my classes filled to overflowing, the school had to double my classroom sizes, and I allowed several audits per semester. A few years later, when I sadly announced to my classes that my contract was complete, the departmental chair received more than 200 signatures on two petitions to keep me on. I couldn't ignore such a request, nor could he.

Okay, so I wasn't that bad a teacher, but the university had more skillful, more knowledgeable teachers whose classes never did score above 72 percent.

The difference wasn't my skill; it was that the students learned to use the debugger very early. Instead of spending hours, head in hands, wringing wet over their next assignments, they would turn on the debugger, find the problem, and still have time to understand what had gone amiss!

The alternative, without the debugger, was to panic around for hours until something worked by chance, wonder why it worked, and go party in relief. Students caught in the latter scenario didn't understand entire crucial points of the language. When it came time to answer similar questions on an exam, they often couldn't perform.

Anyone can memorize some Java syntax. If you truly want to know how Java works, what its side effects are, and what things can "getcha," become intimate with debuggers. If you want to be more productive on the job, and who doesn't, get to know your debuggers better than you know Java. If you want to be the peer who's always answering questions, instead of asking them… 'nuff said.

Java Debugger (JDB) Is Free

Even if you own or plan to own a great third-party debugger like Assure, JProbe, Jtest, TogetherJ, or the tools that come with JBuilder and Visual Café, you should get to know JDB, the debugger that comes with your Java Development Kit. It's excellent, powerful, and can serve as the basis for an extended debugger that you write.

This section will begin with an overview of the JDB. It will discuss the commands, and then extend the discussion into sophisticated ways to use those commands.

If you're familiar with UNIX, you may know the gdb debugger. Java's JDB is similar to gdb.

Installing

JDB installs with your Java Development Kit. There's no need to do anything special.

Overview

JDB is text-based and command-line oriented. It's not a GUI product. Like **javac**, you run it from the DOS prompt. However, it would be relatively easy for you to wrap a GUI blanket around it. In fact, doing so is an excellent project if you want to master the language! The JDK Commander product has done exactly that, and it's free!

Compile your program with the **–g** option. If you don't, the Java Debugger will usually, but not always, request that you do so. You may notice that your program runs more slowly, so before you release it for general consumption, recompile without the **-g** option.

```
javac -g MyProgram.java
```

Invoke the Java debugger this way:

```
jdb [ options ] class
jdb [ -host hostname ] -password password
```

For example:

```
jdb MyProgram
```

Here are the things you can do:

- Get help on using the debugger.
- Stop your code at any spot you choose by setting a breakpoint.
- See a list of threads and thread groups, and examine any thread in the list.
- Suspend, and then resume any or all threads.
- See a list of fields and their contents.
- View the call stacks and their individual entries.
- Step forward one or as many lines as you choose, and then stop again.
- Check memory usage.
- View the source code near a specified line.
- Ignore various exceptions that you specify.
- Force the garbage collector to run.
- Print various items for reference.

Command Reference

Square brackets, such as **[item]**, denote that the item is optional. **(s)** denotes that one or many items can be specified.

CLASSPATH [path]	This command gives you a list of directories and ZIP files that the JDB will search for class definitions. If you specify a path, the JDB searches your path first, then the system path. You can override CLASSPATH with the –classpath compiler option.
!!	Shorthand for the last command entered. You can append additional text if you desire.
catch [exception class]	Sets a breakpoint whenever a specified exception is thrown. If you just type catch without a class, this command lists the exceptions that are currently being caught. Then, you can optionally use ignore to cancel those breakpoints. Note that you can throw your own exceptions and catch them in the debugger.

classes	Lists all loaded classes.
clear [class:line]	Removes the breakpoint at the class:line you specify. If you just type clear, you get a list of current breakpoints and the lines where they are set, making it easier to clear the ones you want. Note that typing clear doesn't clear all breakpoints. It just lists them for you.
cont	Continues at full speed, after a thread is stopped by a breakpoint.
down [n]	Goes down n frames in the call stack. n defaults to 1 if you leave it off.
dump fd(s)	Prints the values of all fields in fd(s). If you specify a class name for fd, you will see all class (static) methods and their variables. You'll also see the superclass and the implemented interfaces. Specify objects and classes by name, or by their eight-digit hex ID numbers. Specify threads with the shorthand t@thread-number.
exit	Stops the debugger. quit also stops the debugger.
gc	Forces the garbage collector to run.
ignore exception class	Ignores the fact that an exception class would cause stoppage at a breakpoint. You have to specify the exception class to ignore.
list [line number]	Lists the source code line number specified, as well as several lines above and below it. If you don't specify a line number, it lists the line number of the current stack frame and current thread.
load classname	Loads the specified class into the debugger. You must specify the class name.
locals	Shows a list of local variables in the current stack frame. Note that you must compile with the –g option to use this feature.
memory	Shows a memory usage summary.
methods class	Lists all of the methods for the class you specify. The class name is required.
print fd(s)	Invokes the toString() method to print the contents of what you specified in the fds. They can be classes, objects, fields, or local variables. You can also use the t@thread-number shortcut to refer to a thread.
quit	Stops the debugger. Same as exit.
resume [thread(s)]	After one or more threads have stopped at breakpoints, this command restarts them. If you don't specify a thread, all are resumed.
run [class][args]	Runs the main() method of the class you specify, using the args you list. The default is the class and args you specified when you ran jdb.
step	Runs only the current line of the current thread and gets ready to run the next line.
stop [at class:line] [in class:method]	Either sets a breakpoint at that class and line, or at the first line of that class and method. If you just type stop, this command lists all of the current breakpoints for you.

suspend [thread(s)]	Stops the threads you specify. If you don't specify any, this command suspends all threads.
t@thread-number	A shortcut that identifies a thread.
thread thread_id	Sets the current thread to the one you specify in thread_id. The thread_id can be the thread name or its number. Other JDB commands act on the current thread, so you use this command to say some thread is the current one.
threadgroup name	Sets the current thread group to the one you specify in name.
threadgroups	Lists all of the current thread groups.
threads [threadgroups]	Lists all of the threads that are in the specified threadgroup, or if you don't specify one, the current threadgroup.
up [n]	Moves up n frames in the current thread's call stack. If you don't specify n, it moves up one frame.
use [source-file-path]	Tells the JDB where to look for source files. If you don't specify a path, this command shows the one being used.
where [thread] [all]	Dumps a stack trace for the thread you specify. The default is the current thread. You can specify all and see stack traces for all threads.

Design Tip *In DOS, a small program named doskey is useful. It lets you use your* UP *and* DOWN *arrow keys to flip through a stack of the last commands you've entered. When you find the command you want, the* ENTER *key reexecutes the command on the screen, saving you the typing. I always install doskey in my autoexec.bat file. It's found in c:\windows\command, and is particularly handy when you use the debugger.*

Third-Party Debuggers

If you can purchase a great debugger for, say, $300, and your company spends, say, $60 an hour on your salary, equipment, benefits, workspace, lights, heat, etc., then tell me quickly: How many hours must such a product save before it begins to pay for itself? Five?

How often have you built a program and spent more than five hours debugging it? Once every three months? More often than that, I'd guess.

If this $300 debugger can save you half of your debugging time, it pays for itself every six months. If you invest $300 and the investment pays for itself every six months, you're getting about 145 percent interest, compounded! If the debugger costs $2,500 and you're the only user, it's still a 17-percent investment.

Yes, software tools are outstanding investments for companies, and yes, their prices are all over the map.

Most companies have different accounts for software than for your salary, benefits, and environment. There may be a tight budget for software, making it difficult for you to convince your leader that you need a copy of that "Chrome Plated, Diesel Powered, Whiz Bang Debugger." But to the stockholder getting a check, all things come out of the same corporate pocket. The stockholders have the correct view. Why shouldn't you have the best tools on the market? Certainly not merely because the company's software pocket is empty, while some other corporate pocket is semifull. That's my opinion, anyhow.

Frankly, I've only succeeded about a third of the time with such arguments. But I always make them. After all, the answer is no if you don't ask! As a consultant, I have no qualms about spending my hard-earned money for the best tools, because doing so makes me far more productive and valuable.

Here are the best points of some popular debuggers. If I don't mention your favorite debugger, it's not that I think it's inferior. You'll have to draw your own conclusions about usability. Although I'm not about to plug any particular product, I do like each piece of software that I mention next in alphabetical order.

Please be aware that there's not enough space to illustrate all features of any product. Before purchasing any of these, you should visit Web sites, try demonstration versions, and talk to people who use them.

Assure

Assure, by Kuck Associates, is a dynamic analysis tool, not a static one. It is a GUI system, complete with bar graphs, error listings, and annotated source code windows. You can see the runtime call stack and a Call Tree window. You can set your colors and numerous other preferences to tune Assure to your work habits. It includes reports for documentation or communication to other team members.

Assure works on applets and applications. It temporarily replaces your JVM, so it can watch your code better. You can use it with any compiled .class file from any Java compiler. However, you shouldn't use the **–O** (optimize) compilation flag to optimize your code, because this removes line numbers. In that case, Assure can only report what methods contain errors, instead of identifying exact lines. Also, optimizing creates excessive inlining, which hides the bugs in the middle of excessive output.

It's best to have the source code available to Assure, but the program will even run without it. In this case, the results are a bit more obscure, but at least you have results.

Assure inspects running code, as opposed to JLint, which examines static source code. As such, Assure only reports problems in sections of code that have executed. It does four things to check your programs.

- Detects multithreading data race conditions
- Detects thread deadlock situations
- Detects potential thread stall situations
- Monitors lock acquisition cycles

Data races can occur when at least two threads have access to the same variable and at least one modifies the variable. The classic example of a race is a shared bank account. Say it has $1,000 in it and one thread withdraws $900, but another thread can access and withdraw money before the first one completes its transaction. In that case, the second thread might get away with more than the allowed $100.

Deadlocks are fatal errors that occur mostly in **synchronized** code. Two or more threads are deadlocked when each one requires a resource that another has locked. No thread can proceed, and without proceeding, no thread can release a resource—which some other thread needs. While other threads in the program may continue, these are stuck.

Thread stalls look similar to deadlocks, but are more difficult to detect. In the paragraph above, if there is another thread that can reach in and release one of the required resources, then the threads that appeared to be deadlocked were actually stalled. It is nearly impossible to prove that a piece of code includes a stall, but Assure can show that a program has a high probability of containing threads that can stall.

Sometimes, stalls are deliberate. For instance, a thread might be waiting on a port for a message, and several threads might be waiting for the first thread to finish executing. All are stalled until the message arrives. That might be by design, or maybe not. Be sure!

By monitoring lock acquisition cycles, Assure can detect the fact that a program can deadlock, even if it never has done so. This is because deadlocks are cyclic by nature. Say you have a situation in which the following conditions can occur, autonomously.

- Lock A is held when trying to acquire Lock B.
- Lock B is held when trying to acquire Lock C.
- Lock C is held when trying to acquire Lock A.

If all three conditions occur at the same time, you have a deadlock. However, they must occur at the same time. All three might occur, but at different times, and there is nothing but a potential deadlock. Later, the program might deadlock. This kind of situation can become tiresome, because a deadlock may not occur for months, and then may happen to your CEO three times—on the day before your wedding!

You do know, don't you, that Murphy invented computers?

Assure watches as your code acquires locks, looking for cycles. If it finds them, it alerts you to the possibility of a deadlock, even if one has never occurred. Thus, Assure cannot guarantee that a deadlock will occur. But it does indicate that you need to look at the code.

If you have a program with ten threads, and each thread can assume one hundred states, the entire program can assume 100^{10} or 100,000,000,000,000,000,000 states. In any production program, that means the number of possibilities for thread conflict nears infinity. This fact makes it impractical for any program to report all potential problems. Assure takes a smooth and rational approach, reporting the difficulties that have the highest probability of being actual bugs you need to fix.

Assure has a **–limit** option (the default), which tells it to disregard errors it uncovers in several specific classes. Most messages reported from these classes are safe, or are not fixable by developers. You can see these messages by not using the **–limit** option. In keeping with the best debugging practices, Assure lets you concentrate on the areas that most probably need your attention.

Swing and some other core classes are not thread-safe. This is by design. Their methods lack the synchronization needed to keep them thread-safe, because using **synchronized** can incur a hefty 4:1 performance penalty. When using such classes, you must either provide your own synchronization or use a single thread.

 *You can often make Swing code thread-safe by using the **invokeAndWait()** or invokeLater() methods in SwingUtilities.*

Assure works best when you use it to stress your code. Make your application work as hard as you can. Create as many threads as possible by clicking rapidly. Be sure to try every branch in your code, because Assure only tests code as it executes.

The Assure demo program shows three kinds of problems the product is designed to uncover:

- The classic "dining philosophers" problem demonstrates a deadlock. Five philosophers are seated at a round table with five meals in front of them, and five forks placed between them. Because of their peculiar upbringing, it takes two forks for any philosopher to eat. Each philosopher thinks a random length of time, and then picks up the left and right fork, if possible. If there is just one fork available, he picks it up. However, if both forks are available, the philosopher eats a while, then puts both forks down. A waiter immediately replaces the forks with clean ones. (I added that part.) If the philosophers cooperate, they will all get to eat, one or two at a time. However, if all of them happen to pick up their right forks (or left forks) at the same time, they will all starve in a deadlock, because they will never put down a fork until finished eating.

Assure's example is misprogrammed on purpose. All five philosophers should be in a single thread, but they are in five separate threads. Sooner or later, they will deadlock.

- The rectangles demonstration shows a data race. One thread draws randomly sized rectangles, and another colors them blue by setting the red, green, and blue colors. Occasionally, because not all three colors are set before the next rectangle starts being drawn, you'll see a red square instead of a blue one.

- The counters demonstration shows synchronized and unsynchronized incrementing. There is one counter of each type. The synchronized counter always updates when a thread says to, but the unsynchronized one will miss an increment at times. What actually happens is that after an update, two threads can poll a variable at the same time, obtaining its value. Then each thread updates the unsynchronized counter with the same value. Instead, each thread should wait until an update, then in synchronized fashion obtain that variable's value.

Here's Assure's demo, after running a few minutes. The philosophers have not yet deadlocked, but they will. The square is red and the counters are not equal. The demo illustrates not the debugger but, rather, three kinds of errors you can expect Assure to trap.

When You Run Assure

Assure is menu-driven. You'll find the familiar menu items that let you open and close files; seek, view, and sort errors; set your preferences, etc. It has an excellent help system, which is fortunate because of the sheer number of its features.

Assure's main window lists your source code, with each line flagged by a color. The colors indicate Error, Caution, Warning, and OK. The window gives you a bar graph summary of errors. Here's a screen shot of the main window, taken from Assure's documentation.

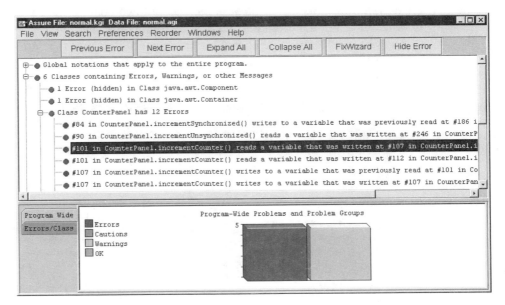

Have you ever wanted a compiler to include an option named "On Error, Fix?" Oh, dreamer!

It seems to me, however, that while a compiler can never fix all errors, any compiler that can detect the absence of a semicolon could insert that semicolon. It should tell you what it did, of course, in case the missing semicolon wasn't the true problem. Perhaps such a compiler could suggest the most probable fixes in a sorted drop-down box, and let you double-click on the one you desire.

Assure approaches that idea. It includes a FixWizard button in the main window's menu, which gives a more verbose error description, and when possible tells you ways to correct the problem. You still must incorporate the fix into your code.

You can hide all errors whose text matches that of any error you select. This hiding is rule-based, and you can edit the rules. For example, you might remove certain characters in a rule and generate a more general rule for hiding errors.

The Call Tree

Since Java is threaded, many errors that get past the compiler are state-dependent. That is, they occur with some combinations of program calls, but not with others. Assure records the exact call sequence that results in an error, and color codes them in its Call Tree window, shown next.

The Call Tree window lets you examine all method calls that have occurred in the current run. This hierarchical listing can help you determine coverage—that is, whether or not the program executed every module.

The window's entries are clickable, letting you follow through various methods backward until you find the most suspicious ones. This is an example of the Call Tree window:

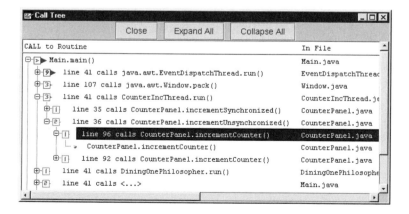

The Source Code Window

This window shows a screen of the analyzed program's source code, with one line boxed. The source code is syntax-colored for legibility. Line numbers are given, and icons indicate where errors probably are. If you click on a line in the call tree display, which was discussed in the last subheading, the Source Code window will display the line that called that method. Thus, you can follow the sequence of execution that led to your bug.

The preprogrammed error in the next illustration lets two threads receive the value of *unsynchCounter* simultaneously. When they do, they have identical values, and each one updates its variable to the same value. Instead, each thread should wait for an update to get a new value, so the various threads would always have different values.

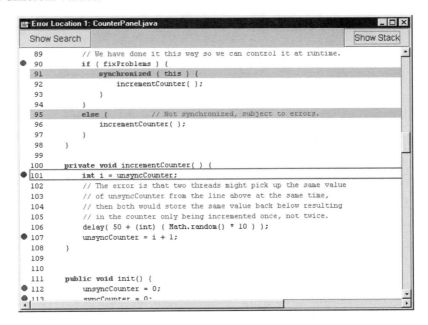

The Runtime Call Stack

Often, there are several ways that the program could arrive at an erroneous line, with only one of those paths able to cause an error. It's not enough to find one path; you need to find the erroneous one. Assure logs the exact sequence of method invocations that caused a particular error, and shows this information in the Stack window. The Runtime Call Stack window looks like this:

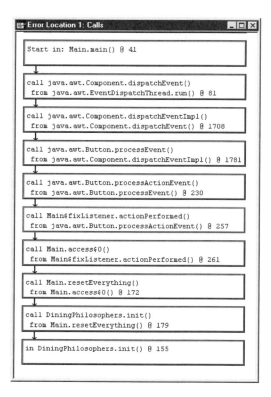

Assure is marketed by Kuck & Associates, Inc., a wholly owned subsidiary of Intel:

> 1906 Fox Drive
> Champaign, IL 61820-7345
> 1-888-524-0101 (KAI-0101) or (217) 356-2288
> 1-217-356-5199 FAX for Purchase Orders
> http://www.kai.com/assurej/ is their Web site. They accept MasterCard and Visa.

Assure comes with a 30-day money-back guarantee—if you're not fully satisfied, you can return Assure and they will refund your money. A 15-day free trial version is available for downloading.

JBuilder

Borland's JBuilder is far more than a debugger. It is a GUI, Integrated Development Environment (IDE). It is a set of visual development tools. JBuilder specializes in producing high-performance applets and applications, and in generating code that is remarkably free of excess verbiage.

JBuilder can build efficient, small systems, but it can also generate networked, database connectivity systems; client/server systems; and enterprise-wide, distributed multitier computing solutions. Its open architecture lets you add new JDKs, tools, add-ins, and JavaBeans to its tool set.

It can also import existing systems to let you enhance or debug them, but first it's best to turn them into Java Project (.jpr) files, the kind generated by JBuilder.

JBuilder's Debugger

JBuilder detects logic errors and runtime errors, leaving syntax errors to the compiler and programs like JLint.

Logic errors, as you know, cause your program to do something unexpected, such as take the wrong path. Variables may contain incorrect values, graphic images might look odd, or the output may be incorrect. Logic bugs are troublesome because they epitomize one of my "21 Laws of Programming": "The trouble is not where you are looking, or you would have found it by now." See Appendix C.

If your program compiles successfully but throws runtime exceptions, or hangs when you run it, you have a runtime error. Your program contains valid syntax, but the statements cause errors when they're executed. For example, your program might be trying to open a nonexistent file, or divide by zero. Runtime errors are a bit easier to find than logic errors are, because the program generally stops or hangs when it finds them. However, your only clues might be how the output looks or the contents of a cryptic error message.

 Some people group errors into two classes: compile time and runtime. They include logic errors into a class of bugs they call runtime errors.

Debuggers like the one in JBuilder are necessities for finding logic and runtime bugs, unless you enjoy things like line-by-line code reviews and receiving floggings.

The next illustration shows some source code from JBuilder's chess program example:

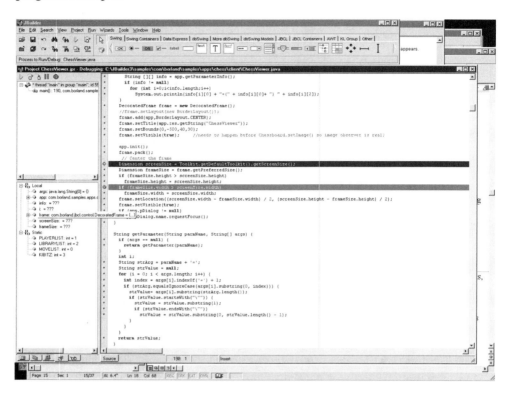

The mouse cursor is resting on a variable name, and the debugger has displayed the variable's value in a yellow box.

I have single-stepped the program to the **Dimension** statement, which is the top one highlighted. Below that, you can see another highlighted line. That one is a breakpoint, which would stop the code if it were running at full speed.

You have complete access to the JBuilder editor when the code is stopped. For example, this box shows that you can search for text:

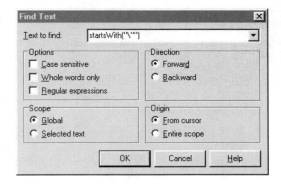

When you're debugging, it is often useful to know what classes are loaded. You might suspect that you're using the message box from the wrong class, for example. JBuilder shows you all loaded classes in a window like this:

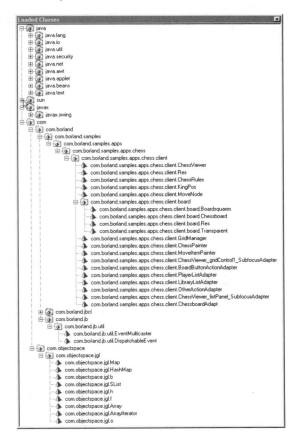

JBuilder in Practice

When you run your program under the control of the debugger, the program behaves normally. It displays windows, accepts user input, calculates values, and produces output. Graphical images move on the screen. The only differences are a slight decrease in performance, and the fact that you can stop the program to examine its variables and state.

You can pass parameters to a program, and you can use HTML with it, so you can debug applets.

When you run JBuilder's debugger, you'll notice that it adds two tabbed pages, named Debug and Watch, to the AppBrowser window. You can also access debugger features through the Run and View menus.

You can tell the debugger when or where to pause your program as it runs. When it stops, you can view the values of class variables, instance variables, local variables, method parameters, and properties (getter/setter method pairs). You can examine and change the values of data items with the following JBuilder windows (panes,) discussed in more detail later in this section:

- Threads and Stack pane
- Data pane
- Watch pane
- Inspector window
- Evaluate/Modify dialog box

You can even edit paused code!

The ability to change program data values is a powerful tool. You can change values according to what potential bug fixes might do, and test further. If your program runs properly, you can modify the code this time, save the breakpoints, and retest to see if the program still runs correctly. Then, when satisfied, you can remove the breakpoints, recompile, and proceed to the next test. Here's how easy it is to use JBuilder to debug existing programs.

To import an existing project, click File | Open in the main menu, then navigate to any .java file, such as one of the files included in your JDK. You will probably want to convert a .java file to a JBuilder Project (.jpr) file. You can actually open any text-based file, but .java and .jpr files are more interesting.

You'll immediately notice how comments are in green text and keywords are in bold font. Things like constants and quoted strings are in blue. You can change the colors to suit your fancy, or to agree with another program.

Compile it in JBuilder, using debugging information. To do that, click Project | Properties. On the Compiler page that appears next, check the Include Debug Information option.

Then compile by clicking Project | Rebuild (or Make, after you've initially compiled the program.) Alternately, you can click Run, which will compile your program if it needs it. You have toolbar buttons for all of these options. You don't have to leave JBuilder and go to the DOS prompt. The compiler will identify any syntax errors at this time. Fix any errors, and consider whether or not to fix any warnings. You can have JBuilder turn off all warnings, but I prefer to leave them turned on.

Two panes (windows) at the left, named Navigation and Structure, help you navigate through the program, by showing all classes, methods, objects, imports, etc. Clicking on any listed item takes you directly to it, or to its first line as appropriate.

Install a breakpoint by putting your cursor on a line and clicking Run | Add Breakpoint. Another method is to click the vertical bar to the left of the line. The line turns scarlet. Click the bar again to remove the breakpoint. F5 also sets a breakpoint.

The F7 function key is for "Trace Into." Thus, you can press F7, which compiles and runs the program, stopping it at the first executable line. F7 doesn't insert a breakpoint there; it merely executes the program's first line, doing any compiling it needs to do along the way. Repeatedly pressing F7 steps you through your program one line at a time. This is an excellent way to see that your code visits the correct methods.

To create the next illustration, I loaded Borland's sample chess program named ChessViewer and pressed F7 (Trace Into), which took the program to the first line. Then I clicked Run in the menu, to show the powerful debugging options you have.

You may also notice two extra tabs at the bottom left of the screen. Clicking on one will give you the Threads, Stacks, and Data pane, while clicking the other will show you the Watch pane where you can see the contents of specific variables. Back to the Run drop-down box:

which lists the following features:

- Run "ChessViewer" (F9) compiles and runs the program without debugging it. You can run partial programs by unchecking the Make Packages Stable option, after clicking Run | Parameters, and selecting the Compiler tab.

- Debug "ChessViewer" (SHIFT-F9) compiles and runs the program with debug options turned on.

The debugger mode also displays panes for viewing data watchpoints and such context information as threads and calls.

Parameters lets you establish various defaults. The next illustration shows how the debug parameters look on my test machine. Other tabs let you set JBuilder paths, compiler options, coding styles, and servlet paths.

- Step Over (F8) runs the entire methods and stops. This option is handy for getting to problem areas quickly. If you have several methods on a single line, a practice I don't recommend, F8 steps over them all. In a way, "step over" is a misnomer, because F8 does run each method. It just doesn't show you each line as it executes it, like F7 does.

- Trace Into (F7) runs one line at a time. F7 runs any library methods and other methods that do not contain debugging information at full speed and then stops. To examine a specific part of your program, you can disable Trace Into for all of the files used in your project and then enable Trace Into on just the files you want to trace.

- Run to Cursor (F4) lets you highlight a line and run just that far. You'll find this especially useful when you suspect a bug lies a few dozen lines away. You can page down, highlight a line, and press F4 to see if some crucial variable has changed value.

- Run to End of Method does just that. If you have traced into a method and have found that it does not contain the problem, this option quickly takes you back to the line immediately after the one that called the method.

- Show Execution Point is for the times you have paged all over the source code and want to return. You can also press F7, but that executes another line. Sometimes you don't want to execute any more code, because that would destroy the values in some critically buggy variables. Show Execution Point is for such situations.

- Pause, or CTRL-ALT-SYSRQ, may become your good friend. When you are debugging, a new Pause button also appears in JBuilder's Navigation pane. When your program is doing something forever, or at least doing it for a long time, you can click Pause or press CTRL-ALT-SYSRQ to stop it. You may have to press that key combination a number of times before you time it just right! However, when the program pauses, you'll be paused in the middle of your "do-a-long-time" code. At that point, you can single-step through the code and see why it "does-a-long-time."

- Program Reset (CTRL-F2) stops your program cold, closes all files, and releases its memory. You can't view the contents of variable things after you press CTRL-F2. However, it retains all breakpoints and watchpoints, to make it easier for you to resume debugging tomorrow. Borland mentions that when you have numerous exceptions, your program can become unstable. If this happens, you shouldn't merely reset the program. You should stop and reload JBuilder. When you are debugging, a new Stop button also appears in JBuilder's Navigation pane.

- Inspect lets you enter a symbol or an expression for JBuilder to evaluate. You can also right-click an expression to inspect it. Inspector windows are extremely valuable because they let you see the contents of variables, so long as they are still in the program's scope. They show the data in the original format. You can inspect an array or, via a second Inspector window, its details. If the array has too many elements for convenience, you can restrict the range by opening an Adjust Range box.

- Evaluate/Modify is the box that opens when you right-click an expression or variable. You can edit the value of a scalar variable by clicking on the value. A scalar is any single number. Highlight and right-click the variable, choose Modify Value, and enter the new value.

- Add Watch lets you tell JBuilder to monitor the value of a variable, and display that value when the program stops. Some debuggers use watches to stop the program when a variable assumes a particular value, or when it changes, but JBuilder reserves that idea for breakpoints. You can monitor all kinds of variables, and even save the results to a file for later inspection.

- Add Break lets you tell JBuilder where or why to stop. You can specify a line, a Boolean condition, or a pass count, which is the number of times the program goes past a certain line. An alternative way to set a breakpoint is to click on a line of code and press F5. You can use breakpoints and watchpoints in conjunction for powerful debugging tactics. Set a breakpoint for when a variable reaches a particular value, and set watchpoints to inspect all of the critical variables' values.

Of course, after working with such an excellent demo, one really must let it run to completion. Here's the chess game, in the middle of a Stonewall attack, black to move:

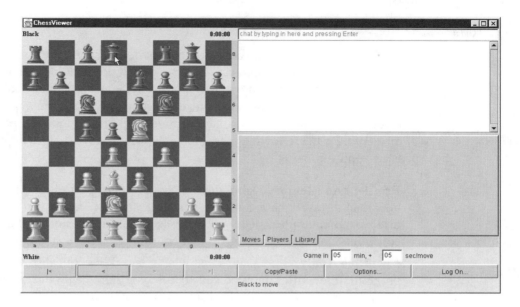

After working with such a powerful set of tools for a short while, it becomes difficult to recall how tough the old ways were. What JBuilder does is essentially the same as what the debuggers did when I taught computer science. It frees you from much of the drudgery and frustration inherent in finding bugs, helping you understand the language and your program much better. It gives you time to create better code, write sterling documentation, and generally impress your users.

JBuilder is marketed by Borland.Com, a Division of Imprise Corporation:

100 Enterprise Way
Scotts Valley, California 95066-3249
(831) 431-1000
http://www.borland.com

A light, but very capable, version is free for downloading.

JProbe

Whereas JBuilder is a complete development environment, JProbe concentrates on probing your applets and applications for errors. It does not include an IDE, but instead integrates seamlessly with Webgain!/Symantec's Visual Café and/or IBM's VisualAge. If you want to use one of these with JProbe, you must install it before you install JProbe so the installer can make all of the required linkages.

JProbe contains the following main elements, which work on java applets as well as on applications:

- **Profiler and Memory Debugger**   Records where your program has run, how long it stayed there, and how much memory it required while there. It discovers memory leaks (yes, they can occur in Java, despite garbage collection) and memory hotspots that consume excessive amounts of RAM.

- **Coverage Analyzer**   Ensures that you've tested the critical parts of your program. It identifies untested code before you ship the product, helping you prevent errors. Chapter 13 discusses JProbe's Coverage Analyzer.

- **Threadalyzer**   Identifies deadlocks, data races and thread stalls. This tool pinpoints their causes and locations in code, making it much easier to correct them. Chapter 11, "The Threaded Environment," discusses the JProbe Threadalyzer.

Profiler and Memory Debugger

The JProbe Profiler and Memory Debugger watches your program in execution, timing and counting. It allows you to use Just-In-Time (JIT) compilers, and provides a GUI front end so you can launch it from a remote computer. You can have it launch on a schedule and profile a program in the middle of the night, unattended. The Profiler and Memory Debugger lets you locate such things as:

- **Inefficient memory use, also known as memory hotspots**   These are areas in the program that temporarily consume large amounts of RAM. They are the sources of many performance problems, because the machine slows down when inordinate amounts of RAM are consumed. One reason is that a program may start using the hard disk swap file to alleviate its memory shortage. While the computer probably has plenty of swap space, a hard disk operates at least 1,000 times slower than RAM. Any time the computer needs to swap something to the hard disk, it slows by a factor of at least 1,000.

- **Inefficient algorithms** One of my "21 Laws of Programming" is that you should always use the most efficient algorithm. Do you wonder what kind of loop runs faster? Write a program that does nothing but loop, perhaps 100,000 times, using each kind of loop, and profile it. You'll find out quickly. Are you interested in which file access method is fastest? Profile them all and find out. How about conditionals. Is a nested **if** faster than the equivalent **switch**? Is a series of non-nested **if** constructs even faster? Profile them and see. Do comments really make no difference? Can you introduce all the whitespace you want? Can you put braces on separate lines with impunity? Does code run faster if you have several statements on a single line? The profiler will tell you. However, the profiler's main job is to tell you where your program is inefficient, or waiting on scarce resources.

- **Excessive creation of objects** This can cause "memory leaks." The garbage collector has its own timing, and you can't control it. You can influence when it will collect, but you can't control it. If you create too many objects, you increase RAM usage, and can force the computer to resort to using its hard disk swap file. That always slows things down. Many times a computer that seems to be locked has only been forced to swap huge amounts of programming in and out of the hard disk. If the hard disk light is glowing and the disk drive is beating its head against the stops, your computer may recover when the garbage collector reclaims enough RAM. That's why shutting down programs in a stuck computer can sometimes free it and let it return to normal.

- **Excessive method calling** If you find a method being called far too many times, look for ways to remove it from a loop or from recursion. See if it is being called but its results are not being used.

- **Input and/or output obstructions** A profiler will tell you if a method seems stuck on a port, because that method's execution time will be extremely high. This might be okay, because threads commonly wait at ports for messages. However, it might mean something else went astray and failed to make it to the correct port, at least on time.

- **Memory leaks** Leaks aren't actually leaks, but appear to be so. Objects that are not garbage-collected tie up RAM, so the available RAM is lessened. It's as if some of that expensive RAM has leaked off the motherboard.

The Profiler and Memory Debugger measures performance. You can turn on any or all of the following metrics:

- **Time each method takes to execute**   It makes little sense to improve a method's execution time by a factor of 1,000 when that method only takes 1/100th of a second to execute and another method takes 100 seconds to execute. Expend your effort on the consumptive methods. However, see the next point.

- **Number of calls**   If a method is called 1,000 times and takes one second each time, it's an expensive method that cries for optimization.

- **Number of methods called**   If you have 100 methods and only 30 are called during a test, your coverage is incomplete. The coverage analyzer needs to be run.

- **Average method execution time**   This metric is valuable when compared to individual execution times.

- **Average method object count**   The more objects a method keeps open, the harder it works the computer.

- **Average cumulative time**   This is the average time for a number of runs. You can run JProbe 20 times over your program and get an average. If one of the runs deviates significantly from the cumulative average, it bears investigation.

- **Average cumulative object count**   As in the previous bullet, this is an average over a number of runs.

- **Cumulative time**   The total time consumed by a number of runs.

JProbe gives you a color-coded graph showing what objects hold references to other objects. You can click and drill down on these objects, all the way to the source code.

The product also lets you take snapshots of the code's current performance, and of its memory usage. These data can be invaluable when compared with stack traces made at the same time. You can take snapshots manually, such as when a screen turns red, or you can set automated snapshot triggers. Method entry and method exit are particularly good places to set snapshot triggers.

You can save all snapshots, so you can analyze them later at a more leisurely pace. Lest you conjure up Frankenstein pictures of core dumps in your mind, JProbe is user friendly, not user vicious. Five powerful windows help you analyze your program's memory and performance. Each window has various ways to sort and select the pertinent data. The windows are described next.

Runtime Heap Summary

The Runtime Heap Summary (memory) window gives you a graph of how the heap was used in real time. You can see the heap size, memory usage, and objects created, sorted in various ways. Heap usage normally rises for a while and then, when garbage collection occurs, it falls. However, very frequent garbage collection may mean you have a problem. For example, a rogue thread may be generating too much garbage.

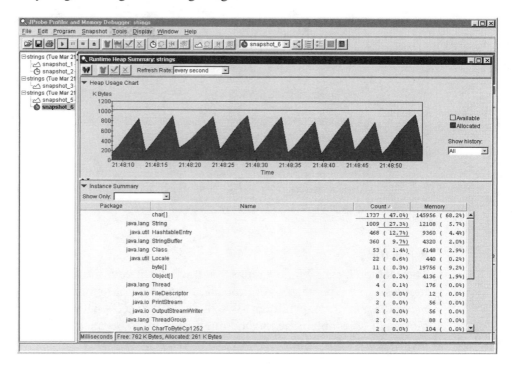

Call Graph

The Call Graph window shows the calling relationships between all of your methods. You can see which methods take the most time, or which ones create the most objects. In fact, the Call Graph highlights them for you by default. This lets you find your most expensive methods, so you can concentrate on panning pay dirt instead of mere dirt. You can position the cursor on these methods to drill down for more information. A drop-down box appears, listing the method's name and metrics.

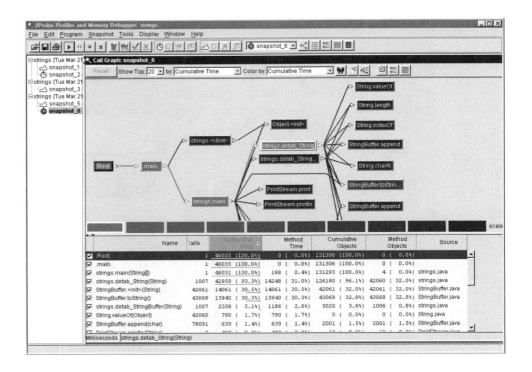

Method Detail

The Method Detail window helps you track down your most expensive methods. It gives you the percentage of time and the amount of memory allocation for any method's parents and children. You often want to see what parent or child has the most calls. A problematic method might only be so because it is being called unnecessarily, for instance.

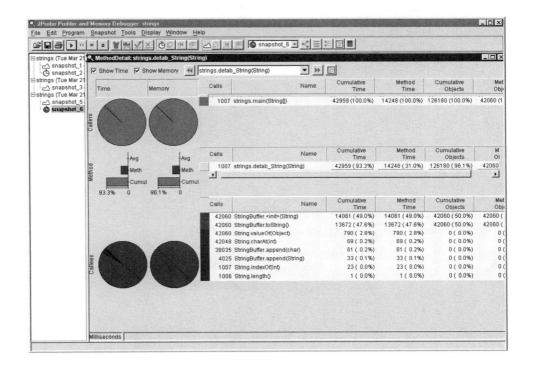

Heap Browser

The Heap Browser is a powerful tool for discovering memory leakers—that is, methods that stick around, doing nothing. This window gives summary and detail information about all objects in memory at any given time. It looks as follows:

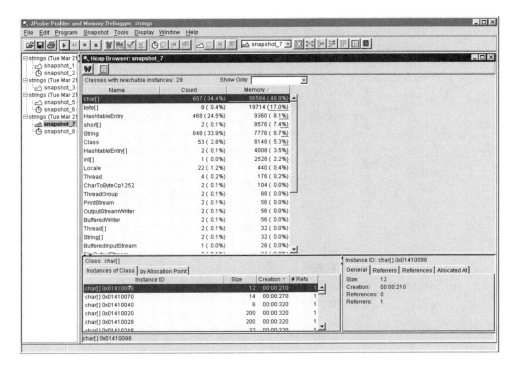

Source Code

The Source Code window may be the best tool of all. It tells you how long each line of your code takes to run, and how many objects are in memory. Each method has one line that is the most expensive, and the Profiler highlights it for your scrutiny. Expense is listed in terms of calls, method objects, and cumulative objects, as raw numbers or percentages. This window is the one that will tell you which kind of loop is fastest.

Threadalyzer

The Java designers deserve all the medals we can bestow on them for including threads. Multithreading is the most powerful aspect of Java, but it does come with a downside. You can't turn it off. This stubborn fact forces you to ensure all those autonomous threads don't interact improperly with each other.

While many Java classes are thread-safe, some (notably in Swing) are not. The reason is that thread safety ordinarily requires developers to use **synchronized** methods, which hurts performance. It's no trivial task to be sure your threads work perfectly and perform speedily.

At times, conflicting threads can ruin Java's lofty goal of "Write Once, Run Anywhere™."A program with potential deadlock problems may run fine on one JVM, but miserably on another.

JProbe's Threadalyzer seeks potential deadlocks, actual deadlocks, thread stalls or long waits, and data races. When it finds these conditions, it points you to the source code causing or potentially causing them. This obviously saves you debugging time.

Since Chapter 11 covers threads in detail, JProbe's Threadalyzer is discussed more fully there.

Coverage Analyzer

JProbe's Coverage Analyzer software measures how much code has been tested. Its reports make it easy to locate individual lines or modules of untested code. The software does the following:

- Identifies and quantifies untested code
- Uses advanced filters to define specific code to be tested
- Merges coverage data from multiple runs of your program
- Lets you browse, share, and print the results as text, or as HTML documents
- Helps you test server-side code (ServerSide Edition of JProbe Coverage only)

Chapter 13 discusses JProbe's Coverage Analyzer more fully. JProbe is marketed by KL Group, Inc.:

260 King Street East
Toronto, Ontario, Canada M5A 4L5
http://www.klgroup.com
(800) 663-4723
(416) 594-1026

Visual Café

This product is powerful in the extreme. Because of its breadth and depth, Visual Café is an excellent choice for an enterprise-wide development suite. It is far more than a debugger.

Visual Café's core capabilities are as follows:

- Visual, form-based development. If you're also a Visual Basic or Visual C++ developer, you'll enjoy this feature. Drag components onto forms and set their properties. Set connections to other objects, the databases, other networks, or the Web.

- Quick creation of component connections with the Interaction Wizard.

- Two-way development so that the visual tools and Java code always match. Change the code and the visual tools match. Change the visual tools and the code matches.

- Database connectivity through a three-tier architecture and the JDBC standard.

- Support for major database servers.

- Database wizards for simplified form development.

- Hierarchical view of database cataloging information with the dbNAVIGATOR.

- Simplified Java database connectivity through data-bound components. These components connect to a database automatically. You only need to tell the components what database, what tables, what fields, etc., to use.

- Backward compatibility for JDK 1.1, support for portable JavaBeans components and Java Archive (JAR) files. JAR files are compressed for smaller storage, yet they don't need to be decompressed for use, because Java reads them directly.

- Quick creation of component interactions.

- Integration with the Visual Page HTML editor. Make superb Web pages quickly.

- Fast compilation by way of WebGain!/Symantec's speedy, Just-In-Time compiler.

- An advanced debugger that includes expression evaluation.

The Visual Café debugger's features include the following:

- Syntax checking
- Drag and drop command execution
- Data tips
- Stop just before the first executable line
- Stop when you press the pause button

- Run to the cursor
- Run to the end
- Expression evaluation
- Conditional breakpoints
- Watch variables
- Graphical view or data structures
- Incremental debugging
- Method restarting
- Decompilation support

To use the Visual Café debugger, you must first compile your program, since the debugger works on .class files only. That's no problem, of course, because you can use the Visual Café JIT compiler. If the source code isn't available, you can use the decompiler to replicate it unless the source has been scrambled with an obfuscator program.

If you have the Professional or Enterprise edition, you can do runtime editing. That is, you can make code changes and press on without leaving the debugger. Visual Café recompiles, rebuilds, and saves your files automatically. Otherwise, you'll need to stop the debugger, recompile, rebuild, and then start the debugger again. Restarting the debugger is only a two-click process.

After editing a paused program, you can have the code continue from that point or pop back to the method that called the currently active method and issue another call. Visual Café saves the program's state when it calls methods. You'll use this feature abundantly, because it saves you from having to run through all of the various screens that brought you to the present error. Your program merely returns to the state it was in when it called the current method and lets you start debugging again.

Error Watch *Restarting the active method is not a total undo operation, because if the active method has caused side effects, they remain intact. For example, you may find that your current method has corrupted the contents of your variables enough that it's better to restart the program and run it to a breakpoint.*

Often enough, you'll find a problem and realize it's caused by a bug inside another method, which resides somewhere else in the call stack. When you edit, recompile, and save, you get a dialog box asking you to choose one of these options:

- Restart the entire program
- Restart the active method
- Continue the old code until the next time it becomes active, ignoring breakpoints until it becomes active
- Exit the debugger

The debugger even recommends an action for you.

If you're debugging native code, you can add new methods, but if you're debugging bytecode, you can't do that.

These windows assist you in resolving problems:

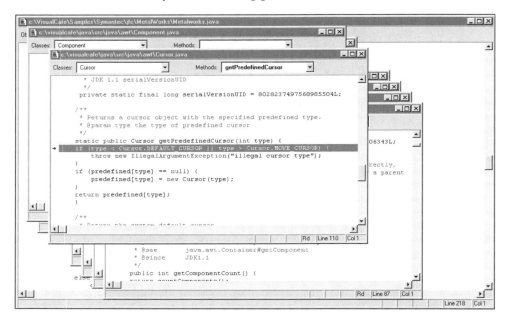

Source Code Window   Here, you can edit java source, HTML, or any text file. The Source Code window is always available when you're debugging, except that the window won't open if Visual Café doesn't have access to the source code you want to see.

You can examine variables and evaluate expressions by selecting them in the Source Code window. You can also tell the debugger what variables to watch, and you can modify breakpoints here.

Watch Window   You often want to see the contents of variables, and this window shows them anytime you pause your program. When the program is paused, you can enter any variable's name and if it is in scope, you see the contents.

You can drag a variable from the Source Code window to the Watch window, or use cut and paste, or type its name.

When you want to test the program with some variable near its limits, this window can become extremely convenient because you can set the variable contents here. If you have an integer that must not go below zero, for instance, you can test it at 1, 0, and –1 to see that the program performs sanely in all conditions.

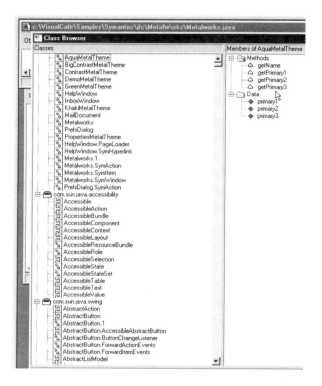

Class Browser   This three-pane window lists the following:

- The Java classes in your project. This and the next pane support keyboard incremental searches. As with Visual Café's help system, when you type a character, the pane immediately lists everything that matches that character. Type a second character, and the list refines itself while you type further, until you've found what you seek. Life should be so easy! A variety of filters and views help you find what you want.

- The methods and data members in each class. Use keyboard incremental searches here as well.

- The source code for that class. You can edit any code that's currently in scope.

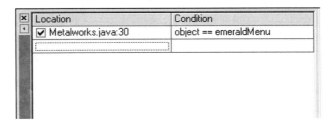

Breakpoints Window   This window lists all currently defined breakpoints in the entire project. This is an add/change/delete window. You can also disable one or more breakpoints without removing them. A check box next to each breakpoint tells whether or not it's enabled.

Set simple breakpoints that stop the run at a particular line or method by clicking that line, by entering a line number or method name, or by pressing F9 with the cursor in that line or method.

Set complex breakpoints that halt your program, based on some condition becoming **true**. You can use any legal Java condition, such as **(a >= 1000)** or complex conditions such as **(((a == "Here") or (b == "There")) and ((c <= 0) or (c >= 1000)))**.

Error Watch   *These conditional expressions are evaluated! If you erroneously write* **(a = "Here")** *instead of* **(a == "Here")** *you'll assign "Here" to a, instead of comparing a to "Here". This is a sure way to confuse yourself, because later the comparison* **(a == "Here")** *will succeed, even though your program never did assign "Here" to a. The debugger did it!*

When your program pauses, you can step line by line, step into a method, step over a method, or step out of the current method to the one that called it. Often, you'll want to step into a method to see how it handles itself. Just as often, you won't. For example, the **println()** method works correctly and is complex. It's senseless to step into it every time your code comes to it. If you mistakenly step into it, you can always step out.

Design Tip   *Just once, you might want to step into such methods as* **println()** *that are known to be correct to see how they work. This can help you understand the Java language better.*

Handily, Visual Café saves breakpoints along with the source code. The next time you open the project, your carefully formed breakpoints are intact, along with their active/inactive status.

Design Tip *Some other kinds of debuggers set conditional watchpoints, using the same process as setting conditional breakpoints in Visual Café. If you want to see the contents of several variables whenever some condition becomes **true**, Visual Café makes that easy, because the Variables window is viewable when the program pauses.*

Variables	Type	Value
incRate	static int	100
TOP_ALIGNMENT	public static final float	0.0
CENTER_ALIGNMENT	public static final float	0.5
BOTTOM_ALIGNMENT	public static final float	1.0
LEFT_ALIGNMENT	public static final float	0.0
RIGHT_ALIGNMENT	public static final float	1.0
serialVersionUID	private static final long	-764411451271461975O
serialVersionUID	private static final long	461379757891990634 3
WHEN_FOCUSED	public static final int	0
WHEN_ANCESTOR_OF_FOCUSED_COMPONENT	public static final int	1
WHEN_IN_FOCUSED_WINDOW	public static final int	2
UNDEFINED_CONDITION	public static final int	-1
KEYBOARD_BINDINGS_KEY	private static final String	"_KeyboardBindings"
TOOL_TIP_TEXT_KEY	public static final String	"ToolTipText"

Context: com.sun.java.swing.JComponent.<init>()

For Help, press F1

Variables Window   Here, you can examine all variables that are currently active. This includes globals, locals, objects, array elements, and simple data types. You can also check a variable's type, which can be revealing information when, say, a large number suddenly goes negative. That change often indicates an overflow condition. If the variable is an **int**, you can change it to a **long**, recompile, and see if it still goes negative.

If you want to change the value of a variable at runtime, you can do so in this window.

Design Tip *The Variables window can be an invaluable testing tool. Remember how bugs cluster around limits? You can use this window to reset a variable's value near, at, or past a limit, to check that your program performs properly during all of those conditions.*

×	Method	Class	VM
	getPredefinedCurso	java.awt.Cursor	main
	<init>()	java.awt.Component	main
	<init>()	java.awt.Container	main
⇨	<init>()	com.sun.java.swing.JCo	main
	<init>()	com.sun.java.swing.Ab:	main
	<init>()	com.sun.java.swing.JM	main
	<init>()	com.sun.java.swing.JM	main
	<init>()	Metalworks	main
	main()	Metalworks	main
	run()	symantec.tools.debug.N	main

Calls Window   Like any Virtual Machine (VM), Visual Café maintains a call stack. If method A calls method B, which calls method C, the call stack could be thought of as being like a stack of dinner plates with C on top and A on bottom. When method C returns to its caller B, the VM removes C from the stack, leaving only B on top of A. Thus, it's relatively easy for the debugger to show you a list of all methods leading up to the currently active one. It merely dereferences the call stack.

Design Tip   *Examining the call stack helps you find many kinds of problems. For instance, you might notice that a parameter is erroneous, and need to know which method called the current method with a bad value. Merely check the call stack via this window.*

You will find the call stack invaluable for another reason. You can display the contents and the types of all parameters passed to each method on the stack. You can also see the values and types of all variables that are within the program's current scope.

Want to see the source code of a method on the call stack? No problem. You're about two clicks away from it.

Hierarchy Editor

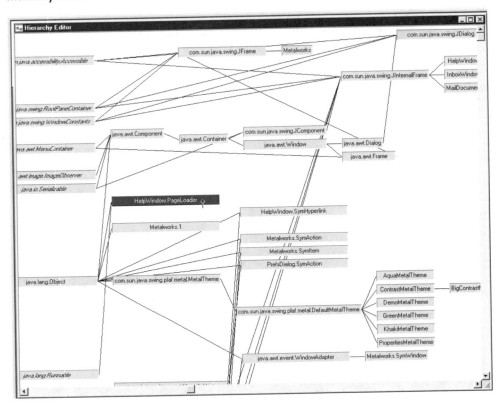

This graphical window shows everything that calls anything else. If you double-click on an item, you go directly to that item's code.

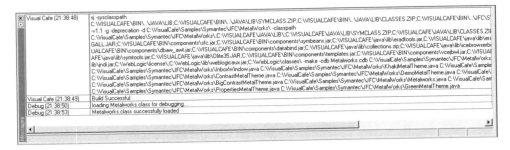

Threads Window   This window is indispensable when you have more than one thread running, which is the case in almost any useful program. In the Enterprise edition, it's called the Processes window. Sometimes, when I want to evaluate an odd expression, such as the 30th number in the Fibonacci series, I'll write and run a tiny, single-threaded Java program instead of popping up the calculator. However, most Java programs have at least two threads.

The Threads window lists all currently existing threads, along with their states. You can click any thread to select it.

 If a user-created thread you seek isn't in the list, that thread has not come to a breakpoint yet.

You can examine the source code for any thread in the list. You can also tell the Calls window or Variables window to update itself with the current thread's call stack or variables.

You can even see a particular thread's call stack.

Your program has a primary thread, which the Threads window annotates with a bold arrow in the margin. This is the thread that the operating system creates when it creates the application. A nonbold arrow indicates the thread from which the debugger grabbed control.

The window lists thread numbers, and the status (frozen or thawed) of each thread. You can suspend a thread or resume it. Suspending a thread can help you discover whether or not that thread is participating in a deadlock or data race. You can suspend or resume any or all threads with a couple of mouse clicks.

Messages Window   This is the window that displays all informational and error messages from Visual Café. It can also display anything you write to System.out so you don't have to go to DOS to see those messages. You can double-click any message and go to whatever generated it, a very useful feature. You can configure it to show or hide the following:

- Itself and/or other windows
- Progress messages that appear as the compiler works
- Compiler warnings
- Deprecated classes and members the compiler encounters
- File dependencies such as imports

- The Sun Java compiler's self-diagnostics
- The first part of each message, such as "Compiling with SJ…"

Hiding various options saves compile time. Showing them obviously gives you more information to help you debug your program.

Exception Handling

When the Java runtime system finds an error, the current method creates an exception component and passes it to the runtime system, which tries to find the code to handle the error. The Java system looks for the proper **catch** block, one that matches the exception's name. If none is found by the time the system returns to itself, the Java system handles the error by terminating the Java program and the runtime system as well.

You can set your own exceptions and tell the program to stop when any exception—yours, the program's or Java's—is thrown. In this case, the program pauses for you, whether or not the exception is caught and handled.

Visual Café's Remote Debugging Ability

You are not restricted to debugging on the development machine, or even the machine into which you've plugged your keyboard. On the contrary, you can debug a number of VMs simultaneously, by merely attaching to them. Visual Café Enterprise is designed for exactly this idea.

The computers have to be networked together with TCP/IP. The computer you're debugging does not have be running Windows. You can debug to a computer running a different VM than Visual Café uses.

The class files you are debugging must reside on the remote machine, and have to have been compiled for debugging. The project and source files need to be on the local computer.

Error Watch   *Visual Café doesn't let you debug native applications or DLLs remotely.*

Debugging via a Waiting Debug VM   When a Debug VM has not yet launched a Java program, it's known as a "Waiting VM." It can reside either on a local or a remote computer. Visual Café lets you attach your current debug session to such a Debug VM. Visual Café sends the main class filename to the VM, starting the program from the very beginning.

There are times you will want to use this technique of starting a remote program from the beginning, rather than debugging a work in progress. For example, you might need to enter a specific user ID and password.

Attaching to a Running Program   The VM you are debugging must be running in debug mode. It can either be on a remote computer or the local one. By clicking File | Attach to Process, you can debug it. The source files can be on either VM.

Many people use this technique to test cross-platform compatibility, and that the application or applet runs okay with various JDKs. This technique also lets you ensure that all of the system resources are available on the other machine.

Design Tip   *We have various kinds of CDs available for our Clean Machine, so we can quickly install most operating systems and environments. If we need a new environment, we generate a new CD for our Clean Machine. Often, we run directly from the CD, which is about four times as large as the hard disk and not too much slower!*

Run In Debugger   Just as easily as starting a local program in debug mode, you can start a remote program in this mode. You merely specify the remote computer and its program name. In this case, you don't use the local machine's class loader. Instead, you use the class loader for the remote machine. That can be an important distinction if, for example, you want to check the class loader's performance, or you want to use classes that Visual Café doesn't support directly.

24x7

I installed a very limited computer onto our network. We call it the "Clean Machine." It acts as a lowest common denominator for developmental testing. Anyone may use it for any purpose, but a sign states that unless they post a note when they leave the keyboard, anyone else is free to reformat the hard disk for another purpose. The idea is that if a program will run on this physically limited machine, it will probably run fine on the customer's system. You probably have such a $50 machine lying about, awaiting salvage. Add an obsolete network card and an old CD-ROM, and you're set.

Attaching to Multiple Programs   When you are debugging a multitier system, Visual Café's ability to attach to several VMs becomes invaluable. You can set things so the product will attach to various processes automatically. This way, as a tier becomes active, you can examine it thoroughly.

You can choose to start your debugging session from within a Visual Café project, or from the command line.

Visual Café is marketed by Webgain!/Symantec:

20330 Stevens Creek Blvd.
Cupertino, CA 95014
1 (888) 822-3409
e-mail: sales@webgain.com
http://webgain.com/Purchase

CHAPTER 9

Debugging Stratagems

It's interesting that this book exists in a near vacuum. There is almost no published information on debugging Java, and not much on debugging in general for that matter. That's interesting, but not too surprising. Would you rather show your friends a clever applet that flashes and dashes across the screen, or the equally clever, but broken, line of code you wrote and then had to fix? Programmers don't like to debug, even though most spend up to half of their time doing it.

It makes sense, then, to improve your debugging strategies, so you'll have more time to create flashy, dashy programs. Debugging, like testing, benefits from doing things the smart way, and from using the best resources available.

Assemble the Best Resources

"My program's acting funny."

"Okay, ...'

"No, it's not okay at all."

Sometime a voice can sneer. "Yes-s-s, I understand that. What's it doing funny?"

"It's not acting like it did last month."

"Nobody has touched that program in six months."

"I told you about the problem a week ago, and it's going to get serious quickly."

The conversation outside my office was becoming heated and heading downhill fast, so I invited the antagonists in. I asked someone else if he'd please bring in four cups of coffee and join us.

The user, a departmental manager with his Ph.D. in engineering, had noticed some small, but important, anomalies in aggregate results. As a result, certain valves opened $1/10^{th}$ of a second too early or too late. To fix the program, the software developer needed specific answers that the user could not supply.

An afternoon's investigation revealed that the user's program had not received any daily data from a remote site in two weeks! Someone had quit and their computer had been renamed. That broke a script. Fortunately, the serving computer archived everything, so resetting the script restored matters to sanity.

Bug Isolation

The problem was that neither the engineer nor the programmer had enough information, alone, to isolate the bug. When they pooled their talents, they were able to "box the bug."

After you've identified the fact that you have a bug, your first goal is to isolate it. Box it. Constrain it into smaller and smaller boxes until you can see it.

The diminishing-size boxes are usually pieces of code, but that's not always the case. They can be pieces of time. Some bugs might only occur at midnight. Others might occur at least three seconds after a particular thread starts, or when certain threads are operating simultaneously and your shoes are tied. Well, probably not the last condition, unless that also implies it's daytime.

With Java's remote capabilities, and the pervasive use of networks, the bug boxes might be physical. You might need to localize a bug to a particular subnet or computer. In other cases, the boxes include, or are, people. It may be that one person has a preferred, even undocumented, method of operation that nobody else uses, and that method happens to expose a bug nobody else sees.

Somewhat more often, bugs are data related, and you can squeeze the boxes until you can see the bug feeding on data in a particular set of related tables, or even one record. An accountant called me one day with a program crash. She knew what record had caused the crash, and it turned out to have a null input field. The program had been running two years without a glitch, and there were hundreds of ways that field could have gone to null instead of zero. I asked her to change a field to a zero if it happened again. In the meanwhile, I installed a trap to change nulls to zero and log about 20 facts the next time a null came across the wire. Months later, my trap contained a bug, and the data told me the bug was in a supplier's computer. The fix was a phone call away.

No matter what kind of boxes you use, you need to isolate the bug. Sooner or later, you'll probably isolate it to a small section of improperly written code, which should have trapped for erroneous data conditions, methods of operation, timing, or security conditions over the network. Then you can squash the bug.

Programs that abort are being friendly in one way. They usually tell you where they aborted. The bug is usually nearby, and it's almost certainly not past the abort point! Such programs help you isolate the bug.

Programs that merely make mistakes are more tedious to fix, because the searching process can take much longer. There are, however, ways to shorten the search process. It's obviously important to adopt the most cost-effective ways to debug your program.

The next discussion begins with the ridiculous and ends somewhere short of the sublime, as we survey debugging strategies.

Start Changing Things

I arrived at work to find my client had preceded me by an hour. He and I had assembled a small network for development. Windows NT on his PC had grown more flaky than usual, so he decided to save his work on my machine and reinstall NT on his. He moved my work to a backup directory, moved his work to my working directory, and was formatting his hard drive.

I quickly discovered that while the directories were intact, the files were all corrupted, and four weeks worth of work was in jeopardy. You do know, don't you, that Murphy invented computers? Minutes later, the server's hard disk ground to a halt, and all of the backups disappeared. We later speculated that the server was actually the cause of his NT problems.

Nearly everyone falls into a trap like that. I did, once, and then threw out the $200 tape drive that failed me. A few fortunate people hear about someone doing that and bypass the error.

When you have a problem, never just try changing things—especially if doing so could jeopardize anything whatsoever. About the only thing less effective and more dangerous is to turn the source code and keyboard over to a monkey.

Instead, realize that computer programs seldom spoil. Sit back and turn on the brain. Seek the safest way out of your dilemma. If you can back everything up, be sure to test the backup.

Even if the changes are safe, don't make them without investing some thought first. There are five reasons:

- The phrase "trial and error" does not include any form of the word "succeed," and that's significant. A trial-and-error process has a very small chance of success.

- Trial and error has an excellent chance of introducing more bugs. Change A appears to move the program further along, then change B appears to help further. Ten changes later, you discover that you're up a blind alley and the only way out is to reverse all of those changes, which you hope you can recall.

- Your chances of fixing the whole problem are only about 75 percent.

- Trial and error takes an inordinately long period of time.

- Here is the most important reason. If you have no idea why your bug fix worked, that bug will, and I emphasize, *will*, bite you again!

The Shotgun Approach

Use this only when you want to consume a lot of time.

Sequential Println() Statements

One shotgun method resorts to sprinkling **System.out.println();** statements, rather evenly, throughout your classes, hoping you'll come across an odd value in a variable. It looks similar, but is very different from another approach: using binary searches. The shotgun tactic has several flaws:

- You must analyze a prodigious amount of data.

- Almost none of the data is related to the bug.

- As in physics, you can't measure anything without changing it. The **println()** statements change things, especially thread timing.

- The large number of **println()** statements can obscure or cause other bugs.

- The **println()** statements must be keyed somehow to the source code to be meaningful later.

The tactic has merit in one specific case. If the program aborts, the last **println()** statement may have useful information. However, the shotgun approach is best reserved for the times when you've tried every other avenue, with zero results. In other words, never!

Debugging via Reasoning

A detective was asked if the police were really as smart as the TV cops. He replied, "No, but the crooks aren't as smart as the crooks on TV either."

Occasionally, I've likened our profession to detective work. Top detectives know that they seldom find suspects by circulating sketches or putting up extremely expensive roadblocks everywhere. On the contrary, they use established procedures that they know produce good results. They supplement standard police work with ample applications of gray matter, and as a last resort, on particularly heinous crimes, they use the shotgun approach. Reasoning is what solves most crimes.

Most reasoning comes in two forms: general to specific, and specific to general.

General to Specific, or Inductive Reasoning

When you're seeking a bug, probably one whose existence testing has revealed, begin the inductive reasoning process by using the following approach.

Gathering Information   Negative information can be as revealing as positive. The fact that the program ran okay last Monday might be as important as the fact that it fails while Chris was logged on. Continue by seeking patterns, as described below.

Seeking Patterns   Bugs are deterministic. In threaded languages, they can seem to be nondeterministic, but without some kind of random generator, they cannot be. Mathematicians generally agree that pure randomness is impossible, so program bugs are deterministic. That is, the same pattern of conditions will always duplicate a bug.

Okay, that was theory. In practice, the patterns can be so complex that the bugs might as well be random—that is, without pattern. Look for patterns anyhow.

In particular, look for things that repeat, and look for ways to break seeming patterns. See if you can find a Monday when the program fails, or a time that it works with Chris logged on.

Until you have patterns, you have little hope of proceeding. Until you find patterns, keep gathering information.

Not long ago, an accountant noticed occasional small errors in the general ledger. No specific entry was in error, just the sum of several thousands of entries. The errors could have come from hundreds of places, so after looking at data for a couple of hours, I suggested that we needed more information.

Soon, it became apparent that the errors only occurred during reversing entries. That pattern isolated the bug to one-third of the program. Later, the accountant was able to point to specific reversing entries of $0.01 and then another of $0.30 that didn't resolve correctly. She tried several reversing entries and demonstrated the patterns.

Armed with those patterns, a colleague of mine generated two hypotheses, disproved one, proved the other, and solved the problem handily.

Generating Hypotheses   When patterns emerge, it generally takes very little effort to think of possible hypotheses. They fairly leap out at you. In fact, the mental process of pattern-to-hypothesis-to-bug is often instantaneous, and so compelling that people can jump to wrong conclusions. It's important to prove or disprove the hypotheses, usually with test cases. In the general ledger problem, disproving one hypothesis gave my colleague the correct solution, when he might have gone down the wrong path.

Proving Hypotheses   What if there are two causes for seemingly related errors? I've seen programs with two bugs that cancelled each other except for rare conditions of data. If you get one of those, fixing one bug makes things much worse, tempting you to remove a fix that was actually correct!

In the accountant's problem above, what if one error had caused the penny error and another caused the 30-cent error? Repairing only one would not suffice.

It wasn't quite the case, but this could also have happened: One of my colleague's hypotheses could have explained the two errors the accountant saw, while the other explained those as well as suggesting other errors. Actually, there were other errors the accountant had not uncovered, and my colleague's second hypothesis suggested them. Further testing proved one hypothesis and disproved the other. Only then did he apply the repair.

Specific to General, or Deductive Reasoning

In this logical method, the first steps are reversed, but the result is the same: one proven hypothesis. The method is as follows:

Write Down Hypotheses   Consider all reasonable causes for the bug, especially half-baked but reasonable causes. Even toss in some of the off-the-wall possibilities.

Eliminate the Impossibilities   In the accountant's problem, the one-cent error suggested the slight possibility of intentional embezzlement, via rounding errors. You've heard of the story of how an embezzler sent fractions of a cent into his bank account, unnoticed, and then absconded with the money. When the accountant discovered the 30-cent errors, that entire hypothesis took a far back seat. However, it was not impossible, so my colleague didn't eliminate it.

Early hypotheses included all kinds of data entries, but soon the accountant discovered that errors only occurred during reversing entries. That pared away two-thirds of the problem.

Other hypotheses considered the possibility of two entries differing by $0.01 or $0.30, but testing showed that a single reversing entry of $0.01 produced an error.

Some of the original hypotheses may be half-baked, and in need of refinement before you can prove or disprove them. You may never be able to prove or disprove some of them. However, select the most likely hypothesis and try to prove it.

Prove the Hypothesis   In this step, proceed exactly as you do in the general-to-specific or inductive method. Design one or more tests that always duplicate the bug.

Binary Bug Searches

Once when I was the "visiting expert"—you know, the person whose reputation is directly proportional to the miles traveled—a manager asked me why he should use a binary search instead of a sequential one in his five-hour data-processing program. I picked up his phone book and asked him to find his name, which he did quickly. Then I asked him to locate it by searching sequentially, exhaustively, through page 1, then page 2, etc. He nodded his understanding, and I showed him how to write binary record searches. His revised program ran in about three seconds, and in gratitude he bought me a steak dinner that night.

Within reason, try to use binary-style searches for bugs, because you can find the critters thousands of times faster. If you have a large program with a dozen threads, and the program doesn't abort when it makes an error, you might try installing break points at the beginnings, middles, and ends of only half of the suspicious threads. That would give you a reasonable number of breakpoints. Then examine variables when the program suspends. If you find no errors, try half of the other half of the suspicious threads. You should quickly find the errant thread, and even know which half of the thread is causing the problem.

That may give you enough information, or you might want to install a few breakpoints in the offending half of that thread and refine your search a couple more times. At some point, you may want to step sequentially through the code, looking for the spot where something unusual happens.

When debugging a GUI program, you can use pop-up boxes to tell you about the program as it executes. As mentioned earlier, you can adopt a binary manner in deciding where to place them. Otherwise, you'll be building pop-ups until the deadline is past.

In a GUI program, you might write a special thread that continuously displays the values in a list of variables. It could check each one according to some logic you specify, and turn any variable red when it goes outside any bounds you set. It could suspend the program based on other conditions, pinpointing the problem area.

If you write that thread, don't throw it away. Generalize it with parameters or a small database and use it in all of your projects.

Backtrack

If you find an erroneous value at a breakpoint, the bug is probably between that breakpoint and the one previous. However, you should also identify all of the ways that some other thread could affect the code between those breakpoints. Another thread may have changed your variable.

Throw Exceptions

Because an exception is nothing more than a signal from one part of a program to another, you should make good use of exceptions. For example, if a variable should never go negative, you can have your code throw an exception if that ever happens. If a string's length should not exceed 50 characters, you can throw an exception when it does. You should write those kinds of exceptions in your program anyhow, so your system can handle bugs in a very user-friendly manner.

During debugging, you might throw an exception if a variable exceeds a million, even though a million might be a valid value. That can let you examine the program and see if it handles larger numbers correctly. You might throw an exception if a timer goes beyond ten minutes, or if a particular computer or user logs on.

View exceptions not so much as errors, but as signals that something interesting happened. Unless an exception is actually caught, it costs you nothing in performance. So, use them.

Temporarily Synchronize

If you suspect a foreign thread is changing your variables when it should not, **synchronized** is an easy way to stop it temporarily. You can synchronize and unsynchronize entire methods until the problem disappears, and then synchronize in a binary fashion until you localize the bug's entrance.

Sometimes the failure to use **synchronized** is the bug, and your work is done. Sometimes, using **synchronized** is the bug!

Be aware that using the **synchronized** keyword invariably costs your program some performance and makes it less robust. When a thread encounters **synchronized** code, the thread suspends and is unable to do any further processing until released. At that point, your program becomes susceptible to a deadlock or a stall. The **synchronized** keyword causes what's known as a spin-lock. Spin-locks are simple to implement and use, but they are the least efficient means known for managing conflicts. Chapter 11 will demonstrate several better methodologies.

Beware of Regression

Please don't just fix the bug! Prove that the program now works properly, but take another vital step. Test for regression. Regression testing is important in sequential programs, but it is orders of magnitude more important in threaded ones.

It shouldn't be surprising, but it always is, how many times fixing a bug introduces a new one—or uncovers one that was hidden in the same area. Be sure your program has moved forward toward perfection, instead of taking a step backwards.

Bugs cluster and nest. Where you find one, redouble your search in that area. Your chances of finding more are much greater there than elsewhere.

I'll say it one more time for emphasis, because this is such a critical point that I should write it thrice. Where you find one bug, others lurk.

A regression test saves the state of a program before and after the bug fix. Then it compares the two states. The comparison should reveal that not only has the program progressed where the bug was squashed, the system doesn't exhibit new errant behavior. That is, it hasn't regressed in some other area.

The reason that threaded programs are more sensitive to this phenomenon called regression is the possibility that other threads may interact with the thread being repaired. If they depend on the changed thread's new state, they might begin acting poorly.

Regression testing programs for other computer languages automate this kind of debugging. Typically, a regression tester will show you all variable contents that changed from one run to the next, the next being with the repaired code.

JTest and JProbe contain regression testers, which improve with every new release. These are the features I expect you will find in commercial products in the near future. Many of these features are already available. A key design point will be to make the program as unobtrusive as feasible, because the very act of measuring something changes it. Hopefully, the changes will be imperceptible.

User Interaction   The user will have several ways to trigger snapshots. Pressing a user-defined hotkey, for example, or clicking a command button with the CTRL key depressed, will trigger one. The user will be able to set static snapshots, like setting breakpoints, when user-specified conditions become **true**. As with cameras, time-delayed snapshots can be valuable. The user might want one 0.5 seconds after an event fires, for example.

The user will be able to limit the scope of a snapshot, but the default state will be to examine everything.

Typically, the user will want to take snapshots at one of five times:

- The start of a process
- The end of a process
- While something modal is happening, such as while a window is awaiting input
- When some condition becomes **true**
- A specific time period after something happens (event fires, condition becomes **true**)

Program Initialization   The program will examine the code for the names of all variables within any scope the user has specified. It will write these variable names, not their contents, to an array. It will initiate and suspend a snapshot thread, which knows what scope the user has specified.

Snapshots   When a snapshot is triggered, the thread will awaken. The program will retrieve the variable names from its array and save the current contents of them all. It will also save key environment data, such as the date and time and/or other run identification. At user request, it might list the threads running, threads frozen, etc. Then the thread will suspend, awaiting the next trigger.

Review   At review time, the program will compare the results of two or more runs the user specifies. When the contents of any variable have changed, the program will identify the variable and the two runs. Some statistical analysis might be applied. For example, the program might sort the output by variable name, class name, variable contents, or percent of change in the variable's value.

At user option, the entire set of variables and their contents will be available. The user should be able to flag variables as nonreportable.

Of course, the program will be able to save the results to disk, present reports, publish to email, etc. Since sensitive data might be involved, there should be provisions for removing all references to specific variables, at initiation, at runtime, and at review time.

Testing

Forgive me if I left the wrong impression in Chapter 1. It's true that testing, alone, cannot possibly lead you to all bugs. However, intelligent testing remains your most important tool for showing that bugs exist.

Testing during the debugging phase serves a different purpose. It attempts to prove or disprove hypotheses. You can generate new tests, or you can refine existing test cases, becoming more and more specific with your tests.

As noted earlier in this chapter, you should use a binary-style refinement. As a trivial example, say you know there's an erroneous number somewhere between 1 and a million. First, eliminate half a million possibilities, then half of the remainder, etc. In 20 binary tests, instead of a million sequential ones, you will have isolated the number.

Write Test Stubs

Java 2 has more than 5,000 classes. Other vendors have added thousands more, and you've created not a few of your own. Choosing the best class for a task can be a daunting task, especially since some of the classes are imperfectly documented. In defense of the class authors, perfect documentation is as elusive as perfect programming. However, that fact fails to make your choice easier.

When you need to choose from several possible classes, a test stub often helps. Write a small program that implements the class, runs it with input, and presents the output data that interests you. Often, you will seek information about performance or side effects.

A profiler, such as the ones included in JTest and JProbe, can tell you how much memory and time the class consumes. By setting breakpoints, you can see the values of variables. By adding various threads, and by running other classes, you can check interaction. When the data is extensive, your stub should save the data to a disk or printout.

When you have enough data, insert a different class into your test stub, and repeat the process.

Never discard your test stubs! Archive them, because you'll want to use them again, usually with modifications. Archive the modifications and build a library of test stubs. I've written hundreds of test stubs to prove or disprove points for this manuscript.

Right about now, my popularity halo is going to slip some ten degrees to the right. Oh well, that has happened before. Document those test stubs! Invest the brainpower necessary to invent long, descriptive names for your files, classes, and variables. Never use names like test1, test2, and test3. If you do, I'll know, and you'd better hope your gorilla is bigger than the one I'll send to thrash you.

Use Javadoc. Run your Javadoc to make sure it says meaningful things about your test stubs. Then, file and index your Javadoc results.

Use a "Holey" 3 × 5 card deck, or write a searchable JDBC application to contain your results.

In any critical pursuit—be it aviation, firefighting, mountain climbing, or meeting a deadline—minutes and seconds can become precious. Many is the pilot, fire fighter, or mountain climber who, given five seconds at a critical time, could have saved his or her life. Pilots, fire fighters, and mountain climbers gladly spend hours (even years) of preparation and practice, knowing that their preparation can yield a few lifesaving seconds of time.

When you're up against a deadline, the preparation you've put into such systems as your library of test stubs can save you a critical hour or week. So, while you have time freedom, prepare for when you will not. As you know, you must avoid time pressure, because it creates hosts of bugs.

Examples   "Hello world!" is the trivial test stub. Millions of programmers have used it to demonstrate to themselves that they could write a tiny program in some language, usually C. In Java, it looks like this:

```
public class helloworld; {
  public static void main (String args[]) {
    System.out.println("Hello world!");
  }
}
```

You knew that. It can become your first test stub. The next can be a slight modification that proves some syntax works. Here's another trivial example:

```
public class helloworld; {
  public static void main (String args[]) {
    int a, b;
    a = 5;
    b = 5;
    a = b = 10;
    System.out.println(a);
  }
}
```

It prints 5. You knew that too. I'm being trivial because I have no idea what you want to test. The idea is to deliver a paradigm, not a suite of test stubs.

Let's say you want to include a financial calculator in your stock-management program. You realize that exhaustively testing such a calculator is impossible. A reasonable test suite would be one that builds on past results, much like mathematical expressions do. If you know that (a + b) works, and negation works, then you can apply similar tests to $(a - b)$, then to various versions of $(a + b - c + d - e)$, etc. Next, you can extend the calculations to multiplication, division, roots, and powers. You can test iteration for evaluating infinite series. Test stubs can help you do all of that until you're confident that your algorithms for present value, future value, interest, and time periods always work. Once again, the idea is to demonstrate a paradigm. The test stubs you write will be far more sophisticated than these.

If you're using GUI tools for development, test stubs are good ways to prove the characteristics of a tool's events. One of the first things to do when trying a new (to you) GUI tool is to install a test stub in every event. That stub tells you when each event fires, and may reveal the contents of some variables. This way, you discover the time sequence of various events, and whether or not you can actually trigger all of them. Often an event requires certain conditions to be present before you can trigger it. If it doesn't fire when you expect, you can investigate before relying on the event.

Ask Questions When You're Stuck

Ask your user via interviews.

Ask your program via testing.

Ask technical support. Even if it's expensive, one $50 call that saves you ten hours is a bargain.

Search the Web. There are many excellent Java sites, and several may have your solution. Appendix B has a good list of Web addresses.

Ask colleagues, especially those versed in other languages. After all, there are only about six things a language can do (sequential processing, looping, assignment, recursion, etc.) and your CoBOL friend might have your answer. Even if that's not the case, I find that the act of explaining the problem points me to its solution more than half of the time.

Ask yourself after a break. One of the wiser pieces of advice I've received is never to look at a page of code for more than ten minutes. Get some refreshment to refresh your mind. You'll probably meet someone willing to listen to your dilemma. If that won't work, take an overnight break, but have a notepad at your bedside in case you awaken with the solution!

It's a shame that having a bed in one's office is viewed with disfavor. At home, I can lie across the bed and solve the most difficult of computer problems in mere minutes. At most offices, I'd be let go for appearing to take a nap. It's a strange profession we have!

CHAPTER 10

Testing

The first chapter of "Debugging Java" shows that testing, alone, is insufficient to find all bugs. That's true, but testing remains your strongest ally in the war against program errors.

This chapter begins by discussing multiple ways to test. It shows how to and how not to conduct those tests, and the huge difficulty involved. It contains a number of proposals for software that could automate those tests.

Finally, it presents JTest, a commercial product which prevents and detects errors in Java classes, automatically.

Localize and Squash Bugs

A license plate on a new VW Beetle reportedly reads "IH8RAID."

If you turn on the kitchen light and something small moves in the middle of the kitchen floor, your generalized test was successful. Instantly, your eyes begin a more specific test for what moved. In a more specific search, you spot a roach, and your specific tests were successful. The critter is doomed.

If, however, the roach makes it to the baseboards before you can pinpoint it, the bug will probably elude you. You must localize a bug to squash it.

Similarly, you use code instruments to help you localize the program bugs that your generalized testing has revealed.

Instrument Your Code

Just as an airliner has hundreds of specialized physical instruments to tell the pilot if something goes wrong, you can install specialized virtual instruments in your code. However, you wouldn't install a compass to measure the exhaust gas temperature of a jet engine, nor an airspeed indicator to monitor fuel quantity. Be thoughtful about how you instrument your program. After all, you must build most of your instruments, and the ones you buy can cost serious money. Java instruments come in many varieties, for example:

- Breakpoints in a specially instrumented compile that is created by a debugger
  - When reaching a particular line
  - When reaching a particular method
  - When a counter assumes or goes beyond a particular value
  - When some Boolean condition you define becomes **true**

- When the code throws a particular Java exception
- When the code throws a user-declared exception
- Watchpoints to show the values of variables
- Logging routines, which write information to disk files or printouts
- Recorders that trace where your program goes as it executes
- Pop-up boxes that display something that looks interesting
- Counters that tell you how many times various pieces of code execute
- Timers that tell you how long it takes to execute bits of code
- Instruments that change the values of variables when they go astray, letting the code continue but logging the action they took
  - Watchers that track threads, looking for various kinds of conflicts
  - Watchers that keep an eye on memory usage and other aspects of the computer environment
  - Disk usage trackers
  - Network usage trackers that seek time and usage bottlenecks
  - Sensors that wait at ports for Java-controlled peripherals to report problems
  - Dozens more not mentioned here, including specialized instruments you'll invent

Some of these instruments, such as **throws** and **try**, are cheap and small. Others are quite expensive in terms of performance, programming effort, or money. Part of our programming art is choosing the best instruments. That generally means balancing simplicity with the ability to garner the most bugs.

Conditional Compiling

C, C++, and (in recent years) Visual Basic include conditional compilation. The idea was so powerful that the first examples of C++ were written in C, by using C's conditional compiler. As a simplification, Java abandoned that whole idea of conditional compilation for the more powerful **try-catch-throw-throws-finally** concept. With its version 7, Visual Basic has finally adopted this more sophisticated idea.

Any language can include error traps and imbedded debug tools, turned on or off with a common flag. One improvement conditional compiling made over that idea is that when the condition is turned off, the compiled version no longer contains the conditional code. In other words, you can install any number of conditionally compiled error traps and use them for development. Then by flipping a software switch, you can remove them entirely when you build a version for your user. However, they remain in the source code, ready to use at the flip of a software switch.

The **try** block doesn't disappear from compiled Java, but the code suffers no performance penalty from having it there until an error is actually caught. You can test this claim with a profiler. Moreover, **try** is computationally small.

As shown earlier, the true elegance of the **try-catch-throw-throws-finally** idea is that it doesn't obscure the meat of the program like traditional error traps and imbedded debug tools do.

Where the Bugs Are

If bugs were evenly distributed, random testing would be a fine way to discover some of them. However, they are not, and that's fortunate. By knowing where to look, we can maximize our efforts, rather like a gold miner, panning the streams of California instead of the Missouri River.

Bugs Cluster Around Limits

There are many reasons why bugs cluster around limits, but the primary one is that programmers don't live, mentally, around those limits. And, face it, programmers write nearly all bugs.

Put another way, bugs are more prevalent in unfamiliar mental territory. For example, we all know that 12 + 14 gives 26. Those numbers are well within the normal range of human computational capability. We don't even have to "carry the one." By inspection, within 1/10th of a second, one has the answer. But what does 16,543 + 16,432 give? It might take someone ten or a hundred times as long (1–10 seconds) to calculate the result mentally. One can't even verbalize the answer in 1/10th of a second. So, it's easier for a person to prevent a bug in a calculation that results in 26 than one that results in 32,975.

Whether or not there is a bug depends on the kind of number the result is. If it's a **byte** with a maximum of 32,767, then in summing 16,543 + 16,432, you automatically have a bug. If it's an **int** or **long**, any problem in the code is a bit more subtle.

Once, I received a trouble call that a report had stopped working after about five years. It turned out that the report depended on a file that was created several times a day, and that file wasn't being updated. But why not?

The mainframe (a DEC VAX) had a very nice feature. Files had version numbers. When the operating system wrote a file with the same path and name as another file, it erased nothing. It gave the file a new version number and retained the old file until something deleted it.

In the case of my trouble call, the program wrote the new report to the directory, verified that nothing had failed, and then erased the old one. Thus, Report.Txt;111 became Report.Txt;112 an hour later, etc.

The trouble occurred when the version number reached 32768. The operating system reached a limit and refused to create a new file. So, a perfectly running program aborted for the first time in five years. As usual, finding the bug was difficult, but the fix was trivial.

Mentally, the programmer didn't live around that obscurely documented limit. Who would?

Off-by-One Errors Are Among the Most Common

Off-by-one errors generally involve limits. For example, the following Java snippet

```
for (counter = 0; counter < 10, counter++) {
  // Other code here
}
```

iterates from zero through nine. Most bugs in its code block will be found around counter values zero and nine. If an array uses counter as an index, does it have a zeroth and ninth entry? It's more likely to have a bug there than in a fourth and fifth entry. Does it erroneously have a tenth entry the loop doesn't address?

Other Kinds of Limits

Bugs cluster around file limits, around string beginnings and endings, around the maximum and minimum sizes of numbers, and around the limits of their precision. Anywhere you find a limit in your program, beware of bugs trying to hatch.

Most tests should run near limits of some kind. Here are some limits to consider:

- File sizes on various kinds of media. Floppy disks, CDs, and hard disks all have size limits, at times imposed by the operating system or the computer's BIOS. Some large storage media have limits in the 2-gigabyte and 8-gigabyte range.

- Filename limits. Some software, such as some Novell networks, still require the 8.3 filename convention. Some operating systems only allow 255 files in the root directory of a floppy diskette, but 65K files in subdirectories. That's the number of files, not their sizes. Some systems allow, and some disallow, various nonalphabetic and non-numeric characters, such as spaces. Some systems disallow a number as the first character of a filename. Some allow, and some disallow, capital and/or mixed case filenames. Some make filenames case sensitive and some do not. Since Java runs on nearly all systems, these differences can make your program nonportable.

- File versions. Some operating systems like VMS let you have a version number on the filename, such as Myfile.Txt;111, but impose a limit of 32767 on the version number.

- Some operating systems let you play with the dates files were created or modified. Dates have their own peculiar limits. Is Feb. 30th or March 55th allowed? Is Feb. 28th in the proper format? Is 01/02/03 January 2nd, or February 1st, and what is the exact year?

- Some operating systems let you change a file's ownership, mode, etc., imposing various limits on such activities—often depending on your program's or user's privileges.

- Some programs, such as Word, save a host of user information with the file. If your software does this sort of thing, what limits are there on such information?

- Numbers have limitations, which in Java are easy to memorize because the numerical limits do not vary from platform to platform.

- Strings have limitations, some subtle. Strings have lengths, of course. Strings also have beginnings and ends, and the end of the string might be assigned a special character, as it is in C. Strings may have delimiters between words or between fields. The delimiter is usually absent at the beginning and ending of the string. So, the number of delimiters is usually, but not always, one fewer than the number of words or fields. That can be a limit.

- Are you noticing about now that any property is a limit? Anything that characterizes something, anything that describes its properties, is a limit. Anything that tells about how something does something—that is, describes its methods—is a limit. By that logic, a class' properties and methods are, themselves, limits.

- There are limits on any object's properties and methods. Those limits are the list of properties and the list of methods, as distinguished from properties and methods themselves. If you try to address a text box's

OnError method, you'll probably find it doesn't have one. Some boxes don't have captions. They have list or text properties instead. Most picture boxes don't have RecordSource properties.

- Data conversions always have strict, and oftentimes obscure, limits.

- Numeric casts can lose data when one kind of number exceeds another's limit. If you cast a huge **int** to a **byte**, you may lose information because of the size limit in a **byte**.

- Taking the value of a string like "123 Main Street" costs you data. You retain the number 123 but lose the street name. That's a limit. What about 123 45th Street? How would your program handle that? Could a bug that erroneously exchanges dots for spaces cause that value to be interpreted as 123.45? I saw that oddity happen once.

- Input data imposes limits on its target system, and any target system imposes limits on the input data. These limits are often ill understood.

- People change their names, in particular due to marriages. People leave jobs. Computer names on the network change accordingly. If a program relies on mail going to specific people or computers, that's a limit that is easy to overlook during testing. Granted, hard coding a person's name into a program is poor practice, but sometimes you'll inherit someone else's work.

- Many processes have time limits. A thread, waiting at a port, may time out or die. A login may or may not time out. A login that never times out imposes a sort of reverse limit, because things that are waiting on it stall.

- People impose many kinds of limits. Human-factor research shows that a person begins to get uneasy if nothing happens for three seconds, and thinks the computer may have stalled at seven seconds. After waiting thirty seconds with no activity from the computer, most users are thinking in terms of rebooting the beast or calling the help desk. At the least, they're getting ready for a cup of coffee or a conversation with their peers.

- Many people are color blind. This imposes limits on your graphical user interface. There is a lot of blue in a green traffic light, to help color blind people distinguish it from red. Most color-blind people can tell blue from red, but blue vs. green or green vs. red are often indistinguishable to them. Color blindness varies a lot.

- Do you have a flashing red error box? Epileptics might not appreciate that! It's a limit that bit me once.

- Personal handicaps impose limits. You may need to consider visual acuity limits, or limits imposed by the lack of a mouse.

- Touch screens have their own limits, especially with resolving the exact spot of the touch. Just today, I saw how a small Start button in the bottom-left corner of a Windows touch screen is nearly impossible to activate with a finger.

- The physical box may have limits. What if your system must run in 120-degree heat in the middle of a desert dust storm? What if it needs to run in a factory atmosphere laden with microscopic oil particles (forget using a roller-ball mouse) or run in an atmosphere of explosive, hexane gas used for extracting the oil from soybeans? Can it handle a dusty environment? What if it needs to run in the radiation of outer space? Do you need to devise something to handle such limits? Does your software need to consider them?

- Budgets impose limits. Usually, that's a good thing! Sometimes, it's not.

- Politics—within your company, among your customers, and even internationally—impose limits. Can your new 256-bit encryption software be exported? Are your graphics legal or proper in other countries and cultures? Will your text offend an entire religious group? You wouldn't want to have to go into hiding.

- Windows graphics have some limits (standards) that many programmers don't know to consider. For example, any 3-D object on the screen should be shadowed as if the light were coming from above and 45 degrees to the left of the object. Are your command buttons shadowed one way and your screen banners shadowed another?

- Your audience is a limit. Programs produced for children have different textual, style, and visual limits than do programs produced to attract investors to a dot.com company.

- Screen size is a limit. CAD programs typically use huge screens and could always use more screen real estate. Screen resolution is another limit. Some software, particularly for games, simply cannot run well on a 14-inch monitor because a magnifying glass would be needed.

- Number of colors is a limit. Do you need to write for 16 colors, or do you need to specify more? Is black and white okay?

- Reports have limits. Do you need to stuff 256 characters on a 10-inch landscaped line, yet keep the font readable? Good luck! Do you need to keep everything on one page? That can be a challenging limit.

- Does your software require a color printer? There's a limit. Do you need to specify the font and color? Those are limits. Some printers may not work with your software.

- Your software may require special drivers, which may not work on all hardware—more limits.

- Thread interactions impose limits. Multithreaded software that runs fine on some platforms can perform miserably on others due to how the JVM sequences threads.

The first chapter made a puzzle out of finding new bug classes. Similarly, you can add to the previous list of limits. Make it a game and keep a file of your results. When you want to devise test cases, pull out your limit list and let it inspire you.

Bugs Cluster Around Other Bugs

In some respects, this proven phenomenon is counterintuitive. After you remove twenty bugs from one piece of code and two from another, you might think that the first piece is more bug-free, and you might be correct, but rarely so.

Research shows that the code where you found the most bugs still has the most left!

The conclusion is obvious. In a "where there's smoke there's fire" sort of mentality, you should look for more bugs where you've already found some.

When you consider the factors that cause bugs, it becomes obvious why bugs cluster in special places. Those causative factors are relatively long term, so they tend to produce many bugs in pockets of code. Among such factors are:

- Deadline pressure, which tends to increase the bug ratio in the last modules being developed

- Inadequate understanding of an algorithm, which may make it buggy anywhere it is found

- Few personal or office programming standards, which tend to make some programmers more bug-free than others

- Failure to follow established standards, which may help you find bugs based on who signed the code, or who reverses the vowels in words like "receive."
- Some major source of irritation, causing preoccupation
- A ton of e-mail after a vacation
- Learning curves

These factors don't go away in minutes or even hours. While someone is programming under their influence, the chances for bugs increase. Thus, when one bug crops up, more are liable to be abounding. On the other hand, if you examine a routine carefully and find no errors that will deflect the project, the chances are good that other routines written by the same person at about the same time have few, if any, bugs.

There is a fairly wide variation in people when it comes to writing error-free code. Recently, I performed upgrades on a smallish system written over the years by at least five programmers, one at a time. Two of them signed their work and three didn't. After considerable experience with the code, I found I could look at the signatures and predict many of the kinds of bugs I'd find. When I found one particular signature, which I'll call ABC herein, I'd shudder. I knew that the bugs in this clever person's code would be particularly difficult to find, and that they would be nasties.

ABC wrote the infamous Field13 bug. He rarely gave his objects meaningful names. He just called them things like Text12, Text13, Text14, etc. But first, a bit more background.

One of my tasks was to update a large number of forms to a universal, brighter, and more friendly look. They all had to have a similar theme. I chose colors and fonts and cleared the basic design with the users. Then I built a template header consisting of two labels, slightly offset to give a nice 3-D look, and added a version label. Over each old header, I copied the new one, changed two captions, and was done. Or so I thought. One form compiled but refused to work right. A subform wasn't getting information, and was complaining that the data should be coming from a mysterious Field13.

There was no Field13, so I checked the original code. After considerable effort, I found the culprit. It was not a field at all, but a text box that ABC had hidden behind three labels in the form heading, and one of those obscuring labels was exactly the same size and placement as Field13.

There was no need to hide the text box in the first place, because at runtime it was invisible.

A month later, I was working on another ABC form that had four text boxes and four labels. The labels and text boxes had the same names, and were elements of an array. He wanted to ensure there was something in each text box when the user clicked the OK button to perform some laboratory analysis. Instead of writing four lines to test the four boxes, he put all eight objects in an array and wrote seven lines of code to step through that array on the even numbered objects only, checking for null input. There was, after all, no need to check the labels—just the text boxes. To make matters worse, he emitted an error message constructed from properties on the text boxes and their labels, along with several characters to which he referred only by their ASCII values.

This overly clever scheme worked fine until someone had to figure out what he was trying to accomplish. I consider that a bug, simply because he didn't use a straightforward approach, which would have been three lines shorter!

Thankfully, ABC usually signed his work, because he gave me clues about the kinds of bugs to seek. In his work, you can find bugs clustering around his great inventiveness.

Another programmer, who doesn't sign his work, had an entirely different class of bugs in his code. However, that person has difficulty spelling words with "ie" and "ei" in them. When I found a misspelled word like "archieve" for "archive" or "recieved" for "received," I knew to seek bugs in his interfaces with the database, because I'd find them, even in code that had run for years.

Reality Checks

My manager put down his book and came to my office. "How much water pours out of the Mississippi in a day?" he asked. I must have had a blank look on my face, because he said, "I really want to know. Figure it out and come tell me."

So, I called someone in New Orleans, and about four calls later had a pretty good estimate from some official with the State of Louisiana.

My manager looked at me, and said something I'll never forget. "That fits what I just read in this book. So if you can do that, why are you estimating 20 times too high in this paper you gave me last week?"

I walked around his desk to look. My estimate was too high because it relied on another estimate that was grossly erroneous. My manager's book was open to a page where the author's manager had once pulled that same stunt! My manager had sandbagged me to make an unforgettable point. I had failed to perform a reality check.

I resolved at that time always to give an estimate the cold test of reality, and eventually I became rather good at making quick, accurate estimates.

If you're pointed straight down in a fighter at 400 mph, at what minimum altitude must you must start pulling out of the dive? Err on the wrong side of reality and, if you're lucky, someone may be picking pine boughs out of your landing gear when you arrive. If you're unlucky, someone else may be carting you out of the pines. Your programming estimates seldom need to be so exact, but what if your program were to cause a Mars lander's engines to shut off a hundred feet above the ground? Could a reality check have found the bug caused by one group using metric and another using English measurements in that failed lander's failed predecessor?

Say you have a crucial file to transfer to Kansas City, which someone says will take nine hours on your 56K line. Say it's six hours faster to have a driver take a CD there. Better order a car right now!

It's reality check time. How big is the file? 4 megs? Well, at perhaps 15 minutes a meg, don't you think it would take about one hour instead of nine?

Here's an odd way of looking at something. At 15 minutes per meg, how fast does a 20-meg file travel 300 miles? Well, 15 * 20 = 300 minutes, or 5 hours. Then, 300 / 5 = 60 miles per hour. That file only travels 60 mph? Whatever happened to the speed of light?

That's rather like asking when a mile-long train traveling 30 mph passes the train station if the engine arrives at 9:00 A.M. Did the train pass at 9:00 A.M. or 9:02 A.M., or sometime in between? In the file's case, the so-called "train" would be millions of miles long, except that the "engine" started arriving at the destination hours before the "caboose" left the origin. We don't usually think in those terms, do we?

The point is that people don't often live, mentally, among some kinds of limits. So, results like an electronic message traveling a mere 60 mph, instead of some 186,000 miles per second, seem bizarre. However, bugs are liable to cluster around any kind of limit, and especially so around bizarre ones.

Black-Box Testing

Chapter 1 began with an example of black-box testing, in which an implementation of Heron's formula is tested solely with input and output. The program, viewed as a black box, accepts input and is supposed to produce a certain kind of output. Without caring how the program works, the tester is supposed to deduce from the input and output that the program works.

The objective is to find as many bugs as possible per test. For this reason, tests should cluster where the bugs are. That's an excellent reason for maintaining, and appending to, a personal list of limits. It helps you live, mentally, where the bugs are.

White-Box Testing

This kind of testing is concerned with "how" a program works, not so much that a particular set of inputs produces a certain kind of output. White-box testing relies on the presumption that the compiler is correct, and that a given statement will always produce the same results within its normal set of parameters, which are well defined. In threaded languages, those presumptions may be rightly questioned. However, white-box testing is invaluable to developers. For now, let's accept those presumptions.

Given those premises, a programmer can often prove that a piece of code is correct, or that it's not. For example, say a loop has exactly one entry point, exactly one exit point, exactly one entry condition, and exactly one exit condition. You can say with certainty that if the loop is entered and you prove the exit condition will be met eventually, then the loop will be exited. That's not enough to prove the loop is correct, but it's part of the proof of correctness. You still need to know that the loop does what it should, with each iteration.

An often-overlooked point occurs when the loop index must be set properly when the loop exits.

The classic code walk-through is one example of white-box testing. A group, composed mostly of programmers, reviews a programmer's work, looking for places where it might or will fail to produce proper results.

Alone, white-box testing is insufficient, because people find it difficult or nearly impossible to predict the results of a set of code. Where this is possible, it may be far beyond human endurance to do so. For example, white-box testing would have failed to find the bug that caused my student's program to erroneously round 101.001 to 101.01 instead of 101.00. White-box testing presumes the compiler is correct, which wasn't the case that day. It mattered to the student and the instructor that the code was provably correct, and I gave him 100 for that exercise. However, had Neil Armstrong's computer relied on that program, he might never have walked on the moon.

Another Set of Eyes (It's Time to Strut)

White-box testing must be set up correctly if it is to work well, because egoless programming is a myth. One programmer told me, "I'll never let anyone know it, but I have a tremendous ego." Because of egos, the testing session itself has failure modes that can override the ability of white-box testing to find bugs. The manager and the group must work diligently toward success.

The group manager establishes the meeting because a meeting's caller is the meeting's de facto authority. The manager establishes the agenda, the attendees, and the time limits.

All meetings should have published agendas, although many managers neglect this action—possibly because it is a courtesy that requires careful thought. Code reviews, in particular, need agendas, and the agenda needs a note at the bottom, stating that it will be followed strictly. Code reviews are stressful enough, and the structure such a note adds is very reassuring.

A typical set of attendees will include the developer, possibly a trainee or two, several peers (including a couple from another project), a respected and senior programmer, and the manager. One of the attendees may be designated as recorder, or an outside recorder may be brought in. When I'm the manager, I prefer to act as recorder. Some say that a user's input is valuable, but invariably I've found that a user's presence disrupts the ideal process, because nobody wants to reveal a bug in the presence of a user.

The great imperative is to forbid anything resembling a personal attack. The agenda should say so, clearly, as a "given." Generally a programmer's peers will avoid snide remarks. For one thing, they know they're next. However, the manager enjoys the luxury that their code will probably not fall under scrutiny. Moreover, a manager's words carry more weight than a peer's. The manager is the one who must choose words and voice tones very carefully.

The agenda states that the meeting's primary purpose is to find bugs, which everyone acknowledges will be present. Everyone knows that nontrivial code is never bug-free. Everyone acknowledges that no single person—and for that matter, no single group—will find all bugs. However, the meeting's purpose is to find as many bugs as feasible.

You may find it useful to include a note that a number of bugs have been carefully "seeded" into the program (more on that idea later).

The secondary purpose is training. The person who wrote the code conducts the review, line by line, explaining the reasoning for each line and why it works. The peers learn, at least, what that piece of the project does, and usually a few new programming concepts. Similarly, the code's author will usually learn a few new and possibly better ways of programming. The recorder's notes should include ways that each bug can be prevented in the future, and the recorder should feel free to ask the team, "How's the best way to prevent this kind in the future?"

When a bug is discovered, the attitude of the team, including the author, should be, "Great! That's one the customers will never find." High-fives are cool, and the finder can select a piece of candy from a pile. Knowing the code better than the peers, the author will discover about two-thirds of the bugs.

I oversaw one code review in which the author's voice began dropping in volume until it was inaudible. He paused a moment, then reached out and pulled the whole pile of candy to his corner of the table. He sat down, sheepishly, to a chorus of "What? What?"

We all looked at him and then the program that lay on the table. Right in the middle of the page was an error so magnificent that it made the rest of the session moot. I said something like, "I think John won the rest of the candy." Bernard quipped, "He's gonna need it. Midnight snacks for a week over this one!"

Bernard wasn't jesting. Time was tight, so he stayed late, four evenings, to help John fix the problem in time for the next deadline. Bernard never did tell me about doing that.

The agenda does not specifically include time for fixing bugs, but does allow attendees to suggest three things:

- Possible bug locations
- Ways to localize the bug further
- Potential repair methods

The session should last for about 45–90 minutes. If it goes much longer, people begin to fidget, losing concentration. Since debugging is one of the more cerebral activities in programming, adjourn the meeting if interest flags.

The worst time to hold such a meeting is half an hour before quitting time, because the idea is to find bugs, not to overlook them! The next worst time is an hour before lunch. The third worst time is right after lunch, because people must be mentally sharp. The fourth worst time is the middle of the afternoon. That leaves 9 A.M. Question: Was that inductive or deductive reasoning?

If you run a team of afternoon people, then 2 P.M. is best.

All Logic Testing

The course of a thread is driven by logic. The idea behind All Logic testing, and its cousin, All Branches testing, is simple. Let the computer find runtime errors by ensuring that it exercises every branch of the program.

In a program that has menus, a tester might start with the left-hand menu item's first drop-down item and see how that works. If it contains other subconditions, the tester would check each of them. In a menu-driven program, the depth-first process is easier to perform than a breadth-first test would be.

Sometimes, a menu item will be disabled. For example, File Save might be grayed out until a file is opened. The tester would have to open a file and then see if it saves properly.

The program's user manual should be available for this kind of testing. The most common kind of bug will be a minor discrepancy between what the user manual says and what the program does. However, it's a bug.

Last week, preparing for a business trip, I installed my external CD recorder on a client's Windows NT system so we could take a clone of the c: drive on the road. My user manual says that installing on Windows NT is identical to installing on Windows 98, and shows the Control Panel with the Add Hardware icon circled. When the NT machine's Control Panel appeared, there was no Add Hardware icon.

Whenever I call a company's tech support team, I like to ask the technician a simple question: "Tell me, what two problems give you the most calls?" In this case, the lead technician told me that each member of her team of three spends about an hour a day handling this particular question. While installation on an NT box is straightforward, this bug costs their company at least $15,000 a year in tech support salaries. The program should do exactly what the manual says it does, or one of the two needs changing.

Something many commercial products miss is ensuring that their help system accurately describes what the program does or does not do, and that it actually offers helpful help. Several people should test this aspect, people who have different levels of familiarity with the program.

All Logic and All Branch testing have inherent difficulties. They presume the logic is correct, so they can't always test incorrect logic. If you write **And** where you mean **Or**, your program will test the wrong path, and possibly report that everything is running just fine. If your parentheses are wrong, these kinds of tests can't discover the error.

You can use a manual version of all logic testing to check your logic. Merely step through the program. At each decision point, check the value of the logical condition to ensure it is correct. Then check that the program goes down the intended path. That, of course, is taking the test a step beyond the original premise that the program is correct if all paths are tested.

Build Better Fly Swatters

Did you ever try digging a ditch with a spoon? Of course not! A ditch digger machine nearly automates the process.

Similarly, why not automate the tedium of testing, even if you have to build the tool? Personally, I don't think any of the following would be especially difficult to write. They could be written in any language, including Java. Many commercial software tools already incorporate the best of these ideas:

Macro Recorder

A tool that records keystrokes, mouse positions, and button clicks can help you this way:

- Record a long test scenario until encountering a bug
- Fix the bug
- Play back the test scenario to see if:
  - The bug is fixed
  - Fixing it caused no further bugs (regression)

Such a tool should have an editable test script. You should be able to edit it three ways:

- Via a text editor
- By running an existing script to a given point and recording from there
- By combining several scripts into one hierarchical test suite for your application

A macro recorder has other important uses. During development, for example, it can help you automate the typing of entire sections of code.

Many years ago, I even used a standard macro recorder to build a translator from one computer language to another. These things are powerful tools.

Best Practices Analyzer

This kind of package would analyze your source code and do the following:

- Suggest better, or equally good, alternative algorithms to the ones it finds, or that you highlight
- Show several alternate ways to write any loop it finds or that you highlight
- Show other reasonable ways to write any conditional branch
- Regarding the three bullets above, it should:
    - Present drop-downs that list titles of the substitute algorithms, loops, or conditions, best one first
    - Let you reorder the list of titles, according to best speed, best memory usage, best disk usage, or best network usage
    - Retain the last-chosen ordering for the next time the drop-down is used
    - Let you click on a title to see suggested source code
    - Let you drag a title to your source code, replacing yours with the analyzer's
    - Let you edit the results and do a test compile on the spot
    - Let you revert, stepwise, back to the original, via clicks on an Undo icon, or by selecting an intermediate step from a drop-down box
- Locate error-prone practices, such as:
    - Potential data races
    - Potential deadlocks
    - Potential stalls
    - Entering the middle of a loop
    - Casts that remove precision
- Find potential performance hogs
- Show high users of memory and list ways to improve memory usage
- Identify potential memory leaks and show how to fix them
- Estimate disk utilization, in terms of space, and numbers of reads and writes
    - List ways to reduce file sizes
    - Show algorithms that reduce reads and writes
- Examine your database methodologies and suggest different ones with better speed or file usage
- Optionally, finish writing your entire application for you—just kidding!

Static Coverage Analyzer

A tool that examines the source code and traces each logical branch helps you locate dead code. The Java compiler can find dead code, but it's not difficult to write dead code the Java compiler can't find. Merely include a data-driven condition that only you know will never become **true**, for instance. Since you can write code that fools the best static coverage analyzer, how about a dynamic coverage analyzer as a supplement?

Dynamic Coverage Analyzer

A tool that watches your code as it runs, and catalogues everywhere the program has gone, helps you find dead code that a static coverage analyzer cannot. Such a tool might do the following:

- Begin by showing your source code in black type, comments in green
- As the compiled version runs, change the corresponding source code to a red font
- At the end, let you scroll through your code, looking for black lines that have not yet been executed
- Save a copy of the changed source code in a format like Rich Text that supports colored fonts
- Let you make changes to the source, in a paused program, recompile, and continue testing (this would be an advanced feature)

Such a tool will show you exactly what code has executed, letting you devise tests that will execute the rest, or decide whether or not the rest of the code is correct.

Bug Tracker

This kind of tool's purpose would be to help you with the clerical work. It would manage a small database and accept the following, mostly optional, information.

- Bug number, autoincrementing, never reused, even for other projects
- Project name, which defaults to the last bug's project name

- Formal, short, bug description
  - This description would go into formal bug-report summaries
- Detailed bug description
- Module where found, from a drop-down list of current modules
- Who and/or what test suite found the bug
- Date and time it was found, which defaults to "today"
- Potential bug-localizing tactics the bug's finder might suggest
- Potential fixes
- To whom to report the repair
- Workarounds
- Date or release scheduled to fix the bug
- Date it was repaired, which defaults to "today"
- Actual fix
  - Any entry here would optionally suppress the bug from to-do screens and reports
  - This entry would pass to official bug-fix reports
- Date the retest was successful
- How this bug might be prevented in future projects

Input would be via a gui computer screen, or from flat files with entries preceded by the keywords listed above in parentheses, with the Bug Number being the only required field. Extensible Markup Language (XML) could drive such input. For example:

```
<?xml version="1.0"?>
<ID>123
  <Fix Date>12/25/2000</Fix Date>
</ID>
<ID>125
  <Short Description>The menu item |Tools |Options |Flags is disabled
if no files are loaded.</Short Description>
  <Finder>ABC</Finder>
  <To Localize>Run with tracer on, load a file, click on
|Tools |Options |Flags, stop program, locate flag that disables the
menu item. Search for that flag's initialization routine and
change the flag's default value.</To Localize>
  <Workaround>Load a blank file before setting program flags.</Workaround>
</ID>
```

Output would be to various reports, as well as screens of those reports.

A screen with a number of buttons would manage the system. Managers would be concerned with outstanding bug lists. Developers would be interested in detailed descriptions and suggestions for locating/fixing bugs, as well as the suggestions for improving their craft. Users could see a list of bugs and workarounds on the company's Internet site.

Test Data Assistant

Developing test sets is cerebrally tedious, if that's not an oxymoron. In any case, let's reduce the tedium. Once you develop data to test something, you can use that data as part of your next test suite.

Beware, however, of using it exclusively, for that practice might allow a class of bugs to crawl into all of your programs! Any bugs immune to that suite won't be found in the future, either. I find it good to let a team develop at least half of their unique test suite, and then to give them access to various saved suites.

A test data assistant would let you select tests that you and others have designed, and would then help you tailor them for your current project. It would use XML documents to manage such optional information as this:

- Mandatory test ID, autoincremented, never reused
  - Alternately, a date/time stamp could be used. In case of collisions, the later test added could have its time incremented by one second.
- Short description of the test
- Long description of the test
- Purpose
- Author
- Test value set
- Fixed or delimited data
- Data field length
- Value delimitation character
- Tested in what program or suite
- Recommendations for enhancement

The assistant would offer other features:

- A sophisticated find system, that employs grep-like regular expressions, helping you find tests of interest
- Ability to edit tests, adding new data
- Flag any tests that have recommendations, or that have not been used
- Extensibility, so you can add features to it

When to Stop Testing

Stop when all bugs are found! What a fine ideal, except that it's difficult to approach that goal. For one thing, economics intervene. You can test software forever and not find all bugs. Some bugs have to be prevented, and most vendors seem to rely on their users to report bugs, a phenomenon I call "Charlie" testing. You know, Alpha, Beta, Charlie, except that the users are the "Charlies." Wouldn't it be nice to know how many bugs there are left? Then you might be able to make some kind of economic decision about when to stop. Here are three experimental methodologies, based on statistical analysis.

Remainder Curve

This method is simple in concept, but rather expensive to implement, because of the number of test sessions involved. It is useful when ultra high-quality software is needed. You track the number of unique bugs reported during several testing sessions, between which you've fixed all known bugs.

Then you find a second-degree polynomial or spline curve that fits the numbers of bugs found. Hopefully, the graph of that polynomial will converge toward zero. Many curve-fitting programs are available to reduce the tedium of solving various curve-fitting equations. I use a simple one that I purchased for $19 over the Internet.

For instance, if your first test session found 100 bugs, then the next found 25, and the next found 10, you would seek a polynomial that fit these three points (1,100) (2,25) (3,11) and plot it on a graph. In this contrived but representative case, the polynomial is approximately:

```
y = 100 / x^2
```

Where the curve crosses 4 on the y-axis, you would find the number of bugs you expect to find in the next test. Or, you could merely substitute x=4 and solve the polynomial, expecting to find about six bugs in the next test.

Multiple Group Testing

If two groups test the same large piece of software, the following six things will happen:

- Both groups will find some of the same errors.
- Both groups will miss some errors entirely.
- Group A will find errors that group B misses.
- Group B will find errors that group A misses.
- Both groups will find some of the same errors, but they will apparently have found different ones.
- Both groups will multiple-report some bugs, unknowingly.

Think with me here.

The latter two cases can happen easily, because one bug can have several pathological side effects. If a bug causes two or more error conditions, each group could zero in on separate conditions, apparently reporting different bugs. Also, one group might see two or more side effects of the same bug and report them as separate bugs. I'll explain why the last two cases are important shortly.

Say a piece of software has 10,000 randomly scattered bugs, a fact that only God knows. Say, further, that after a bout of testing, group A finds 8,000 bugs and group B finds 9,000 bugs. One would expect both groups to find mostly the same bugs, because there are only 10,000 to find.

Say, instead, the software has 1,000,000 randomly scattered bugs, and that after some obviously incomplete testing, group A finds 8,000 bugs and group B finds 9,000 bugs. In this case, one would expect that few of those bugs would be cofound by both groups.

This indicates that there is a way to estimate the total number of bugs in the program! That, in turn, indicates whether or not you have tested adequately.

Calculate a ratio of the number of bugs reported by both groups to the total number of unique bugs found. We'll call this the "commonly-found" ratio, because it's the ratio of bugs found in common to the total number of bugs found.

If that commonly-found ratio is near 1, you have found nearly all of the bugs. If it is near 0, you have found very few of them. This happens regardless of the total number of bugs out there.

Assertions like "nearly all" and "very few" are imprecise, but at least they are helpful in determining when to stop testing. Except for other factors that compound the uncertainty, random number theory could predict how many bugs remain, within as many standard deviations as you desire. However, other factors intervene:

- A bug can be reported twice by the same group because it has multiple symptoms, and testers discover most bugs from their tracks—their symptoms.

- A bug can be reported once by each group, for the same reason.

- A bug can be reported multiple times by one group and once by the other.

- A bug can be reported multiple times by both groups.

- The groups will have a human tendency to find the same bugs, and to miss the same bugs as well. This is especially true if the groups adopt the same testing methods. If they use the same test sets, they might as well be a single, larger group, invalidating this kind of analysis.

- The bugs are never distributed smoothly throughout the code.

In a simulation, I created a table of 10,000 sequential numbers, representing 10,000 bugs. The simulator program randomly selected 5,000 numbers for testing group A. I allowed numbers to be selected multiple times. Then, it did the same for group B. The two groups selected 1,583 numbers in common, and 6,312 total numbers were selected. This gave a commonly-found ratio of about 25 percent, just what statistical theory predicts.

In this simulation, testing groups A and B are equally efficient at finding bugs. The idea here is to generate data based on various percentages of bugs actually found and then use that data to predict the number of bugs that exist. I ran many more tests, obtaining the averages in Table 10-1. Each time there were 10,000 numbers from which to select, representing 10,000 random bugs, but I had the simulated test groups find different numbers of those bugs.

It's important to reiterate that the results in this table are flawed by those multiply reported bugs. Here's what the columns in Table 10-1 mean:

- **Total Bugs Found**   This number, ranging from 1,000 through 10,000, is the number of bugs I told the simulator to "discover" for each group, at random. Of course, selecting 10,000 numbers at random doesn't mean that all possible 10,000 will be selected, because some will be selected multiple times.

- **Found by A** Since the simulator allows a number to be selected multiple times, this column contains the count of different bugs found. If only one bug were selected twice, this column would be one less than the Total Bugs Found column.

- **Found by B** This column is the same as column A, except that the numbers are slightly different. This difference is caused by randomness in the selection process.

- **Found by Both** Any bug found by both groups is tallied once here, even if it is found multiple times by one or both groups.

- **Found by Either** This tally gives the total number of bugs found by either of the groups, or by both of them.

- **Ratio Both/Either** Here we have the predictor ratio. The higher it is, the better the bug-finding process has gone.

What's Wrong with this Picture?

From the table, you'll immediately notice that due to duplication, neither group reports more than two-thirds of the actual bugs, even though it thinks it has found 10,000 bugs. Because of this duplication, the predictive ratio doesn't quite reach 50 percent. If both groups found all 10,000 bugs, the ratio would be 100 percent. We'll work on that flaw momentarily.

Total Bugs Found	Found by A	Found by B	Found by Both	Found by Either	Ratio Both/Either
10,000	6,311	6,342	4,004	8,649	0.46
9,000	5,892	5,955	3,544	8,303	0.43
8,000	5,478	5,528	3,073	7,933	0.39
7,000	5,021	5,070	2,492	7,599	0.33
6,000	4,556	4,483	2,070	6,969	0.30
5,000	3,904	3,953	1,497	6,360	0.24
4,000	3,314	3,303	1,087	5,530	0.20
3,000	2,612	2,623	653	4,582	0. 14
2,000	1,814	1,823	327	3,310	0.10

Table 10.1 When to Stop Testing

It would be wonderful, wouldn't it, to be able to predict exactly how many bugs remain? Unfortunately, that's not quite going to happen. It's conceivable, but highly improbable, that both groups could find exactly the same group of 9,999 bugs, missing just one. It's even less probable that they both could miss the same 100 bugs. But it could happen. So, there are no guarantees. Here are some reasons the data can be skewed:

- Earlier, I noted that a single bug can have multiple symptoms, and that groups detect bugs by their symptoms, or side effects. Thus, it's easy for each group to think they've found 11,000 bugs, when only 10,000 exist, and still miss several hundred!

- Both groups might use the same set of tests. In this case, their results will be artificially similar, or even identical.

- Even though the groups test identical code, Java has threads. That means different bugs surface due to differences in the dynamic test environments. There are probably no guarantees regarding which threads run in what order.

- Both testing groups come from the same backgrounds, and they have similar mental bents because they are composed of programmers. Thus, they will tend to find the same bugs, and will tend to miss many of the same bugs, regardless of the test suites they design.

- Bugs are not universally easy to find. Some leap out at their finders, and some hide in extremely subtle ways. I've mentioned some of the more subtle bugs I've encountered. I'd guess that you haven't seen all of those, and also that you've seen a number of kinds of bugs I'll never encounter. Moreover, the more subtle bugs tend to be the most costly to find, and to fix.

However, this flawed method has a second wind. The analysis we've discussed so far takes place before the bugs are fixed, and thus, before anyone knows which reported bugs are truly duplicates.

After the bugs are localized and identified, that critical information is known. We know which bugs have been double-reported, and which not. We can revise the numbers, and thus improve the estimate. When deriving the data for Table 10-1, I also kept track of the true numbers of bugs found. Playing the role of omniscient, I knew beforehand which bugs were reported multiple times. When I removed those factors that confuse the issue, Table 10-2 was the result.

In Table 10-2, the numbers in the first two columns run in increments of 1,000 because I didn't allow duplicate selections from the random bugs. The table shows how good this system could become with perfect knowledge, which nobody would have in practice. However, some retroactive analysis can approach this ideal.

As you localize bugs, you can determine which bug reports are duplicates. Do that for each team, and find a new number of unique bugs reported by each team. Then figure out how many of those both teams found, and how many total bugs were found by either but not both teams. Then calculate a new commonly-found ratio.

Enter the following graph with that number and you'll have a decent idea of what percentage of the program's bugs remain. For instance, say you find a new ratio of 0.75. Find that point of the bottom scale and ascend vertically until

Found by A	Found by B	Found by Both	Found by Either	Ratio Both/Either
9,000	9,000	8,100	9,900	0.82
8,000	8,000	6,419	9,581	0.67
7,000	7,000	4,922	9,078	0.54
6,000	6,000	3,655	8,345	0.44
5,000	5,000	2,498	7,502	0.33
4,000	4,000	1,572	6,428	0.24
3,000	3,000	878	5,122	0.17
2,000	2,000	412	3,588	0.11
1,000	1,000	109	1,891	0.06

Table 10.2 Theory

reaching the curve. Then go straight left, and you see you have found about 85 percent of the bugs. Thus, about 15 percent remain hidden.

How many errors are there?

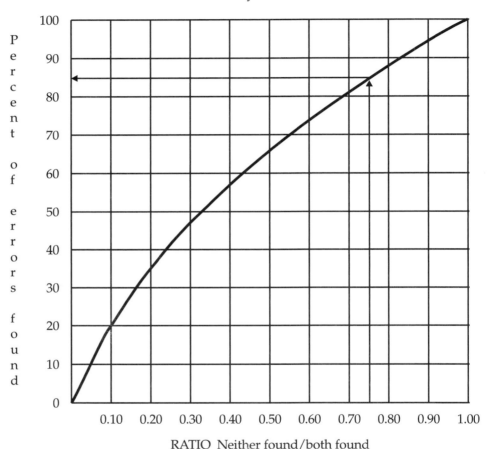

RATIO Neither found/both found

Remember, of course, the prime caveat regarding this method. You've eliminated most duplicate reporting. However, if the bugs you've found are mostly "ordinary" in some sense, and not, shall we say, "subtle" bugs, then all this method can tell you is that 15 percent of the ordinary bugs remain. It can't tell you much about the "subtle" bugs. The next section will explain more about how the range of subtle vs. ordinary bugs affects the solution.

Sowing Error Seeds

Here's an alternative method that exploits the same statistical principles. In that same piece of code with 10,000 bugs, say you insert 1,000 known bugs intentionally and then turn a single testing group loose on the code. If they find 900 of your known bugs, you could argue that they probably found 90 percent of the total bugs. On the other hand, if they found 250 of your known bugs, you'd suspect that they only found 25 percent of the total bug count.

A psychological advantage of this tactic is that it lets the developer off the hook. Any given bug might be one you inserted. So, seeding with errors helps you inch toward that elusive goal of egoless programming.

This estimation method has another interesting advantage. You can actually control the subtlety of the bugs you estimate. That idea bears some explanation.

In the exercise/puzzle of Chapter 1, some of the kinds of bugs we sought were easy to find. However, some were sophisticatedly subtle and specialized, more so than the simple Heron's formula usually would merit. For instance, who but a researcher into how subatomic string theory describes space-time tears and repairs would be concerned with something like 10-tuples, representing a triangle in 10-dimensional space?

Your program might run in such an esoteric arena, or it might be designed for the 2-space of a two-dimensional piece of paper. If you seed a hundred 10-space errors in your program and your testing team finds 30, then you can expect 70 percent of the unknown bugs remain. If, on the other hand, you only seed 2-space type errors, you have no idea now many 10-space errors remain, but that may be just fine for your program's application.

Thus, by tailoring the kinds of errors you seed, you tailor the results you want. This can be a huge advantage or a disadvantage, because you also must tailor the seeds.

You can control the accuracy of your estimate as well. The more errors you seed, the greater your accuracy, up to a point. When your seeds start to overwhelm the code, you've definitely passed the point of best accuracy. Personally, I like to plant enough seeds that they'll represent a few percent of the total bugs.

Of course, you must remove all intentional bugs before delivering the code. Otherwise, what a massive mess you'll have generated!

This simple idea works rather well. However, it does have problems of its own:

- Introducing new bugs changes the code in ways you cannot quite control.
  - The very introduction of new bugs might generate further new bugs that your team would have to discover, possibly corrupting your results.

- New bugs have a tendency to hide, or hide behind bugs that are already present, potentially preventing your team from finding either kind.
- It requires considerable thought to place 1,000 bugs in a program.
    - You need to make some easy to find, and some subtle.
    - If you expect, say, 30 percent of the real bugs to be easy to find, about 30 percent of your faux bugs should be easy to find.
- Someone has to expend time placing those bugs in the code.
- The developers who wrote the code will instantly recognize most errors that you insert. Therefore, an original developer cannot participate in debugging.
    - Unfortunately, the developer is the one person most qualified to understand and explain the code.
    - Of course, that's an outstanding reason for demanding good documentation . . .
    - Not having an original developer available, the debuggers must understand the program more thoroughly.
    - In code walk-throughs, the developer finds the majority of the total bugs that are found.
- This is a relatively expensive undertaking, although it may turn out to be the best investment you can make in your project. Speaking of investments, you probably need to invest in more and better hardware and software.

You Need a Second Computer

Sometimes I pull my friend's leg a bit too hard. One slightly askew conversation went like this:

"Man, I need a 30-hour day!" he remarked.

"No way. Remember back when we had 18-hour days?"

"Huh?" He grinned, sure that I was baiting him.

"Look what they did with the 24-hour day when I invented that! There's no way I'm going to invent the 30-hour day for the world."

The strongest reason I have for using two computers is that the second one helps me be more productive. Greater productivity frees up time. Time with one's family is beyond value, but some argue time can be equated to money. That money could be considered the return on an investment, and if you do that, the return is extraordinarily high.

For example, several computers churn as I write these words. I'm using my second box for 50 automated JProbe sessions, which test for errant threads in a Java program for this book. My aging laptop is quietly researching the Internet for articles on some obscure parts of Java. In an hour, I'll stuff its dismountable disk full of files, preparing for a business trip. A fourth computer on my home network is scheduled to consolidate our mail every half hour. My son is using it to play a game, and he barely notices it dialing out in the background. A Solaris machine is poised to check out some commercial software as soon as I click its mouse a few times, but it is technically idle. My older print server is also idle, but it could just as easily be printing something for my editor. Since it's always running, two computers regularly back up crucial files to its large hard disk.

Alternately, I could do less than the above on one single computer, taking as much as four times as long. So, in a way, this is a good start toward inventing the 30-hour day. All one would have to do to invent the equivalent of a 30-hour day is to free up another six hours! So I wasn't totally teasing my friend.

How to Convince Your Boss You Need a Second Computer

Here are some facts that you already know. The trick is assembling them in a persuasive manner, and that's your chore.

Bosses have projects and they have budgets. The budgets consist of money to get resources. One of the ways bosses are evaluated is how much they get done for how little money. So, it's natural for bosses to be concerned with spending less and getting more done.

You and your computer are an investment in your company's future, or you wouldn't be working there.

Say your desired new computer is a beauty that costs $2,100 after tax write-offs.

Design Tip *QVS makes a product called a "Heavy Duty Dataswitch" that lets you manually switch one monitor back and forth between two computers. It costs about $20 for a two-computer model, and $30 for a four-computer model. You also need video cables. For under $100, you can find an automatic box that switches your monitor, keyboard, and mouse from one computer to another, via a keystroke or the click of your mouse. One of these devices can let you purchase one large, high-resolution monitor and use it with 2–4 computers, one at a time.*

Your computer will last at least three years before becoming obsolete. At that rate, it costs about $700 a year. You cost the company a lot more than that per year. Salary consumes the lion's share of that amount, and the rest goes for benefits, floor space, lights, facilities, lost time, computers, software, network support, licenses, administration, HR support, picnics, Christmas parties, and the like. If your salary is $40,000, then the company spends around $60,000 to keep you around. If your salary is $60,000, the company spends nearly $85,000, and if your salary is $100,000, figure they spend $130,000 a year on you. Let's say your company spends $70,000 a year on you. In that case, a miniscule 1 percent of that cost is for your computer hardware.

Say they were to spend another $700 a year to buy you that second computer. It must pay for itself, just as you must be a profit center for your company. The question an investor asks is how quickly does that new box pay for itself? Anything under three years would be good. Three years' return on investment equates to stuffing the money into a savings account at about 25 percent interest, a rate most people would accept.

Will that second computer save you an hour a week—that is, one hour in 40?

Over time, I've formed some habits around having two or more computers on my desk. Some careful records I've kept confirm that I use the second computer around 18 percent of the time, mostly when I'm waiting for something to happen on the primary box. However, nearly 50 percent of the time the primary box becomes ready before I'm done with the secondary task, and I continue with the secondary task anyhow. Put another way, 50 percent of 18 percent is 9 percent, and so that second computer lets me add about 9 percent more work to every day.

That equates to about 3.6 extra, free hours per week. So it sounds quite reasonable that a second computer will save anyone one extra hour a week.

What's that hour worth? If your company spends $70,000 to keep you, that equates to $35/hour. When you've had that new computer 60 weeks, it has saved the company $2,100.

To be a good investment, a computer would have to pay for itself in less than three years, or 152 weeks.

In this scenario, the actual return on investment hovers around 60 percent, even given the extremely conservative estimates of how much time the new box would save you. To gain a 25 percent return on investment, it would only need to save you about 20 minutes a week.

It may sound pretentious, but oftentimes you simply think faster than a computer. Even if you don't, what are you doing while it compiles, boots, or has a slow screen loading?

The more important question is "What could you be doing, and of course, what would you be doing?"

Surrounded by glowing machines, what geeks we must seem to be! Efficient ones?

Convincing Your Spouse

Is your spouse of a logical or investment bent? Then the arguments above might persuade. Does your spouse trust you for being logical and for finding good investments? Then, also, the arguments might persuade. If you're consulting, merely divide the cost of the computer by your hourly rate and see how much extra cash that new box should bring into your household. Remember that, as a business tool, it's probably tax deductible.

However, may I respectfully suggest that you approach this issue as a team? Then persuasion is much less necessary. Becoming a team if you aren't one involves two people truly becoming as one. A large portion of romance never hurts; however, allow me to suggest that romance with an ulterior motive lacks integrity. Plan the purchase together, and include software on it that intrigues everyone in your family.

Network the computers, and you can use many of the second computer's features while someone else is playing a game on it. For instance, you can use a small amount of the game computer's spare hard-disk space as a backup for the inevitable time that your primary hard disk will crash.

Commercial Software Tools for Java

Testing linear programs is tough enough. It's tedious. It's an arcane art practiced by a few. The harness, or wrapper, code needed to test each method or class must be written by someone, and can seldom be reused. Harness code often exceeds the size of the code it tests!

Testing is seen as a sinkhole for time, one that is exceedingly expensive. Research studies indicate that the average company tests only about 32 percent of the software it releases to the public, and to hear users grousing at the lunch counters, that number seems realistic!

I'd never drive an automobile that only had 32 percent of its components tested during development. The reason isn't safety. The reason is that the car would never make it off the dealer's lot!

Testing probably represents 30 percent of the software's total cost of development. Testing 90 percent of the modules, especially at the cost of today's salaries, might price software out of the market! At least, that's what bottom-line watchers seem to believe, but let's do the math and see.

Say that your product retails for $100, and that 25 percent of the development cost is due to testing 30 percent of the modules fully. Those are reasonable numbers. Now, say that you triple the amount of testing, so that 90 percent of the code is fully tested. That might reasonably mean that instead of spending $25 per copy for testing, you'd spend $75 per copy for testing. You'll still spend $75 per copy for all other expenses. In that case, the software needs to be marketed for $150, to recover your development costs with the same number of sales.

By the way, how would you like to test 90 percent of the code for, say, $10 per copy instead of $25 or $75 per copy? Hold onto that thought.

Back to the analysis. The software's shelf price has only risen by 50 percent. Some people would argue that users would snap up such high-quality software, even at twice the price, increasing your profit margin significantly, because you'd make another $50 in pure profit.

I'm in the latter camp.

Say a user is paid $25 per hour, and uses a $99 product that wastes an hour of the user's time per week due to bugs. The product actually costs $199 the first month, and $100 every month thereafter, for the life of the product. At the end of the second month, total cost of ownership is $299. At the end of a year, the product has cost about $1,300 to own.

On the other hand, a product with a $199 price tag that costs one hour a month due to bugs, costs $224 the first month, and $25 a month thereafter. By the end of the second month, the second product has a total cost of ownership of $249 and the higher quality software is the better deal. At the end of a year, the better product has cost about $500, vice $1,300 for the inferior, but cheaper, product.

The original price of software is insignificant, compared to the salary cost of the people using it.

Insignificant!

One would think that your company's marketing people could make a significant amount of hay with that idea. They could sell total cost of ownership, which includes downtime due to bugs. Remember that a good investment pays for itself every 3-4 years. In the software example above, if someone bought the cheap software and invested the difference of $100, they would have to invest at a whopping 280 percent compound interest, just to stay even. That's 10 times the best rate they might ever get in the stock market.

If you can improve your downtime by only ten percent through more rigorous testing, and charge twice as much for the product, your product is still a bargain. It seems that customers buy features, instead of quality and software up-time, but that's because of what marketers push—features. Customers tend to buy what the marketers push.

These arguments are among the best for using Java in the first place. Inherently, Java is less error-prone than older languages, even though their libraries are more mature. Java has advanced the state of the art of software development by disallowing the most error-prone constructs of previous languages. Many of the kinds of errors that abound in languages like CoBOL, PL/I, Modula-2, Ada, C, C++, and Visual Basic simply don't occur in Java. However, Java's autonomous threads change the picture again, because of their sheer, easy-to-use power.

It's not that other languages lack the possibility of threads. Programmers can use any language to implement threads, with a bit of thought. Any language can implement any construct, for that matter. CoBOL doesn't support recursion, but that only means the programmer has to write a few stack procedures by hand, to implement recursion. Each one takes about twenty lines of code. It's a bit less trivial to implement threads, but one merely needs to manage independent processes. System programmers have been doing that for decades, using a variety of languages.

It's just that Java's threads are pervasive. You can hardly get away from them. The simplest "Hello World" program is a thread, by default. The garbage collector operates as a thread, which is why it can run autonomously. You can create as many threads as you desire. Threads are integral to Java, giving it great power as a language.

Programming power attracts bugs, because such power is not easily understood. Computer bugs flee from understanding, even faster than roaches run from light, because a computer bug, understood, is easily squashed.

The most valuable tools for debugging Java tend to be thread-centric. They focus on the difficulties threads give to Java programmers, because a large percentage of Java bugs involve thread interactions. So, before discussing these advanced tools in depth, the book needs to delve into threads.

Chapter 11 discusses the threaded environment and the unique challenges it presents to programmers. Then, Chapter 12 discusses error traps. After those subjects, Chapter 13 returns to testing, to show how automated testing has come to Java. Software has been written, and is being improved, to automate many of the tedious, expensive tests that programmers must perform.

By using automatic software testers like ParaSoft's JTest, you can test nearly all of your code, as you develop it, with only a few clicks of the mouse! This product even examines your classes and generates test cases for you!

Profilers like the one in JProbe tell you where your software performs poorly, so you can concentrate on optimizing those areas. JProbe's coverage analyzer, and the coverage tester in JTest, let you know which parts of your code you have tested, and which you have not.

JLint, discussed earlier, performs numerous static tests on your source code.

Perhaps best of all, these products let you customize them. You can write your own testing rules, and even use these products to enforce office coding standards.

The Threaded Environment

Someone took a historic photograph of the world's very first automobile collision.

Obviously, such a collision could not have occurred until there were at least two cars on the road. Multiple cars brought new dynamics into driving. Now, to prevent collisions, we govern automotive traffic with signs, signals, divided roads, speed limits, etc.

A sequential computer program cannot collide with itself any more than the first car could hit itself. Concurrent programming changes all that. A concurrent Java program can have numerous autonomous threads, which can collide unless something governs them. Such collisions can result in corrupted data, deadlocks, deadly embraces, and data races.

Linear, one-dimensional programs are easy to pick apart and understand. The developer can set a breakpoint and single-step through the code, examining variables along the way. When a variable assumes an incorrect value, often the error is within a few lines of that variable.

However, threads add dimensions. People think in, at most, three dimensions. Or, do they?

Actually, dimensions beyond the usually considered three are nothing unusual. Unknowingly we use them every day.

Today, my wife and I remarked how driving a car occurs in more than three dimensions. Sitting in a parked car, we are concerned with the ordinarily perceived three dimensions of width, breadth, and height. We move a hand in three dimensions to adjust the rearview mirror, or we adjust the seat up-down, forward-back, and in its tilt dimension.

However, as soon as the car is moving, we've involved at least two more dimensions, barely realizing it. In relation to the outside world, we maneuver the car forward and backwards, left and right, so we can turn right at a street corner and not into someone's front yard, so we can drive safely to the grocer and not through the grocery.

As other drivers pass us, and we pass them, we also maneuver in relation to those cars, fitting into other two-dimensional traffic streams and avoiding other cars. Doing that adds two more dimensions of left-right and forward-backward, and we're up to seven. Rarely, such as when a car leaps into the air at a crash scene, yet another dimension becomes relevant. Moving from the fast lane through progressively slower lanes, preparing to exit a freeway, we interact with several independently moving streams of traffic, all moving at varying speeds. We calculate when two or more traffic holes will appear simultaneously, and again we're adding dimensions. We hear the siren of an approaching fire truck, and suddenly all traffic becomes chaotic as drivers try to make way. Suddenly, several more dimensions flood our consciousness.

And we handle it all, without realizing we've passed far beyond the fourth dimension! Amazing.

A sequential program moves linearly in one dimension. At a branch, a second dimension appears, somewhat analogous to left-right. When the program uses nested loops, each nesting can be deemed a new dimension, so 3-D or even 4-D computer programs are relatively common.

In Java, creation of each thread adds another dimension to the "space" of the program. That thread may have loops and branches, adding more dimensions. And we, who somehow manage to handle five, seven, nine, or perhaps fifteen dimensions while driving a car, worry that threads add too much complexity to a program? Hang on. There's a point approaching.

That point is, when moving between traffic lanes, we mostly disregard the three dimensions inside the car. Our feet and hands move almost autonomously as we speed up or slow down and move left or right into another lane. We don't consciously apply 0.75 pounds of force to the accelerator and move the steering wheel ten degrees clockwise. Instead, we speed up and move the car one lane right. That's what is in the mind, speeding up and moving right, as if we did it while running or walking. The car becomes an extension of our persona, letting us disregard the very real three dimensions within it, while we autonomously interact with them too.

On another level, we don't consciously make our biceps muscle contract. Instead, we move our arm and hand in a particular and complicated way that involves perhaps a hundred muscles. In fact, it would be impossible to think about contracting all hundred or so muscles in particular ways to type this sentence. We're able to type because of training, which means thinking in terms of patterns that involve contracting hundreds of muscles very precisely. This training simplifies things so we can do far more complex tasks than we can even program robots to do!

Considered in that light, threads don't complicate simple programs; they simplify complex computer programs. Without autonomous programs such as threads, complex programs like operating systems would be impossible to understand. Threads hide complexity, so we can rely on whole things happening, instead of being overly concerned with minutia. One might think of the hundred or so muscles required to type this line as separate, human threads that simplify an extremely complex task—typing.

As we drive cars, we ignore most of the dimensions around us, especially those represented by autonomous processes. Should we be concerned that since spark plug #3 just fired, and the V-8 engine is running at 3,000 rpm, the #1 spark plug must fire exactly 1/400 of a second later? Of course not! When maneuvering to let a fire truck pass, we'd best not worry about the fact that the driver's seat can move up, down, forward, and back. We drive in relation to the stream of traffic on the right, find a hole, and then find another hole, until reaching the side of the road. We disregard most threads of traffic on the left, except for avoiding someone who wants to swap fender paint with us. We disregard the threads involving the driver's seat, the spark plugs, the valves, the heater fan, and dozens more. We do that because we can, and because they don't affect what we're trying to accomplish at that moment.

Similarly, in a threaded computer program, we can disregard the thread that's writing a file to the disk, except when we're actually concerned with writing to the disk. If that's our concern, we can disregard most other threads in the program. Being able to do that simplifies our programming tasks to the point that we can handle them. We can actually build an operating system, and even understand it—one piece—one thread at a time.

Despite the fact that multiprocesses allow mankind to create far more complex programs than we otherwise could, Java's inherently threaded environment does add new dimensions of difficulty to debugging. This happens because, although we have excellent tools to encode our threads, we have very few tools for encoding their interactions.

Sometimes, it seems the best we can do is to create threads as intelligently as we can, turn them loose, and hope. All is not lost, however.

This chapter discusses the kinds of bugs you can expect from multiple threads, how to prevent them, performance penalties for doing so, more sophisticated threading techniques than the JDK offers natively, and specialized tools for isolating potential threading bugs.

Ancient Parallel Algorithms Revisited

The Monroe calculator was a mechanical marvel in its day. It could divide! Before it died, my antique example produced about one digit of precision per second, but calculated incorrectly about 2 percent of the time, probably because some wheel had a worn cog.

The U.S. Army once employed roomfuls of people running noisy Monroe calculators, to grind out the trajectories of artillery shells. To speed the computations, the algorithms were broken into pieces, and all of the pieces were calculated simultaneously, in parallel. As an error check, a group of six people would perform identical calculations on one-tenth of the trajectory, while other groups of six calculated other tenths of the trajectory. If four of the six people running one calculation arrived at the same answer, it was deemed correct, and they could move to the next calculation. When all of the calculations were complete for a particular shell fired at a particular angle, the information went into a printed trajectories table for artillery officers to use.

The advent of digital computers changed all that. Calculating far faster than any reasonable group of people could, even a PC has no need to perform parallel computations on artillery trajectories. The calculations are deterministic and repeatable. Parallel algorithms, which were used up to World War II, have largely been supplanted by algorithms that are better suited to high-speed calculators.

However, as wise King Solomon observed, there is nothing new under the sun. In such diverse fields as astronomy, particle physics, aerodynamics, entertainment, and encryption, certain algorithms are so complex, or the calculations are so numerous, that the fastest computers can require weeks or years to produce results. In such disciplines, the obvious way to get faster results is the same as the obvious way to calculate artillery shell trajectories quicker. Use more calculators. In the case of computers, that means using more CPUs, or computers, running in parallel.

The first Connection Machine shocked the information world by approaching supercomputer speed with an array of 64 ordinary PCs. Later, an instance of the Data Encryption Standard (DES) that was considered so complex a Cray would take years to crack it was reportedly found vulnerable when thousands of programmers used the interconnectivity of the Internet to crack it in a few weeks. The power of parallel computing is enormous.

Java is bringing antique parallel algorithms back to the fore, because it allows parallel computing.

Strictly speaking, a Java implementation on one single-CPU machine does very little in parallel. Peripherals, such as the disk drive, are able to perform tiny tasks while the CPU does other things. For instance, a CPU can set a disk drive head to moving, and instead of waiting for the head to arrive at its appointed cylinder, the CPU can put a pixel on the screen. Then, having some of its own "smarts," the disk can interrupt the CPU, saying it's time to transfer some more data. Those things happened in parallel.

However, the idea of ten simultaneous trajectory calculations being governed by one CPU is not yet possible. Instead, the CPU allocates a tiny slice of time to each thread, then moves on to the next thread. So, one might think that the multiprocessing power of Java is lost on an ordinary single-CPU PC. That's not so, because other factors enter the picture.

Most peripherals, such as disk drives, have intelligence built in. Drives can perform small tasks, such as moving a drive head to cylinder 123 autonomously, perhaps cache what's there, and then send a signal that it is awaiting further instructions. Some printers have large amounts of memory. Most new monitors have intelligence. The list goes on: modems, network cards, scanners, cameras, joysticks, keyboards, even mice, commonly have computer intelligence. While peripherals are performing their tasks, the CPU can be directing some other thread to start its task. Thus, many things can be happening at once.

Another factor is the human operator. While you read what's popping onto the screen, your Java program can be doing a host of things. In fact, that's one key to writing "quick" programs. Give the user something interesting to read whenever a slow process is executing. For example, if you ever run across my résumé on the Web, you might find my photo. It takes a few seconds to load, so I put a small amount of text behind it to entertain the reader.

Parallel Computing Bugs

Even the simplest program uses a thread, and in general, a program runs until all threads are finished.

Daemon and User Threads

You can specify threads that must run in the background and never stop. Such threads might perform data cleanup, for instance. You declare threads that you want to run forever as **daemon** threads, using the **setDaemon()** method, as follows:

```
Public final void setDaemon(boolean on)
   throws IllegalThreadStateException
```

If the parameter *on* is set **true**, then the thread is a **daemon** thread. If **false**, the thread becomes a **user** thread. Thus, you can convert a thread from **user** to **daemon** and back. You can determine whether a thread is **user** or **daemon** with the **isDaemon()** method.

When the JVM detects that all **user** threads, excluding **daemon** threads, have terminated, it terminates the program, and of course, the **daemon** threads terminate with it.

Daemon is an ancient computer term meaning Disk And Execution MONitor. The first daemons were small, independent programs that watched over the disk and programs as they did their work. Today, operating systems use daemons for all manner of tasks, such as delivering messages from one part of the system to another.

Java's Inherent Protection

If a maverick thread, perhaps a **daemon** thread, could put all other threads to sleep, change their priorities, or worse yet, terminate them, the results could be disastrous. Fortunately, Java won't allow that to happen. Threads can only manipulate threads in their own thread group or subgroups, letting you restrict their power. Here's how it works.

Each thread has an associated **Runnable** interface. That interface can even be the thread itself. The interface calls a **run()** method, which contains the thread's programming.

Error Watch *You can create a thread without a **Runnable** interface, but in that case, the thread merely uses itself as the **Runnable** interface. In that case, because the **run()** method's default action (in the **Thread class**) is to return, nothing happens.*

You should always specify a **Runnable** interface. This is one way:

```
public Thread(Runnable threadName)
```

In this case, the **run()** method is invoked in *threadName*, and the current thread's group gets a new thread. Threads in this group can interact with each other, but not with threads in other groups.

When you want to assign a thread to another group, you do so at thread creation time with a line like this

```
public Thread(NewThreadGroup group, String threadName)
```

where *threadName* is optional, and advisable, so you and your debugger can isolate it more easily if necessary. In this case, the new thread can only interact with threads of *NewThreadGroup* or, as mentioned, any of its subgroups.

Loop Parallelization

Some processes, such as loops and recursion, cry out for simultaneous computation. If you have a loop that iterates 1,000 times and you have a computer with ten CPUs, in theory, you might have one CPU run the first hundred loops, while the second CPU runs the second hundred loops, etc. The result is a calculation that runs in 1/10 the time.

Not all loops can benefit from this idea. A loop in which each iteration's result depends on the results of prior iterations, such as a sort or a search, is not a candidate for parallelization. However, a loop that reads data from one file to another certainly is.

Although it is threaded, Java does not have automatic loop parallelization. However, that power is surely coming!

Similarly, some recursive processes can be parallelized. In some depth-first searches, one CPU might begin to handle the first level, and send the next available CPU scurrying off on each second-level node. In turn, that CPU might use the next available CPU for each third-level node, etc.

Java won't do that for you automatically, either. However, you can write parallelized loops and recursion into your code, and on a multiple-CPU machine you can usually take advantage of all the CPUs.

What Java does is run separate threads for things like the mouse, the disk IO, and various classes. It allots a tiny amount of time to each thread in turn, so they all seem to run simultaneously. The difficulty that presents to you is that you have no easy way to know which thread runs when. More importantly, you need special tools or techniques to know when two threads try to conflict with each other.

Fortunately, thread analysis software exists to help you.

Handling Input and Output

The **read()** method, using **System.in** to specify the user's computer, accepts user input. During a **read()**, the computer waits until the user provides some input, such as by typing a character. Then the program resumes running, perhaps testing that character against a list of characters allowed at that point. Commonly, the next step is to take an action based on that character. The action might be to read another character, like my word processor is doing right now. I may press nearly any key on the keyboard and the program will accept it, and then wait for the next. If my next characters were ALT-F, the word processor would open the File menu, which would restrict the keystrokes the program would accept to a smaller set.

Each time the statement **read(System.in);** is executed, the program blocks. If the input is from a user, blocking is probably good. If the input is from a network, blocking is probably just the opposite of what you want to happen, because you don't want the program to stall, waiting for the network to deign to offer up a bit of input. It would be far better to let the computer read data from the network as it comes in and, meanwhile, allow the user to get some other work done on the same machine. So, dedicate a thread to reading input. There are several techniques you can use, among them the following.

Polling for Input

Java's **available()** method in the **FilterInputStream** class lets you implement polling. In this technique, the program tests whether or not data is available. If not, the program can do other things. If data is available, the program can process it and perhaps return to polling duty. You can implement polling easily with a **while** loop, or a **do while** loop.

24x7

When polling a socket, create a special thread. Allow that thread to block when no data is available at the socket. That way, other threads can run the rest of the program unimpeded.

Signaling that Input Is Available

Java doesn't support this "monitor and semaphore" technique directly, but you can write Java code to signal that input is available. Arrange for the input source to send an asynchronous signal when data arrives. Let the signal interrupt the program, forcing the program to process the data before resuming. Signaling is often better than polling for two reasons:

- In polling, a process tests the input periodically. That takes CPU cycles. On the other hand, the signaling technique relies on the presence of data to let the computer know the data has arrived. The difference is rather like calling someone on the phone every now and then to see if they're home yet vs. leaving them a note to call you when they return. If data is nearly always there, such as on a fast network, then polling is a fine choice.

- Polling is a measurement, and all measurements change whatever they're measuring. Most likely, the changes are inconsequential in this case, but signaling doesn't change the input data.

Multiplexing Multiple Kinds of Input

Java's **select**() method can let a program know when data arrives. You can combine all kinds of input. Then your program can handle input just as if it came from the user. You may need to have each packet of information identify itself in some manner, so you can decode from whence it came.

Output Can Block

If you are uploading data over a modem, you typically have a speed problem. In this case, your computer can outspeed your modem by an order of magnitude. You've probably seen cases in which your computer seems to lock until your modem catches up. This is a case of output blocking.

24x7

If you've created a thread for input, you probably need another one for output.

Asynchronous Tasks

Due to its threads, Java is artfully made for asynchronous behavior.

I used to turn off autosave in my word processor, because now and then my keyboard would lock. It was frustrating to drop the train of thought (right brain) and figure out (left brain) what was happening, then try to return to that train of thought. My favorite word processor has no such difficulty. Autosaving occurs completely in the background, probably run by a thread.

Various kinds of servers need to perform asynchronous tasks, as does an operating system. If ten people address the print server within a single second requesting printouts, the print server must asynchronously schedule the jobs.

Schedulers

Many print servers have more than one scheduling mode. To satisfy the most users the quickest, one popular mode reschedules all pending jobs so that the shortest begins first. This mode satisfies the most people the fastest. However, if you send all of the chapters of a book to the printer as separate jobs, the "shortest first" mode can mix up the chapters. Instead, you can set your printer to operate in first-in-first-out (FIFO) mode.

Operating system schedulers often default to emphasizing programs that are heavy with IO, and deemphasize those heavy on math. A company dealing with complex calculations might opt for just the opposite in their computers. So, when you write that diesel-powered, chrome-plated, never-fail operating system, you need to allow for various scheduling methodologies. One possibility is to write a thread for each scheduling mode and let the system administrators select which one to activate.

Whatever the scheduling mode, your program should probably create separate threads for the asynchronous tasks so that if one blocks, the rest can continue. Also, build threads that unblock blocked threads at the click of a mouse.

Java has a default means of scheduling threads. Whenever a thread suspends, waits, or goes to sleep, Java looks into the thread pool and runs another. You can give threads various priorities via the **setPriority()** method, and the JVM picks the one with the highest priority to run next. If several have the same highest priority, it merely chooses one.

Threads receive a default priority value equal to **Thread.NORM_PRIORITY**.

Error Watch   *The thread's priority has limits, which are **Thread.MIN_PRIORITY** and **Thread.MAX_PRIORITY**. An **IllegalArgumentException** occurs if a thread priority gets outside the limits. Algorithms, such as used in operating system or print job scheduling, that raise or reduce thread priorities must check that they stay within the allowed range. Check a thread's priority with the **getPriority()** method.*

Various JVM implementations can choose their own minimum and maximum thread priorities. If your code should run on Windows, UNIX, and MAX operating systems, you should test it on all three.

It's possible to set thread priorities without knowing the values of **Thread.MIN_PRIORITY** or **Thread.MAX_PRIORITY**. Here's how:

If the minimum is 1 and the maximum is 10, then you have 10 possible priorities (Max – Min + 1). You can normalize this difference to a scale of, say, 1–100 and choose your own priority on that 1–100 scale by dividing the 10 possible priorities into 100, getting a factor of 10. Then, to set a priority of, say, 30, on your 1–100 scale, divide 30 by 10, getting 3, and add that 3 to the minimum of 1, then subtract 1. Set the thread's priority to 3. While you may want to use floats or doubles and casts, instead of integer division, the pseudocode is as follows:

```
//Set priority to 30 on a scale of 1-100, as an example.
priority = 30;

range = (Thread.MAX_PRIORITY - Thread.MIN_PRIORITY + 1);
factor = 100 / range;
newPriority = (Thread.MIN_PRIORITY - 1 + (priority / factor));
Thread.setPriority(newPriority);
```

JVM Differences

If you rely on thread priority to keep things synchronized, it is important to test on various classes of JVM. It's also important to test Java applications vs. applets, because you will find differences.

Timers

Your program can set timers running, and then resume execution. When the time runs out, the timer can send a signal to the program, interrupting it, thus telling it to do something like backing up a file, dialing the modem again, or putting a notice on the screen.

Error Watch *Don't count on too much timer precision. In the **Thread** class, the **sleep(long)** method lets you specify times to nanosecond precision, but few computers have clocks that can support such extreme precision. After all, the CPU cycles in a gigahertz microprocessor occur one nanosecond apart! Most computers merely round nanoseconds to the nearest millisecond and implement that, if they even support millisecond precision. Some don't.*

Time-Sensitive Thread Bugs

Time-sensitive bugs occur when two processes conflict, such as by competing for the same resource. With a few exceptions, Java is careful not to let two processes have the same resource at the same time. However, this precaution allows new things to go wrong. The problems occur when your idea of what a resource should be differs from Java's. It's a matter of granularity. One atomic (indivisible) grain in Java is assignment. Except for **long** and **double** numbers, no two threads can try to assign a value to the same variable at the same time, for the results would be indeterminate.

In the case of **long** and **double** numbers, two threads can assign values to them simultaneously. The undesirable result is that one thread changes some bits, and the other thread changes the rest. Nothing can predict beforehand which thread will change which bits!

 *Whenever more than one thread can assign a value to a **long** or **double**, you might want to synchronize that assignment for safety.*

Error Watch *Be aware that garbage collection can affect all threads running in a JVM. Garbage collection happens autonomously, and when it does, it can temporarily suspend any and all threads. This can create synchronization problems out of thin air.*

Data Races

You don't want data races in your programs. They cause nasty bugs. When a program runs fine most of the time but locks randomly, you probably have a data race condition. Data races are so time sensitive that your program might work perfectly for everyone except one of your clients. It might run fine for you but not your colleague, on the same machine! There might be no rhyme, reason, or discernable pattern in the blowups. Data might be corrupted only occasionally, and when you step through the program, exactly the same data mysteriously updates perfectly. The program may run superbly, except that the release build version dies randomly.

24x7

If a program runs well in development but crashes consistently in the release build, you may be using a different kind of memory allocation. You probably have uninitialized variables to fix, not a race condition. Race conditions generally cause random crashes.

Data races can even be sensitive to how fast you double-click your left mouse button. Now, try to debug that!

The thing about data races is that the data is actually part of the program. More specifically, how the program acts depends on the data. As a trivial example from an earlier chapter points out, a program that has to build an initial table does so only once. If that table exists, the program does something different. Here's a less trivial example.

Consider a program that highlights a chosen line of text by reversing the colors of its foreground and its background. The colors on a screen can be expressed in terms of red, green, and blue, each having values from 0–255. To highlight a line of text, you might add 128 to each value, modulo 256, so that a value of 60 would become 188, and a value of 250 would become 122. This is a self-reversing algorithm. Run it again and the text returns to its original colors. Here it is in pseudocode:

```
void ReverseColors() {
  foreRed   = (foreRed   + 128) % 256;
  backRed   = (backRed   + 128) % 256;
  foreGreen = (foreGreen + 128) % 256;
  backGreen = (backGreen + 128) % 256;
  foreBlue  = (foreBlue  + 128) % 256;
  backBlue  = (backBlue  + 128) % 256;
  repaint();
}
```

Such a block of code can act incorrectly if another thread can reach into it and subvert the process. That can happen in the above code, because the **repaint()** method does not act immediately. It queues its request. If the repainting happens just before **foreGreen** is reset, for example, the colors will be wrong, at least until the next **repaint()** method acts, because **foreGreen** and the rest will not have been changed yet.

Of course, the solution is to prevent some other thread from changing colors before the first thread finishes. The **synchronized** command makes a block atomic—that is, indivisible. Any thread that wants to reach into the block stalls until the block is finished executing. The new pseudocode could read this way:

```
synchronized void ReverseColors() {
  foreRed   = (foreRed   + 128) % 256;
  backRed   = (backRed   + 128) % 256;
  foreGreen = (foreGreen + 128) % 256;
  backGreen = (backGreen + 128) % 256;
```

```
    foreBlue  = (foreBlue  + 128) % 256;
    backBlue  = (backBlue  + 128) % 256;
}
repaint()
```

Notice that **repaint()** is now outside the code block. With the previous block **synchronized** and atomic, **repaint()** cannot act until the block is finished and all colors are safely set.

The **synchronized** command introduces its own set of difficulties (does this trail never end?):

- The blocked thread can do nothing for a time, impairing its performance.

- Blocking introduces the possibility of locking up the program, or allowing memory leaks.

- A synchronized process runs only about 1/4 as fast as the same process, unsynchronized.

So, the **synchronized** keyword must be used carefully, and sparingly.

Data Race Prevention   To prevent data races, you should monitor every access to every variable. In a limited scope, you can do this. If a variable is accessed more than once, but no common lock exists that can prevent multiple threads from accessing the variable at the same time, you have a potential data race.

In JProbe, the Lock Covers Analyzer does exactly this for all accesses to all variables, and flags potential data races for you.

Deadlock

If thread A locks some **synchronized** code that thread B needs, and thread B locks some **synchronized** code that thread A needs in order to release its lock, the program is deadlocked. Thread A cannot release the lock that would let thread B run and release the lock that prevents...well, you understand the problem.

Deadlocks can involve multiple threads, in a circle:

- Thread A locks code that thread B needs.

- Thread B locks code that thread C needs.

- Thread C locks code that...

- ...that thread N needs.

- Thread N locks code that thread A needs.

It is often, but not always, possible to prove whether or not code will deadlock. It is easier to look for suspicious cases.

Notice that an active deadlock may or may not appear to lock up your computer. If the deadlock occurs between the input and output threads of a Web application, you still might be able to move the mouse and edit what's on the screen, because the mouse and keyboard threads might be operating perfectly. However, if your mouse thread deadlocks, the mouse cursor won't move. If your mouse and keyboard threads deadlock, your computer may seem to need rebooting, even though a 20MB download is running just fine.

It might be that when the 20MB download finishes, a thread terminates, releasing a lock and resolving the deadlock. If that's the case, you had a stall, not a true deadlock.

Deadlock Prevention   Seek situations in which threads try to obtain the same series of locks, but not in the same order. In the above example, one thread might acquire locks in A, B, C order, but another thread acquires them in C, A, B order. In this case a deadlock is possible, but not certain to occur.

In this case, prevention is tedious, but tools like JProbe automate it for you.

Don't let a process go to sleep, such as via the **wait**() method, while it has locks open. If it doesn't awaken, it can't release those locks. JProbe seeks this condition for you as well.

Stalls

A stall is similar to a deadlock. Say two threads can deadlock, but a third thread's job is to release one of the locks. In this case, you have a potential stall condition. The problem is that the third thread may fail to release a lock, since it runs autonomously. It can also die before releasing that lock. Thus the program might run perfectly for a while and then stop. Obviously, such random-seeming bugs are difficult to localize.

Since the action of that new thread might not be deterministic, it can be impossible to prove a stall will occur. Tools like Assure are able to point out suspicious conditions so you can decide whether or not a fix is needed.

A thread may stall for an extended period by design. For instance, it may be sitting on a port waiting for input to arrive. About the best a tool like Assure can do in that case is to tell you that a thread has stalled for a while. The rest is up to you.

Preventing Thread Clashes

There is a classic textbook problem in concurrent programming, known as "Readers and Writers." In one variation, you have a number of fast processes that need to read data that is being written slowly by another process. It's okay for multiple readers to read anything that has been written, but not while anything is being written. How can you implement this?

Here are the ideas:

- Multiple readers may read data at the same time.

- Only one writer may write data at a time.

- While a writer is writing, no reader may begin reading.

- While any reader is reading, no writer may begin writing.

- These ideas boil down to a different set involving a **readLock**, which prevents reading, and a **writeLock**, which prevents writing.

- When set, **readLock** ensures that only one reader locks and unlocks the **writeLock**.

- When set, **writeLock** ensures that only one thread is writing at a time.

- When set, **writeLock** ensures no readers are reading during a write.

  This pseudocode solves the problem:

```
/* Declarations */
Lock readLock;        //Prevent reading
Lock writeLock;       //Prevent writing
int  readers = 0;     //Count readers

/* The Reader method */
read() {

  // Only let the first reader set the write lock.
  lock (readlock);

  // If this is the first reader
  if(readers == 0) {
    // Prevent any writing until reading is done
    lock(writeLock);
  }
  // In any case, increment the number of readers.
  readers++;

  // Get data. Unlock first.
  unlock(readLock);
  /* Read Data */
```

```
    lock(readLock);
    // Finished reading, so decrement readers.
    readers--;

    // Only open the write lock when there are no readers left.
    if(readers == 0) {
      unlock(writeLock);
    }

    // Housekeeping.
    unlock(readLock);
  }

  /* The Writers method */
  write() {
    getDataToWrite();
    lock(writeLock);
      /* Write Data */
    unlock(writeLock);
  }
```

The trick is to implement it in Java! One would think **synchronized** would help, and it does, but there's this small problem. The **synchronized** keyword does not implement a lock. It implements what's called a "critical section." It makes that section atomic. If a thread enters a critical section, no other thread can enter until the first thread exits. Since we want multiple reader threads to read the data at the same time, we cannot merely synchronize the reader method because that would lock out all readers but the first one.

Design Tip   *You can use **synchronized** to link critical sections, and thus build a mutual exclusion system, also known as a "mutex," but the idea of having multiple readers is elusive.*

Spin Locks to the Rescue!

A spin lock is one way to make a process wait until another is finished. The spin-locking process continuously polls the blocked process to see if it is unblocked yet. It's rather like dialing a radio station's phone line continuously, hoping to be the tenth caller and win that new Ferrari.

The simplest way to implement a spin lock is with a loop. In the **write()** method below, the spin lock's mechanism is in bold text:

```java
public class ImplementingSpinLocks {
  private Integer readLock = new Integer(0);
  private int readers = 0;    // Count the readers.

  /* The Readers method */
  public int read() {
    int readData = 0;

    // Lock out other readers
    synchronized(readLock) {
      // The first reader locks out the writers

      // This is what the pseudo code says
      //  if(readers == 0) {
      //     lock writers
      //  }

      // Synchronized will not allow multiple readers in,
      // so the writer implements a spin lock on readers

      // Increment the number of readers
      readers++;
    }

    // Unlock readers
    /* Read the data here. */
    // Lock readers

    synchronized(readLock) {
      // Decrement the number of readers
      readers--;

      // This is from the pseudo-code
      //  if(readers == 0) {
      //     unlock writers
      //  }
      // Instead, let the writer poll the readers until there are
      // no readers left.

    }
    // Unlock readers
    // Send back the data
    return readData;
  }
```

```
/* The Writers method */
  public void write(int x) {
  /* Strategy:  Lock writers
            Write
            Unlock writers
    However, we must use spin locks.
  */

    // "while" implements a nice spin lock.
    boolean success = false;
    // Wait until there are no readers left
    while(!success) {
      synchronized(readLock) {
        if(readers == 0) {
          // There are no readers, and readLock is set
          /* Write the data here. */
          // Break out of the while loop
          success = true;
        }
      }

      if(!success) {
        // Keep spinning, because there is at least one reader left.
        // yield() to give other threads their time in the limelight.
        Thread.currentThread().yield();
      }
    }
  }
}
```

Locks Using Monitors and Semaphores

It's quite obvious that a continuously running **while** loop in the **write()** method consumes CPU cycles. What if you could avoid that problem neatly? Here's a lock class that relies on the **try** and **catch** keywords of Java. In Chapter 3, I recommended that you not use **try** and **catch** to exit from loops, because doing so subverts the basic tenets of structured programming. That's still good advice. However, here is one place outside of error traps that **try** and **catch** can validly be used for performance reasons.

Monitors are things that go to sleep, consume very little CPU power, and awaken only when notified that something interesting happened.

Semaphores are message carriers, or signalers. The code below uses monitors and semaphores:

```
class Lock extends Object {
// Purpose: Implement a boolean lock
  private boolean blocked = false;     //Tells whether or not the lock is set.

  public synchronized void lock() {
    // If a thread has locked this object, then wait.

    if(blocked) {
      do {
/*
  Normally, I would not recommend using try this way. However, it is
  a very efficient mechanism, in that it doesn't consume the CPU.
  This code temporarily removes itself from being synchronized.
  When notify() is called, the program will perform another
  synchronization and continue. Notice how exceptions are handled.
  If they are not caught, an exception can ruin the lock.
*/
        try {
          wait();   // Go to sleep, waiting for notify()
        }
        catch(InterruptedException e) {
          e.printStackTrace();
        }
        catch(Exception e) {
          e.printStackTrace();
        }

      // Wait while the other thread has this one blocked.
      } while(blocked);
    }
    // Set a block for this thread.
    blocked = true;
  }

  public synchronized boolean lock(long milliSeconds, int nanoSeconds) {
  // Comments for this method are similar to the above.
    if(blocked)
    {
      try {
        wait(milliSeconds, nanoSeconds);
      }
      catch(InterruptedException e) {
        e.printStackTrace();
      }

      if(blocked) {
        return false;
      }
    }
```

```
    blocked = true;
    return true;
  }

  public synchronized boolean lock(long milliSeconds) {
  // Comments for this method are similar to the above.
    if(blocked) {
      try {
        wait(milliSeconds);
      }
      catch(InterruptedException e) {
        e.printStackTrace();
      }

      if(blocked) {
          return false;
      }
    }

    blocked = true;
    return true;
  }

  public synchronized void releaseLock()
  // Setting blocked to false releases any lock that was set above.
  {
    if(blocked) {
      blocked = false;
      notify();
    }
  }

  public synchronized boolean isLocked()
  {
    return blocked;
  }
}
```

By importing the **Lock** class above, it's possible to solve the Readers and Writers problem without using **synchronized**. Finally, here's a way to implement that pseudocode example in Java:

```
import Lock;
public class ReadersWritersUsingLocks {
  private Lock readLock = new Lock();
  private Lock writeLock = new Lock();
  private int readers = 0;                    // Count the readers


  // The Readers method.
  public int read() {
    int readData = 0;
```

```
    // Disallow reading.
    readLock.lock();

    // The first reader locks out all writers.
    if(readers == 0) {
      writeLock.lock();
    }

    // Increment the number of readers.
    readers++;

    // Allow reading.
    readLock.releaseLock();

    /* Read the data here. */

    // Disallow reading again.
    readLock.lock();

    // Decrement the number of readers.
    readers--;

    // If there are no more readers, allow writing.
    if(readers == 0) {
        writeLock.releaseLock();
    }

    // Allow reading again.
    readLock.releaseLock();

    return readData;
  }

  public void write(int x)
  {
    // Block other writers.
    writeLock.lock();

    /* Write the data here. */

    // Allow a new writer in, if one arrives.
    writeLock.releaseLock();
  }
}
```

More on Monitors and Semaphores

Monitors and semaphores are more efficient than spin locks. With these devices in use, a process that wants access to a blocked process goes to sleep, via **wait()**, until notified by the blocked process, via **notify()**, that it's time to awaken. A sleeping process consumes very little CPU power. It's like leaving a note on a friend's front door instead of camping on the doorstep.

Above, **wait()** and **notify()** comprise a monitor system, and the variable *readers* is a semaphore that various processes can test, increment, and decrement, thus signaling information to each other.

A few more comments are in order. These are important details!

In the **lock()** method of the **Lock** class above, **wait()** and **notify()** seem to play fancy with **synchronized**. In fact, they do. The **wait()** and **notify()** commands must be in synchronized blocks to work as a monitor system. The **wait()** method stops its synchronization before it goes to sleep. Otherwise, **notify()** could not reach into the block and awaken it! When the **notify()** message arrives, **wait()** restarts **synchronized** and continues, with the locked condition being over.

Distilled to its essence, the **wait()** and **notify()** mechanism looks like this:

```
Object o = new Integer(0);

// Go to sleep.
synchronized(o) {
  o.wait();
}

// Awaken the sleeper.
synchronized(o) {
  o.notify();
}
```

Some of the Best Thread Practices

In any language, there are good, bad, and downright ugly ways to do things. This section lists some practical ways to help threaded code shun bugs.

Stopping a Running Thread

Error Watch *You can find a **start()** and a **stop()** method in both the **Applet** and the **Thread** classes. **start()** has the same parameter list (signature) in both classes, and so does **stop()**. The methods have different functions, so take care when using **start()** and **stop()** with thread applets! **stop()** is deprecated in Java 2, alleviating some of the potential confusion.*

When you **run()** a thread, you should terminate it by letting it return from the **run()** method, if feasible. That is, arrange for it to run to completion.

Java 2 (JDK 1.2) deprecated the alternative method, **stop()**, because developers have had serious trouble with it. **stop()** does exactly what its name says—immediately, without taking care of housekeeping. That can trigger security problems, deadlocks, and memory leaks. If you use earlier versions of the JDK, I recommend that you terminate a thread by letting its life span run out—that is, by letting it return from its **run()** method. There are various ways of terminating early when you need to do that, such as by setting a flag or using the **isAlive()** or **isActive()** method of the Applet class.

The ThreadDeath Exception

Java lets you **catch** the **ThreadDeath** error if necessary. However, you should use the safer **finalize()** method instead. If you do **catch ThreadDeath**, be sure to throw it from the method that catches it. If you don't, guess what? Your thread won't die after all!

isAlive() vs. isActive(), and join()

The instant your program calls **start()**, the thread is alive but not yet active. This is a subtle but critical point. Some short span of time later, the thread starts running. When the thread is terminated via **stop()**, or because the thread returns from its **run()** method, it is no longer active but remains alive for a short time. The methods **isAlive()** and **isActive()** differ by those short time spans on either end of a thread's existence. A thread can be alive and not active, but not vice versa.

You can loop on the **isAlive()** or **isActive()** method to see when it's time to do something, but often the **join()** method is preferred. For instance, if you create a thread to send something through a socket, you can do other processing while that happens. A bit later, you can use **join()** to wait for that socket thread to finish. When the thread is no longer alive, **join()** returns. The **join()** method lets you specify a maximum time to wait for the socket thread to complete, and best practice is to use that parameter, avoiding a potential deadlock or stall.

The nicer things about **join()** are as follows:

- It doesn't do any polling, improving performance.
- It has no effect on the joined thread, reducing potential for bugs.
- It can join numerous threads, via a loop.

Here's a simple example of using **join()** in which the program spawns a new thread to calculate a large factorial, returns to the screen for the next number to calculate, and then returns to wait for the first calculation to finish:

```
double answer;         //The calculation's answer will go here.
Thread calculator = new CalculateLargeFactorial(answer);
calculator.start()
  //Code that gets the next number to be calculated, from the screen
calculator.join()    //Wait for the calculation to finish.
```

Error Watch *Don't bother trying to join a thread to itself. You'll wait until the **time** parameter runs out and then nothing will happen. Similarly, don't bother testing **isAlive()** on the current thread, because the test will always return **true**. The current thread is always alive, although it might not be active.*

Error Watch *Don't bother trying to restart a stopped thread. If you use **start()** on a stopped thread, nothing much happens. The **run()** method isn't called, **isAlive()**reports **false**, and no exception is thrown, with one exception. If your program calls **start()** during that small amount of time before the thread actually stops, you see an IllegalThreadStateException, just like you get if you try to **start()** any thread that is already active. However, you may call **stop()** on a stopped thread.*

Forcing Threads to Be Good Citizens

You probably don't want a thread like *calculator* in the previous example to hog the CPU, because your user will probably call you about it—at the most inopportune time. Many Java Virtual Machines allow preemptive scheduling, in which other threads get a chance to run, even when one is being a virtual hog. Not all JVMs schedule preemptively, so when you program potential CPU hogs, or a profiler like JProbe identifies one, you should make allowances.

As also shown in the Readers and Writers example above, the **yield()** method gives other threads a chance to run. Here's a smaller example:

```
double answer = 0;
for (int i=0; i<10000, i++) {
  for (int j=0; j<10000, j++) {
    answer = ((answer * i) + j) / j;
  }
Thread.yield();
}
```

Performance Issues

Face it. Poor performance is a bug. It might take another bank of memory or a faster CPU, or a larger hard drive, to squash the bug, but it's a bug.

Garbage Collection

Each time the garbage collector runs, it consumes a considerable amount of CPU time, but only for a short while. Then the CPU operates much more efficiently, until garbage begins piling up again. JProbe has a screen that shows you the garbage collection cycle, and their documentation wisely notes that if garbage collection occurs too often, that fact can signal a problem. The problem can be that something is creating too much garbage.

I've found the garbage collector works admirably well with threads. The system knows when all threads are running, and reclaims most resources when they stop. In some cases, however, you may want to dereference a thread manually to let garbage collection proceed.

Slow Synchronized

In Java, use of the **synchronized** keyword may be the wrong way to go for performance reasons, because it blocks threads from doing anything at all. When you use synchronized, you actually stop Java from multithreading! You force it to single-thread its processes. Moreover, my tests reveal that synchronized processes run about 1/4 the speed of unsynchronized processes.

Thread Safety

Some processes are not thread safe. With a few documented exceptions, **Swing** classes are not thread safe. That is, the usual restrictions and safeguards placed on threads are not in place. This is not to say you should avoid using the invaluable **Swing** classes, just that when you use them, you must be particularly careful with your threads. When you see erratic behavior in **Swing** classes, the first thing to suspect is that you have a wild thread or two.

Prevention

At the start of the chapter, I tried to make a case for the idea that threads simplify programming, as I wrote about driving on the freeways amidst five to fifteen dimensions of activity. I believe that the best drivers are those who stay aware of the multiple facets of driving, and thus avoid situations where they must consider too many dimensions at a time. Similarly, the finest pilots are those who never let themselves get into situations where their superb skills are necessary.

In programming, it seems that the more we can expand our consciousness, and the more we can be aware of various facets of programming (often threads), the less we react, and the more we act purposefully. Part of the key to writing bug-free threads is adopting an attitude that threads simplify programming. The rest of the key is experimenting in sterile environments, so you can find processes that always work for you.

After all this reading, if you still have one or two errors, you need to enlist your users. You need to get them to help you stomp out those last bugs. The next chapter gets into ways you can do that.

CHAPTER 12

The One That Got Away

L ook to grass-roots humor when you want to understand frustration.

How Users Perceive Bugs

You've seen the famous cartoon that shows a user brandishing a large mallet, about to "Hit Any Key!"

I saw a photo of a disk drive with a deep, .45-caliber bullet dent in it. Someone had sheepishly returned it to the factory, requesting data recovery.

There's a priceless office surveillance video being passed around. It shows a man kicking a PC off his desk and then jumping up and down on it, smashing it to bits!

A friend of mine took a keyboard to the corner of his desk, breaking it in half. I pocketed the "X" keycap as a souvenir of witnessing that incident.

People who shoot drives or who smash computers—sometimes costing themselves their jobs—graphically demonstrate the frustration the rest of us feel. Such people almost rise to folk-hero status.

We literally invest parts of our lives using computer programs, only to discover that the software has squandered those very parts of our lives. It's robbery of the worst sort.

I'm not immune. My boss' boss talked me into upgrading my new laptop from Windows 3.0 to the brand new Windows 95. A month later, a potential client asked how old that computer was when it took six minutes to boot. I replied it was three months old, but it had Windows 95 installed.

She quipped, to my embarrassment, "Want to know how to speed up Windows 95?" I answered, lamely, that I had very few ideas. She replied, without smiling, "Upgrade to Windows 3.0."

Four months later, having spent $450 on RAM, out of necessity, I took the laptop on a business trip, because I needed to touch up a novel during the evenings. I had to submit it in the most popular word processor's format, but I had used the second most popular program to write it. So, I bought the other word processor and imported the novel, but the import process failed. Then I discovered importing had corrupted my original file as well! My backup was some 500 miles away.

I soon had technical support from both companies on two phone lines, and heard each one blame the other company. We got nowhere on that issue, except that they agreed that it was a known problem, and there was no way to recover the novel until I got home.

Hoping to make some use of my evenings in the motel, I used the new word processor to retype and correct an offered contract. Then I used my original software to import it from the new program to the old, as a backup, and guess what. The reverse transfer process corrupted both copies too!

More phone calls. This time, better informed technicians in both companies told me they had patches I could download and prevent the problem, but that nothing could recover my files. I downloaded the patches, and they mostly worked, but underscores never did transfer. That was maddening because in a fiction manuscript, one uses underscores to denote foreign-language words, etc.

Six years later, the problems remain. Yesterday, I tried to import a novel from one of those word processors into another, using the latest versions, and the conversion failed! When I changed fonts, every line mysteriously acquired an "A" at its beginning, and the apostrophes changed to equal signs. Amazing!

Microsoft salesmen claimed that my Windows 95 woes would be over if I upgraded to Windows 98. My poor laptop lacked the disk space for Windows 98, so, foolishly, I opened my wallet, spending about $2,500 for new hardware. Then, I probably expended $15,000 worth of otherwise billable consulting time keeping the new machine running and learning how to tiptoe through the minefield commonly known as the "blue screen of death."

Today, my most stable machine, of the six in my network that run Windows, is a 486/33 running Windows 3.0. Next is that slow, little Windows 95 laptop, and even it locks up occasionally. Several times a week, at least one of my screens goes blue without warning. My latest computer has Windows 98, Word 2000, and Java software installed. Nothing else. It has a fast CPU, sports 256 megs of RAM, and has a huge hard drive. It's nearly as bad as the rest, and so it's slated for Linux when this book is finished.

When Windows 2000 shipped, independent testers logged about 65,000 bugs in it, and Microsoft admitted to more than 30,000! It had a distressingly short list of supported peripherals, and a number of companies reverted to earlier versions of Windows, or gave up and installed something else.

It's not just Microsoft producing such software. Users gather at the soda machines and turn the air blue about low-quality software from all sorts of manufacturers. Managers look at the billions of dollars literally wasted, due to faulty software, and some file lawsuits. Scores of class-action lawsuits are in the works against the largest software houses in the nation.

Technical support often runs out after 90 days, and becomes expensive thereafter. When you take a look at the alternative, which is wasted salary, an expensive call to technical support is cheap. I've resorted to a less expensive option on occasion. I go to the store and buy a new copy of the software, register it, and never use it, just to get another 90 days of support!

A colleague of mine made a sobering observation a few months ago. He said, "You know, the Japanese nearly dismantled the American auto industry over a single issue. Quality."

During the period between Microsoft's conviction over antitrust laws and the judge's announcement of punishment, you could hardly toss a rock without hitting some pundit who was offering the judge advice in print. The cleverest idea of that period was to require Microsoft to offer absolutely free technical support for all products, forever. That profound idea would encourage the company to produce dramatically higher quality software. Of course, what's good for Microsoft is good for the rest of the industry. I, for one, would welcome that kind of legal requirement, because for 20 years, I and several of my colleagues have guaranteed software to specifications forever. Although that's not an especially easy task, we're proof it can be done, and done profitably.

Read almost any software license agreement. It says that you don't own the software, and that the company who wrote the software offers no guarantees whatsoever. In my humble opinion, it's a win/lose situation that such licensing agreements are legal. At best, they belie the advertising, which claims it does everything from washing your dishes to forecasting the future—seemingly, at least.

That kind of license, which absolves software houses of any liability for quality, changes the rules of the marketplace. Nowadays, software that sells is the software that has the most advertised features, whether or not they work all the time. Bloat makes software more and more complex, adding more and more potential for bugs, and making billions of dollars worth of PCs obsolete.

That's how users perceive bugs.

Are you any different, or do you leap for joy when you get a blue screen? Do you delight in the sheer challenge that an error message offers? If you don't, may I respectfully ask you to strive for perfection in your code? Doing so puts you on the path trod by heroes.

Make Your Client Love You

If a pack of wolves has surrounded you and a wolfhound trots up, chases the wolves away, and wags its tail in friendship, now tell me: Who are you gonna love?

If all of the software your client owns is buggy and costs them tons of money—except for the software they buy from you—now tell me: Who are they gonna love? There's a saying that goes like this: "The bitterness of low quality remains long after the sweetness of a low price fades."

A very few innovative companies endear themselves to their clients in a clever way. All of a sudden, their team arrives at the client's door. The team presents credentials and tells the manager that they've remotely detected a problem in the manager's server, or a client's machine, or whatever, and then they go about fixing the problem. If possible, they do it while the user is at lunch! Sometimes, nobody in the client's company even knows a problem or potential problem ever existed, because the software manufacturer fixes the problem remotely!

In that case, was there ever a bug?

When all other companies produce software that requires you to hire a staff of in-house technicians to maintain, and these people show up, who are you gonna love? Whose products will you buy next time? Who will get your upgrade money next year?

Master orator Zig Ziglar holds up his thumb and forefinger, one quarter of an inch apart, as he asks his audience, "How much difference is there between the very best and all the rest?" His point is that it only takes a small amount of extra diligence to become the very best at something. Paul the apostle called such excellence going the extra mile.

As a Java developer, you should remember that your problem and your solution lie in the fact that you're competing with developers who, for whatever reason, are driven by ever shortening time-to-market pressures. The first one to market gains the lion's share of that market. However, being first to market often means selling partially tested software that lacks some of the features the advertising people claim it has.

Fortunately, you've gotten this far in *Debugging Java*, *Debugging VB*, *Debugging C++*, etc., and you have acquired a few hundred ideas that shorten your development time. These ideas are enablers. They enable you to be competitive with high-quality software.

You might not yet believe that you can write bug-free software. I disagree, but until you believe it, you're correct. So, you may need to enlist the help of your users. When you install the best kinds of bug traps, your users will help you in many ways, and be happy to be on your team.

Build a Better Bug Trap

Yes, pity the poor user who is pressed to deliver a document to the CEO by noon, when a small window appears saying: "Undefined Error." There's an OK button, and the user knows, without a shadow of doubt, that clicking the button will reboot the computer.

That's when the user is tempted to stomp the computer, or call the corporation's chief legal counsel, neither of which will help the CEO get that document faster.

Design Tip   *Why do we always have to back up files, anyhow? What an adverse comment on the state of computer software that is! If the problem is in the operating system, why not buy or write a reliable one? If it's your database system, why not buy or write a reliable one? Make utter reliability a prime tenet of your canon of ethics. Require it, contractually, from your vendors, and eschew those vendors who won't sign such contracts. Everyone has competition, and sometimes vendors need to be reminded of that stubborn fact.*

The poor user is caught in a trap. There's no way out. The document is lost, and of course there's no backup. That means the CEO will blame the user, not the real culprit, who is the nameless software developer.

The first of my "21 Laws" is simple. "Software Must Never Abort." More fully, its meaning is that only the user is allowed to stop the software from running. All situations that would otherwise cause a fatal abort must be trapped and handled sanely before the abort can occur.

The solution for both you and the user is to think carefully about your error messages. Give the user plenty of well-written information about how to solve the problem, and prevent yourself from waking up at 3 A.M. due to a phone call.

When you install a bug trap, make answers to the following kinds of questions available, either onscreen or at the click of a "More Info" button. Some or all of the information should also be logged to the disk, and possibly emailed to the developer. Give the user a Print button that prints this information for later reference. Post this list near your computer. It's okay with us if you want to photocopy this one page.

Components of the Perfect Error Message

- What happened?
- Why did it happen?
- What will happen next?
- What can the user do about it right now?
- What can the user do about it in the future?
- Where can the user get help right now?
- How can the user help the developer improve the situation?
- What similar problems have occurred in the user's software recently?
- What should the user tell a technician about the problem?
- What restitution does the software developer offer to the user?
- What was the computer's state when the problem occurred?
- Is the bug in the client or the server?
- What databases, tables, and fields are open?
- What program, what module, what method, and what line triggered the error?
- What threads are active at the time?
- With as much precision as the computer supports, when did the problem occur?
- Who is the logged-on user?
- Further into this chapter, the book discusses each topic in detail.

Debugging Java, copyright 2000, Will David Mitchell, all rights reserved. Debugging Java is published by Osborne / McGraw-Hill. We grant permission for you to photocopy this single page, so long as the copyright notice is attached.

All of that information is far too much to install in an ordinary error message box. Your bug traps need to be concise and to the point. "Undefined Error" is too concise. It reveals too little information. However, few users, especially those pressed for time, will read an error message that includes all of the bullets above.

The key to a great error message is to have all that information readily available, just not on the screen yet.

One solution is to provide a button that brings up more data, possibly organized in a hierarchy. Another is to borrow the sidebar idea from Web pages. Sidebars help organize large amounts of data for Web sites, and can do so in your bug traps. Error messages adapt well to HTML code.

You need to give the user enough information to make a good decision, and you only have a few seconds to present it.

Have you ever seen a user press CTRL-ALT-DEL or the Power button, when you knew ALT-ESC or ALT-TAB had a decent chance of saving the document? Several times, I've nearly shouted, "No!," but a half-second too late. Once, I physically stopped a lady's right hand as she was about to push the Power button. She was insulted, until I showed her a way to recover her document after all. Later that day, she gave me a nice card of thanks.

When your intelligent error message gives a user a way out of the trap, suddenly you're the hero—even though your software had a bug.

Bugs Confuse, by Definition

If it were not so, they'd be fixed quickly.

This means that your poor user is in an abnormal, confused mental state when your error message pops up. Thus, you have a tightrope to walk. Without talking down to your user, you have to explain everything a bit more simply than you might otherwise.

Often, error messages exist to tell the user a better way to do something. If you feel the need to write those kinds of messages, then:

- Why write the message in the first place, if you can detect a probable user error? Either accept the alternate way the user is doing things or rewrite your software to avoid the confusion. That may not be possible, but I've often found it easy to do.

- Drop the language a couple of grade levels. Keep it easy to understand, because your user has already failed to understand something important.

- Think of all the ways the user might have done something wrong to get to that point. Here's a chance to be creative.

- Explain things extremely clearly and precisely. Allow nothing to chance.

What Else Can Go Wrong?

Adopt an attitude. Pretend that something else has gone wrong and ask yourself what it was. Then adjust for that, and ask yourself the same question until you have no more answers.

Ask someone else. Get a fresh insight.

Writing great error messages is a very creative process that requires a good dose of logic. In other words, you must use both hemispheres of your brain.

Elements of the Perfect Error Message

Great error messages must communicate. They must soothe. They must do things that keep your user working productively. But most important of all, they should not exist! An error message always begs the question: "If you can predict that a user might make a mistake where you just inserted an error message, why not fix the problem instead?"

I'll be practical, however. I realize that error messages are facts of programming. I write them, because I know I can't test for all errors, and I can't write code that users cannot break. So, I rely on error messages to trap the rest of the bugs. Here's how to write an error message.

Speak the User's Language

"Invalid Page Fault" means little to a user who hasn't studied operating systems. It means little to most programmers! If you can explain page faults, and invalid page faults, you probably have at least one college degree in computers.

"General Protection Fault" means only one thing to the user: It's gonna crash! It would be better for your message to say, "Your program is about to crash!" That would be an improvement because it's written in the user's vocabulary, but it's insufficient. The user needs more information.

Eschew Concision

Write your error messages in complete, easy-to-read sentences. Direct your language a step or two below your user's expected level of expertise.

Even though "File Not Found" doesn't specify the path and filename, it means a lot to a programmer. It means little to a novice. For the novice, you should begin with something like the following: "The program was looking for the file 'test.cat' in the folder named 'c:\temp\' and could not find it."

That, of course, is only a start. You might mention that 'c:\temp\' does exist, and that 'test.cat' might be misspelled. A great message might notice that '.cat' is a lot like '.bat' and suggest '.bat' for the file's extension, after first checking that 'test.bat' exists.

Choose Words Carefully

I saw a magenta error message in commercial software once that contained two words, the latter of which was obscene, to the effect of "You're toast."

Sure enough, the moment I moved the mouse, the computer rebooted. I thought I had a virus, because nobody would put obscene words in a commercial error message.

The manufacturer's technician sheepishly told me, and I quote: "An errant error erroneously slipped into production. We have issued a recall. We will ship you a free, new version, and we will send you a postpaid mailer to send the original disks back to us. May I please have your address?" He was obviously reading a script. I was so impressed that I asked him to read it again so I could copy it down.

If the company only sold 100,000 copies of this popular program, that single word cost them a million bucks! It probably cost me the original price of the program in time lost.

When you write an error message, ask someone else if they can think of two ways to interpret it. If they can, the message is ambiguous, and you must rewrite it. There are dozens of ways to interpret "File Not Found," including one that involves metal working, another that involves manicures, and yet another that involves filing cabinets. Hey, there are people who didn't know what a computer file was the first time they saw that message!

The best way to avoid ambiguity is to use complete sentences that contain precise verbs and nouns.

Be Sure to Spell a Word Wrong

Just checking. Don't do that. I say again, don't do that!

If you must emit an error message, thus admitting to a bug, at least get the spelling and grammar right!

If you have trouble with "I before E except after C, and when sounding like A as in neighbor and weigh," there's an English major sitting three cubicles to the south of you. The CEO has a secretary who can probably quote most of Webster's Dictionary from memory. K-Mart sells a small, electronic dictionary made by Franklin for about $10. Get a bit of help before you spell "recieving" in an error message. Use an error-correcting word processor or editor to write your code. My word processor kept AutoCorrecting that intentional misspell for me!

If your native tongue is not English, I heartily commend you for speaking my native language far better than I can speak yours. But, remember how long it took to perfect your own tongue? English is not an easy language to master. It has thousands of irregularities. You might want to ask a native to check your error messages. If you speak English and are writing for the German audience, you should ask a native German to check your messages. For that matter, English spoken in various countries has enough local variations that you should ask a native to check your work, especially your spelling of words like "color" and "colour."

Contriteness Never Hurts

Erich Segal wrote in *Love Story* that love means never having to say you're sorry. It was a great line in a lovely book, but I'm sorry, Erich erred. In an error message, as in love, an apology never hurts and always helps.

Putting the word "sorry" in an error message removes much of its sting. So does inserting the word "please." Your users are already upset with you, so why egg them on?

Total Disclosure Is Best

If you're traveling halfway across the state to a vacation spot you've never visited, you'll probably consult a map. You know that spending a small amount of time planning may save you an hour or two of driving later.

Similarly, if you plan your error messages and take the time to disclose every reasonable detail to your user, you'll probably save valuable time later. My friend told me a year ago, "You haven't lived until you've received a 2 A.M. trouble call from someone in Hong Kong!"

Your User Is in a State of Near Panic

I saw a clever sign posted above our copier. It stated that this copier had the latest version of a "panic detector" installed, so that when it detected a user's state of panic, it could jam.

Whether or not a data race turns destructive can depend on subtle things such as how fast you double-click your mouse. A user who's under the gun does things differently, and that fact introduces new dynamics into your program. Software that works fine under ordinary circumstances may find a panicked user trying innovative ways to squeeze a bit of extra performance out of it. That's when the user may misclick or get into poorly tested environs. That's when threads can unexpectedly collide.

Your messages must be able to reassure a panicked mind and supply speedy relief.

Error Messages Must Soothe

One of the world's most famous error messages was, "Houston, we have a problem." I heard a recording of the original, and it was spoken just like it was in the movie *Apollo 13*, with a soothing, professional voice that meant business. Those five words galvanized hundreds of people into purposeful, thoughtful, lifesaving action.

Never intentionally turn the whole screen blue with white text. You'll have legions of users pushing Power buttons unnecessarily! Similarly, never turn a whole window's background red or bright yellow. Those colors can generate emotions that range from rage to terror, at the worst possible time.

Write your messages so that the user will take a deep breath, move into left-brain thinking, and take the correct action. Black text on a light-gray screen is best.

Avoid Anything Condescending

The Scandisk screen, which appears upon reboot after an improper shutdown for any reason, was obviously well-intentioned. However, people should have considered the wording more carefully. "Because Windows was not properly shut down, one or more of your disk drives may have errors on it. To avoid seeing this message in the future, always shut down the computer by clicking the start button."

Of course the user would like to avoid seeing that screen in the future, because it's up for a long time while the system repairs itself. An error message is no place to chide a user.

What is especially irritating to an impatient user is that the screen appears after every spontaneous reboot, and the user has no control of that. The reboot was the operating-system programmers' fault, not the user's. Had the operating system been more stable, that message would never have gained the status of infamy.

Standardize Phrasing

Some systems, particularly large ones, select the message text from a common pool, by number. This is useful when a number of modules interact, such as in an enterprise-wide manufacturing system. This technique is also useful when one message can be used in a dozen places throughout the system. It saves space. The most important reason for not using this kind of a system is that the program does a poor job of showing a maintenance programmer exactly what messages are being presented to the user. A line like this tells the maintenance programmer very little:

```
DisplayErrorMessage(2137);
```

You need an explanatory comment near the message, but if you insert a comment, you might as well substitute the comment for the error number. You can build a line that tells much more by using standard strings whose names indicate their contents. Such strings might look like the following:

```
msgFileNotFound = "Sorry, couldn't find the file: ";
titleFileNotFound = "File Not Found ";
msgPathNotFound = "Looked in the directory: ";
```

If you're careful, you can construct most of an error message from standard strings. It's easy to assemble components of the message into a whole, depending on parameters you pass to the message system.

You already pass parameters into your message box. In the box's method, you can detect what parameters you pass in. Accordingly, a **switch** statement can concatenate such sentences as "The program aborts next. Please save all open files. " or, "Clicking 'Yes' will stop the program. " or, "The program will continue." The same **switch** statement can change the color of the title of your message box and its title. It can append words like "Fatal Error" to the title.

The following pseudocode may not set colors and messages according to your taste or office standards, but it gives some ideas of what you can do:

```
//Some standard messages that you can append and prepend, are shown below:
//Also notice the inclusion of spaces after all punctuation, even where not
//necessary. This is a good habit to adopt, because it helps you avoid the
//possibility of run-together sentences during concatenation.

abortTitle = "Program Aborts Next ";
abortMessage = "Fatal error. \n" +
    "    Sorry, but the program must abort next. Please save all open files " +
    "before clicking the OK button. \n" +
    "    Alt-Tab will switch between running programs so you can save files. ";
```

```
questionTitle = "Info Needed ";
continueMessage = "The program will continue next. ";

switch(parameter) {
  case 1:                   //Critical error
    MsgBox.Title = MsgBox.Title.Caption + abortTitle;
    MsgBox.TitleBackColor = red;
    MsgBox.TitleForeColor = white;
    MsgBox.Caption = abortMessage + MsgBox.Caption;
//I don't recommend a red and white box, unless you really
//want to get the user's attention, that is, it's nearly panic time.
    MsgBox.BackColor = red;
    MsgBox.ForeColor = white;
    break;

  case 2:                   //Question
    MsgBox.TitleCaption = MsgBox.Title.Caption + questionTitle
    MsgBox.TitleBackColor = yellow;
    MsgBox.TitleForeColor = black;
    MsgBox.BackColor = lightgrey;
    MsgBox.ForeColor = black;
    MsgBox.Caption = MsgBox.Caption + continueMessage;
    break;

  case 3:                   //Information
    MsgBox.TitleBackColor = blue;
    MsgBox.TitleForeColor = white;
//Please do not turn the whole message box blue with white text!
    MsgBox.BackColor = lightgrey;
    MsgBox.ForeColor = black;
    MsgBox.Caption = MsgBox.Caption + continueMessage;
    break;

  default:
    break;
}
```

The Button Captions

When you install captions on buttons, be sure the captions adequately answer any questions the error box asks. For instance, a box that says "Please enter filename:" would reasonably sport an OK button. However, a box that asks "Do you want to continue or stop?" shouldn't have OK and No buttons, or even Yes and No buttons. It should have Continue and Stop buttons.

- "OK" can be confusing, so I seldom use it, except for informational messages on modal boxes. A frustrated user can find "OK" particularly galling in a box that merely states something like: "Program aborting, OK?" It's not one bit okay with the user! It would be much better to say please, and sorry, and thank you, and to make nice. You might explain that the program has paused for the user's convenience, to let the user attend to any final tasks, such as saving files. Then, the user can click a button in the error box that will eventually reboot the computer. How you say that, in 25 words or less, depends on the task at hand.

- "Yes" or "No" should mostly be used when the box asks a question. In some cases, you should add a "Help" button for the user to pick.

- "Cancel" can be confusing. Is the user canceling the box, the error, the program, the session, or even rebooting the computer?

- "Retry" should give the user some way to affect the program before the retry takes place, which implies an explanation in the text. If you need a Retry button in a box that asks for the user to locate and copy a file, then you should give hints on locating and copying the file.

- "Abort" should be explained. What's being aborted? Is it the screen, the report, the form, the write, the read, the module, the whole program?

Formatting an Error Message

An ordinary message box delivers an error message handily. However, you may want to program your own custom box so you can add exactly the buttons you want, accept the parameters you desire, change colors, etc. For example, most message boxes restrict the designs and number of buttons you can install. Write your own and turn it into an object so you can use it over and over.

Forming a good error message is akin to writing a great magazine advertisement, except that your error messages operate at a disadvantage: ads use graphics.

As in an ad, you must grab your user's attention with the first few words, and somehow induce the reader to finish the first sentence. That sentence, somehow, must force users to read the rest of the important text so they can make an informed decision about how to handle the problem.

I've experimented with turning the background color red for critical errors, and other colors for other messages. The experiments succeeded, but too well. After seeing users nearly have apoplexy, I reverted to black text on light-gray boxes or occasionally black text on very light, pastel backgrounds, barely tinted with red, yellow, green, or blue. I do like to turn the titles bright colors, but I never flash them.

Once, I asked a colleague to test a program that emitted a blue-screen error message. To my shock, the instant his screen flashed blue, he hit CTRL-ALT-DEL twice and aborted the program. I explained that my program was supposed to turn the screen blue, and I merely wanted to see how he liked the color scheme. He explained that his computer had already "blue-screened" three times that morning, and he thought it was just another occurrence.

Microsoft has inadvertently set a new standard. Even Microsoft marketers talk about how their later products reduce blue-screening. A blue screen with large, white text tells most users that the computer is about to reboot spontaneously, or already has. If you make your error message emulate the blue screen of death, you'll have users pushing their Power buttons unnecessarily, before they read your carefully crafted text.

Contents of the Error Message

Earlier in this chapter, I presented a list of questions the error message should answer. This section discusses them in greater detail.

What Happened?

The message should explain, in soft-spoken, plain language, why the error message appeared in the first place. In my opinion, an error message's title bar should be programmed to show a tight abstract of the error. "Error" is not sufficient. "Error: File Not Found" is about right, even though that's about all some programmers ever put in the message text. The text should explain what file wasn't found, etc.

What often passes for an error message, such as "File Not Found," belongs in the title of the message box, not its text. In this case, the text should name the file that was not found and name the path. However, reserve verbose details for the More Info button you'll put into the message box. You want the text to read quickly, so it will be read in the first place!

Why Did It Happen?

This informational bit is an extension of the previous one. It's one of the toughest bits to write, because if you can write it, you can probably prevent that error message from appearing. Write it to inform the user, but also write it to see if you can discard an entire error-message scenario.

What Will Happen Next?

Is the computer going to reboot? The user certainly needs to know that!

Yours may not be the only program running. Your user may have a spreadsheet program open, and may have launched your program to seek additional information, or to surf the Net a while. If your program reboots the computer, your user may lose hours of work on that spreadsheet.

It may still be possible to save the files that are open in a concurrent program. If your program has detected an error that might crash the operating system and was able to report the problem, your user can usually save files, perhaps by pressing ALT-TAB or clicking on the program bar. You should alert the users to those options, instead of relying on them to think of it.

Often, it's possible to shut down the current program and relaunch it. Just as often, that's an unsafe thing to do, because some of today's operating systems are remarkably fault intolerant. In many cases, you should advise the user to save all files and try to shut the computer down normally, while apologizing profusely, requesting user help, and offering to fix the software speedily.

What Can the User Do About It Right Now?

Obviously, the user can click any button in the error message box. Give the user information regarding what the various buttons do, because if you don't, most users will just press the OK button and hope. Remember, a user looking at an error message is in an altered mind state—and it's your fault.

If you haven't used hover boxes before, or if you call them something different, these are small, usually yellow, boxes that say a few words about whatever object is under the mouse cursor. You should install hover boxes that appear when your user hovers a mouse cursor over your buttons. If you do that, make the hover boxes appear immediately, not in 1–2 seconds as they normally do. You want the user to be acutely aware of what those buttons do.

All of this activity reinforces the idea of programming a special version of a message box so you can use context-sensitive programming techniques to explain the effects of the buttons. If you don't want to go to that effort, at least explain what the OK, Cancel, etc. buttons really do.

If the user can cure the problem, perhaps by launching a concurrent program and moving a file to the directory that needs it, say so. If you can identify the file and locate it, say so. Better yet, have your program offer to move or copy it for the user, thus preventing a future error.

Some help pages do a fine job of listing complicated processes to follow, and then disappear when the user does anything other than scroll the help page up and down. While a few users may feel complimented that you believe they can memorize a 12-step process, most feel frustrated when you ask them to do that. Leave your help page or message box on the screen for reference until your user clicks it off.

Install a Print button so your user can print the page.

You might want to allow copy-and-paste functions so your user can pull salient parts of the error message into the offending document, fixing it.

If there's a complicated procedure the user should have followed, perhaps you can redirect the user to your Web site, or to a specific place in your help system.

What Can the User Do About It in the Future?

Here's a good place to watch your words very carefully.

Remembering that you can install error traps for nearly anything, also remember that those error traps must detect errors first. If you can detect an error, you can often correct it on the spot. For example, if you're checking that a user inputs a date properly, it's very simple for you to add a leading zero for the month for your user. It's equally simple to allow either two-digit or four-digit years, correcting the information before writing it to the file.

If you're concerned about the user entering a date in YY/MM/DD or DD/MM/YY or MM/DD/YY format, your input box can prompt for the desired format. If you're further concerned, you can write a date-checking routine that catches most erroneous dates and requests clarification in the case of ambiguity.

You certainly don't want to bug the user with such a query every time a date is entered. Instead, you might put radio buttons on the form, letting the user select the preferred format.

Where Can the User Get Help Right Now?

Hopefully, you're brave and confident enough that your users can call you day or night, because there will be no bugs!

Error messages should tell the user where to find more help. You may want to point them to the proper page in the instruction book. If help is available on their computer, a button should be able to bring it to the screen. If it's available on the Internet, a button should be able to contact that exact page on your Web site. Make certain you don't move that page!

If help is available at your technical support section, its toll free number should be available when users press the More Info button.

Don't falsely be cost conscious with your technical support. I always prefer mediocre software that does the job but has great technical support I can reach over great software I have difficulty understanding, and whose technical support is incommunicado for whatever reason.

How Can the User Help the Developer Improve the Situation?

This is the holy grail of error messages.

Most users would love to help you, because they can feel they are a part of the process. If you can induce them to do what they'd love to do, you have improved your product, and have probably gained a few more customers for life.

I was absolutely thrilled when my antivirus software once asked me, please, to send certain files to the antivirus software manufacturer, because it had detected a new strain. Even nicer was the short email dialog I had with a technician, helping her understand how a virus nearly infected my computer system. I hope that information helped them track the virus back to its source. Because of that simple thing, I decided to use that kind of antivirus software on all of my computers that didn't have it, whether or not another company produces an equal product.

Since that particular virus activity happened at the DOS level, the antivirus maker didn't have an opportunity that you do have. You can install a button that will send the error message back to you via automated Internet email. You may get a ton of email, but you can set your email filters to take care of that detail. Merely give each possible error message a unique number in its subject, and your filters can redirect the mail based on subject line.

Most users don't know that in Windows 3.0 and later, ALT-PRINTSCREEN or just PRINTSCREEN copies a window or screen image into the Windows copy-and-paste buffer. Users can launch Word, Write, Paint, PowerPoint, etc., and paste the buffer's contents into the newly launched program. There, they can print the window's image—error message and all. The user can annotate the printout with a pencil and fax this information to your technical support staff. Or, the user can annotate the file with any of the programs mentioned above and email it to your people.

You might want to mention those options in your instructions to the user. Every time I've informed users of that trick, my hero status has ratcheted up a notch.

If you install a Print button on the message box, your user can print all information the computer has collected about the error for further reference or for faxing to you.

If you use the circular queue idea explained in the next heading, the user can e-mail you the file that contains that queue, and you'll have the user's last 100 error messages. You can even install a button to make it easy for the user to do all that.

What Similar Problems Have Occurred in the User's Software Recently?

Computers keep track of innumerable things, so why not let it track the errors your software produces? One reason is that an infinite loop of errors might cause yet a larger problem. The logger might overflow the free space in the hard disk! Fortunately, a simple solution to that detail exists. It's called the circular queue. You can write a data structure to implement such a queue, or you can save the information in a self-paring Oracle database, but there's a simpler and better way.

For one thing, it's preferable that any ordinary editor or word processor be able to read the file. Thus, common ASCII text is best. Here's a slick way to implement a circular queue for this particular purpose:

1. Install the latest set of error information into the first element of an error array. Each element of the array would have a number of fields. It's up to you how to implement that, but I'd suggest quoted, comma-delimited strings.

2. From the second element to the end of the error array, or to the end of the error log file on disk (whichever comes first), read error information into the array. If the error log file doesn't exist, just create a blank one and you have nothing to read in.

24×7

You don't want to name the file in a way that attracts undue attention, or that might get it deleted. Certainly, .TMP should not be its extension. Nor should it reside in one of the disk's several temporary directories, because many users routinely erase anything found there. For a program named Mirage, MIRAGE.FIL would be my choice. I put the file in the executable's directory. I make sure the filename has no more than eight characters and the extension has no more than three, for greatest compatibility.

Design Tip *If you're writing a DOS text file, you want to avoid a "File Not Found" error. Opening an open file gives you that error. You can close any DOS file with impunity, even if it's not open, so before opening the file, perform a precautionary close.*

3. Close the input file, and reopen it for output.
4. Write the entire error array back to the disk, as comma-delimited, double-quoted ASCII text.
5. Close the file, of course.

This kind of queue has a number of advantages, but the main one is high versatility. If you restrict the array's size to 100 elements of up to 250 characters each, the disk file can never grow beyond a mere 25KB in size. Moreover, since it's ASCII text, any editor, word processor, or other program that can import common text can read it. The file is easy to print, easy to forward, and easy for you to parse when you receive a copy.

What to Do with the Information

When the same error occurs several times, why not give the user the option of pressing a button on the screen and sending the error log to you as email? All the user has to enter is contact information, along with optional comments. You've nearly automated one of the more onerous tasks that confronts a user: the necessity of waiting on the phone for a neck-cramping quarter of an hour, hoping that you will even be able to understand the explanation of what went wrong, hoping that you can make the wound better.

I suppose most people dislike public speaking more than that, but not much more.

So, you receive an email of the last 100 messages, presorted by date/time, along with a comment or two from your user. To conserve email traffic, you might arrange for the software to send you just the last 10 messages, and any duplicates it finds in the last 100. In any case, you have most of the information you need.

Obviously, you autoreply that you've received the information and that you're looking into it immediately. Incidentally, your autoreply must be from an email account that can receive messages! Few things incite irate users to riot more than not being able to reply to email from technical support. Always sign your messages, even if you have to invent a pseudonym.

Occasionally, your software will be able to pinpoint the fix and give you a canned message that you can proofread, sign, and send.

Software at your end should be able to flag bugs in the message according to several choices:

- All occurrences of the last bug logged

- All occurrences of any bug that the user reports in the comments

- All occurrences of the most common bug, the second most common, etc.

- Bugs that appear to be related for some reason. You might have a table of related bugs, or the software might glean relationships from some of the fields reported in the message.

Onward Toward the Holy Grail

Now that you have a way for your client's computer to send you its symptoms, obtain your client's permission to treat the problem. Let that computer email you an error message if ever your software generates one. Then, you can show up at the door, present your credentials, and fix the client's machine over the lunch hour, or whatever suits your customer's fancy.

If you know your customer's system intimately, you might arrange to use a Remote Method Invocation (RMI) session to fix your customer's computer from afar.

Instantly, instead of being a goat, you're a hero!

Error Watch *Don't push unrequested updates onto your customers without permission. People react strongly to that practice. Consider this scenario that happened to a client of mine. The client had his browser installed in a nonstandard directory, thinking that doing so would help thwart some kinds of Internet attacks. Not a bad idea, actually. His server's c: drive had 47 megabytes of free space, which was adequate. The d: drive had about 14 gigabytes left. Along came an automatic, unrequested, unwanted update from his Internet Service Provider (ISP), which consumed 46 megabytes of his server's c: drive and put his company out of business for a day! He and most of his employees have bumper stickers that read "Friends Don't Let Friends Use XXX" where XXX is that ISP's name.*

What Should the User Tell a Technician About the Problem?

How does the user know what to tell a technician in the first place? The user is already confused, or the trouble call would be moot. This is a reason that Frequently Asked Question (FAQ) systems can fall short of their potential. The difficulty is asking the right question.

Why Not Use FAQ Systems?

Disregarding the fact that FAQ systems can be tedious and unrewarding to the user, they only seem to have the answer about half of the time. Most users prefer talking to a human about a problem, because of one thing. It's called discussion. A FAQ file has great difficulty asking the correct question of the user, because it's designed to provide information, not to ask questions. A good technician can ask a few questions, ask the user to try a couple of things, and often pinpoint the error quickly.

I've tested beta software that has never been user tested but that arrived with a long list of FAQs in an automated software system. So, who had been asking the questions? Actually, some technical writer thought a while about what questions users would probably ask, and wrote up some good answers. Questions aren't frequently asked unless they're asked frequently!

If rocket scientists cannot yet program a robot to land on Mars unerringly, why do we mortals think we can write software that automatically answers questions about bugs that we weren't sharp enough to prevent in the first place? A long list of FAQs is little more than an unresolved bug list, which certainly should be printed if the bugs are there, but which also may mean the software is too immature for release.

In a pure world, there should be no frequently asked questions, and for that matter no need for a technical support staff. Okay, the world isn't pure, but that only means we should strive for software so nearly error free that it requires almost no support. If a question is truly asked frequently, perhaps something isn't written clearly enough, or a ten-step process can be automated.

In general, if anything in commercial software requires more than 3–4 clicks of a mouse, it's bordering on being too complex. It's no coincidence that your phone number and social security number are expressed in groups of 3–4 digits. Most intelligent people can remember 3–4 step processes, but have difficulty with longer things.

How Can the User Get More Information?

Install a hotspot on the user's main screen. It can be anything that is clickable, such as your customer's logo. Occasionally, I've put an invisible clickable image about the size of a postage stamp in the upper left-hand corner. One way to make it invisible is to turn its background the same color as that of the main screen.

When the user double-clicks or right-clicks on that hotspot, the computer pops up a scrollable box with the entire error message file, which it reads from the disk. Of course, no scrolling is necessary to view the current error. You can add all the frills you want, such as the following:

- Clicking on any field's header sorts the info on that field, first ascending, then descending, then ascending again, as the user clicks multiple times.

- Dragging a header left or right changes the column order.

- Selecting two or more column headers and double-clicking on any one of them implements a major/minor sort, based on the order the headers were selected.

- Buttons along the bottom of the screen let the user print highlighted items, or print all items, or send them all to you.

When your customer calls technical support, your technician can ask the customer to double-click on the hotspot and read the results. If the program is completely broken, your technician can ask the customer to run any editor or word processor, load the file, and read the results over the phone.

The Chat Room Help Room

Have you ever considered a chat room for technical support? One technician can talk to at most one person at a time on the phone. However, that same technician can probably handle four to six chat queries at a time! That would mean you didn't have to hire so many help technicians.

Chat rooms are easy to install on Web pages. Most newer Web authoring tools include chat room wizards. You can even find companies to whom you can outsource chatroom-style help support!

What Restitution Does the Software Developer Offer to the User?

I'm kidding, right?

Actually, no. I've been known to offer bounties for bugs. I've offered $5 bills to bug finders, with the following caveats: The claimant had to be the first to report the bug, and the definition of "a bug" was that the program operated differently than the user manual said it did. Did I go broke? In fact, my client probably sold more software than he would have otherwise, and there've been no bug reports so far. Well, I sort of saw to that!

I've offered free software upgrades to reporters of bugs. I've even offered free upgrades for life. Again, no takers.

I have some software available on the Web. What it is doesn't matter here, but one title comes with a few hundred records. The data changes when companies move or go out of business, so to keep the information more or less up-to-date, I offer free upgrades when people report data changes. In two years, I've had about 20 claimants, and my data stays relatively current while demanding less research on my part. It's not a perfect system, but it's close.

What Was the Computer's State When the Problem Occurred?

If your error trap can glean it, such information as percentage of memory being used, names of threads running and their priorities, other users logged in, and free disk space can be invaluable in some cases.

Is the Bug in the Client or in the Server?

Sometimes your error trap cannot even localize a bug this precisely, but always include as much isolation information as you can. If you can identify the computer hosting the buggy program, name it.

What Databases, Tables, and Fields Are Open?

Your Java program is probably data-dependent. It may be that a particular bug is not related to data, but your program can easily determine what data is available. Such information may be the key to isolating a bug.

What Program, What Module, What Method, and What Line Triggered the Error?

Unfortunately, some errors are not trappable. When feasible, avoid programs and operating systems that produce untrappable errors. Since this is seldom feasible, ask the user to help your technical support staff.

If feasible, include something unique that pinpoints the exact line of code spawning the message. It could be a line number, as well as the method, class, program, etc. Ask the user to write it down or make a screen print, via the ALT-PRTSCRN method, and give the information to technical support. ALT-PRINTSCREEN copies the screen into the Windows buffer so it can be pasted into any program that can print graphics.

This idea requires foresight that often obviates the error. After all, if you can identify that a particular line of code might cause an error, why not change that line of code to something more robust? If that's not possible, can you jump to a routine that will correct the problem? For instance, instead of saying "File Not Found," can you jump to a routine that does the following:

1. Creates the missing file or finds the correct one and copies it where it goes.

2. Resets the error.

3. Goes back a line and reexecutes the line that caused the error?

If so, you have a self-fixing bug, and your user never sees the error message. If a user never sees a bug which fixes itself, was there ever a bug?

What Threads Are Active at the Time?

It's a simple matter to poll the system and develop information about active threads. Just use the **isActive()**, **isAlive()**, **enumerate(Thread[])**, **getName()**, or **getPriority()** methods. This code lists all active threads and their priorities in a program that creates threads for some purpose that doesn't matter here:

```
public void run() {
  Thread listThreads[];                    //Declare an array of threads
  while (Thread.activeCount() > 1) {
    listThreads = new Thread[Thread.activeCount()];
    Thread.enumerate (listThreads);

//List thread information.
    System.out.println("The Following Threads Are Active:");
    for (int i=0; i<listThreads.length; i++)
      System.out.println("Thread Name: " + listThreads[i].getName() +
      "   Priority: " + listThreads[i].getPriority());

  }  //while
}
```

With as Much Precision as the Computer Supports, When Did the Problem Occur?

Time of occurrence helps you track the bug sequence. It also helps you analyze other data, seeking patterns that isolate bugs. For instance, you might find that a particular bug rarely occurs after 9 A.M. Perhaps it only occurs as people log in and run your program the first time. Bugs that occur on particular days of the month may be associated with end-of-month processing. If a company has price rollup processing every Wednesday morning at 2 A.M., then miscellaneous bugs that occur weekly around that time may be triggered by or otherwise be involved in the price rollups.

You can try to get the system's time to the nanosecond, but most computers will round such precision to the nearest millisecond. For most purposes, that is enough precision. In fact, rounding to the nearest second is often enough.

Some bugs that involve thread clashes are more easily resolved if you know exactly when the bug occurred. For instance, you might have three bugs reported a few milliseconds apart. You might find that the first caused the other two. Perhaps fixing the first will ensure the other two never occur. On the other hand, the other two bugs might be truly autonomous, requiring fixes of their own.

Often, time will tell.

Who Is the Logged-On User?

Query the operating system or network.

What to Display on the Screen or Report

The message should answer these questions for the user:

- What happened? Commonly, this is the only information a user gets, and even this information is too sparse. For instance: "File Not Found" only confuses the user. The error-message text should give details, such as what file wasn't found and possibly why the program needs the file. It's often helpful to tell the user where the computer looked for the file. Perhaps the user can correct the problem by merely copying a file, or the computer can offer to do the copying automatically. What can the user do about it? Obviously, the user can press one or more buttons on the error box. Give the user information regarding what those buttons do. This usually means programming a special version of a message box so you can use context-sensitive programming techniques to explain the effects of the buttons. Lacking that, the message text should explain what the "OK", "Cancel", "More Info", etc., buttons really do. The user might be able to launch a concurrent program and correct the problem on the spot.

- What's going to happen next? If a fatal abort is about to occur, that can be crucial information for the user. For example, the user might want to launch another program, such as the Windows Explorer, and try saving the work lest the computer corrupt its operating system next. In such a case, warn the user if that's possible. If data will be lost, warn the user. If it's safe to continue, but the last data entered will be lost—perhaps because it was invalid data—tell the user. If the user has several options, explain them. There's nothing that says an error message cannot include a Help button!

Guarantee Your Software to Specifications, Forever!

In my early 20s, I was a foreign-car mechanic. I recall disassembling my first Porsche engine. Engraved inside the case were the German words for "Assembled by Hans Gregor." Whether Herr Gregor was just proud of his work or the Porsche factory required him to do that, I never discovered.

I told my father about that engine, and learned a wise life lesson. "If you always sign your work, you'll do your best," he counseled. Ever since, I've imprinted my name where it will be found if something breaks. That includes source code. A decade ago, I acquired a personal, toll-free phone number and began including that as well.

Deciding to guarantee your software to specs, forever, is not a decision to be considered lightly. It means you must write high-quality software, or resign yourself to calls at all hours.

Along the higher trail, rocks are sharper and slips are more costly. But from there, you can see so much farther.

PART III

Performance

CHAPTER 13

Use the Best Testing Strategy

Most large programs consist of several modules. In Java, each module may be a class or may be composed of several classes. A new Java compiler might have a module for each keyword. An accounting package might have separate modules for accounts payable, general ledger, payroll, etc. A manufacturing system might have hundreds of modules grouped into submodules for administration, accounting, development, legal, inventory, receiving, shipping, shop floor, etc.

When testing such programs, the strategy you employ will affect the results, as well as the time required to test the system. The obvious conclusion is that you need to employ the best strategy.

Incremental vs. Module Testing

Incremental testing is additive. You test a module. Then you add another module and test the entire system, with most of your tests focused on the added module. You proceed that way until you've tested the whole system.

Module testing, on the other hand, is the more traditional method in use. You test each module separately, as a stand-alone program, and then combine the modules into one unit.

Incremental Testing's Advantages

Incremental testing has several advantages over the traditional strategy of module testing. Among the advantages are the following:

- With incremental testing, you will detect interface errors earlier (on average 50 percent earlier), when they are less expensive and less time-consuming to repair. Because errors due to interoperability between modules are not evident until modules are combined, traditional testing strategies do not expose them until the end of the testing phase.

- Because interface errors do not surface until the end of the project, and because more projects are late than not, deadline pressure often encourages the team to take shortcuts with these kinds of bugs. This is probably why interoperability errors have always existed in office suites, except for the few suites like StarOffice that were designed as suites from the start. It is difficult make several separately developed modules speak the same computer language. Often, you must write translators to do that.

- With incremental testing, interoperability errors are easier to locate because, on average, they will occur after half of the modules are tested. This localizes the bugs and makes them easier to squash.

- Incremental testing is inherently more thorough. As you test each new module, you test its interfaces with modules that are already tested, but which might not have been tested completely enough. Chapter 1 showed the futility of trying to develop a comprehensive set of input/output tests, and the same difficulty carries over to other forms of testing. It is common for users to find errors in well-tested code. The more times you subject a module to testing, the more errors you will find, and the fewer you will leave for your users to discover.

- Incremental testing requires less test code—that is, fewer test stubs— because many of the test stubs can be reused along the way.

Module Testing's Advantages

On the other hand, traditional module testing has a pair of advantages:

- Module testing offers more opportunities for you to test several modules in parallel.

- Parallel testing can come at a time when you probably have the maximum number of people on the project anyhow.

Integration Testing

If you are building a very large project, especially if you have modules and submodules, you might find you must combine the two testing strategies. You might have ten teams of ten programmers building the hundred modules of a heavy manufacturing package, for example. As modules are finished and tested, an integrator team might merge them with what has already been tested and check the results. Such a dedicated team would probably have plenty of work to do, because testing could consume 20–50 percent of the entire project.

Top-Down vs. Bottom-Up Testing

Let's presume you have a project similar to the partial model in Figure 13-1. As we'll see later, this diagram is flawed.

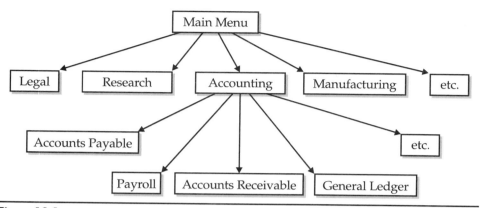

Figure 13.1   Manufacturing system

In Figure 13-1, each module could be a stand-alone program. Even the modules shown under Accounting can stand on their own. They are integrated into an expensive package you are building. In what order should you be testing the modules?

Top-Down Testing

The top-down approach has you beginning at the Main Menu, then progressively moving to the next level. But in that case, should you use breadth-first testing— that is, test the Legal, Research, Accounting, Manufacturing, etc., modules before testing the submodules under Accounting? Or, should you use depth-first testing? In that case, after you test Accounting, you would bypass the other modules on its level, and go straight to its submodules of Accounts Payable, Payroll, Accounts Receivable, General Ledger, etc.

In traditional top-down testing, there is a single inviolate rule for selecting what module to test next. A module's parent must be tested already. There are numerous other considerations, however, which don't have the force of a rule:

- Risky modules should be tested early, because they are more likely to have fatal flaws requiring major design changes.

- Input and output modules should be tested as early as feasible. Doing this makes it easier to feed test cases to the system, and to capture their output, such as to files and printouts. The presence of tested I/O modules also facilitates regression testing, which detects whether or not a system has "regressed" to a less stable state after being improved. In one form of regression testing, you feed a module a set of inputs and notice the results, and then you revise the module. Later, you feed the module those same inputs again. You examine the output to ensure the revisions didn't break earlier good code, and that the code has progressed from its former state.

- Top-down testing can bear a siren song. After a few modules are completely tested, it becomes too easy to think that design can proceed concurrently with testing. This idea generally prolongs the process of producing software, rather than shortening it. The act of designing lower-level modules all too often sparks design changes in higher-level ones. If they are coded and tested, the impetus for making the higher-level modules as good as possible wanes. At best, the enhancements wait for a new version, and at worst, they are never implemented. This is not to say coding and testing must occur at separate times. The design, however, should be finished before any but the most rudimentary testing of an overall framework begins.

- A module being tested will usually need to rely on the existence of modules further down the chain. In this case, programmers can write stubs to simulate those nonexistent modules in a process called "creating a harness." However, when modules replace stubs, retesting is mandatory because the calling module usually expects far more than the simple "Got This Far" kind of message that a stub would return. The called module might return several rows and columns of a table, which the caller must process further. Any stub that could simulate activity that intricate might as well be the finished module anyhow. In most cases, a stub must be more complex than at first seems to be necessary. A typical set of harness code equals the size of the source code being tested!

Why the Flowchart Is Flawed

Figure 13-1 is a typical chart, with a typical flaw. Many lines of communication are missing. For example, the Legal module interfaces with nearly every other module in the system. None of those lines are drawn. In fact, if all the possible lines of communication were drawn, the chart would be overwhelming and useless.

Computer systems must manage the white space on the organizational chart—that is, the space between modules—just as much as they do the boxes and drawn lines. The interface between Legal and Accounting may be as informal as reviewing a printout. It might take the form of limits that Legal places on prices, or triggers in certain accounting modules which might precipitate legal attention on selected supplier accounts.

The same kinds of statements argue for software connectivity between Accounting and nearly every phase of a manufacturing system. Research typically interfaces with Manufacturing, because the latter helps Research stay within the bounds of what's physically possible in the plant. Testing must evaluate the white space on the flow diagram, because if Legal can't interface with Accounting, for example, the project is likely to fail. This requirement places even more stress on the top-down testing model, because of the myriad of submodules, which must be present when any particular module is being tested. If they are not present, a myriad of stubs must simulate them, and regression testing must be performed when the stubs are replaced with working code.

One crucial reason to consider top-down testing, however, is that the overall framework can be demonstrated very early in a project's development cycle. This enhances the team's ability to attract funds and people for the project. It's a political reason, but like most political reasons, it's reality. With strictly bottom-up testing, the opera isn't finished until Samson pulls the temple down. That is, the overall framework isn't ready for demonstration until the whole product is ready.

Bottom-Up Testing

If you code and test the bottom-level modules first, and then their parents, you are doing bottom-up testing. The inviolate rule for selecting a module to be tested is simple: All modules that the candidate calls must be coded and tested.

Nearly every objection to top-down testing becomes a strength of bottom-up testing, and vice versa.

As with top-down testing, there are important ideas to consider. High-risk modules should be tested as early as feasible, to lessen the possibility that fatal flaws lurk inside them.

Input and output modules should be scheduled for coding and testing as early as feasible, so testers can use them to feed the system test data and observe the results.

As mentioned above, bottom-up testing does not yield a preview of the program early in its development. In most development, this is a requirement. It certainly is if you're to employ Risk Factor Analysis (RFA) as detailed in Chapter 4.

When any module is tested, all of the modules it calls are in place and tested. That means you seldom, if ever, need to write stubs, much less sophisticated ones.

The siren song of designing lower-level modules while testing higher-level ones goes mute, by default.

A Compromise

The following process generally smoothes the way toward your ultimate goal.
It is a combination of top-down and bottom-up testing.

- Use RFA to identify the design modules to the desired granularity. That will
  help you give accurate resource estimates early.
- Build an entirely separate demonstration based on those modules. Testing it
  ensures that the skeleton is sound and gives you tools to help sell the project.
- Design the entire system based on the skeleton.
- Develop and test bottom up, selecting critical modules first, and then input
  and output modules. After that, the modules can be selected in about any
  order, so long as selection follows bottom-up testing's inviolate rule that
  requires all submodules to be finished and tested.

Testing Philosophy

Remember that finding bugs is a good thing! Testing's goal is not to show that a
module works right, but rather to localize the bugs that are known to lurk there so
they can be squashed.

A module test that fails to reveal any bugs has failed, utterly. Measure a test's
success by the number of bugs it finds vs. the number believed to exist. See
Chapter 10 for that procedure.

Testing a Flowchart's White Space

Imagine you're developing a competitive replacement for the world's most
popular office suite. You know what your company's salespeople will face in the
field. To be successful, your program will need to offer more value than its
replacement, and value is a difficult commodity to quantify. Your program will
need marketing edges in some of these areas to succeed:

- **Low total cost of ownership** You can manage that via your licensing
  schema and your bug ratio.
- **Intuitive to use** That may mean borrowing the best ideas from the
  competition. Since ideas cannot be copyrighted, but they can be patented,
  that may prove troublesome.

- **Easy to use**   The more often a feature is used, the easier it should be to find. Pressing a single key A–Z on the keyboard is the easiest action a user can take. Pressing a special key or number is next. Pressing a function key follows, followed closely by dual-key combinations like CTRL-X. After that come things that require you to move your hand, like to the keypad and then to the mouse. Last of all are the items that require several mouse clicks on several drop-down menus that may be difficult to memorize. That's one theory, but novice users subscribe to another. They dislike memorizing keystrokes such as CTRL-H and prefer using the mouse. You must know your audience.

- **Shallow learning curve**   People learn things more easily when they look familiar. A radical new way of programming may be years ahead of anything on the market, but unless people can learn to use it easily, it will fail. That's the main reason Java looks like C, instead of, say, APL, which is an elegant language but one that is relatively unknown.

- **Excellent interoperability between modules**   Information from your spreadsheet should import seamlessly into your word processor, your database, your presentation program, your image program, etc., in several formats, without your needing to select formats.

- **Reasonable cost of development**   You may need to turn a profit.

- **Extensibility**   You need to be able to enhance the product, responding to competitive changes. On another level, your users need the ability to customize your system to their needs. In Chapter 5 this book shows how to extend Word, turning it into a Java editor, without digging into the actual programming language in which Word was written. No, Word wasn't written in VBA. It incorporates VBA to help you customize your usage of Word. Similarly, the components of Star Office can be reprogrammed.

- **Availability**   You need to make it easy for users to get copies of your suite.

- **Easy installation**   Until Caldera pioneered an easy-to-install system for Linux, for example, most Linux users were wizards, and they were few in number. The legions of office workers ran Windows.

Not one of these points deals with whether or not a module works. They all presume the modules work flawlessly. However, your potential users will be put off by software that doesn't address these ideas and others. To your potential users, the lack of any of these features is a bug. Your users see a water-tower-sized bug if they can't even get your system installed, or if they can install it but it won't interface with their video, modem, or printer drivers. While some users might forgive a system that turns the screen blue once a week, they'll return one that they cannot get to run after installing it, and will probably refuse to consider its successor.

You must think at the system level. Most programming flowcharts address none of these points, but your system testing must. Thus, you should do the following:

1. Brainstorm your users' needs and desires, remembering that a user sees little difference between the two.

2. Measure the cost of satisfying each need and desire.

3. Look for conflicting needs and desires.

4. Try to pull in ideas from company experts you can find in several other diverse departments, such as Legal, Advertising, Marketing, Production, Human Resources, Accounting, Engineering, Art, Customer Relations, and high-level management. You'll be surprised at the insights your CEO's personal secretary can offer.

Of course, these kinds of people should influence the original system design. However, at testing time, it's wise to gather them again for their ideas.

Automated Testers

Chapter 1 expended a fair amount of ink showing how difficult it can be to write sets of test data, and then the text moved into ways to make generation of such data more efficient. Jtest, by ParaSoft, does that for you, at the class level.

Jtest fully automates three primary kinds of testing:

- White-box testing
- Static analysis
- Regression testing

You only have to tell Jtest what class or classes to test, click the Start button, and look at the test results.

The product automates much of a fourth kind of test, black-box testing. In black-box testing, you may want to add your own inputs, and you must indicate the correct input/output relation for each class, but that's it.

As soon as you compile a class, you can let Jtest pass judgment on it for you. Jtest will examine your class and build a comprehensive set of tests for it. Jtest also builds a "harness" for that class, saving you the difficulty of doing so and ensuring that the harness tests all aspects of your class.

The real power of Jtest, however, is what it enables—you. Since you don't need to spend hours upon hours generating the test harness, and building a set of test conditions for each class, Jtest encourages you to test each class fully. Before Jtest arrived on the Java scene, such comprehensive testing was impractical. Now, it's easy, because Jtest automates the entire process.

You can even run Jtest in batch mode, letting it work while you sleep.

The effect is that your software quality will improve dramatically, while your development costs will drop.

This is the Jtest Class Testing window, after a test run on their demo program:

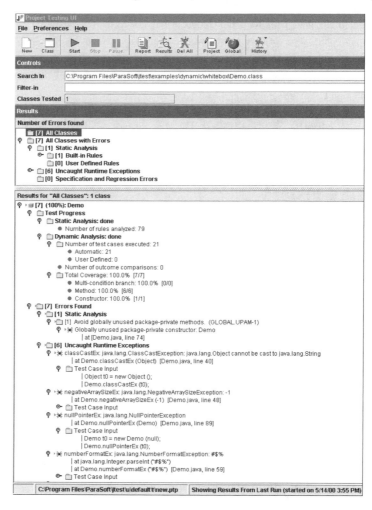

As you can see, the product found seven errors, one of which was caught by static analysis of the source code and six of which were uncaught runtime exceptions.

The window shows that the testing covered 100 percent of the test program, including all multicondition branches, all methods, and the single constructor.

Since Jtest is able to locate specific errors, it only makes sense that it would give you access to an editor so you can correct them. You merely click the error to go directly to that line. Jtest uses WritePad as a default editor, since that editor is bundled with Windows. You can specify any editor you want to use, including the special version of Word you may have built according to the ideas in Chapter 5. The next illustration shows Jtest running an editor to fix a found bug.

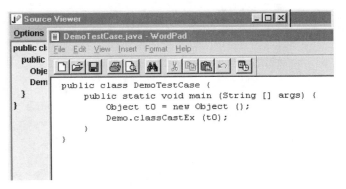

Not everything Jtest flags is truly an error. For a good reason, you might decide to program a **switch** without any **break** statements in it. Some constructs in computer science, such as "state machines," can benefit from the fact that a Java **switch** allows the code to fall through to the next **case** statement if there is no **break**. Since a missing **break** statement is normally an error, Jtest will flag it as such. While testing your new interpreter, you might want to suppress this kind of reported error, and possibly others. The next illustration shows how easy that is accomplished.

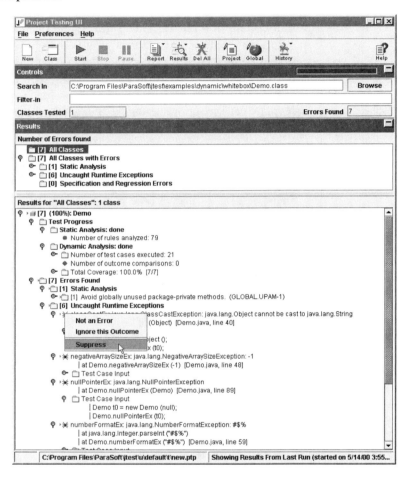

Jtest helps you with the errors and potential errors it flags. It gives clearly written descriptions of what the problems might be, shows examples, and even lets you see how the rule is constructed. This illustration shows a **NullPointerException** that Jtest caught red-handed.

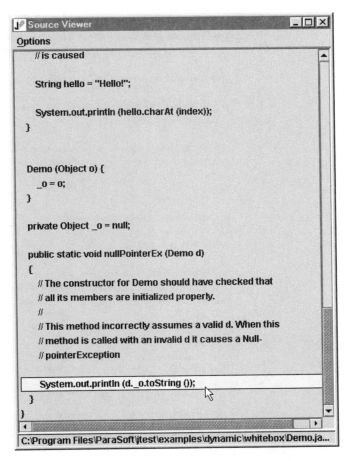

```
// is caused

   String hello = "Hello!";

   System.out.println (hello.charAt (index));
}


Demo (Object o) {
   _o = o;
}

private Object _o = null;

public static void nullPointerEx (Demo d)
{
   // The constructor for Demo should have checked that
   // all its members are initialized properly.
   //
   // This method incorrectly assumes a valid d. When this
   // method is called with an invalid d it causes a Null-
   // pointerException

   System.out.println (d._o.toString ());
}
}
```

C:\Program Files\ParaSoft\jtest\examples\dynamic\whitebox\Demo.ja...

Below is a Jtest rule. You can edit or remove any of the rules, and you can add new ones. Adding new rules lets you enforce programming standards.

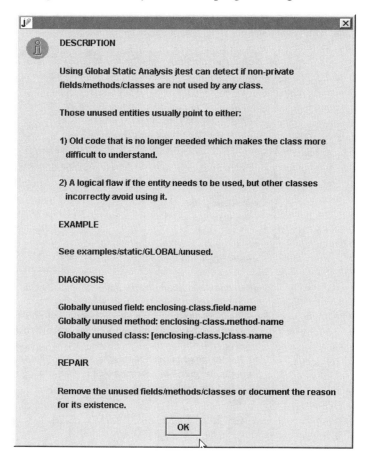

Automated Black-Box Testing

In traditional black-box testing, you write a series of inputs, based on the program's specifications. In the Heron's formula example of Chapter 1, the challenge was to write sets of inputs that would result in expected output. No knowledge of the program's internal structure was given or allowed. Generating such a set of tests is an intractably difficult task.

Jtest generates such a set of black-box tests for you, although not as complete a set of tests as you could generate from your set of specifications. Jtest uses a unique, and patented, approach. It analyzes the bytecodes of each class to build a core set of inputs, to which you should add your own.

The product presents the set of inputs in a tree fashion, looking like this:

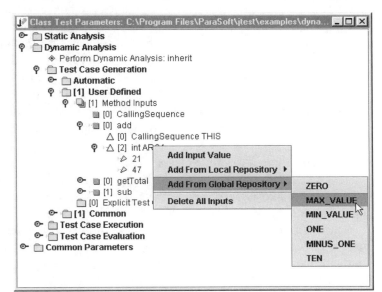

As the illustration shows, you can add input values, as well as adding data from specified local or global repositories. In the illustration, user values of *21* and *47* have been typed in, and *MAX_VALUE* is about to be added from the global repository. You can add data to any node in the tree of input data.

If you run several black-box tests sequentially, Jtest tells you when specification or regression bugs occur.

Automated White-Box Testing

In white-box testing, you examine the class' structure and generate tests that will exercise everything that can possibly generate a crash. Programs written in most languages terminate when this happens, but Java's ability to catch runtime exceptions helps it avoid most crashes. This is not generally a good thing, however, because of unwanted side effects such as database corruption or erroneous output to the screen or printer, while the program gives your user no indication that anything has gone wrong.

The developer, of course, does a considerable amount of white-box testing as the code is being written. However, the developer is concerned with making something work, not breaking it. Thus, more testing is required. When it is not performed, bugs will abound.

Jtest executes each class with a symbolic Virtual Machine, seeking uncaught runtime exceptions. It uses patented technology to create test cases that execute every branch in the code. When Jtest finds an uncaught runtime exception, it reports an error, including a stack trace and the call sequence for that line of code.

Classes are not hermits. They do not exist in isolation. They interface with external files and databases. They use resources like the Common Object Request Broker Architecture (CORBA) and Enterprise Java Beans (EJB) libraries. To test these linkages, Jtest automatically generates inputs from any external resources the class uses. The tests are designed to be comprehensive, exercising the class in every way possible.

Jtest isn't limited to single classes. It also lets you run sets of classes through its testing engine, so you can check the integration between classes. Even when testing groups of classes, you don't have to write test cases or scripts, write harnesses or stubs, or modify your source code especially for the test.

The latter condition is particularly important because when you modify your source code to test it, you can hide bugs, and you can generate new faux bugs in the process. Threads that previously ran perfectly may no longer synchronize the way they should. Moreover, your stub or harness is just as susceptible to bugs as your code is.

There are four kinds of uncaught runtime exceptions Jtest reports to you:

- **Incorrectly behaving methods**   The method is throwing an exception for the derived arguments, but should not be doing so. You must fix this code.

- **Unexpected arguments**   The method is not expecting one or more of the arguments that are being passed in. The calling routine is expecting the method to operate differently than it does, so either the caller or the callee must be changed.

- **Correctly behaving methods**   The method is operating properly, in that it is designed to **throw** an exception; however, the exception being thrown needs to be written into the method's **throws** clause. This is more of a maintainability issue than an error that causes output difficulties. By installing the exception into the **throws** clause, you won't wonder in the future whether the exception is a bug or not.

- **Developer-use-only methods**   In these cases, the developer is the only person using the method, and should not be passing the arguments out of the method. The method should probably be made private.

Jtest lets you save these test cases after using them, because they are valuable for regression testing.

Automatic Regression Testing

Regression testing's goal is to ensure that modifications have not caused the code to regress to an earlier, more erroneous state. When a running program breaks, the smart developer wants to know what has changed, because changes attract bugs. Java's threads make it feasible for code to run fine for several months, and then fail due to a data race that ran foul. However, changes cause more errors than data races do.

When you want to enhance a program, you can ensure against regression by using Jtest. Let Jtest construct a set of tests, or reuse the tests it built while white-box testing. Run those tests and let Jtest save the results. Then, enhance the program and run the tests again. By comparing the results, you will know whether or not your enhancements broke something.

On the positive side, regression tests let you know that the code has progressed after your enhancements have been compiled. You run the same set of inputs before and after, and check to see that the outputs, before and after, are just what you want.

With Jtest, you do not need to specify the desired output, although you may do so. The product remembers the output from each test, compares the results, and flags anything that has changed. Then, you verify that the changes in the output are all positive.

Running a regression test requires but a few clicks of the mouse.

Automatic Static Analysis

Static analysis has one purpose. It enforces coding standards. These standards can range widely in what they enforce. Violations of these standards might address the following:

- Syntax errors, which would never pass the compiler
- Possible coding errors, which might be indicated by indenting and seemingly misplaced braces, parentheses, or semicolons
- Style variations, such as where the opening brace for a code block is placed
- Preferred loop construction methods
- Preferred algorithms
- Highly localized standards for a particular set of classes

Static analysis lets you enforce coding standards so your team will write bug-shunning code from the start. It only makes sense to do that, because all bugs are written into code. Bugs that are never written never have to be removed, saving the time spent to write them—and the time spent in removing them. Quality increases, and so does production, when you write to shun bugs from the start.

When a team adheres to a good set of coding standards, sick time and vacations have less effect on production because it's easier for another team member to step in. Moreover, when enhancement time comes, the original coder does not necessarily have to be available to do the work. This makes scheduling easier.

The often-sought and seldom-realized goal of software reusability requires a good set of coding standards, used commonly among all team members. So when a programming shop begins using common standards, another productivity door opens.

Don't fall into the trap of extreme rigidity. In legislating tough programming standards, you can legislate innovation right out of your team! (Remember my little adage that rules and laws exist so that people don't have to think.)

JLint, covered in Chapter 6, is a static analyst. It examines the source code according to a set of rules and flags possible violations. You can customize JLint's set of rules, and the product is free.

Similarly, Jtest performs rule-based static analysis for you, and it's considerably easier to use, but the product is not free. Jtest gives you a graphical tool, called the RuleWizard, for creating custom rules.

The authors of Jtest recognize two kinds of coding standards, termed "traditional" and "global."

Traditional standards apply to constructs inside the class under test. For example, use of the **==** operator, instead of the equals keyword, when comparing strings, is probably an error.

Global standards ensure that projects use fields, methods, and classes as desired. The errors that global standards prevent include the following:

- Logic bugs
- Unused fields, methods, or classes
- Overly accessible fields, methods, or classes

Whether or not you use the product, you can learn a large amount about debugging by examining Jtest's rules and how it implements them. Like JLint, it parses the Java source of classes that are to be tested. However, because Jtest uses **.class** files instead of **.java** files to enforce the programming rules, you can use Jtest to perform global static analysis even when you don't have the **.java** source code.

Jtest has a large number of rules that test your code. The product can report too large an error set for convenience, so it assigns severity levels of 1–5 to rules, where 1 is the highest severity. It defaults to reporting violations of rules with severity levels 1–3, but you can change which levels are reported. You can also disable or re-enable individual rules, or rules in any severity category. All it takes is a click of the mouse. This way, you can prune the error list to those that are most relevant to your team or project.

This is the extensive list of test rules that Jtest uses. ParaSoft is adding rules continually. They let you add custom rules to the set, and acknowledging your expertise in Java, they've automated a way for you to help improve the product by suggesting new rules.

- Unused (dead) code:
  - There is an unused private static field.
  - An interface has an unnecessary modifier.
  - A private field is not being used.
  - A variable is not used.
  - A parameter is not needed.
  - The **java.lang** package is imported explicitly.
  - A private method is not being used.

- Coding standards:
  - Variables of different types are declared in one statement.
  - Group members with the same name are physically separated.
  - An abstract method is called from a constructor in an abstract class.
  - A **switch** statement has a large number of **case** statements.
  - The **main()** function is not first.
  - The class **Exception** is thrown directly.
  - Either **Exception** or **RuntimeException** is in a **catch** clause.
  - **Error** is being directly thrown.
  - Constants are not defined in interfaces.
  - "L" should be used instead of lowercase "l" for a long integer.

- Initialization:
  - Static fields are not initialized explicitly.
  - A constructor doesn't explicitly initialize every data member.

- Possible bugs, in code that compiles:
  - A **switch** statement has a bad case.
  - A **for** statement has an empty body.
  - An **if** statement has an empty body.
  - A method appears to need overriding.
  - **equals** should probably be used in place of **==**.
  - An **else** statement has an empty body.
  - A primitive data type is being cast to lower precision.
  - A text label is inside a **switch** statement.
  - There is a variable assignment within an **if** condition.
  - A **switch** statement lacks a **default** clause.
  - There is an embedded assignment.
  - Floating-point numbers are being compared.
  - A loop control variable is abruptly changed within a loop.
  - Method parameter names conflict with class member names.
  - The **+** operator may be confused with **String** concatenation.

- Object-oriented programming:
  - Inherited static member functions are hidden.
  - Classes may be nested too deeply.
  - Inherited instance variables are hidden.
  - A **private** method is overridden.
  - An inner class is not associated with or visible to the class that contains it.
  - An instance variable is **public**, or in a **package**.
  - **public** or **package** methods and data are not listed first.
  - An interface is either implemented trivially, or is not **abstract**.

- Naming conventions:
  - A class name doesn't comply to standards.
  - An interface name doesn't comply to standards.
  - An exception name doesn't comply to standards.
  - A method name doesn't comply to standards.

- A static field name doesn't comply to standards.
- A static method name doesn't comply to standards.
- A method parameter name doesn't comply to standards.
- An instance field doesn't comply to standards.
- A local variable name doesn't comply to standards.
- A final static field has lowercase letters in it.
- A method returning a Boolean isn't preceded by "is" or "has".
- An interface member field contains lowercase letters.
- An unconventional variable name is used.

- Optimization:
  - A **finally** block has an unclosed stream.
  - A **for** loop is used to copy an array, instead of using **System.arraycopy()**.
  - There are unnecessary **instanceof** evaluations.
  - There is unnecessary casting of variable types.
  - An abbreviated assignment operator can be used.
  - **StringBuffer** is used for a constant string, instead of using **String**.
  - A loop condition is overly complex.
  - The negation operator is used too frequently.

- Garbage collection:
  - **finalize()** doesn't call **super.finalize()**.
  - A finalize method's finally block doesn't call **super.finalize()**.
  - **finalize()** is called explicitly.
  - When converting primitives to **String**, unnecessary temporary variables are used.
  - **Date[]** is used where **long[]** should be used instead.

- Javadoc comments:
  - There is a misused Javadoc tag.
  - There is poor distinguishing between Javadoc and ordinary comments.

- Threads:
  - **synchronized** is used, slowing performance.

- Global static analysis:
  - **package-private** fields are too accessible.
  - **package-private** methods are too accessible.
  - **package-private** classes are too accessible.
  - **public/protected** fields are too accessible.
  - **public/protected** methods are too accessible.
  - **public/protected** classes are too accessible.
  - Global **public/protected** fields are unused.
  - Global **public/protected** methods are unused.
  - Global **public/protected** classes are unused.
  - Global **package/private** fields are unused.
  - Global **package/private** methods are unused.
  - Global **package/private** classes are unused.

- Enterprise Java Beans (EJB):
  - The bean class is not defined as **public**.
  - The bean class is erroneously defined as **abstract**.
  - The bean class is erroneously defined as **final**.
  - The bean class implements an **ejbCreate**() method.
  - The bean class erroneously defines the **finalize** method.
  - The **ejbCreate**() access control modifier is not defined as **public**.
  - **ejbCreate**() in **SessionBean** does not return a **void**.
  - The finder method's modifier is not defined as **public**.
  - The finder method's return type is not a primary key, and is not a collection of primary keys.
  - **ejbPostCreate**() has an access control modifier that is not **public**.
  - **ejbPostCreate**() does not return type **void**.

- Miscellaneous:
  - Member fields are hidden in member methods.
  - A loop's counter fails to increment.
  - A **for** statement does not contain a Boolean condition.
  - A **clone()** method exists that doesn't invoke **super.clone()**.
  - A **for** statement lacks a code block.
  - A method parameter received an assignment.

You can add to this long list of rules. Jtest has a RuleWizard that gives you a simple way to construct new rules, via point-and-click, without having to learn how Jtest's parser works. Dialog boxes let you customize the new rules at will. Thus, you can implement any kind of coding standards you feel necessary and Jtest will enforce them for you.

Let's say you want to add a rule that says all instance variables must begin with underscores. This illustration shows how you get to the RuleWizard with three clicks.

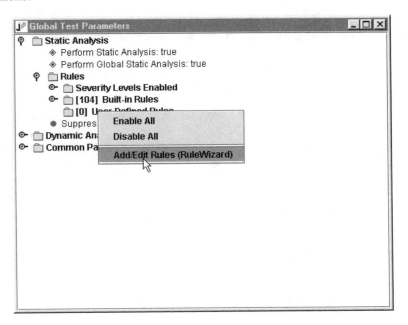

First, you select a field node upon which to build the rule. You can choose any kind of Java entity and build a rule on it. In this case, the rule will first check that the field is not static. Then, by entering the regular expression ^_. you specify that at the beginning of the name you want an underscore, and that only the first character is to be matched. If you haven't studied regular expressions, Jtest tells you all about them.

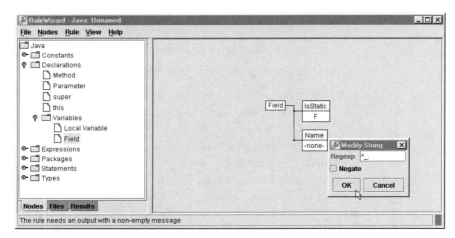

The next illustration shows how you can enter the text you want to display when the rule you've entered is violated. Be clear in these statements, lest you confuse an already confused developer. You might even want to cite a printed source document that gives full details.

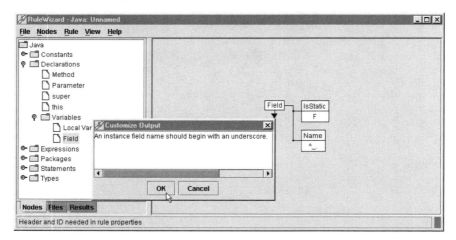

The RuleWizard also requests information about the rule's:

• Accessibility—that is, whether **public**, **private**, **protected**, or **package** code can be tested by it.

- Type, context, and initializer. In these areas, you can create a "collector," which can specify the set operators Union, Intersection, Difference, and XOR. It can specify labels. It can contain a hit counter or it can trigger specific output. It can maintain a count based on various expressions.

- Line number. Install whatever line number you want here.

- FileName. You can store rules under various filenames.

As you build your rule, a message bar at the lower-left corner lets you know what else is needed to complete it. When your rule is valid, a small red box at the lower-right corner turns green.

Automatic Coverage Analysis

JProbe, by the KL Group, contains an automatic coverage analysis tool. Its purpose is to identify and quantify untested lines of code. As mentioned in Chapter 8, the software does the following:

- Identifies and quantifies untested code

- Uses advanced filters to define specific code to be tested

- Merges coverage data from multiple runs of your program

- Lets you browse, share, and print the results as text, or as HTML documents

- Helps you test server-side code (ServerSide Edition of JProbe Coverage only)

When you take snapshots of your program in JProbe's Coverage Analyzer, a series of drill-down screens takes you to the root of any untested code, that is, any code that has not executed during the test run. The following illustration demonstrates this:

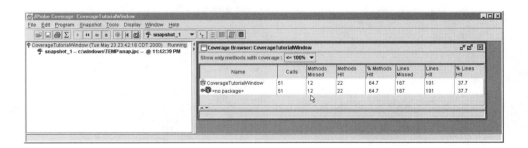

This highlights some suspicious activity. While 22 methods have been hit, 12 have been missed. The question is why. Clicking the icon next to **\<no package>**

takes you to the class level, where more information is available, as shown in Figure 13-2.

At this point, you can see that only 50 percent of the **super linked list** has been covered. Other items have uncovered areas as well, but drilling down into the **super linked list**, you find the screen shown in Figure 13-3.

Now, two culprits, **iterator()** and **containsObject()**, are identified as being missed by the coverage analysis. This might be because they cannot be executed. Double-clicking on the iterator method in the bottom window lets you see the source code, with lines color-coded. Red lines are missed, and black lines are hit. (See Figure 13-4.) You can change the colors to anything you want.

Where the arrow cursor is, you'll see what JProbe is rendering as a red line. Notice there are no calls to this particular line.

At this point, you can revise your test suite, or install a new one that is designed to hit the heretofore missed lines of code. After you do that, you can rerun your coverage test.

The importance of running tests like these throughout the development cycle is seldom emphasized enough. The next major section shows how the cost of fixing a bug rises dramatically the later it is found. This only makes sense, because a late bug requires the developers to redo much more work than an early bug does.

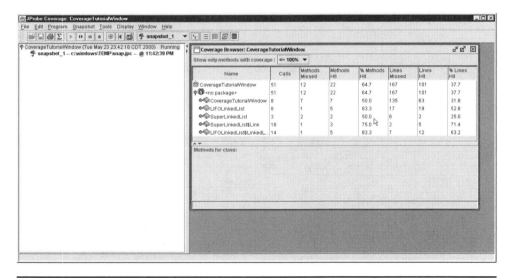

Figure 13.2 JProbe class level

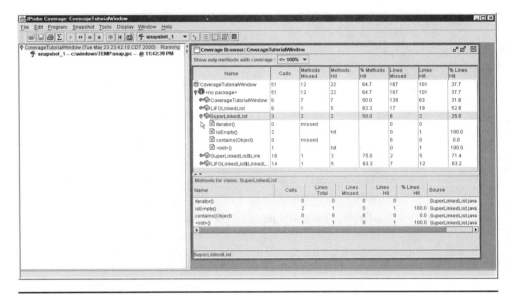

Figure 13.3   Coverage Browser

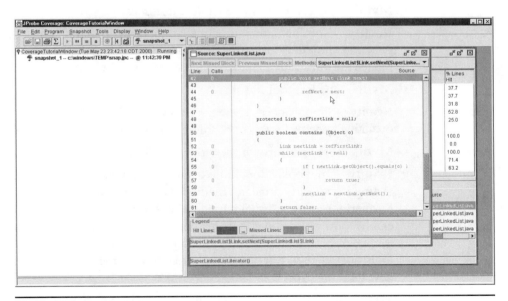

Figure 13.4   Identifying methods missed by the coverage analysis

Find your bugs as early as possible, by testing early and often. JProbe's Coverage Analyzer helps you ensure you're testing all pieces of the code.

False Expectations and Myths

You might be amazed at some of the myths surrounding automatic testing. To give you a bit of ammunition the next time someone tries to get you to cut your budget or manpower by giving you an automation tool, here are a few myths, in print, so you can point to them:

- **Myth**   Spend a few bucks to buy an automatic test tool, and a delayed project will automatically jump back on track.

- **Reality**   Test tools need to be used as soon as code begins to be written. Test each class, and test the system as each class is added to it. This way, you catch errors very early when they are cheap to fix. Table 13-1 shows how bugs become dramatically more expensive the later they are found. If you implement automated testing later in the game, you will still see positive results, but nothing like the results obtained when you begin a project with automated testing.

- **Myth**   The test tool will generate a test plan.

- **Reality**   Nothing commercially available can do that, to date. Jtest can generate numerous test cases, but nothing as comprehensive as a full test plan. Test tools only enhance manual testing, albeit strongly.

- **Myth**   One test tool fits all.

- **Reality**   Simply not so. There are currently too many kinds of computers and operating systems for this to be true. Several tools are needed, for portability.

- **Myth**   Testing effort will be reduced, cutting costs.

- **Reality**   The tools allow more testing to be done, but since far too little testing is currently done, all that will happen is that quality will increase. Furthermore, any test tool has a learning curve. A testing-savvy developer can become operational with Jtest or JProbe in a morning, and proficient in a week, but the art of testing software is not a trivial one to learn. Automatic tools operate in a different thought realm than manual methods do, and new thinking processes must be learned.

- **Myth**   The tools almost use themselves.

- **Reality** Actually, a tool like Jtest can perform sophisticated checks on code with no manual intervention. However, black-box testing is an integral part of software testing, and a complete suite of black-box tests cannot be generated automatically. Testing products typically requires the user to write scripts, or at least to tweak what the test tool records, before the scripts are robust enough to use.

- **Myth** Tools test everything.

- **Reality** Not quite. Test tools have difficulty with third-party add-ins, graphical user interfaces, and custom features like spin controls. A test tool can verify that a printout is being created, but a human must walk to the printer, check that it's not out of toner, retrieve the paper, and verify the results manually. A user halfway around the world might need to prepare input to transfer over the wire, verifying that the wire transfer works.

- **Myth** Automated tools can perform exhaustive tests.

- **Reality** Not during our lifetimes can this happen. For instance, a few quadrillion possible passwords are possible in a typical six/eight-character system. Testing all of those might require years, and thus be entirely infeasible.

Cost of Bug Removal

Table 13-1 shows how the cost of eliminating bugs increases the later they are found. It illustrates the importance of using automated testing throughout the software development life cycle.

Development Phase	Cost
Definition	$1
High-Level Design	$2
Low-Level Design	$5
Code	$10
Unit Testing	$15
Integration Testing	$22
System Testing	$50
Post-Delivery	$100, or much more

Table 13.1   The Rising Cost of Bug Removal

Other Kinds of Tests

So-called "monkey tests" are conspicuously missing from the text up to this point. If you set a chimp at the keyboard, sometimes the animal can break your code, but inputting random data is rarely effective. Here are ten more kinds of tests you will find yourself running from time to time.

Quality Gates   Management should implement gates and install gatekeepers whose purpose is to ensure that before software is accepted, it passes certain quality tests. Only then is the software allowed to progress to the next phase.

Deliverable Tests   Anything delivered from one team to another, or to a customer, should be tested at that point. It makes little sense to deliver something to a team that is expecting adherence to a set of specifications without testing it. The receiving team doesn't have access to nearly as much of the design and code thinking that the sending team has. Furthermore, when defects are found, the receiving team must decide whether they are actually defects or something else. That process can cost an inordinate amount of time.

The receiving team should, however, test what they receive against the specifications they are given.

Fault Insertion   Similar to the idea of seeding code with bugs to see how many remain, fault insertion seeds bugs, but with a different purpose. The idea is to see that the code behaves sanely when a disk is full, RAM is low, a file goes missing or becomes corrupt, etc.

Memory Leaks   This kind of testing tries to find where the program is not releasing resources properly. Stalled threads can cause memory leaks, for instance.

Performance Testing   These tests measure how fast or efficiently the program runs. Often, performance tests are interested in the speed of input and output, CPU utilization rates, query response times, and number of I/O actions.

Stress Testing   To stress test a system, you load it down. You run multiple copies of the program amidst other programs and see how the system handles the results. This is a kind of performance testing, but it occurs on a highly loaded system.

Data Integrity   This kind of testing checks that data types, field names, field lengths, and amounts of precision are correct on both ends of a data transfer. Data security gets involved in these tests, as does data corruption.

Backup Testing   Data will need to be backed up, because systems are imperfect. Not only that, data needs to be recovered. It can be relatively simple to test a backup system for data integrity, because one merely backs up, recovers, and then checks that no data have changed. There can be a bit more to backup testing, however. A daily backup that consumes 25 hours is obviously unacceptable. I had to fix one such situation. A recovery process that takes days may be unacceptable, even if all of the data returns perfectly. In case disaster strikes an entire building, the backup system must allow for recovery by keeping the archives elsewhere.

Compatibility Testing   Often enough, a system must interface with other systems. An excellent example of this is an office suite, wherein a word processor needs to be able to import a spreadsheet and then be passed to a presentation manager. Unless the systems have common file formats and similar ways of accessing those files, the interfaces will fail, and the programs will be incompatible.

User Testing   Users need to be involved early and throughout the development process. While I contend that a system should be developed according to what is in a user manual, at the end of the day, the user, not just the manual, must be satisfied. Typically, a board of users will test the system according to the specifications and either accept or reject it.

How Many Bugs Remain?

As good as products like Jtest and JProbe are, one wouldn't expect them to be perfect. They aren't designed to catch design bugs, for example. Also, the problem of generating a complete black-box suite of tests is beyond current technology. So, one wouldn't expect them to find all bugs.

Since you can't rely on these products to find all bugs, how do you know that you're done debugging? By applying the statistical techniques in Chapter 10, you can forecast how many bugs remain in your project. Do it this way:

1. Run Jtest across the program and catalog the bugs.

2. Submit the program to a test team's art.

3. Calculate the sum of all bugs found by either method—that is, find the mathematical union.

4. Calculate the total number of bugs that both the team found and Jtest found—that is, find the mathematical intersection.

5. Create your commonality ratio by dividing the intersection by the union.

6. Enter the graph shown here, reproduced from Chapter 10, and estimate the percentage of bugs that have been found.

How many errors are there?

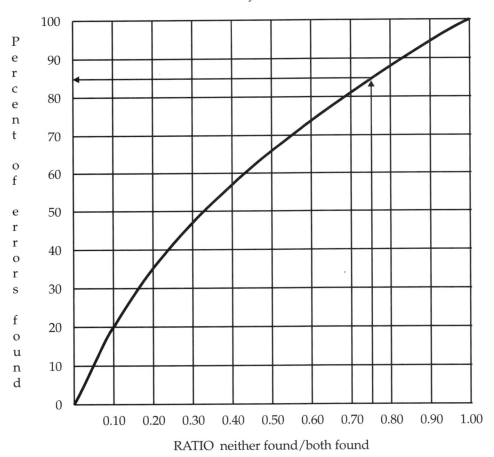

RATIO neither found/both found

May your coffee's aroma be heady, your work days sweet, your leisure times long, and your code ever free of bugs.

Commercial Software

Not a day goes by without scores of companies trying to purchase others. While developing this book, two of my favorite software titles changed hands. That's probably good. Surely some of the companies listed below will have changed vital information during the few weeks it takes Osborne/McGraw-Hill to run the presses and distribute the book to the stores.

This isn't a list of recommended products. It's just a list of products that may help you find exactly the right one for your particular needs. They are listed in no particular order.

If your favorite company isn't listed below, or if it is and the information is typed wrong, please accept my apology.

Add-In Libraries

ProtoView

ProtoView Development Corp.
www.protoview.com
800-231-8588
2540 Route 130
Cranbury, NJ 08512

Rogue Wave Software

www.roguewave.com
800-487-3217
5500 Flatiron Parkway
Boulder, CO 80301

Artificial Intelligence

Amzi!

www.amzi.com
913-425-8050
5861 Greentree Road
Lebanon, OH 45036

Browsers & Browser Tools

4thPass LLC

www.4thpass.com

Escape

Espial Group, Inc.
www.espial.com

Netscape

Netscape Communications Corp.
www.netscape.com

BrowserHawk

CyScape
www.cyscape.com
800-932-6869

Aviva

Eicon Technology, Inc.
www.eicon.com
800-803-4266
2155 Chenault Dr., Suite 503
Carrolton, TX 75006

Code Generators

Access Converter (Access to Java)

Diamond Edge, Inc.
www.diamondedge.com
801-785-8473
184 South 300 West
Lindon, UT 84042

Applet Designer (VB to Java)

Diamond Edge, Inc.
www.diamondedge.com
801-785-8473
184 South 300 West
Lindon, UT 84042

Aonix

www.aonix.com
800-972-6649

Gen-It

Codagen Technologies Corp.
www.codagen.com
514-288-4802
2075 University St., Suite 1080
Montreal, Quebec, Canada H3A 2L1

Mini Packs

Demicron
www.demicron.com
+46-8-289450
Hogklitavagen 9
172 64 Sundbyberg, Sweden

Tango

Pervasive Software, Inc.
www.pervasive.com
512-231-6000
12365 Riata Trace Parkway, Building II
Austin, TX 78727

WinA&D & WinTranslator

Excel Software
www.excelsoftware.com
515-752-5369
P.O. Box 1414
Marshalltown, IA 50158

Collaborators

StarBase

www.starbase.com
888-782-7700

iam

www.iam-there.com
212-580-2700
200 West 72nd Street, Suite 35
New York, NY 10023

Compilers and Interpreters

Smalltalk/JVM

Mission Software, Inc.
www.SmalltalkJVM.com

Data & Web Data

PointBase

www.pointbase.com
877-238-8798

IBM WebSphere Transcoding Publisher

IBM
www.ibm.com/developer
914-499-1900
New Orchard Rd.
Armonk, NY 10504

Java Blend

Sun Microsystems
www.sun.com

Sybase

www.sybase.com
800-879-2273

ObjectFX

www.objectfx.com
800-762-7748

ThinAccess

ThinWeb
www.thinweb.com
877-844-6932

DBArtisan

Embarcadero Technologies
www.embarcadero.com

Javelin

Object Design, Inc.
www.objectdesign.com/javelin
800-962-9620
25 Mall Road
Burlington, MA 01803-4194

Poet

www.poet.com/downloads
800-950-8845

CodeBase

Sequiter Software, Inc.
www.sequiter.com
780-437-2410

JServer

Oracle
www.oracle.com

VantagePoint and DataVista Pro

Visualize, Inc.
www.visualizeinc.com
602-861-0999

Relational Object Framework

Watershed Technologies, Inc.
www.watershed.com

ACL-Base

Plyasys, Inc
www.plyasys.com
617-354-8115
2285 Massachusetts Ave., Suite 204
Cambridge, MA 02140

WebXi Data Server

WebXi.Inc
www.webxi.com
781-272-1111
83 Cambridge St.
Cambridge, MA 01803

DataDirect SequeLink

Merant
www.merant.com

JClass HiGrid, Livetable, Field, and DataSource

KL Group
www.klgroup.com
888-328-9396
260 King Street East
Toronto, Ontario, Canada M5A 4L5

InterBase

InterBase Software Corporation
www.interbase.com
800-451-7788

SpacialVision

Sedona Geoservices
www.sedonageo.com
610-495-6701
649 North Lewis Road, Suite 220
Limerick, PA 19468

Jasmine

Computer Associates
www.cal.com
888-752-7646

JYD Object Database

JYD Software Engineering Ply Ltd.
www.jyd.com
+61-2-9980-7812
P.O. Box 744
Pennant Hills, NSW 1715
Australia

Debuggers

Metamata Debug

www.metamata.com
510-796-0915
Metamata, Inc.
2140 Peralta Blvd., Suite 2138
Fremont, CA 94536

JBuilder

Borland/Imprise
www.borland.com/jbuilder
831-431-1000
100 Enterprise Way
Scotts Valley, CA 95066-3249

JProbe Suite

KL Group
www.klgroup.com
888-361-6205
260 King Street East
Toronto, Ontario, Canada M5A 4L5

JTest

ParaSoft, Inc.
www.parasoft.com
888-305-0041

DevPartner

NuMega
800-468-6342

SilkPilot

Seague Software, Inc.
www.seague.com
800-287-1329
1320 Centre St.
Newton Centre, MA 02159

AnyJ

NetComputing GmbH
www.netcomputing.de
+49-0-721-9715480
Erzbergerstr. 131
Karlsruhe 76133
Germany

Documenters

DocJet

Tall Tree Software Company
www.talltree.com
512-453-4909
3104 King Street
Austin, TX 78707

VisiComp

www.visicomp.com

Utility+

WoodenChair Software
www.woodenchair.com
905-479-2243
8 Kemsing Court
Markham, Ontario, Canada L3R 4P7

DocCentral

QuickStream
888-768-9898

CommentMaster

Objectsoft, Inc.
www.objsoft.com
888-625-7638

---

eCommerce

eWave

Unify Corporation
www.ewavecommerce.com
408-451-2000
100 Century Center Court, 3rd Floor
San Jose, CA 95112

BankFrame

Eontec
www.javabanking.com
781-229-5848

Cysive

www.cysive.com

Segue

www.segue.com
800-287-1329

ObjectSwitch

www.objectswitch.com

Jsales

Sales Vision
www.salesvision.com
800-275-4314

Editors

DevPartner

NuMega
www.compuware.con/numega
800-468-6342

Multi-Edit

American Cybernetics
www.multiedit.com
602-968-1945
1830 W. University Dr.
Tempe, AZ 85281-3248

Graphics Development

JLOOX

LOOX Software Inc.
www.loox.com
650-903-0942
4962 El Camino Real, Suite 206
Los Altos, CA 94022

INT

Interactive Network Technologies, Inc.
j-extreme.int.com
713-975-7434

KAL espresso

Espial
Espial.com

J/Carnac

Interactive Network Technologies, Inc.
www.int.com
713-975-7434
2901 Wilcrest, Suite 100
Houston, TX 77042-6011

RasterMaster for Java Imaging SDK

Snowbound Software
www.snowbnd.com
617-630-9495
29 Crafts St., Suite 550
Newton, MA 02458

Jimi Pro

Activated Intelligence
www.activated.com
212-896-8220

EspressChart

Quadbase Systems, Inc.
www.quadbase.com
408-982-0835
2855 Kifer Rd., Suite 203
Santa Clara, CA 95051

Help Authoring

JavaHelp

Blue Sky Software
www.bluesky.com
800-559-4423

IDEs and Development Tools

JBuilder

Borland/Imprise
www.imprise.com
831-431-1000
100 Enterprise Way
Scotts Valley, CA 95066-3249

Visual Café

Symantec Corporation
www.visualcafe.com
408-254-9600
20330 Stevens Creek Blvd.
Cupertino, CA 95014

Sun

www.sun.com

JClass Enterprise Suite

KL Group
www.klgroup.com
416-594-1026
260 King Street East
Toronto, Ontario, Canada M5A 4L5

Kalos Architect

Espial
www.espial.com

Elixir IDE

Elixir Technology
www.elixirtech.com

JdesignerPro

BulletProof Corp
www.bulletproof.com
800-505-0105
20533 Biscayne Blvd., Suite 451
Aventura, FL 33180

ArcStyler

Interactive Objects Software GmbH
www.io-software.com
+49-761-400730 (Germany)
Basler Strasse 65
D-79100 Freiburg

Cerebellum

Cerebellum Software
www.cerebellumsoft.com
412-208-6500
600 Waterfront Drive, Suite 250
Pittsburgh, PA 15222

Components by Design

Flashline.Com
www.flashline.com
1300 E. 9th St., Suite 1310
Cleveland, OH 44114

SwingBuilder

SwingSoft
www.swingsoft.com
+44-0-208-469-0827
Suite 81, Grosvenor Gardens House
Grosvenor Gardens
London, United Kingdom

SynerJ

Forte' Software, Inc.
www.forte.com
510-869-3400
1800 Harrison
Oakland, CA 94612

jbAssist for JBuilder

Instantiations, Inc
222.instantiations.com
800-808-3737
7618 SW Mohawk St.
Tualatin, OR 97062

NetBeans

NetBeans, Inc.
www.netbeans.com

Vision JADE Developer Studio

Vision Software Tools, Inc.
www.vision-soft.com
800-984-7638
2101 Webster St., Eighth Floor
Oakland, CA 94612

Elixir IDE

Elixir Technology Ple Ltd.
www.elixirtech.com
+65-532-4300
20.21B Circular Rd.
Republic of Singapore 049376

Simplicity for Java

www.datarepresentations.com

FastJ

DiabData
www.ddi.com

Installers & Deployment

InstallAnywhere

222.zerog.com

InstallShield

www.installshield.com
847-240-0618
900 National Parkway, Suite 125
Schaumburg, IL 60173-5108

BulletTrain

Natural Bridge LLC
www.naturalbridge.com
650-327-6544
648 Menlo Ave., Suite 12
Menlo Park, CA 94025

JPacker

InetSoft Technology Corp.
www.inetsoftcorp.com
732-235-0137
559 Buckingham Drive
Piscataway, NJ 08854

KAWA & JFORGE

www.tek-tools.com

Internationalization

Emule

Slangsoft
www.slangsoft.com

I18n Expeditor

OneRealm
www.onerealm.com
303-247-1284

Internet

WebLogic

BEA
www.beasys.com

HOW

Riverton Software Corp.
www.riverton.com
781-229-0070
1 New England Executive Park
Burlington, MA 01803

SynerJ

Forte'
www.forte.com
800-903-6783

JumpStart

The Theory Center
www.theorycenter.com
888-843-6791
1 Winthrop Square
Boston, MA 02110

Java Beans & Enterprise Java Beans (EJB)

alphaBeans Suites

IBM
www.ibm.com/developer
914-499-1900
New Orchard Rd.
Armonk, NY 10504

Flashline

www.flashline.com
800-259-1961

JFCSuite & JSuite

ProtoView
www.protoview.com
800-231-8588

Cool:Joe

Sterling Software
www.cooljoechallenge.com
214-981-1000
300 Crescent Ct., Suite 1200
Dallas, TX 75201

InLine Software Inc

www.inline.com

Cool Beans

The Theory Center
www.theorycenter.com
888-843-6791
1 Winthrop Square
Boston, MA 02110

JClass Enterprise Suite

KL Group
www.klgroup.com
416-594-1026
260 King Street East
Toronto, Ontario, Canada M5A 4L5

Jumping Beans

Ad Astra Engineering
www.JumpingBeans.com
408-738-4616

alphaBeans

IBM Corp.
Alphaworks.ibm.com/alphabeans
914-499-1900
New Orchard Rd.
Armonk, NY 10504

BeansDesigner

Streamgate Ltd.
www.probeans.com
+44-171-580-92-59
11 Conway St.
London W1P 5HD
United Kingdom

J-Adapter

ObjectSwitch Corp.
www.objectswitch.com
415-925-3460
900 Larkspur Landing Circle, Suite 270
Larkspur, CA 94939

Virtual Instrumentation Beans

ErgoTech Systems, Inc.
www.ergotech.com
888-374-6832

IP*Works

www.dev-soft.com

Java Virtual Machines

Jeode for CE

Insignia Solutions
800-848-7677

Java

Sun Microsystems
java.sun.com

TowerJ

Tower Technology Corp.
www.towerj.com
Houston, TX

Jeode

Insignia Solutions
www.insignia.com
800-848-7677

JVM for Windows

IBM
www.ibm.com/java
914-499-1900
New Orchard Rd.
Armonk, NY 10504

JAR Self Extractor

SelfExtract-Pro

EquitySoft
www.kagi.com/EquitySoft
+4-1-1276-47-1255
1 Owen Road
Windlesham Surrey GU2O 6JG
United Kingdom

Mapper

TOPLink

www.objectpeople.com

Messagers

FioranoMQ4

Fiorano, Inc.
www.fiorano.com
408-354-3210
718 University Avenue, Suite 212
Los Gatos, CA 95032

iBus Connection

SoftWired
www.softwired-inc.com/ibus

Java Message Queue

Sun Microsystems
www.sun.com

ebox

Espial
www.espial.com

SonicMQ

Progress Software Corp.
www.progress.com
800-471-6473
14 Oak Park
Bedford, MA 01730

BambooPipe

InetSoft Technology Corp.
www.inetsoftcorp.com
732-235-0137
559 Buckingham Drive
Piscataway, NJ 08854

Modeling, UML, and CASE Tools

Together/J

TogetherSoft LLC
www.togethersoft.com
919-772-9350
1720 Leigh Drive
Raleigh, NC 27603

GDPro

www.advancedsw.com
800-811-2784
7851 South Elanti St., Suite 102
Littleton, CO 80120

Power Design

Sybase
www.sybase.com
800-879-2273

Visual UML

Visual Object Modelers
www.visualobjectmodelers.com
800-900-1902

CC-Rider

Western Wares
www.westernwares.com
970-327-4898
Box C
Norwood, CO 81423

Elixir CASE

Elixir Technology Ple Ltd.
www.elixirtech.com
+65-532-4300
20.21B Circular Rd.
Republic of Singapore 049376

ClearCase and Rational Suite

Rational Rose
www.rational.com

TOPLink

The Object People
www.objectpeople.com
613-569-8855
99 Bank Street, Suite 100
Ottawa, ON Canada K1P5A3

Jvision

Object Insight, Inc.
www.object-insight.com

MetaEdit+

MetaCase Consulting, Inc.
www.metacase.com
+358-14-4451-400

System Architect

Popkin Software
www.popkin.com
800-732-5226
11 Park Place
New York, NY 10007

WinA&D

Excel Software
www.excelsoftware.com
505-771-3719

Softeam

www.objecteering.com

ObjectDomain

ObjectDomain Systems, Inc.
www.objectdomain.com
919-461-4904
200 Laver Drive
Cary, NC 27511

Obfuscators & Optimizers

SourceGuard

4thpass
www.4thpass.com

DashO-Pro

Preemptive Solutions, Inc.
www.preemptive.com
800-996-4556

JCloak

Force5
www.Force5.com

Optimize It!

Intuitive Systems, Inc
www.optimizeit.com

JOVE

Instantiations
www.instantiations.com
800-808-3737
7618 SW Mohawk St.
Tualatin, OR 97062

Condensity

Plumb Design
www.plumbdesign.com
888-237-5862
636 Broadway #1202
New York, NY 10012

Mako

Blue Lobster Software
www.bluelobster
408-371-5300
2005 Hamilton Ave., Suite 270
San Jose, CA 95126

Object Request Brokers (ORBs)

ORBacus

www.ooc.com/notify
978-439-9285
44 Manning Rd.
Billerica, MA 01821

Profilers

JProbe

KL Group
www.klgroup.com
416-594-1026
260 King Street East
Toronto, Ontario, Canada M5A 4L5

Report Makers

Elixir Report

Elixir Technology
www.elixirtech.com

Enterprise Reports

EnterpriseSoft
www.EnterpriseSoft.Com
510-742-6700
7573 Waterford Drive
Cupertino, CA 95014

Java Printing Components

InetSoft Technology Corp.
www.inetsoftcorp.com
732-235-0137
559 Buckingham Drive
Piscataway, NJ 08854

JClass Page Layout

KL Group, Inc.
www.klgroup.com/pagelayout
888-328-9599
260 King Street East
Toronto, Ontario, Canada M5A 4L5

JavaReporter

ObjectWave Corporation
www.objectwave.com

Elixir Report

Elixir Technology Ple Ltd.
www.elixirtech.com
+65-532-4300
20.21B Circular Rd.
Republic of Singapore 049376

Security

RSA Security

www.rsasecurity.com/go/jumpstart
800-782-5453

Soteria

Aurora Enterprise Solutions
www.aurorasim.com
703-391-9534
12310 Pinecrest Rd., Suite 200
Reston, VA 20191-1636

HiT SSL Server

HiT Software, Inc.
www.hit.com
408-345-4001
4020 Moorpark Ave., Suite 100
San Jose, CA 95117

Servers & Servlets

TomCat

Apache Software Foundation
www.jakarta.apache.org

ProSyst

www.prosyst.com
678-366-5075

ServeletExec

New Atlanta
www.ServeletExec.com

WebSphere Application Server

IBM
www.ibm.com/software/soul/websphere
914-499-1900
New Orchard Rd.
Armonk, NY 10504

ServletExec

New Atlanta
www.newatlanta.com

SilverStream Enterprise Applications.Server

SilverStream Software

PowerTier

Persistence PowerTier
www.persistence.com

IServer

Servertec
www.servertec.com
210-998-1048
18 Oakwood Ave.
Kearny, NJ 07032

SITEFORUM

SFS Software
www.sfs-software.com
+49-172-471-4485
Wolff Strasse 6
99099 Erfurf
Germany

Progress Apptivity

Progress Software Corp.
www.progress.com
800-471-6473
14 Oak Park
Bedford, MA 01730

ServeletExec

New Atlanta Communications, LLC
www.newatlanta.com

Voyager Application Server

ObjectSpace, Inc.
www.objectspace.com
800-625-3281
14850 Quorum Dr., Suite 500
Dallas, TX 75240

Software Development Kit (SDK)

Sun Microsystems

www.sun.com

Spreadsheet

Formula One

TideStone
www.tidestone.com
800-884-8665

Testing Tools and Suites

Jtest, by ParaSoft

www.parasoft.com

TETware

The Open Group
tetworks.opengroup.org/datasheet.html

WebLoad

RadView

WinRuner

Mercury Interactive

SilkTest

Seague Software, Inc.
www.seague.com
800-287-1329
1320 Centre St.
Newton Centre, MA 02159

Trackers, Project Managers

Track

Soffront
www.soffront.com

PR-Tracker

Softwise Company
www.prtracker.com
425-513-0413

Voice Recognition

SpeechKit

Chant, Inc.
222.chant.net
310-3410-9895
8820 S. Sepulveda Blvd., Suite 204
Los Angeles, CA 90045

Word Processor in Java

Jword

SIC Corporation
www.sic21.com

J-Spell

Wall Street Wise Software
www.wallstreetwise.com/jspell.html
P.O. Box 852
New York, NY 10268

XML

Bolero

Software AG, Inc.
www.softwareag.com/bolero
925-472-4900
1990 N. California Blvd. Suite 950
Walnut Creek, CA 94595

Enhydra

Lutris Technologies
www.revolution.lutris.com

Breeze Commerce Studio

VSI
www.vsi.com/breeze
800-556-4874

eXcelon

Object Design, Inc.
www.objectdesign.com/javelin
800-962-9620
25 Mall Road
Burlington, MA 01803-4194

XwingML

Bluestone Software
www.bluestone.com
888-258-3786
1000 Briggs Rd.
Mount Laurel, NJ 08054

Java Resources

Y ou might notice that the various resources are listed in alphabetical order. If your favorite resource is missing, or you find a typographical error, please accept my apology.

Books

If you want to find nearly all books that are available on the subject of Java, the best source for information and prices is on the Internet, at a single Web site:

http://www.evenbetter.com

You can't buy books from the EvenBetter Web site. Instead, the Web site searches numerous sites where you can buy the books. Then it gives you the prices and shipping times. When you select an option, you go to the vendor's Web site.

When you find an intriguing title, the EvenBetter Web site will list a number of places where you can buy the book at excellent discounts, or pay a premium to have it shipped overnight.

You must check your final arrangements. One book I wanted immediately for some XSL research was deliverable in one day. Perfect! That was according to information a vendor gave EvenBetter. In the fine print at that vendor's Web site, the one-day delivery was after a seven-day delay to get it out of their own warehouse! I ended up getting it in two days from Amazon, at a much better price.

Magazines

Dr. Dobb's Journal

www.ddj.com
Subscriptions: 800-456-1215
 400 Borel Avenue, Suite 100
San Mateo, CA 94402-3522

Java Developer's Journal

Subscriptions: 800-513-7111
Editorial offices:
39 E. Central Avenue
Pearl River, NY 10965
914-735-7300

JavaPro

www.java-pro.com
Subscriptions: 303-945-5282
P.O. Box 54584
Boulder, CO 80322-4584
Editorial offices:
650-833-7100

Fawcett Technical Publications

209 Hamilton Avenue
Palo Alto, CA 94301-2500

Java Report

www.javareport.com
Subscriptions: 800-361-1279
Editorial offices:
1250 Broadway, 19th Floor
New York, NY 10001
212-268-7766

JBuilder Developer's Journal

Subscriptions: 800-513-7111
Editorial offices:
39 E. Central Avenue
Pearl River, NY 10965
914-735-7300

E-Zines

Java World

http://www.javaworld.com

Javology

http://www.javology.com/javology

Newsgroups

I hesitated before including this category, because the flame wars there waste so much time. However, most of the information that flourishes around them is invaluable.

alt.www.hotjava	comp.lang.java.help
comp.lang.java	comp.lang.java.machine
comp.lang.java.advocacy	comp.lang.java.misc
comp.lang.java.announce	comp.lang.java.programmer
comp.lang.java.api	comp.lang.java.security
comp.lang.java.beans	comp.lang.java.setup
comp.lang.java.databases	comp.lang.java.softwaretools
comp.lang.java.gui	comp.lang.java.tech

Web Sites

http://babylontown.softseek.com	http://www.apache.org
http://café.symantec.com	http://www.bluestone.com
http://cirrus.sprl.umich.edu/javaweather	http://www.cetus-links.org
http://debuggingjava.com	http://www.davecentral.com/java.html
http://developer.javasoft.com/developer/early/Access/jdk12/idltojava.htm	http://www.developer.com/directories/pages/dir.java.html
http://developer.netscape.com/library/documentation/javalist.html	http://www.developer.java.sun.com/developer/index.html
http://info.fuw.edu.pl/multimedia.html	http://www.enhydra.org
http://java.miningco.com	http://www.freecode.com
http://java.miningco.com/msubbsrc.htm	http://www.gamelan.com
http://java.sun.com	http://www.homeideas.com/applets
http://java.sun.com/beans	http://www.ibm.com/java/jcentral/basic-search.html
http://java.sun.com/beans/software/bdk_download.html	http://www.ibm.com/java/jdk/jdkfaq
http://java.sun.com/docs/books/tutorial	http://www.imprise.com/appserver
http://java.sun.com/docs/books/tutorial/servlets/TOC.html	http://www.inside-java.com
http://java.sun.com/jde	http://www.internethelpers.com/java
http://java.sun.com/products/ejb	http://www.io.org/-mentor/

http://java.sun.com/products/java-media/2D	http://www.jars.com
http://java.sun.com/products/java-media-jmf	http://www.javacats.com
http://java.sun.com/products/jdbc/jdbc.drivers.html	http://www.javadevelopersjournal.com/java
http://java.sun.com/products/jdk.rmi	http://www.javalobby.org
http://java.sun.com/products/jdk/1.2	http://www.javashareware.com
http://java.sun.com/products/jdk/idl/index.html	http://www.javasoft.com
http://java.sun.com/products/jfc/jaccess-1.2/doc	http://www.javasp.com
http://java.sun.com/products/jfc/swingdoc-current	http://www.microsoft.com/java
http://java.sun.com/products/jfc/tac	http://www.netcraft.com
http://java.sun.com/products/servlet/index.html	http://www.netdynamics.com
http://javaboutique.internet.com	http://www.omg.org
http://jcentral.alphaworks.ibm.com/Internet/power.htm	http://www.oracle.com/asd/oas/oas.html
http://k2.scl.cwru.edu/-gaunt/java/java-faq.html	http://www.sigs.com
http://ncc.hursley.ibm.com/javainfo/hurindex.html	http://www.silverstream.com
http://sunsite.unc.edu/javafaq/javafaq.html	http://www.software.ibm.com/webservers/appserv
http://sunsite.unc.edu/pub/multimedia	http://www.sun.com/software/jwebserver/index.html
http://weblogic/beasys.com	http://www.sybase.com/products/application_servers
http://world.std.com/%7Emmedia/lviewp.html	http://www.teamjava.com
http://www.afu.com/javafaq.html	http://www.weblications.net

Training

Absolute Software Co., Inc.

www.abssw.com
760-929-0612
5620 Paseo Del Norte #127
Carlsbad, CA 92008-4444

AvantSoft, Inc.

www.avantsoft.com
408-530-8705

Digital Frontier

www.yourpace.com
800-765-9270
Box 561
Brookline, MA 02146

Dunn Systems, Inc.

www.dunnsys.com
800-468-3866

GemStone

www.gemstone.com

Kenetiks, Inc.

www.kenetiks.com
888-536-3845

Knowledge Exchange, Inc.

www.joineel.com
212-742-2225
55 Broad Street, 7th Floor
New York, NY 10004

Number Six Software, Inc.

www.numbersix.com
202-625-4364
1101 30th Street, NW, Suite 500
Washington, DC 20007-3700

Object Mentor, Inc.

Objectmentor.com
800-338-6716

Pillar Technology Group, Inc.

www.knowledgeable.com
248-357-2021

Sysnetics, Inc.

www.sysnetics.com
800-270-6099
150 153rd Ave., Suite 3008
Madeira Beach, FL 33700

The Middleware Company

www.middleware-company.com/ejb

The Object People

www.objectpeople.com
613-569-8855
99 Bank Street, Suite 1300
Ottawa, ON Canada K1P5A3

Valtech

www.valtech.com
972-789-1200
5080 Suite 1010 West
Dallas, TX 75001

Wirfs-Brock Associates

wirfs-brock.com
888-927-1700

Twenty-One Laws
of Computer Programming

1. Fatal aborts are never allowed.

This is the cardinal rule! The user is the only person who's allowed to stop a program. If a fatal abort is about to occur, you must trap the error, inform the user, let the user do whatever is necessary to save other data, and then let the user press the final button to kill the program. This means that the operating system is never allowed to give the user an error message, because operating system messages are nearly always fatal.

2. Write in this order: User manual, specifications, help, source code.

With this process in force, you will have a nice set of specifications by the time you begin designing. Involve your users closely in writing the user manual. You will meet deadlines more consistently, and your users will be delighted that your design fulfils what they wanted in the first place.

You can fit other things, such as technical documentation, where you want them, but the user manual, specifications, help, and source code should be written in that order.

3. Unless you use Risk Factor Analysis (RFA), a program takes twice as long to develop as you think it will—recursively.

Yes, recursively. If you double the project's time estimate to account for research, you'll still be unpleasantly surprised.

The difficulty RFA solves is time of research. All programmers underestimate how long research will take. We seldom have the luxury of knowing how to do everything in the project. So, we often must estimate how long it will take to do something we don't even know how to do! RFA gives you a handle on research time.

4. Coding should comprise no more than 20 percent of development effort.

If you code to a great design, the actual laying down of code can take as little as 10 percent of your development! When you find yourself spending more than 20 percent in the coding process, you can nearly always trace the difficulty to a poor initial design.

5. Testing should comprise at least 30 percent of the project.

When you estimate your project, be sure to add 30 percent for testing. Even if you use automated testing, and you should, you need to spend 30 percent in the testing phase. Automated testing merely allows you to test more completely, but not completely enough. If you spend less time than 30 percent, it's usually because of deadline pressure, which causes bugs and leads to awful documentation.

6. Comments should comprise at least 20 percent of the source.

Maintenance will consume half of a program's life, whether it's fixing problems or adding enhancements. Make it easy on the enhancer by documenting every variable declaration. Any nontrivial method should note its purpose unless the method's name is sufficient. Comments should also list the author, the version date, and perhaps most often missed, the modification history.

Consider putting a large portion of your comments in Javadoc form, so Javadoc can save you a lot of typing.

7. An error message must tell what happened, what the user can do about it, what the program will do next, and what line of code caused the problem. It may also note the time, username, and environment.

What usually passes for an error message generally goes in the error message's title! Give the poor user a chance to love you, instead of hating you.

8. Good programs automatically send recent error messages to permanent media.

Log the messages in a circular queue, so the messages won't consume the disk. Use quoted, comma-delimited ASCII text, so any editor or word processor can read it.

Make provision for your user to be able to send you the messages, at the click of a button if possible.

9. Call a routine thrice? Hide it. Call it once? Don't hide it.

Never hide a routine that you only use once. Insert it inline in the source code. However, if you use a routine several times, turn it into a method, give it a descriptive name, and call it.

10. Routines need exactly one entry and one exit. Exceptions include menus and error traps.

None of the authors of *Structured Programming* espoused the absence of **goto** statements. Instead, they demanded single entries into routines. They only allowed multiple exits for exceptional cases, such as menus and error traps.

Java handles these exceptions so elegantly that its **goto** keyword is not needed.

11. Document code with clear names for variables and routines.

The best documentation of all is not the comments, but how you name your variables, methods, classes, and packages. It's good to adopt conventions. The Hungarian naming convention may be unpopular with some Java programmers, but it helps you keep variable types straight. Moreover, it helps your maintenance programmers with their half of the program's life cycle.

12. Databases should be relational.

Tiny files, and the file that logs your error messages, can be sequential, flat files. However, if you plan to make significant use of your data, take the time to devise a relational database for the tables. You will generally save development time, consume less disk space, and improve performance.

The greatest savings come at enhancement time, especially if you must convert from flat files to a relational system. That usually means recoding the entire program!

13. Always use the best algorithm.

You must define "best" in terms of performance, disk usage, CPU usage, footprint, etc. However, the range of worst to best can be thousands-to-one.

14. Optimize the slowest routines first. Use a profiler to identify them.

This is a matter of concentrating your energy where it will do the most good. It makes little sense to halve a 1-second routine, when for equal effort you could halve a 100-second routine.

15. The best language is usually the one with the shortest development time.

There is an important proviso here. If you are enhancing a program, tend to stay with the original language because it has important time advantages. However, time-to-market is typically a huge factor in deciding whether or not to fund the project, and that means choosing the language with the shortest development time—even if it's a new language.

If you'd like to convert VB or VBA to Java, remember that the Applet Designer and Access97 Converter programs exist.

If you develop a program for more than one platform, you have a strong incentive for choosing Java.

16. Require customer sign-offs.

Would you buy a house without a contract? Would you buy a used car that way? Then why commit to building a computer program that costs that much, or more, without a firm understanding of what you need to do? Contracts, after all, are only tools that finalize and articulate understanding. They are not papers written preparatory to a lawsuit. The contract says what you and the user will do, and you both can refer to it later.

17. Program the more risky modules first.

Doing this lets you get bad news earlier, when it costs less to make changes.

18. Make easy maintenance your guiding light.

Go beyond a great set of comments. Use simple, clear algorithms. When complex processes are in order, use plenty of well-named temporary variables so you can comment the steps along the way. Such variables also help your maintenance programmer inspect intermediate values, looking for where things went astray.

19. Sign and spell check everything you write.

Be proud of what you do, proud enough to sign your name. Hope that someone will call you some day and congratulate you on the fine job you did with a program. That's one of the greatest feelings in the world.

20. Don't write any program you can replicate with a 3 × 5 card deck!

There are some things never to program. For example, you can pick up the phone and dial a single number in about two seconds. If you have a computer do it for you, you have to boot the computer, load a program, type in a number, and click a mouse button. Of course, if you are a telemarketer, a computer is a wonderful asset.

A 3 × 5 deck of cards is at least a table in a database. Sorting the deck is a method. Looking through it for Jane's address is another method. It has input, output, and storage. Combined with your mind, the deck is a manual computer, and a very efficient one. Its size is about the smallest thing you should ever automate with silicon.

21. Know when anything is done.

Scope creep is the bane of projects. Avoid it. Refuse it. Cast it into the next phase so you can come to a complete halt and say with relief, "This project is done!" Then, go get a cup of java, deliver the project, and start discussing enhancements.

22. No list is ever complete.

And that's no joke!

23. The difficulty is not where you are looking.

If it were, you would have found it by now.

24. Rules and laws exist so people don't have to think.

...at least not so hard.

Java Glossary

This glossary is of terms used in *Debugging Java*, and is certainly not exhaustive.

Abstract Window Toolkit (AWT)   The collection of classes used to implement platform-independent graphical user interfaces.

ActiveX   Formerly VBXs, then OCXs. A set of Microsoft technologies based on the Common Object Model (COM). These technologies are the means that Microsoft applications use for communication and automation.

API   See Application Programming Interface.

Application Programming Interface (API)   The libraries, classes, methods, and functions that let a developer write applications at a higher level than they could otherwise.

Argument   A variable or constant parameter passed into a method by whatever calls that method.

Array   An indexed group of variables with a common name.

ASCII   The standards committee that defined how 8-bit text is implemented.

Atomic   Not divisible, as atoms were once thought to be. In Java, an atomic section of code cannot be entered by two threads at the same time.

AWT   See Abstract Window Toolkit.

Base Class   The superclass from which other classes inherit members.

BDK   See Beans.

Bean   A piece of reusable software that can be manipulated visually inside a builder tool. Beans understand specific properties and events, and although their inner workings are hidden, these properties and events can be made public.

Beans   Beans Development Kit (BDK). From Sun, a toolkit that helps developers create reusable beans.

Black Box   A form of software testing in which nothing is known about the inner workings of a process, except how it is supposed to process data. Specific inputs are fed to the black-box process, and specific outputs are expected.

Block   A piece of source code beginning with a left curly brace { and ending with a right curly brace }.

Boolean   A variable that can have only the values **true** or **false**.

break   A Java keyword stating that program control should be transferred to the statement just after the innermost loop or **switch** statement that encloses the **break**.

Buffer   An area of read-only memory (RAM) or other storage that will hold information. The copy-and-paste buffer of Windows is an example.

Bytecodes   Compiled Java code that is portable to any Java Virtual Machine (JVM).

case   An essential part of any nontrivial switch statement. The case clauses hold values that switch compares with an outside variable before choosing the case clause that should execute accordingly.

Cast   Force one data type into another, whether or not bits of data are lost.

Class   One kind of Java object.

Class Library   A group of **class**es that are reusable code useful to programmers for building applications. Also known as **package**s.

Class Variable   A **private** variable in a **class** that only the **class** can access.

Client   A program that relies on a server computer, or possibly a server program in the client's computer, for other services. Typically, servers will hold data or perform services such as printing, and clients will hold the primary programs needing the data or service.

Compiler   In Java, a computer program that reads source code and creates a new file containing bytecodes, which the Java Virtual Machine on any computer can read. Compilers in other languages produce "object code," which, after further processing, becomes machine bits the hardware can understand.

Concatenate   To string together, such as strings of characters in Java.

Conditional   A Boolean expression that results in a value of either **true** or **false**.

Conditional Statement   A Java statement that uses the results of a conditional to decide whether to perform one process or another.

Constructor   A method that creates an instance of a class.

continue   The Java statement that instructs the program to jump to the point immediately after the last statement of the loop that contains the **continue** statement.

Copy-and-Paste Buffer   A place in RAM that the operating system (such as Windows) reserves for miscellaneous data storage. You copy something into the buffer, navigate to another program or another part of the current one, and paste that entity from the buffer into the new program. This buffer serves as a sort of universal translator, because it can accommodate many kinds of data.

Critical Section   A set of statements that is atomic, or indivisible. While one thread is in a critical section, all other threads are blocked from entering it.

Data Type   The kind of data stored in a variable, such as an **int**, a **char**, or a **String**.

Debugger   A program that assists in finding errors. The Java SDK contains a good debugger, and more powerful debugging tools are discussed extensively in the book *Debugging Java*.

default   An optional but important part of a **switch** construct that tells the program what action to take if no **case** statement matches the value passed into the **switch**.

Deprecated   A status given to Java methods that have been replaced by newer methods, for whatever reason. Older deprecated methods are usually supported by later JDKs, but may be dropped. They should be replaced by their newer cousins.

do   The first statement of one kind of loop.

Documentation Comment   A special kind of comment introduced by **/**** and ended by ***/**, which the Javadoc utility can understand when it documents a Java program.

else   An optional clause in an **if** construct that executes whenever the conditional is **false**.

Event   A component of a Java object that is triggered when something happens. Commonly used events are click and activate.

Exception   An abnormal condition. Also, lowercased, a message from one part of the program to another that something abnormal has happened.

Expression   A group of variables and operators that evaluate to a datum, such as **true**, 12.0, or "Hello World!"

Factory   A pattern for creating class instances without needing a constructor.

finally   A member of the **try** methodology of error trapping. Any code in the **finally** block will execute, regardless of whether or not a **catch** block catches an exception.

Finalizer   A method called immediately before a class is garbage-collected.

Flush   To write any output data that remains in an output buffer to the output object. Flushing is usually performed just before closing a file or stream so that no data is lost.

for   The first statement of one kind of loop.

Garbage Collection   The process of releasing unused blocks of memory for reuse. Java automates this process, but not perfectly, which can result in memory leaks.

Graphical User Interface (GUI)   An easy way for users to control their computers, commonly via use of graphics and pointer devices as well as other devices.

HyperText Markup Language (HTML)   The computer language in which Web documents are written. A language that can contain imbedded Java applets.

Debugging Java: Troubleshooting for Programmers

HyperText Transfer Protocol (HTTP)   The set of computer rules that govern World Wide Web documents and how they are constructed and processed.

IDE   See Integrated Development Environment.

Identifier   A name for a class, method, or variable.

if   The first word of a construct that takes one of two branches, depending on whether the conditional (which immediately follows **if**) evaluates **true** or **false**.

Inheritance   The ability of a class to extend the definition of its parent superclass. By default, the class inherits the variables and methods of the parent, but it may override those functions or variables.

Instance   An object that has been declared, as opposed to a pattern of an object that has not been declared yet.

Instance Variable   A private variable inside a class. Notice that when a new instance of a class is instantiated, it has variables of the same name, but these are copies of the instance variables inside the other classes. No class can access instance variables belonging to other classes.

Instantiation   The process of creating a class according to its pattern.

Integrated Development Environment (IDE)   You can use an editor to write any Java program, but an IDE gives you a thousand tools to make it easier, faster, less error-prone, and more profitable. An IDE gives you a graphical way to write most of the program, dragging controls onto a frame, setting their properties, and having method stubs written for you.

Internet Service Provider (ISP)   A company that provides equipment that lets users connect their computers to the Internet.

Interpreter   A program that reads source code and executes each command, one line at a time. Interpreters are slower than compilers, because compilers can optimize programs far better than interpreters can.

Java Archive (JAR) File   A compressed group of files. Interestingly, Java can access these files without the user ever having to decompress them, because Java handles the decompression selectively and automatically.

Java DataBase Connectivity (JDBC)   The system of programs that implement connections to relational databases.

Java Development Kit (JDK)   The programs that let you write Java code, test it, compile it, and execute it.

Java Virtual Machine (JVM)   A computer program that appears to Java bytecodes to be a physical computer able to interpret those bytecodes. The JVM does interpret the bytecodes, running them as machine code on the host physical computer.

JavaBeans   Sets of Java objects that are reusable and can link with objects in other languages.

JavaScript   A different language that shares the first four letters of its name with Java. JavaScript shares may other features with Java, but it is definitely a different language.

Just-In-Time (JIT) Compiler   A compiler that verifies bytecodes and converts them to native CPU instructions before execution time. Such compilers speed up Java programs by a factor of up to 20.

Method   The part of a class that acts. Analogous to a verb in English. A member function.

Modifier   An entity that changes classes, methods, and variables. Analogous to an adjective or an adverb in English.

Multiple Inheritance   Java does not implement this directly, but the same results can be accomplished. This is the ability of a class to inherit methods and variables from more than one class.

Multithreading   Allowing more than one independent task to be running in a program.

Nesting   Including things inside similar things. For example, nested loops are loops within loops.

null   A value that means no object. Entirely different from zero.

Object   A software analogy to a noun in English. Objects have characteristics and behaviors. One common analogy is a dog (object) that can bark (method) and has a bark (property). Notice that having a bark and barking are two different things.

Object-Oriented Programming (OOP)   A software methodology that focuses on objects and their relationships as smaller, more understandable programs.

Overloading   Having multiple uses. For instance, the + sign is overloaded, because it can mean summation as well as concatenation.

Package   A collection of related classes.

Parent class   Superclass.

Polymorphism   The ability of one object to operate on many different types.

Primitive   A data type, such as **int**, that is not an object. Note that **String** is not a primitive.

Property   An attribute of a control, such as a frame. Properties include such things as colors, captions, and sizes.

Rapid Application Development (RAD)   A method of program development characterized by letting one programmer handle as many aspects of development as feasible.

Recursion   The process a method uses in calling itself, but actually an exact copy of itself. Recursion simplifies many kinds of sorting, searching, and binary tree work, as well as algorithms like series, which have repeatable aspects. Most loops can be solved recursively, resulting in simpler code that is more difficult to understand deeply. Most recursive algorithms can be solved iteratively, but this commonly means writing extremely long programs. Recursion, like looping, can become infinite, but infinite recursion usually consumes all available RAM.

Scope   Analogous to the field of view in a telescope. The area of a program in which a variable exists. A variable cannot be used outside of its scope, which is the block in which it was created.

Servlet   A small server-side program, similar to an applet but running on a server.

Signature   A unique description of a method, including the name, arguments, and return type. When overriding an inherited method with another of the same name, you must change the signature in some way, which means changing the argument list or the return type.

Socket   A piece of software that connects a network to the application.

Source   The raw Java code before being compiled. Source is a text file in nearly all languages.

Stack   A data structure that uses last-in-first-out processing. In recursion, you push an instance of a method onto a stack each time you call it. When it's time to back out of recursion, the last method instance that was pushed onto the stack emerges and runs to completion. Then, the next to the last method instance does the same thing, etc.

State   Analogous to the word "is" in English. A program's state consists of everything within the physical computer that defines the program at any given time.

Statement   A line of code.

Stream   A sequence of bytes flowing in or out of a program.

Stub   A small method that has nothing or very little in its body, so that it can quickly take the place of a full method of the same name. A stub lets you make program calls to something that exists, without generating a call error. Stubs are replaced with full methods as development continues.

Superclass   A class from which other classes inherit their attributes.

Swing   Classes in Java that can expand upon the Abstract Windowing Toolkit's graphical user interface. Swing classes are not, in general, thread-safe.

switch   A sort of multiple **if**. Whereas a single **if** statement considers a Boolean condition that can have only two possible values, a **switch** statement considers an expression that can have many values. Each value is typically handled by a **case** statement.

Thread   A single flow of control within a program. A thread can be considered autonomous, because it acts without regard to other threads. A thread can enter an operation, such as an assignment, or a **synchronized** block of code, which then blocks other threads from entry until the first thread is out.

Unicode   The 16-bit, international set of characters, roughly analogous to the 8-bit ASCII set but far more extensive. Unicode allows use of Chinese pictograms, for instance.

while   The first word of one kind of loop.

Word Macros

Chapter 5 contains numerous customization tips for turning an ordinary word processor into a fine Java editor. Part of that process involves programming the word processor with macros, such as these.

Bookmark and GoTo

This quartet of macros helps you navigate within a Word document, whether or not it is a Java program. These macros are best implemented with four toolbar buttons, as indicated in Chapter 5.

Say you are writing an output routine that is similar to an input routine you have already written. Perhaps you've identified several new fields that need to be put into the input routine. It would be handy to be able to jump back and forth between the output and the input routine, cutting, copying, and pasting.

Set a "B" bookmark, where you are, so you can return. Look for the previous area, and set an "A" bookmark there. Now, you can copy and paste back and forth with the click of an icon. Here are the macros. Chapter 5 shows you how to place them on toolbars as icons.

```
Sub BookMarkA()
'Purpose:  Establish a bookmark named "A" in a document, for later return.
'Version:  1.0
'Author:   Will D.Mitchell
'Mod Hist:

    With ActiveDocument.Bookmarks
        .Add Range:=Selection.Range, Name:="A"
        .DefaultSorting = wdSortByName
        .ShowHidden = False
    End With
End Sub


Sub BookMarkB()
'Purpose:  Establish a bookmark named "B" in a document, for later return.
'Version:  1.0
'Author:   Will D.Mitchell
'Mod Hist:

    With ActiveDocument.Bookmarks
        .Add Range:=Selection.Range, Name:="B"
        .DefaultSorting = wdSortByName
        .ShowHidden = False
```

```
    End With

End Sub


Sub GoToA()
'Purpose:  Return to a bookmark named "A" that the reader has set.
'Version:  1.0
'Author:   Will D.Mitchell
'Mod Hist:

    Selection.GoTo What:=wdGoToBookmark, Name:="A"
    With ActiveDocument.Bookmarks
        .DefaultSorting = wdSortByName
        .ShowHidden = False
    End With

End Sub


Sub GoToB()
'Purpose:  Return to a bookmark named "B" that the reader has set.
'Version:  1.0
'Author:   Will D.Mitchell
'Mod Hist:

    Selection.GoTo What:=wdGoToBookmark, Name:="B"
    With ActiveDocument.Bookmarks
        .DefaultSorting = wdSortByName
        .ShowHidden = False
    End With

End Sub
```

Hiding Text

There are many reasons to hide text within a document. One is that you can include notes that you will want to remove before publication. You can tell your word processor to show, or to hide, "hidden" text, either on the editing screen or on the printer.

If you try to record a macro for the RedHidden work, it will be considerably longer than this version. The recording will try to set your text to a number of default states. You probably do not want that to happen, because it might change your font name and size, underlining, bolding, etc.

If you highlight some text and execute this macro, the text turns red and hidden. If it disappears, you can click Tools | Options and select the View tab, where you can check the Hidden box. On the Print tab, you can check whether or not to print hidden text.

If you click this macro and start typing, the word processor conveniently sets what you type to red and hidden text.

```
Sub RedHidden()
'Purpose:  Set text Red and Hidden, while not changing other attributes.
'Version:  1.0
'Author:   Will D. Mitchell
'Mod Hist:

    With Selection.Font
        .Hidden = True
        .Color = wdColorRed
    End With

End Sub
```

You need a companion macro that will return red, hidden text to its former state. For one thing, if you start typing red, hidden text, you need to be able to start typing normal text later. The following macro presumes that the former state's color is "automatic" and that the text was not hidden. It changes nothing else.

As did the **RedHidden**() macro, this one will set any highlighted text back to automatic color and unhidden:

```
Sub NotRedHidden()
'Purpose:  Set text Red and Hidden, while not changing other attributes.
'Version:  1.0
'Author:   Will D. Mitchell
'Mod Hist:

    With Selection.Font
        .Hidden = false
        .Color = wdColorAutomatic
    End With

End Sub
```

One of the reasons for hiding text is so that you can remove it all before publication. This macro seeks all hidden text and deletes it. You can save the results under a new filename if you wish.

```
Sub RemoveHidden()
'Purpose:  Remove all hidden text.
'Version:  1.0
'Author:   Will D. Mitchell
'Mod Hist:

'Be sure some previous formatting doesn't interfere.
    Selection.Find.ClearFormatting
    Selection.Find.Font.Hidden = True
    Selection.Find.Replacement.ClearFormatting
    With Selection.Find
        .Text = "^?"
        .Replacement.Text = ""
        .Forward = True
        .Wrap = wdFindContinue
        .Format = True
'Don't restrict the findings to anything.
        .MatchCase = False
        .MatchWholeWord = False
        .MatchWildcards = False
        .MatchSoundsLike = False
        .MatchAllWordForms = False
    End With

'Replace all hidden text with nothing.
    Selection.Find.Execute Replace:=wdReplaceAll

    End Sub
```

Personal Comments

The letters "QQQ" seldom occur in documents. When you want to send yourself a note, you can type these characters followed by that note. Later, you can search for the note by its three-letter identifier of QQQ.

In Java, while you are busy writing code, you will often be hit by an inspiration. Just type **/* QQQ** with your self-note, followed by ***/**. Doing this helps you stay in your right-brain mode of operation, enhancing your creativity.

The following macro makes that process a small amount easier:

```
Sub QQQ()
'Purpose:  Install /* QQQ */ and move the cursor to just before the */ part.
'Version:  1.1
'Author:   Will D. Mitchell
```

```
'Mod Hist: Added a space after QQQ and moved cursor back 3 spaces instead of 2.
'
    Selection.TypeText Text:="/* QQQ  */"
    Selection.MoveLeft Unit:=wdCharacter, Count:=3
End Sub
```

Green Keywords

This macro finds all Java keywords and turns them green, even if they are in strings or in comments. It has a lot of typing, but the copy-and-paste buffer simplifies that.

```
'Purpose:  Turn all Java keywords green,
          whether or not they are in strings or comments.
'Version:  1.0
'Author:   Will D. Mitchell
'Note:     This macro can be implemented with far less code by using a small
'          dataset and a loop. This version runs much faster.
'          However, the main reason for not using a dataset is that it would
'          have to accompany the macro externally.
'Mod Hist:

'Allow no previous formatting to interfere.
    Selection.Find.ClearFormatting
    Selection.Find.Replacement.ClearFormatting
'Color the replacement text green.
    Selection.Find.Replacement.Font.Color = wdColorSeaGreen
    With Selection.Find
        .Text = "boolean"
        .Replacement.Text = "boolean"
        .Forward = True
        .Wrap = wdFindContinue
        .Format = True
'Be sure to only match the whole word, including case.
        .MatchCase = True
        .MatchWholeWord = True
        .MatchWildcards = False
        .MatchSoundsLike = False
        .MatchAllWordForms = False
    End With
    Selection.Find.Execute Replace:=wdReplaceAll
    With Selection.Find
        .Text = "char"
        .Replacement.Text = "char"
```

```
        .Forward = True
        .Wrap = wdFindContinue
        .Format = True
        .MatchCase = True
        .MatchWholeWord = True
        .MatchWildcards = False
        .MatchSoundsLike = False
        .MatchAllWordForms = False
End With
Selection.Find.Execute Replace:=wdReplaceAll
With Selection.Find
        .Text = "byte"
        .Replacement.Text = "byte"
        .Forward = True
        .Wrap = wdFindContinue
        .Format = True
        .MatchCase = True
        .MatchWholeWord = True
        .MatchWildcards = False
        .MatchSoundsLike = False
        .MatchAllWordForms = False
End With
Selection.Find.Execute Replace:=wdReplaceAll
With Selection.Find
        .Text = "float"
        .Replacement.Text = "float"
        .Forward = True
        .Wrap = wdFindContinue
        .Format = True
        .MatchCase = True
        .MatchWholeWord = True
        .MatchWildcards = False
        .MatchSoundsLike = False
        .MatchAllWordForms = False
End With
Selection.Find.Execute Replace:=wdReplaceAll
With Selection.Find
        .Text = "short"
        .Replacement.Text = "short"
        .Forward = True
        .Wrap = wdFindContinue
        .Format = True
        .MatchCase = True
        .MatchWholeWord = True
        .MatchWildcards = False
        .MatchSoundsLike = False
        .MatchAllWordForms = False
End With
Selection.Find.Execute Replace:=wdReplaceAll
```

```
    With Selection.Find
        .Text = "double"
        .Replacement.Text = "double"
        .Forward = True
        .Wrap = wdFindContinue
        .Format = True
        .MatchCase = True
        .MatchWholeWord = True
        .MatchWildcards = False
        .MatchSoundsLike = False
        .MatchAllWordForms = False
    End With
    Selection.Find.Execute Replace:=wdReplaceAll
    With Selection.Find
        .Text = "int"
        .Replacement.Text = "int"
        .Forward = True
        .Wrap = wdFindContinue
        .Format = True
        .MatchCase = True
        .MatchWholeWord = True
        .MatchWildcards = False
        .MatchSoundsLike = False
        .MatchAllWordForms = False
    End With
    Selection.Find.Execute Replace:=wdReplaceAll
    With Selection.Find
        .Text = "long"
        .Replacement.Text = "long"
        .Forward = True
        .Wrap = wdFindContinue
        .Format = True
        .MatchCase = True
        .MatchWholeWord = True
        .MatchWildcards = False
        .MatchSoundsLike = False
        .MatchAllWordForms = False
    End With
    Selection.Find.Execute Replace:=wdReplaceAll
'Note that widefp and stringfp are provisionally introduced in JDK 1.2.
    With Selection.Find
        .Text = "widefp"
        .Replacement.Text = "widefp"
        .Forward = True
        .Wrap = wdFindContinue
        .Format = True
        .MatchCase = True
        .MatchWholeWord = True
        .MatchWildcards = False
```

```
        .MatchSoundsLike = False
        .MatchAllWordForms = False
    End With
    Selection.Find.Execute Replace:=wdReplaceAll
    With Selection.Find
        .Text = "stringfp"
        .Replacement.Text = "stringfp"
        .Forward = True
        .Wrap = wdFindContinue
        .Format = True
        .MatchCase = True
        .MatchWholeWord = True
        .MatchWildcards = False
        .MatchSoundsLike = False
        .MatchAllWordForms = False
    End With
    Selection.Find.Execute Replace:=wdReplaceAll
    With Selection.Find
        .Text = "void"
        .Replacement.Text = "void"
        .Forward = True
        .Wrap = wdFindContinue
        .Format = True
        .MatchCase = True
        .MatchWholeWord = True
        .MatchWildcards = False
        .MatchSoundsLike = False
        .MatchAllWordForms = False
    End With
    Selection.Find.Execute Replace:=wdReplaceAll
    With Selection.Find
        .Text = "new"
        .Replacement.Text = "new"
        .Forward = True
        .Wrap = wdFindContinue
        .Format = True
        .MatchCase = True
        .MatchWholeWord = True
        .MatchWildcards = False
        .MatchSoundsLike = False
        .MatchAllWordForms = False
    End With
    Selection.Find.Execute Replace:=wdReplaceAll
    With Selection.Find
        .Text = "this"
        .Replacement.Text = "this"
        .Forward = True
        .Wrap = wdFindContinue
        .Format = True
```

```
        .MatchCase = True
        .MatchWholeWord = True
        .MatchWildcards = False
        .MatchSoundsLike = False
        .MatchAllWordForms = False
    End With
    Selection.Find.Execute Replace:=wdReplaceAll
    With Selection.Find
        .Text = "super"
        .Replacement.Text = "super"
        .Forward = True
        .Wrap = wdFindContinue
        .Format = True
        .MatchCase = True
        .MatchWholeWord = True
        .MatchWildcards = False
        .MatchSoundsLike = False
        .MatchAllWordForms = False
    End With
    Selection.Find.Execute Replace:=wdReplaceAll
    With Selection.Find
        .Text = "if"
        .Replacement.Text = "if"
        .Forward = True
        .Wrap = wdFindContinue
        .Format = True
        .MatchCase = True
        .MatchWholeWord = True
        .MatchWildcards = False
        .MatchSoundsLike = False
        .MatchAllWordForms = False
    End With
    Selection.Find.Execute Replace:=wdReplaceAll
    With Selection.Find
        .Text = "else"
        .Replacement.Text = "else"
        .Forward = True
        .Wrap = wdFindContinue
        .Format = True
        .MatchCase = True
        .MatchWholeWord = True
        .MatchWildcards = False
        .MatchSoundsLike = False
        .MatchAllWordForms = False
    End With
    Selection.Find.Execute Replace:=wdReplaceAll
    With Selection.Find
        .Text = "switch"
        .Replacement.Text = "switch"
```

```
    .Forward = True
    .Wrap = wdFindContinue
    .Format = True
    .MatchCase = True
    .MatchWholeWord = True
    .MatchWildcards = False
    .MatchSoundsLike = False
    .MatchAllWordForms = False
End With
Selection.Find.Execute Replace:=wdReplaceAll
With Selection.Find
    .Text = "case"
    .Replacement.Text = "case"
    .Forward = True
    .Wrap = wdFindContinue
    .Format = True
    .MatchCase = True
    .MatchWholeWord = True
    .MatchWildcards = False
    .MatchSoundsLike = False
    .MatchAllWordForms = False
End With
Selection.Find.Execute Replace:=wdReplaceAll
With Selection.Find
    .Text = "break"
    .Replacement.Text = "break"
    .Forward = True
    .Wrap = wdFindContinue
    .Format = True
    .MatchCase = True
    .MatchWholeWord = True
    .MatchWildcards = False
    .MatchSoundsLike = False
    .MatchAllWordForms = False
End With
Selection.Find.Execute Replace:=wdReplaceAll
With Selection.Find
    .Text = "default"
    .Replacement.Text = "default"
    .Forward = True
    .Wrap = wdFindContinue
    .Format = True
    .MatchCase = True
    .MatchWholeWord = True
    .MatchWildcards = False
    .MatchSoundsLike = False
    .MatchAllWordForms = False
End With
```

```
Selection.Find.Execute Replace:=wdReplaceAll
With Selection.Find
    .Text = "do"
    .Replacement.Text = "do"
    .Forward = True
    .Wrap = wdFindContinue
    .Format = True
    .MatchCase = True
    .MatchWholeWord = True
    .MatchWildcards = False
    .MatchSoundsLike = False
    .MatchAllWordForms = False
End With
Selection.Find.Execute Replace:=wdReplaceAll
With Selection.Find
    .Text = "while"
    .Replacement.Text = "while"
    .Forward = True
    .Wrap = wdFindContinue
    .Format = True
    .MatchCase = True
    .MatchWholeWord = True
    .MatchWildcards = False
    .MatchSoundsLike = False
    .MatchAllWordForms = False
End With
Selection.Find.Execute Replace:=wdReplaceAll
With Selection.Find
    .Text = "for"
    .Replacement.Text = "for"
    .Forward = True
    .Wrap = wdFindContinue
    .Format = True
    .MatchCase = True
    .MatchWholeWord = True
    .MatchWildcards = False
    .MatchSoundsLike = False
    .MatchAllWordForms = False
End With
Selection.Find.Execute Replace:=wdReplaceAll
With Selection.Find
    .Text = "continue"
    .Replacement.Text = "continue"
    .Forward = True
    .Wrap = wdFindContinue
    .Format = True
    .MatchCase = True
    .MatchWholeWord = True
    .MatchWildcards = False
```

```
        .MatchSoundsLike = False
        .MatchAllWordForms = False
    End With
    Selection.Find.Execute Replace:=wdReplaceAll
    With Selection.Find
        .Text = "synchronized"
        .Replacement.Text = "synchronized"
        .Forward = True
        .Wrap = wdFindContinue
        .Format = True
        .MatchCase = True
        .MatchWholeWord = True
        .MatchWildcards = False
        .MatchSoundsLike = False
        .MatchAllWordForms = False
    End With
    Selection.Find.Execute Replace:=wdReplaceAll
    With Selection.Find
        .Text = "try"
        .Replacement.Text = "try"
        .Forward = True
        .Wrap = wdFindContinue
        .Format = True
        .MatchCase = True
        .MatchWholeWord = True
        .MatchWildcards = False
        .MatchSoundsLike = False
        .MatchAllWordForms = False
    End With
    Selection.Find.Execute Replace:=wdReplaceAll
    With Selection.Find
        .Text = "catch"
        .Replacement.Text = "catch"
        .Forward = True
        .Wrap = wdFindContinue
        .Format = True
        .MatchCase = True
        .MatchWholeWord = True
        .MatchWildcards = False
        .MatchSoundsLike = False
        .MatchAllWordForms = False
    End With
    Selection.Find.Execute Replace:=wdReplaceAll
    With Selection.Find
        .Text = "throw"
        .Replacement.Text = "throw"
        .Forward = True
        .Wrap = wdFindContinue
        .Format = True
```

```
        .MatchCase = True
        .MatchWholeWord = True
        .MatchWildcards = False
        .MatchSoundsLike = False
        .MatchAllWordForms = False
    End With
    Selection.Find.Execute Replace:=wdReplaceAll
    With Selection.Find
        .Text = "throws"
        .Replacement.Text = "throws"
        .Forward = True
        .Wrap = wdFindContinue
        .Format = True
        .MatchCase = True
        .MatchWholeWord = True
        .MatchWildcards = False
        .MatchSoundsLike = False
        .MatchAllWordForms = False
    End With
    Selection.Find.Execute Replace:=wdReplaceAll
    With Selection.Find
        .Text = "finally"
        .Replacement.Text = "finally"
        .Forward = True
        .Wrap = wdFindContinue
        .Format = True
        .MatchCase = True
        .MatchWholeWord = True
        .MatchWildcards = False
        .MatchSoundsLike = False
        .MatchAllWordForms = False
    End With
    Selection.Find.Execute Replace:=wdReplaceAll
    With Selection.Find
        .Text = "return"
        .Replacement.Text = "return"
        .Forward = True
        .Wrap = wdFindContinue
        .Format = True
        .MatchCase = True
        .MatchWholeWord = True
        .MatchWildcards = False
        .MatchSoundsLike = False
        .MatchAllWordForms = False
    End With
    Selection.Find.Execute Replace:=wdReplaceAll
    With Selection.Find
        .Text = "static"
        .Replacement.Text = "static"
```

```
    .Forward = True
    .Wrap = wdFindContinue
    .Format = True
    .MatchCase = True
    .MatchWholeWord = True
    .MatchWildcards = False
    .MatchSoundsLike = False
    .MatchAllWordForms = False
End With
Selection.Find.Execute Replace:=wdReplaceAll
With Selection.Find
    .Text = "abstract"
    .Replacement.Text = "abstract"
    .Forward = True
    .Wrap = wdFindContinue
    .Format = True
    .MatchCase = True
    .MatchWholeWord = True
    .MatchWildcards = False
    .MatchSoundsLike = False
    .MatchAllWordForms = False
End With
Selection.Find.Execute Replace:=wdReplaceAll
With Selection.Find
    .Text = "final"
    .Replacement.Text = "final"
    .Forward = True
    .Wrap = wdFindContinue
    .Format = True
    .MatchCase = True
    .MatchWholeWord = True
    .MatchWildcards = False
    .MatchSoundsLike = False
    .MatchAllWordForms = False
End With
Selection.Find.Execute Replace:=wdReplaceAll
With Selection.Find
    .Text = "private"
    .Replacement.Text = "private"
    .Forward = True
    .Wrap = wdFindContinue
    .Format = True
    .MatchCase = True
    .MatchWholeWord = True
    .MatchWildcards = False
    .MatchSoundsLike = False
    .MatchAllWordForms = False
End With
Selection.Find.Execute Replace:=wdReplaceAll
```

```
With Selection.Find
    .Text = "protected"
    .Replacement.Text = "protected"
    .Forward = True
    .Wrap = wdFindContinue
    .Format = True
    .MatchCase = True
    .MatchWholeWord = True
    .MatchWildcards = False
    .MatchSoundsLike = False
    .MatchAllWordForms = False
End With
Selection.Find.Execute Replace:=wdReplaceAll
With Selection.Find
    .Text = "public"
    .Replacement.Text = "public"
    .Forward = True
    .Wrap = wdFindContinue
    .Format = True
    .MatchCase = True
    .MatchWholeWord = True
    .MatchWildcards = False
    .MatchSoundsLike = False
    .MatchAllWordForms = False
End With
Selection.Find.Execute Replace:=wdReplaceAll
With Selection.Find
    .Text = "class"
    .Replacement.Text = "class"
    .Forward = True
    .Wrap = wdFindContinue
    .Format = True
    .MatchCase = True
    .MatchWholeWord = True
    .MatchWildcards = False
    .MatchSoundsLike = False
    .MatchAllWordForms = False
End With
Selection.Find.Execute Replace:=wdReplaceAll
With Selection.Find
    .Text = "instanceof"
    .Replacement.Text = "instanceof"
    .Forward = True
    .Wrap = wdFindContinue
    .Format = True
    .MatchCase = True
    .MatchWholeWord = True
    .MatchWildcards = False
    .MatchSoundsLike = False
    .MatchAllWordForms = False
```

```
End With
Selection.Find.Execute Replace:=wdReplaceAll
With Selection.Find
    .Text = "native"
    .Replacement.Text = "native"
    .Forward = True
    .Wrap = wdFindContinue
    .Format = True
    .MatchCase = True
    .MatchWholeWord = True
    .MatchWildcards = False
    .MatchSoundsLike = False
    .MatchAllWordForms = False
End With
Selection.Find.Execute Replace:=wdReplaceAll
With Selection.Find
    .Text = "transient"
    .Replacement.Text = "transient"
    .Forward = True
    .Wrap = wdFindContinue
    .Format = True
    .MatchCase = True
    .MatchWholeWord = True
    .MatchWildcards = False
    .MatchSoundsLike = False
    .MatchAllWordForms = False
End With
Selection.Find.Execute Replace:=wdReplaceAll
With Selection.Find
    .Text = "volatile"
    .Replacement.Text = "volatile"
    .Forward = True
    .Wrap = wdFindContinue
    .Format = True
    .MatchCase = True
    .MatchWholeWord = True
    .MatchWildcards = False
    .MatchSoundsLike = False
    .MatchAllWordForms = False
End With
Selection.Find.Execute Replace:=wdReplaceAll
With Selection.Find
    .Text = "extends"
    .Replacement.Text = "extends"
    .Forward = True
    .Wrap = wdFindContinue
    .Format = True
    .MatchCase = True
    .MatchWholeWord = True
```

```
        .MatchWildcards = False
        .MatchSoundsLike = False
        .MatchAllWordForms = False
End With
Selection.Find.Execute Replace:=wdReplaceAll
With Selection.Find
        .Text = "interface"
        .Replacement.Text = "interface"
        .Forward = True
        .Wrap = wdFindContinue
        .Format = True
        .MatchCase = True
        .MatchWholeWord = True
        .MatchWildcards = False
        .MatchSoundsLike = False
        .MatchAllWordForms = False
End With
Selection.Find.Execute Replace:=wdReplaceAll
With Selection.Find
        .Text = "implements"
        .Replacement.Text = "implements"
        .Forward = True
        .Wrap = wdFindContinue
        .Format = True
        .MatchCase = True
        .MatchWholeWord = True
        .MatchWildcards = False
        .MatchSoundsLike = False
        .MatchAllWordForms = False
End With
Selection.Find.Execute Replace:=wdReplaceAll
With Selection.Find
        .Text = "package"
        .Replacement.Text = "package"
        .Forward = True
        .Wrap = wdFindContinue
        .Format = True
        .MatchCase = True
        .MatchWholeWord = True
        .MatchWildcards = False
        .MatchSoundsLike = False
        .MatchAllWordForms = False
End With
Selection.Find.Execute Replace:=wdReplaceAll
With Selection.Find
        .Text = "import"
        .Replacement.Text = "import"
        .Forward = True
        .Wrap = wdFindContinue
```

```
            .Format = True
            .MatchCase = True
            .MatchWholeWord = True
            .MatchWildcards = False
            .MatchSoundsLike = False
            .MatchAllWordForms = False
      End With
'const and goto are reserved for potential future use.
      Selection.Find.Execute Replace:=wdReplaceAll
      With Selection.Find
          .Text = "const"
          .Replacement.Text = "const"
          .Forward = True
          .Wrap = wdFindContinue
          .Format = True
          .MatchCase = True
          .MatchWholeWord = True
          .MatchWildcards = False
          .MatchSoundsLike = False
          .MatchAllWordForms = False
      End With
      Selection.Find.Execute Replace:=wdReplaceAll
      With Selection.Find
          .Text = "goto"
          .Replacement.Text = "goto"
          .Forward = True
          .Wrap = wdFindContinue
          .Format = True
          .MatchCase = True
          .MatchWholeWord = True
          .MatchWildcards = False
          .MatchSoundsLike = False
          .MatchAllWordForms = False
      End With
      Selection.Find.Execute Replace:=wdReplaceAll
End Sub
```

Programming Helps

This macro creates a short stub that you might want to install at the front of any method whose name doesn't fully describe it:

```
Sub MethodBeginning()
'Purpose:  Create beginning comments for a method.
'Version:  1.0
'Author:   Will D. Mitchell
'Mod Hist:
```

```
    Selection.TypeText Text:="// Purpose:    "
    Selection.TypeParagraph
    Selection.TypeText Text:="// Input:      "
    Selection.TypeParagraph
    Selection.TypeText Text:="// Output:     "
    Selection.TypeParagraph
    Selection.TypeText Text:="// Version:    "
    Selection.TypeParagraph
    Selection.TypeText Text:="// Author:     "
    Selection.TypeParagraph
    Selection.TypeText Text:="// Mod Hist:  "
'Move the typing cursor back to the Purpose line.
    Selection.MoveUp Unit:=wdLine, Count:=5
End Sub
```

This macro is somewhat like the previous one, but it installs a longer stub designed to help you begin a new class:

```
Sub MethodBeginning()
'Purpose:  Create beginning comments for a method.
'Version:  1.0
'Author:   Will D. Mitchell
'Mod Hist:

    Selection.TypeText Text:=" // class constants:      "
    Selection.TypeParagraph
    Selection.TypeText Text:=" // class variable:       "
    Selection.TypeParagraph
    Selection.TypeText Text:=" // instance variables:  "
    Selection.TypeParagraph
    Selection.TypeText Text:=" // class methods:        "
    Selection.TypeParagraph
    Selection.TypeText Text:=" // constructor methods: "
    Selection.TypeParagraph
    Selection.TypeText Text:=" // class constants:      "
    Selection.TypeParagraph
    Selection.TypeText Text:=" // main method:          "
    Selection.TypeParagraph
    Selection.TypeText Text:=" // Purpose:   "
    Selection.TypeParagraph
    Selection.TypeText Text:=" // Version:   "
    Selection.TypeParagraph
    Selection.TypeText Text:=" // Author  : "
    Selection.TypeParagraph
    Selection.TypeText Text:=" // Mod Hist: "
    Selection.TypeParagraph
    Selection.TypeText Text:="package "
```

```
    Selection.TypeParagraph
    Selection.TypeText Text:="class "
    Selection.TypeParagraph
    Selection.TypeText Text:="  public static void main (String[] args) {"
    Selection.TypeParagraph
    Selection.TypeText Text:="  }"
    Selection.TypeParagraph
    Selection.TypeText Text:="  "
    Selection.TypeParagraph
    Selection.TypeText Text:="}"
'Move the typing cursor back to the class constants line.
    Selection.MoveUp Unit:=wdLine, Count:=16
End Sub
```

More Macros

You'll be able to find more macros on this book's Web site, at either
http://osborne.com or http://DebuggingJava.com.

Index